THE
THREE-POUND
UNIVERSE

THE
THREE-POUND
UNIVERSE

JUDITH HOOPER AND DICK TERESI

Macmillan Publishing Company

NEW YORK

Macmillan Publishing Company
866 Third Avenue, New York, N.Y. 10022
Collier Macmillan Canada, Inc.

Library of Congress Cataloging-in-Publication Data
Hooper, Judith.
The three-pound universe.
Bibliography: p.
Includes index.
1. Neuropsychology. 2. Mind-brain identity theory.
3. Mind and body. I. Teresi, Dick. II. Title.
QP360.H67 1986 152 85-19780
ISBN 0-02-553680-X

Macmillan books are available at special discounts for bulk purchases for sales promotions, premiums, fund-raising, or educational use. For details, contact:

Special Sales Director
Macmillan Publishing Company
866 Third Avenue
New York, N.Y. 10022

10 9 8 7 6 5 4 3 2 1

Designed by Jack Meserole

All illustrations by Marta Norman, with the exception of Figures 4 and 8, which were drawn by Robert Conrad

Photo editing by Hildegard Kron

Printed in the United States of America

Acknowledgment is made to the following for permission to reproduce copyrighted material from the sources named:

Lyrics from the Jefferson Airplane's "Crown of Creation" on page 25.
Copyright © 1968 by Icebag Publishing Co.
Reprinted by permission of the publisher.

Rainer Maria Rilke quote on page 152.
From "The Tenth Elegy" from *Duino Elegies*
by Rainer Maria Rilke, translated by D. Young.
Reprinted by permission of W. W. Norton & Company, Inc.
Copyright © 1978 by W. W. Norton & Company, Inc.

T. S. Eliot quote on page 162.
From "Preludes" in *Collected Poems 1909–1962* by T. S. Eliot. Copyright 1936 by Harcourt Brace Jovanovich, Inc.; copyright © 1963, 1964 by T. S. Eliot.
Reprinted by permission of Harcourt Brace Jovanovich, Inc., and Faber and Faber, Ltd.

Wallace Stevens quote on page 235.
From *Opus Posthumous* by Wallace Stevens, edited by Samuel French Morse.
Copyright © 1957 by Elsie Stevens and Holly Stevens.
Reprinted by permission of Random House, Inc., and Alfred A. Knopf, Inc.

Lyrics from Bob Dylan's "Stuck Inside of Mobile with the Memphis Blues Again" on page 269.
Copyright © 1966 by Dwarf Music. All rights reserved.
International copyright secured. Reprinted by permission.

Wallace Stevens quote on page 359.
From *The Palm at the End of the Mind, Selected Poems and a Play* by Wallace Stevens, edited by Holly Stevens.
Copyright © 1967, 1969, 1971 by Holly Stevens.
Reprinted by permission of Random House, Inc., and Alfred A. Knopf, Inc.

Special thanks to *Omni* magazine, which first commissioned and published Judith Hooper's interviews with Candace Pert, Karl Pribram, John Lilly, and Robert Heath. Research arising from these assignments was immensely valuable in the creation of this book and quotes from these interviews have been incorporated into the work.

Photographs of authors on jacket are courtesy of photographer John Muth/*Omni* magazine.

The PET scans of an epileptic patient at the UCLA School of Medicine on p. 123 first appeared in *Neurology* 1983; 33:400–413.

PET scans of a "rapidly cycling" manic-depressive on page 124 courtesy of *Archives of General Psychiatry*, May 1985, 42(5), pp. 444–445. Copyright © 1985, American Medical Association.

Contents

List of Art   ix

Acknowledgments   xi

Foreword by Isaac Asimov   xiii

Looking for Consciousness: A Time Line   xvii

1   The Three-Pound Universe   I

THE HARDWARE OF CONSCIOUSNESS

2   Crown of Creation   25

3   The Chemical Brain   68

4   Madness . . . and Other Windows on the Brain   105

5   Electrical Heavens and Hells   145

6   Caligula's Brain: The Neurobiology of Violence   162

7   Memory: From Sea Slugs to *Swann's Way*   185

8   The Many-Chambered Self   218

ALTERED STATES

9   The Hanged Man: Altered States of Consciousness   251

10   Anatomy of Hallucination: Prophets of the Void   258

11   Chuang-tzu and the Butterfly: Dreams and Reality   281

12   Border Stations: The Near-Death Experience   303

13   God in the Brain: Cleansing the Doors of Perception   324

THE BRAIN/MIND CONNECTION

14   Chaos, Strange Attractors, and the Stream of Consciousness   359

Brainspeak: A Traveler's Lexicon   391

Bibliography   397

Index   403

List of Art

PHOTOGRAPHS

The Three-Pound Universe	2
The Conversion of St. Paul by Raphael	3
A cutaway view of a real human brain	26
Phrenology chart	27
Stained nerve cells viewed under a microscope	31
A small neuron of the cortex	33
Neurons of the human cerebral cortex	33
Frances Farmer	41
The cortex of a rat raised in an "enriched" environment	64
Diagram of neurotransmission	71
The visual cortex of a macaque monkey	74
Candace B. Pert	79
Miles Herkenham	82
"The Face of Pleasure"; map of opiate receptors	84
Abnormal neurons in a schizophrenic brain	113
A normal CAT scan	115
A CAT scan of a schizophrenic brain	115
PET scans of an epileptic	123
PET scans of a manic-depressive	124
Dr. Henry Wagner enters the PET scanner	128
The first pictures of living human opiate receptors	129
The deprivation syndrome	176
Marcel Proust	192
The Hanged Man of the Tarot deck	252
Ronald K. Siegel	259
Huichol Indian yarn painting	262
Lattice pattern in Huichol embroidery	263
Spiders' webs woven under the influence of mind-altering drugs	266–267

John C. Lilly, M.D., and friends   273

Stephen LaBerge prepares oneironaut for a night's sleep   282

Arnold J. Mandell, M.D.   331

Relativity by M. C. Escher   340

Dr. Karl Pribram demonstrates a Multiplex hologram   347

The Belousov-Zhabotinski reaction   379

"Headquarters"   384

ILLUSTRATIONS

FIG. 1   Neuron   29

FIG. 2   The human brain   34

FIG. 3   Geography of the cortex   38

FIG. 4   Homunculus   40

FIG. 5   Comparison of human brain with other animals; triune brain   44

FIG. 6   Endorphins and their relatives   87

FIG. 7   Brain waves   133

FIG. 8   Split-brain test   231

FIG. 9   "Devil's tuning fork"   339

FIG. 10   Necker cube   339

Acknowledgments

This book would not have been possible without the nearly two hundred scientists who shared their knowledge and insights with us over the past five years. We owe special thanks to Candace B. Pert, who taught us that neuroscience is really about human nature and whose insights were the initial inspiration for the book. We are also deeply grateful to Alan Garfinkel, Robert G. Heath, John C. Lilly, Paul D. MacLean, Arnold J. Mandell, Karl Pribram, and Ronald K. Siegel, who spent hours guiding us through their particular realms, pointing out the essential truths buried in the data.

We would also like to thank the following researchers, many of whom took us into their laboratories and their homes, all of whom took time away from their own research and their own publications to make the brain accessible to nonscientists:

Ralph Abraham, Robert Ader, W. Ross Adey, Huda Akil, John Allman, Theodore X. Barber, Jack D. Barchas, Philip Berger, Erica Bourguignon, Jonathan Brody, Gerald L. Brown, Monte S. Buchsbaum, John B. Calhoun, Patricia Carrington, Thomas N. Chase, Richard Coppola, Jack D. Cowan, Timothy J. Crow, Glen C. Davis, Arthur J. Deikman, Victor Denenberg, Emanuel Donchin, David Drachman, Ranjin Duara, Connie Duncan-Johnson.

Sir John Eccles, Cindy Ehlers, Burr S. Eichelman, Doyne Farmer, Lester Fehmi, Walter J. Freeman, Glenn O. Gabbard, R. Allen and Beatrix Gardner, Michael S. Gazzaniga, Alan Gevins, Stanley Glick, Gordon Globus, Philip Gold, Roger A. Gorski, Elmer Green, William T. Greenough, Donald R. Griffin, Stephen Grossberg, Jean Hamilton, Fritz Henn, Miles Herkenham, Steven A. Hillyard, Henry Holcomb, Charles Honorton, John Hopfield.

Turan Itil, David S. Janowsky, Joe Kamiya, A. G. Karczmar, Robert Kastenbaum, Abba J. Kastin, Seymour S. Kety, Roy King, Joel Kleinman, Mark Konishi, Stephen LaBerge, John C. Liebeskind, Elizabeth Loftus, Paul J. Marangos, Daniel Margoliash, James Marsh, Steven Matthysse, John Mazziotta, Robert McCarley, Bruce S. McEwen, James L. McGaugh, Michael McGuire, Sarnoff A. Mednick, Wallace Mendelson, Michael M. Merzenich, Joe E. Miller, Allan F. Mirsky, Mortimer Mishkin.

John A. Money, John Morihisa, Bud Mueller, Dennis L. Murphy, Donald A. Norman, Fernando Nottebohm, Karlis Osis, Jaak Panksepp, Steven Paul, Donald W. Pfaff, Michael E. Phelps, David Pickar, Robert M. Post, James W. Prescott, Frank Putnam, Marcus Raichle, Judith Rappaport, D. Eugene Redmond, Kenneth Ring, Daniel N. Robinson, Norman Rosenthal, David E. Rumelhart, Judith Rumsey, Michael Sabom, Joseph J. Schildkraut, Marjorie Schuman.

John Searle, Robert Shaw, Phil Skolnick, Carolyn Smith, Solomon Snyder, Louis Sokoloff, Larry R. Squire, Michael Stanley, Larry Stein, Janice R. Stevens, Stephen Suomi, Charles T. Tart, Lionel Tiger, E. Fuller Torrey, Stuart W. Twemlow, Thomas M. Uhde, Henry N. Wagner, Donald O. Walter, Stanley J. Watson, Thomas Wehr, Daniel R. Weinberger, Herbert Weingartner, Jay A. Weiss, Alfred P. Wolf, Richard Jed Wyatt, Dahlia Zaidel, Eran Zaidel, Marvin Zuckerman.

We would also like to thank Jules Asher, for help and guidance beyond the call of duty; Beverly Kedzierski, for her perspectives on lucid dreaming; and "M. M. George," for sharing her amazing life story.

Foreword

BY ISAAC ASIMOV

Nowadays we take it entirely for granted that the human brain is the organ that controls thought. We say, "He has brains," when we mean that he is intelligent. We tap our temples significantly when we wish to indicate that someone doesn't think clearly. Or else we say, "He has bats in his belfry," meaning that disorderly and unpredictable events take place in the highest portion of the body (the brain), which corresponds metaphorically to the highest portion of the church (the belfry), in which bats might literally exist. This might be shortened to a simple "He's bats."

Yet what we take for granted was not necessarily obvious to the ancients. The brain, after all, does nothing visible. It simply sits there. How different from the heart that beats constantly all the moments you are alive and no longer beats when you are dead. What's more, the heartbeat races after muscular effort, or when you are stirred by deep emotion of any kind, and it slows during sleep, when you seem to be simulating a kind of death.

There is a certain sense, then, in supposing the heart to be the seat of life and emotion. The long ages in which this supposition held sway remains enshrined in our language. A person who is brave is "lion-hearted," while a coward is "chicken-hearted." If we embolden ourselves to dare a difficult task, we "take heart," and if we suffer a sad disappointment in love or ambition, we are "broken-hearted." (Needless to say, the heart has nothing to do with any of this.)

If the heart is central to our life, surely that must be so because it pumps blood. A wound that involves the loss of blood weakens us and, if bad enough, can kill us. Blood surges into our face and reddens it during physical exertion or when we are driven into anger or shame. On the other hand, blood drains from our face leaving it pale when we suffer fear or anxiety.

The importance of blood also leaves its mark on our language. When we act under the stress of emotion, we do something "in hot blood." When it is not emotion but calculation that is the spring of our action, we do it "in cold blood." Someone who is commonly emotional is "hot-blooded," someone commonly intellectual is "cold-blooded." (Needless to say, the blood remains at the same temperature under all nonpathological conditions.)

Organs particularly rich in blood are also suspected of having much to do with one's state of mind. The liver and spleen are two such organs. Blood is pictured as leaving the liver at moments of fear just as it leaves the face. Under such conditions, it is imagined that the dark color of the liver pales, and a coward is spoken of as "lily-livered." The word *spleen*, on the other hand, refers not only to a blood-filled organ of our body but also to such emotions as anger and spite. (Needless to say, the liver and spleen have nothing to do with the emotions.)

But what about the brain? Does it do *anything*? Aristotle, the most renowned of the ancient thinkers, believed that the brain was designed to cool the heated blood that passed through it. It was merely an air-conditioning device, so to speak.

And yet there is one point that might have stirred the suspicions of a careful observer. The abdominal wall contains no bone but is protected merely by a tough layer of muscle. The liver and spleen (and other abdominal organs) are thus not very efficiently guarded.

The heart and lungs, which are located in the chest, are more efficiently protected, thanks to the bony slats of the rib cage. This seems to indicate that the heart and lungs are more immediately vital to the body than the abdominal organs are. However, the protection isn't perfect, for a knife can easily slip between the ribs and into the heart.

The brain, on the other hand, is almost totally enclosed by a closely fitting curve of bone. The brain lies hidden inside the strong skull, well-protected from all but the most powerful blow. It is the only organ so thoroughly protected, and surely this must have meaning. Would a mere air-conditioning device be so tucked away behind armor, when even the heart is protected only by a slap-dash of ribs?

This may have been one of the reasons why the ancient Greek anatomist Herophilus, in the generation after Aristotle, decided that it was the brain that was the seat of intelligence. But his opinion did not weigh sufficiently against the overwhelming prestige of Aristotle, whose word was taken as final for nearly two thousand years.

It was dimly understood that the nerves were important, however, and in 1664, an English physician, Thomas Willis, wrote the first accurate treatise on the brain and showed that nerves emanated from that organ. That book (only a little over three centuries ago) marked the turning point and the beginning of the final realization of the brain's importance.

The more scientists studied the brain, the more complex it seemed to be. In its three pounds are packed ten billion nerve cells and nearly one hundred billion smaller supporting cells. No computer we have yet built contains one hundred billion switching units; and if we did build one with that many there is no way in which we could as yet compact them into a structure weighing as little as three pounds.

What's more, the "wiring" of the brain is far more complicated than that in any computer. Each nerve cell is connected to many other nerve cells in a complex pattern that allows the tiny electrical currents that mark nerve action to flow in any of a vast number of possible pathways. In comparison, the structure of a computer's units is primitively simple and the patterns of flow easily calculable.

Finally, whereas in a computer the units are switches that are either "on" or "off," the nerve-cell units of the brain are themselves magnificently complex objects, each one containing enormous numbers of complicated molecules whose system of functioning is unknown to us, but which undoubtedly makes each individual cell more complicated than an entire computer is.

The human brain, then, is the most complicated organization of matter that we know. (The dolphin brain might conceivably match it, and there may be superior brains among extraterrestrial intelligences, but we have as yet very little knowledge concerning the organization of dolphin brains and none at all concerning those of extraterrestrial intelligences—who might not even exist.) The human brain is certainly more complicated in organization than is a mighty star, which is why we know so much more about stars than about the brain.

Indeed, the brain is so complex, and human attempts to understand how it works have, until now, met with such apparently insurmountable hurdles, that it seems a fair question to ask whether we can *ever* understand the brain, whether it is *possible* to do so.

After all, we are trying to understand the brain by using the brain. Can something understand itself? Can the brain's complexity comprehend a brain's complexity?

If one human brain were alone involved, these questions would be fair and might be answered in the negative. However, not one human brain but many are tackling the subject; not one human being but a scientific team that is scattered over the world is doing so. Each researcher may, after years of work, add only a trifling bit to the sum of our neurological knowledge, but all the researchers together are making significant and in some cases astonishing progress.

Considering that the human brain, thanks to its intelligence and ingenuity, is the greatest hope of humanity; and that the human brain, thanks to its ability to hate, envy, and desire, is also the greatest danger to humanity—what can conceivably be more important than to understand the various aspects of the brain and to learn how, possibly, to encourage those that are constructive and to correct those that are destructive.

In this book, then, Judith Hooper and Dick Teresi tell of the progress in this research and forecast future potentialities. They tell the story of the ultimate peak of human seeking, the attempt of humanity to understand itself.

Looking for Consciousness: A Time Line

c. 40,000 B.C. Human brain evolves to its present form.

c. 430 B.C. Hippocrates, the patron of physicians, calls the brain the organ of thought.

c. 390 B.C. Plato declares that the soul is incorporeal and superior to the body.

c. 335 B.C. Aristotle, watching headless chickens running around, decides the heart is the seat of consciousness.

1637 Réné Descartes divides *res cogitans* from *res extensa*; glorifies the pineal gland.

1748 Julien Offray de la Mettrie says the soul is superfluous.

1810 Franz Joseph Gall, seeking the source of thoughts and emotions, dissects brains, invents phrenology.

1848 Phineas Gage's brain is pierced by an iron rod, making him history's most celebrated neurological case.

1860 Pierre Paul Broca unveils the speech center before the Paris Anthropological Society.

1871 Camillo Golgi, an Italian physician, invents a silver stain that makes nerve cells visible under the microscope.

1874 German neurologist Carl Wernicke identifies an area specialized for speech comprehension in the left hemisphere.

1890s Sigmund Freud grows bored with lamprey nerves, invents psychoanalysis.

c. 1900 Ivan Pavlov's dog discovers the conditioned reflex.

1901 Santiago Ramón y Cajal notices that neurons are separated by tiny gaps, or synaptic clefts.

1906   Sir Charles Sherrington describes how reflexes are "wired" in the brain.

1911   Eugen Bleuler coins the term *schizophrenia.*

1913   John B. Watson sets forth the principles of behaviorism; the brain becomes a "black box."

1921   Otto Loewi identifies acetylcholine, the first known neurotransmitter.

1926   Karl Lashley begins looking for the seat of memory.

1929   Hans Berger records brain waves from a person's scalp.

1930   B. F. Skinner invents operant conditioning, teaches pigeons to play the piano.

1935   Egas Moniz performs the first prefrontal lobotomy on an inmate in a Lisbon insane asylum.

1940s   Some of Wilder Penfield's patients have interesting "flashbacks" during brain surgery.

1943   Albert Hofmann takes the world's first LSD trip.

1949   Donald O. Hebb describes the "neural net."

1950   Lashley gives up on the engram, concludes memories are not localized.

1950s   America falls in love with psychoanalysis.

1952   Robert Heath implants deep brain electrodes in a human being.

1952   Alan L. Hodgkin and Andrew Huxley describe how neurons fire.

1952   Chlorpromazine alleviates schizophrenia; internal straitjackets replace the external kind.

1952   Paul MacLean names the limbic system.

1953   REM sleep is discovered.

1953   James Olds and Peter Milner activate a rat's "pleasure center."

1954   John Lilly invents the isolation tank, experiences "psychological freefall."

1957   Vernon Mountcastle shows that neurons are arranged in columns.

Late 1950s   Harry Harlow rears baby monkeys in isolation; the monkeys develop serious psychological problems.

1959   David Hubel and Torsten Wiesel publish their first studies on the visual system.

1961   The first "split brain" operation is performed by Roger Sperry and Joseph Bogen.

1963   Edward Lorenz finds a "strange attractor" in the weather.

1963   José Delgado becomes the first neurophysiologist/matador, stopping an electrode-equipped bull dead in its tracks via radio remote control.

1964   Rat brains show the effects of cultural "enrichment."

c. 1966   *Aplysia*, a giant sea slug, "remembers" in Eric Kandel's laboratory.

1973   First PET scan shows the metabolic activity inside a dog's brain.

1973   The opiate receptor is discovered by Candace Pert and Solomon Snyder.

1975   John Hughes and Hans Kosterlitz identify enkephalin, the first natural brain opiate.

1982   First human "brain transplant" (actually, a graft of dopamine-rich tissue from the patient's adrenal gland) is performed in Stockholm; fails to alleviate the patient's Parkinson's disease.

THE
THREE-POUND
UNIVERSE

1

The Three-Pound Universe

Everyone now knows how to find the meaning of
life within himself. But . . . less than a century
ago men and women did not have access to the
puzzle boxes within them. They could not name
even one of the fifty-three portals to the soul.
—KURT VONNEGUT,
The Sirens of Titan

For now we see through a glass, darkly; but then
face to face: now I know in part: but then shall
I know even as also I am known.
—I Corinthians 13:12

WATCHING the mauve shadows of dusk move across the sand-
stone cliffs, the traveler felt suddenly weak. The cries of circling
birds filled him with unease, and he sensed a mysterious presence behind him. But when he turned, he saw only the silver shiver of an
olive tree in the breeze. In an instant that was an eternity, a white light
exploded in his head. The outer world disappeared; he could no longer
remember his name or why he had set off for Damascus. As he fell to the
ground a voice cried out, addressing him by name: "Saul, Saul, why per-
secuteth thou me?"

Three days of blindness and several visions later, the Christian-baiting
Saul of Tarsus had become the zealous epistle-writing Paul, apostle of "the
peace of God that passeth all understanding." His conversion occurred
nearly two millennia ago, in a land of goatherds and prophets.

Suppose it happened now. Suppose a modern-day Paul arrived at the
emergency room, blind and babbling about unearthly voices. "Hmmm
. . . a grand mal seizure with interictal spiking," says the neurology resident,
examining the trail of wavelets on the electroencephalograph (EEG) record. (There are, in fact, hints that the biblical Paul suffered from epilepsy.)
Or maybe, "Disorientation, paranoid ideation, auditory hallucinations,
grandiosity, religious delusions," with a provisional diagnosis of schizophrenia. In any case, few neurologists would be persuaded that God really
spoke to a latter-day Paul, at least not from the cerulean heavens. The
"peace of God that passeth all understanding" they'd say—like patriotism,

I

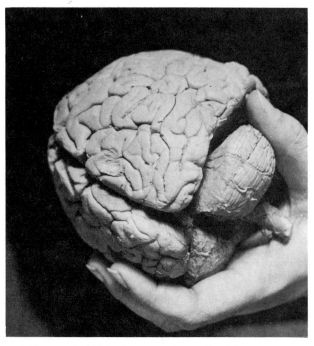

The three-pound universe: You can hold it in the palm of your hand, but a computer with the same number of "bits" would be a hundred stories tall and cover the state of Texas. (*Manfred Kage/Peter Arnold, Inc.*)

phobias, longings, dreams, and dark nights of the soul—is a product solely of the human brain. Are they right? And if so, does that invalidate Paul's vision?

For most of human history, the affairs of the soul fell under the jurisdiction of the local church, temple, or department of philosophy. Today theologians and philosophers still brood on the old conundrums, but the existential secrets seem to lie in the hands of a different sort of people, practical-minded types who wear lab coats and speak of "excitatory postsynaptic potentials" and "central olfactory pathways." When we ask "Who am I?" "What sort of thing is man?" "How do we know what we know?" we are asking about the three pounds of Jello-like tissue in our skull.

This is the Brain Age. The 1930s and 1940s were the golden age of physics. The next two decades saw the flowering of molecular biology, from the unraveling of the double helix to the in vitro bravado of genetic engineering. But the great frontier of the 1980s is neuroscience. Its practitioners come from a dozen or so formerly separate fields, including neurophysiology, neurochemistry, neuroanatomy, pharmacology, psychiatry, psychology, ethology, computer science, electrical engineering, and physics. Some of them run rats through T-mazes; some try to simulate memory processes with a computer; others chart the vertiginous geometries of hallucination. There are brain scientists who impale dreams with superfine electrodes, and those who spelunker in Freudian grottoes. To some the mind is an organ homogenized to a milky froth in a blender; to some it is a little black box of drives and appetites. To others it's an intricate, fluorescent-stained road map of nerve cells or a van Gogh landscape twisted by hallucinations and delusions. All of the above (and more) is neuroscience, for the brain, though the size of a grapefruit, is as vast as the universe. In fact, it *is* the known universe. Everything we know—from subatomic particles to distant galaxies—everything we feel—from love for our children to fear of enemy nations—is experienced and modeled in our brains. Without the brain, nothing—not quarks, not black holes, nor love, nor hatred—would exist for us. The universe exists for us only insofar as it exists in our brains. The brain is our three-pound universe.

There is one point we should clear up before we begin. This book is about the brain, the mind, and the relationship between the two. Most people associate "mind" or "brain" with psychology/psychotherapy or neurology. However, this is *not* a book about the Joyce Brotherses and Ben Caseys of the world, the psychologists and neurologists who get paid by the hour to head off your fourth divorce or to probe your skin with sharp

The Conversion of St. Paul by Raphael: Was the vision on the road to Damascus a temporal lobe seizure? (*The Bettmann Archive*)

instruments in search of damaged nerves. Valuable as these practitioners may be, our focus here is not therapy or doctoring. This is a book about neuroscience.

A neuroscientist may be a psychologist, a neurologist, or a neurosurgeon by training, but he or she is less interested in the early potty-training traumas that set the stage for your present divorce than in the chemical/electrical/physical events that occur in your brain tissue when you file for divorce, move to Kalamazoo, or listen to your favorite Grateful Dead tape.

This book is the result of a four-year journey that was often circuitous and strange, even boring at times. Rather than 36-point-headline news (SCIENTISTS UNLOCK SECRET OF LIFE), we sometimes met with unbelievable tedium, which in an odd way increased our respect for the scientists who do this work. For every brilliant breakthrough there are thousands of "failures to find." For every Nobel prize there are untold hours of painstaking bench-work, figuring out the pH of the solution in which a brain slice is to be rinsed; calculating dose-response curves and standard deviations; staying up all night to watch the graph-paper squiggles that record the firing of a single rat nerve cell. No carpeted offices or panoramic views either. Most brain science is done in places that are about as glamorous as a surgical-supplies store or the audiovisual room in an elementary school. Sometimes there are rank animal smells, too.

Our search for the mind took us to laboratories where "the brain's own Valium" is being sought in mashed cow brains; to gene-splicing factories, dream labs, mental hospitals, and the ersatz sea of an "isolation tank" in California. We talked to specialists in senility, epilepsy, and dyslexia; to neurosurgeons; to electrical engineers who do brain-wave analysis; to psychoanalysts, animal behaviorists, microbiologists, radiation scientists, mathematicians. We met a lot of animals: chimpanzees missing their "memory centers," songbirds tutored by computers, "depressed" rats, monkeys whose circadian rhythms had been derailed by weeks of sensory isolation, mice on cocaine. (Because human brains are off-limits for most experiments, animals are the unsung heroes of this field.) We attended talks on "Enzymes Involved in the Processing and Degradation of Enkephalins in Brain Synaptosomes" and other opaque topics. Our files swelled with journal papers on early childhood development and artificial intelligence, fluid dynamics, depression, the neuropsychology of vision, and linguistics.

Everywhere we went we asked this question: Is the mind the same as the brain? Is this bundle of memories, beliefs, desires, hopes, and fears contained in a bodily organ, a lump of matter? Is *consciousness* only another word for the concerted activity of ten-billion-plus nerve cells? Many of the scientists we met said, *Of course*, where else could the mind be? Others said the question was unanswerable. Some changed the subject to neuroactive peptides.

The business of science is to explain the universe in terms of physical laws. It tells us that lightning bolts are not the weapons of wrathful gods but electrical discharges; that planets revolve around the sun according to orderly gravitational laws; that genetic traits are passed from parents to their offspring along coiled strands of DNA. But what is a human being? Can you be "explained" in terms of mechanics, electromagnetism, physics, or chemistry?

An Ancient Riddle

THE QUESTION wasn't born yesterday. It probably has been around as long as Homo sapiens. Plato saw man as a compound of spirit and matter, with the spirit guiding his actions. The soul was immaterial and eternal, dwelling in the debased house of the body as a disembodied pilot or noble prisoner. Only the soul could know absolute truth and absolute beauty; the corporeal half of man was but a crude contraption of bones, muscles, and sinews. Meanwhile other ancient Greeks, notably the atomist Democritus, said that everything, consciousness included, was material.

Medieval Christianity borrowed the Platonic notion of a godlike soul trapped within a fleshly body. Then in the fifteenth and sixteenth centuries, the natural sciences began to disturb the sacred order, and man became increasingly preoccupied with the behavior of matter. Copernicus proved that our little blue-green planet was not necessarily the apple of God's eye. Galileo, looking through his telescope, saw more planets than the heavenly seven that the Church allowed, and the angels began to retreat from the skies. It remained for Isaac Newton to contribute the stolid new gods of gravity and momentum, and the divine cosmos became a rational, clockwork universe.

Enamored of the new science of mechanics, the mathematician/philosopher René Descartes (1596–1650) thought it likely that the human body was a grand machine, a fancy piece of hydraulic clockwork, whose parts worked according to mechanical laws. But was man *just* a machine? Were all his faculties the work of biological pistons and pumps? Asking himself, "What am I?" Descartes eventually had the epiphany that schoolchildren three centuries later would still be inscribing in their copybooks: *Cogito, ergo sum*: "I think, therefore I am."

The essence of a human being was the faculty of thought, according to Descartes, and thought could not be material. He could see how certain mechanistic functions (walking, eating, digesting food, and so on) could be performed by the clockwork body alone, but understanding, willing, and remembering required a soul. After all, unlike bits of matter, the mind cannot be localized in space; it can't be seen, tasted, or sliced up like a baguette. Besides, Descartes had to reconcile a mechanistic universe with the doctrines of the Church.

By cleaving man into equal parts of matter and spirit, Descartes became the patron saint of *dualism*. He had a problem, though. How do mind and body interact (as they obviously must)? How can something nonphysical have a physical effect? How does an act of will move the muscles of the fingers to write *Cogito, ergo sum*? How, conversely, does a bodily event leave an imprint on the nonmaterial mind; how do mechanical changes in the optic nerve allow one to see the chestnut trees in the Bois de Boulogne? Descartes's search for a liaison between mind and matter settled on the pineal gland, located in the brain behind the space between the eyebrows, at the site of the so-called third eye. Here, he proposed, was the soul's port of entry in the body—the mind/body interface, as moderns might say. Unfortunately the pineal gland didn't really solve the problem.

There are two ways to avoid worrying about the traffic rules between soul and body. You can suppose either that the two do *not* interact or that they are one and the same. Gottfried von Leibniz (1646–1716) took the first route. He declared that the nonphysical mind and the physical body follow separate, parallel courses during a person's life, never meeting and never causally connected. It only *looks* as if the act of pricking a finger causes the mental experience of pain, said Leibniz. Actually, physical events and mental events coincide in time and space only because God keeps the two in perfect synch. This theory, known as *psychophysical parallelism*, isn't much in vogue with the Society for Neuroscience today.

The *idealist* philosophers, on the other hand, saw only one substance in the universe: mindstuff. To George Berkeley (1685–1753), chairs, rocks, tea cakes, carriages, and our own flesh were only bundles of percepts— heat, wetness, sweetness, redness, hardness, shininess, and so on—without any independent existence. We delude ourselves if we think that chairs are more real than the objects of our imagination, according to Bishop Berkeley, for "they both equally exist in the mind, and in that sense they are alike ideas." *Esse* is *percipi*: to be is to be perceived. (Samuel Johnson, Berkeley's contemporary, "refuted" this antirealist doctrine by vigorously kicking a stone.) How does a tree manage to remain in the Quad overnight after everybody's asleep? Well, God is still watching, said Berkeley. In this book you'll read that the idealists were largely right in placing the colors, textures, and odors of "reality" inside the brain, and you'll learn that your neurons convey the features of the outside world more in the manner of highly stylized folktales than a surveyor's report.

A third way out of the Cartesian quandary is to banish the soul from the bodily machine, as the materialist philosophers of the seventeenth and eighteenth centuries did. Their ideas foreshadowed the central gospel of modern neuroscience: that mental states come down to bodily events, and that there is but one substance in the universe—matter. Reflecting on the resemblances between man-made automata and living organisms, Thomas Hobbes (1588–1679) sounds like an early avatar of artificial intelligence. Hobbes reasoned: If machines can simulate bodily motions (or today, if computers can simulate the mind's operations), why regard human beings as anything more than machines?

Seeing life is but a motion of limbs, the beginning whereof is in some principal part within; why may we not say that all *automata* (engines that move themselves by springs and wheels as doth a watch) have an artificial life? What is the *heart* but a *spring*; and the *nerves* but so many *wheels*, giving motion to the body, such as was intended by the artificer?

In 1748 what remained of the soul part of Descartes's equation was irreparably damaged by an influential book, *L'homme machine* ("Man a Machine"), by Julien Offray de La Mettrie, who wrote: "Since the faculties of the soul depend to such a degree on the proper organization of the brain and the whole body . . . the soul is clearly an enlightened machine."

The "enlightened machine" became the glory of the biological sciences, and the soul faded into wan exile. A century later the venerable cell biologist Jacques Monod looked up from his test tubes and proclaimed: "The cell is a machine. The animal is a machine. Man is a machine." In 1949 the late Oxford philosopher Gilbert Ryle caricatured Descartes's philosophy as the "ghost in the machine," a catchphrase that has become a sort of motto of neuroscience. "The idea of an immaterial mind controlling the body is vitalism, no more, no less," psychologist Donald O. Hebb, one of the founding fathers of the field, wrote in 1974. "It has no place in science."

A Preview of Coming Attractions

AT FIRST GLANCE the brain revolution seems to have done it: *proved* that the mind is the brain. No longer is insanity purely "mental"; nor is memory or temperament. What our Victorian grandparents used to call "character" is contained in an intricate matrix of speech centers, motor pathways, and minute electrical circuits.

In the following pages, you'll read about neuroscience's many triumphs along these lines. For example:

· For years psychologists said your character was formed by Dr. Spock, your mother's toilet-training philosophy, and X hours of "Sesame Street." Now it seems that you are shy or dominant, antisocial, alcoholic, suicidal, or predisposed to murder largely because of the chemicals in your brain. Do you suffer from schizophrenia, depression, phobias, obsessions, anxiety? Don't waste years in some analyst's office resolving your Electra complex amid the philodendrons and Mondrian prints. Better to find a good psychopharmacologist to fine-tune your neurochemistry.

· With a new generation of "designer drugs," pharmacologists are proving that a worldview can be quickly changed by a molecule. Out of their test tubes come drugs for a photographic memory, a better sex life, superalertness, an end to anxiety, perhaps even transcendental peace. If selfhood can be altered chemically, is the self a chemical commodity?

· Memory, which the ancient Greeks attributed to a muse and Descartes ascribed to "animal spirits," depends on particular bits of gray matter. Ditto for language, the recognition of familiar faces, the ability to count and read, and many other higher functions. Wipe out one part of the brain and a person speaks fluent gibberish; remove another and he no longer knows his own brother by sight. Brain surgery (or strokes, tumors, and head injuries) can turn a person into a nonperson, or so it seems. Where, then, is the self?

· Twenty years of research on "split-brain" patients (whose two cerebral hemispheres have been surgically disconnected) leave us with the disconcerting possibility that a person can possess two minds in one body. Meanwhile, sophisticated EEG recordings and brain scans show that "split personality" (or multiple personality disorder, as it's known in the textbooks) has a biological basis. The three brains of Eve are neurophysiologically distinct. If every mind requires a soul, do split-brain patients have two? Do multiples have three, ten, fifteen? What about the rest of us?

· Your brain contains pain and pleasure centers as well as control switches for hunger, thirst, and sexual desire. When you stimulate a cat's "fear center" with an electrode, it runs away in terror from a harmless little mouse; when the same is done to a monkey "boss," he loses his rank in the colony. Human beings are not immune. When a mild electrical current is delivered to their "pleasure centers," paranoid, catatonic, or violent mental patients are sometimes converted (temporarily, anyway) into the likes of Ozzie and Harriet Nelson. Does this mean that free will can be overridden and the soul manipulated by electricity?

· Over the last two decades, scientists have methodically demystified perception. We now know that the brightness of a color is exactly proportional to the firing frequency of cells in the brain's visual area. We can identify cells that fire in response to vertical or horizontal lines; others that "recognize" dots or edges. We know the neural coding for sensory messages at each way station on the path from the skin surface to the cerebral cortex. Why assign perception to a hovering soul if we can find it in the biological machinery?

· The mind is the last resort of privacy, of course—unless the new high-tech mind readers invade it. Can Big Brother map your thoughts with ultrasophisticated brain-wave analysis? And what about those new PET (positron emission tomography) scans: Is it true they can see depression in technicolor?

· Three hundred angels dancing on the head of the pin? A Chinese dragon breathing jade-green smoke? The face of God? All visions known to humankind, not excepting Joan of Arc's and the prophet Mohammed's, are products of the brain's wiring. Furthermore, religion is *literally* the opiate of the people; the Godhead itself may lurk in a neurochemical. Or so say some of the scientific connoisseurs of altered states. As for dreams, well . . . Maybe you have a recurrent one about chasing a train that retreats forever in the distance, and maybe you think it means you have feelings of personal inadequacy. Forget it. It's just the cells in your brain stem firing.

With such machinery, do we need a soul?

An Inferiority Complex

DESPITE its Promethean feats, neuroscience has a problem. Its practitioners are modest compared with those in the more established sciences of physics, astronomy, and chemistry. "There is something fascinating about science," Mark Twain once said. "One gets such wholesale returns of conjecture out of such trifling investments of fact." This may be true of physicists, who every time they happen on a minor subatomic particle call a press conference to unveil yet another grand theory—usually in some glamorous place like Geneva.

Neuroscience, in contrast, is data rich and theory poor. It is awash in brilliant discoveries, but you might not guess it from an annual meeting of the Society for Neuroscience, a fest of arid understatement characteristically held in a hotel in Minneapolis. "Speculation" is a breach of etiquette, rather like wearing large gold medallions inscribed with one's initials, whereas one of the favorite buzz words is *parsimonious*, as in: "The most parsimonious explanation for the data is . . ." Those who do venture "beyond the data" to theorize about consciousness risk being considered mavericks or worse.

Why is neuroscience theory-impoverished? One reason may be that the grand scientific theories are generally nourished by higher mathematics, the physicist's second language, and most life scientists aren't at home in advanced math. Brain science is by nature empirical, experimental, and antitheoretical. Another, subtler reason may be this: Like all the life sciences, neuroscience has traditionally occupied a rather low position in the scientific hierarchy. Up at the Olympian levels are the physicists and mathematicians, of course. As the saying goes, physicists answer only to mathematicians and the mathematicians answer only to God. Physicists give grudging approval to astronomers and chemists, and for decades have looked down their noses at biologists and their brethren. Medicine is low on the ladder, psychiatry lower still. And psychology? Don't even ask.

In an effort to make psychology more rigorous, Ivan Pavlov and his behaviorist heirs converted the old "science of the soul" into a would-be exact science of reflexes and salivation rates. Neuroscience, in part because of its association with medical science and psychology, has also suffered from a bit of an inferiority complex. To compensate, it cultivates hard statistics.

Today brain science is on the cusp of becoming a hard science. Its situation might be compared to biology thirty years ago, which was considered a pretty soft discipline before James Watson and Francis Crick came along to unravel the structure of DNA, the master molecule of heredity. Thus molecular biology was born, with its rigorous, quasi-mathematical codes.

There has always been a "hard" side to neuroscience, but in the past it was confined to such matters as ganglion number 21 in the lobster, the stretch reflex in a cat's tendons, and increases in calcium ion conductance relative to cell-membrane depolarization. Real behavior, not to mention consciousness, was so far out in the hinterlands that even psychologists wouldn't touch it. Today, however, brain science is beginning to explain the mechanics of memory, perception, motivation, fear, loathing, and sexual desire. It is tinkering with the regions of nervous tissue where we really live. What it has *not* attempted is any sort of "unified field theory" of consciousness. Physicists openly dream of a theory that would tie together all the forces of nature into a single, elegantly simple formula that, as one researcher put it, "you can wear on your T-shirt."

Neuroscientists in general have shied away from any grand synthesis. Maybe brain events are by nature messier, more inelegant, than physical events, and that is why $E = mc^2$ fits nicely on a T-shirt, while the famous 1952 Hodgkin-Huxley model of nerve-cell excitation would fill a busy ankle-length chemise.

In any case this book will focus on the few synthesizers, theorizers, model builders, and grand dreamers in neuroscience. Interestingly, most of them are interdisciplinary types: physicists-turned-neurophysiologists, computer scientist/psychologists, mathematician/psychiatrists. Some will doubtless be proved either dead wrong or half wrong. One may emerge as the Newton, Einstein, or Watson-and-Crick of the brain. As James Watson put it, "I don't think consciousness will turn out to be something grand. People said there was something grand down in the cellar that gave us heredity. It turned out to be pretty simple—DNA."

Brain as Machine

THAT'S NOT TO SAY that neuroscience lacks metaphors. In science metaphors are called *models*, and they are more than figures of speech, for they shape, direct— and sometimes confine—our knowledge. It's an interesting commentary on the fellowship of man and machine that brain metaphors have historically been drawn from the most advanced technology of the age. Descartes's models were inspired by the ornate water clocks of his day. In the heyday of steam engines, Sigmund Freud envisioned the central nervous system as a hydraulic system in which pressures (drives) built up and required "discharging." In the early 1920s the brain was likened to a telephone switchboard, and not coincidentally Ivan Pavlov, the high priest of the conditioned reflex, began preaching that behaviors were built of layers of reflexes, of hard-wired connections between different brain parts.

With the advent of cybernetic devices (of which your thermostat is a humble example), neuroscientists started hunting for feedback loops in the brain. They found some, too. The neuroendocrine system, for example, is composed of many interlocking feedback loops: Chemical messengers routinely signal back to the brain, "Okay, enough of that hormone; you can shut down now."

The latest model is, of course, the computer, which began to haunt neuroscience in a big way in the early 1960s. Now terms such as *inputs* and *outputs*, *encoding*, information *storage* and *retrieval*, *parallel processing*, and *software* are part of the everyday idiom of the brain lab, as is the concept of the brain as an ultrasophisticated "biocomputer." Artificial brains have even provided a seductive (if imperfect) analogy for the mind/brain relationship. Perhaps mind, a cloud of abstractions, stands in relation to the brain, a lump of matter, as the software of a computer does to its hardware.

A new science of mind, *cognitive science* (a cross between psychology and computer science), was born of the man/machine interface. Cognitive scientists examine the human brain not by inquiring, "What are neurons made of? How do they fire?" but by concentrating on its "formal operations," its "programs," its "software," its "symbols." Just as you don't have to know anything about the physical materials inside an electronic calculator to find the cube root of 473, cognitive science says you needn't get bogged down in the minutiae of cellular chemistry to understand thinking. A thinking machine can theoretically be made of steel, silicon, flesh, or empty beer cans; it could be an abacus, a computer, or a brain. What matters is what it *does*.

The philosopher of science Jacob Bronowski observed in his book *The Identity of Man*, "If all knowledge can be formalized, then the human self can be matched, in principle, by a machine." That is the grand dream of artificial intelligence (AI), and it spawned a peculiar tautology: If a computer can act like a brain, then the brain must be a computer. If the AI whiz kids succeed in building a speaking automaton, they will have proved that speech can be performed by a soulless apparatus—unless we rewrite our metaphysics to allow for machines with souls. (Don't laugh; some pundits have.) So far, the most advanced computer on earth can't duplicate a four-year-old's language ability. It can't even build a bird's nest, as MIT's Marvin Minsky, one of the czars of artificial intelligence, has observed. Yet all this talk of machine intelligence adds a weird dimension to the mind/body problem. "Descartes couldn't see how thinking could be mechanical," says Patricia Churchland, a philosopher of science at the University of Manitoba. "Now we have machines that calculate."

Recently models based on parallel-processing computers and computer networks—which are more brainlike than digital machines—have come of age. The essential question, as Bronowski saw it, is: "Can a brain be both a machine and a self?" Bronowski's answer was yes: Nature creates the machinery, and individual experience fashions a self. There is a lot of truth to that statement, provided we understand that the brain is a Darwinian "machine," not the newest brainchild out of Bell Labs. In this book we'll argue that all knowledge can't be formalized, that human brains are not symbol crunchers. The brain is not really like anything except a brain.

Inside Irving Smith's Brain

NOW IMAGINE a day in the life of Irving E. Smith, *Homo sapiens americans*, from the moment he wakes to the blare of his radio-alarm, cursing the news of a traffic jam on the Brooklyn-Queens Expressway, to the second he falls asleep during the opening monologue on the "Tonight Show." During this particular day, Mr. Smith performs, say, 549,332 different actions: He reads an editorial in the newspaper and gets angry, writes two memos, lunches with a client, orders *boeuf bourguignon*, and tells three jokes; he remembers an old flame, eats and digests several meals, decides to roll over a six-month CD; he buys a new permanent-press shirt, scratches his foot thirty-seven times, glances at the digital time-temperature reading atop the building opposite twenty-one different times, kisses his wife, pats his dog, and so on. The central faith of the Brain Age is that Irving's behavior is the result of neural processes, just as the sun's brightness and heat result from the behavior of hydrogen, helium, and so on.

This doctrine is known as *identity theory*. The idea is that mental (psychological, spiritual) events and brain (physicochemical) events are one and the same. Irving's fit of pique on the expressway is in some sense identical to electrical discharges in his hypothalamus (a part of the brain containing a "rage center"). Instead of two separate sorts of "stuff," mind and matter, there is only one substance. This is called *monism*, as opposed to dualism, and it is the "central dogma of neuroscience," in the words of Johns Hopkins's Vernon Mountcastle, one of the *eminences grises* of this field.

Naturally the physical, electromagnetic, and chemical processes that make up Mr. Smith are extremely complicated. To "explain" two seconds' worth of his behavior—between waking to the sound of the traffic report on the radio and cursing—we'd have to understand how sound waves bounced off the walls of his outer and middle ears and traveled to his inner ear, where twenty-five thousand specialized transducer cells in the organ of Corti converted them into frequency-coded electrical pulses. We'd need to figure out how millions of cells in many parts of his higher brain decoded and understood the English words *bottleneck* and *half-hour delay* and conjured up, in a split second, a whole symphony of related memories and associations.

For the source of his malaise, we'd have to measure the secretion of minute amounts of two hundred different neurochemicals, tracing the flow of salty solutions through tiny porous gates in the cell walls. Then we'd have to diagram the multiple electrochemical events in his neural motor and speech centers that allowed him to articulate "Damn!" This is a pipe dream at best.

Present-day neuroscience can't even explain all the chemical steps that occur in Mr. Smith's inner ear, still less how words, worries about traffic jams, and images of old flames are encoded in his gray matter. Still, if Irving *is* his brain processes, the laws governing his soul are knowable in principle, if not in practice.

Reductionism and Black Boxes

THE MECHANISTIC, post-Cartesian world is ruled by the principle of *reductionism*. Every researcher at his or her bench works within a vast, orderly hierarchy in which subatomic particles congregate into atoms, which congregate into molecules; then into chemical compounds, into biological structures, into organisms, into societies. The scientist's basic modus operandi is to explain the higher in terms of the lower: As, for example, the compound called water is *really* hydrogen atoms coupled to atoms of oxygen in a two-to-one ratio, and those atoms are really an arrangement of electrons, and so on. Thus psychology can be reduced to biology, biology to cellular chemistry, chemistry to physics. At each step down the hierarchy things get successively "harder," while things get "softer" on the way up.

The reductionist dream is to reduce your mental states to the brain's microcomponents, the smaller the better. Aunt Mary's phobia of cats is ultimately reducible to a flow of electrons in her head. (One curious form of scientific reductionism, *sociobiology*, aims to reduce politics, religion, wars, and marriage customs to genes.) In this book we'll tell you that this enterprise is doomed. Even if we could poke an electrode into every single nerve cell in Irving's or Aunty Mary's brain and get a "readout" of its activity—which we can't—we still couldn't predict the thoughts in their minds three minutes from now.

Another "man is machine" philosophy, radical materialism, goes so far as to deny that consciousness exists. It became the credo of *behaviorism*, the anti-introspective psychology founded in 1913 by John B. Watson and elaborated by B. F. Skinner, his most famous disciple. To strict behaviorists, an organism—be it a pigeon pecking keys for food pellets or a second-grader striving for gold stars in "citizenship"—is a behaving machine, a box of conditioned responses. The Skinnerian lab, with its piano-playing pigeons and smart bar-pressing rats, became a showcase for the sort of "intelligent" behaviors that could be built out of simple reflex actions. (Skinner's own daughter, Deborah, spent her first two and a half years in an insulated, glassed-in crib, a sort of Skinner box for humans, reportedly without ill effects.) If there were any mental states inside the inscrutable "black box" of the brain, they were irrelevant to the proper science of behavior. The neuroscience revolution has not been kind to black-box psychology. Mental states are real, even to mainstream neuroscientists, and they do matter.

Which is not to say that every member of the Society for Neuroscience has given these philosophical questions deep thought. Once, in a room in which eight prominent neuroscientists were engaged in a discussion of what makes the human brain special, we asked who considered him/herself a reductionist/materialist. Two of the eight immediately stated they did not believe the mind was totally contained in the brain. The other six didn't understand the question.

Existential Doubt at the Synapse

Yet I have perhaps been inaccurate in speaking of the rock of Pure Matter. In this Pure Matter it is possible that a small quantum of Mind still survived. —MARCEL PROUST, *The Past Recaptured*

AS WE LISTEN to the amplified crackle of a rat's nerve cell—through a little hole in its skull a microelectrode has been sunk deep into the anesthetized animal's brain—a neuropsychologist who has been a "reductionist for a long time" confides to us that he sometimes has "existential doubts." After recounting a vivid telepathic experience he had on mescaline, he wonders aloud: "If you make the assumption that the 'software' [of thought] could separate from the 'hardware' [the brain], could it take up residence in other hardware? How about schizophrenics who hear voices? Some may be tuning in to other people's thoughts." Another scientist, a neuroanatomist known for his methodological rigor, looks up from his nerve-cell maps and says, "I doubt we'll ever get to consciousness from here. . . . Who knows if the mind is even in the brain?"

"The brain may not be necessary to consciousness," a prominent pharmacologist tells us as she measures chemicals into a watery porridge of human brain tissue. "A lot of people believe in life after death. And consciousness may be projected to different places. It's like trying to describe what happens when three people have an incredible conversation together. It's almost as if there were a fourth or fifth person there; the whole is greater than the sum of its parts." An authority on the neurobiology of schizophrenia muses, "I agree with Spinoza that the brain is a vehicle, a prison, for the soul—though I think the prisoner tends to take on the coloring of his prison."

Do unquantifiable mental phenomena still hover, ghostlike, over the Society for Neuroscience on moonless nights? It seems so. At any rate the hard certitudes of the behaviorist age are melting a bit, like Dali's limp watches. One hears words like *consciousness* and *introspection* now. It isn't out-and-out heresy to speak of things that can't be measured in an electrified metal-grid "learning paradigm." And many brain mechanics doubt that the soul is just a collection of electrochemical events.

"I know there's a ghost in the machine," says Daniel N. Robinson, a physiological psychologist at Georgetown University. "What I don't know is, Is there a machine in the ghost?" Translation: The things that remain most "ghostly"—that is, unexplained by neural mechanisms—are the very things that make us human: conscious self-awareness, personal identity, free will, creativity, Paul's vision on the road to Damascus. "Taking a noun out of the speaker and putting it in a neuron doesn't solve anything at all," Robinson adds. "You've still got the problem of how a neuron knows what a noun is.

"The reductionists say, 'Well, after all, we're showing how the brain controls this, that, and the other thing. So what if consciousness falls outside our equations?' *I* say, then forget consciousness and explain perception to me. Explain the experience of blue! Well, we all smile because we know darn well there's no little green man in there reading the back of the retina. And if there was, we'd have to see who was reading the back of *his* retina, and so on. . . . So if the question is, 'Do we understand the mechanisms by which environmental stimuli become transduced into some code that the biological organism can use?' the answer is yes. I think we can put together an account that is good to the fourth place after the decimal. But once you've said everything there is to say about perception, you might not have said anything about experience.

"A totally nonideological science would have to stand up and say, 'We've brought the most exquisite techniques to bear on the organization and functioning of the human nervous system. And we're obliged to report to you that the richest psychological dimensions of human life are not explicable in terms of the biochemistry and physiology as we know them to date.' "

Others have thrown their formidable scientific weight behind the idea that the mind is more than the brain organ. Nobel laureate Roger Sperry, of CalTech, the father of "split-brain" research, states, "To say the mind is the same as the brain is like saying the upcoming ninth wave at Laguna is nothing but another uplift and fall of H_2O and other molecules." Not that the mind is a hovering apparition. Its source is the brain, according to Sperry. But the reason van Gogh cut off his ear can never be found in the firing rates of his neurons, because the whole (e.g., the mind) is greater than the sum of its parts (e.g., cells and parts of cells).

Emergentism, as this viewpoint is called, is the antidote to reductionism. It says that as evolutionary building blocks combined into ever more complex compounds, interesting collective properties came into being that supersede the component parts. Consciousness is such a high-level "emergent property" of the brain, and once emerged, it is in command. The mind's products, including politics, religion, and psychology, exert a downward influence on the brain's physicochemical machinery, pushing the very molecules and atoms around, according to Sperry. "They [ideas] call the plays, exerting downward control over the march of nerve-impulse traffic."

Then there's Sir John Eccles, who won a Nobel Prize in 1963 for his virtuoso research on the synapse (the junction between neurons) and who, after years of listening to the higher nervous system's Morse-code–like song, is convinced that consciousness is not there. A devout Roman Catholic, Eccles believes in a "ghost," a nonmaterial (and immortal) soul animating the computerlike brain. In this view he echoes his former mentor at Oxford, the legendary physiologist Sir Charles Sherrington, who wrote: "That our being should consist of two fundamental elements offers, I suppose, no greater inherent improbability than that it should rest on one alone." At age eighty-one, Eccles continues to write ambitious tomes of neurophilosophy, illustrating his arguments for a nonphysical soul with technical drawings of neuron terminals, charts of "spike amplitudes" from single-cell recordings, and the like.

Eccles's gospel is basically a reincarnation of Descartes's, to wit, that "we are a combination of two things or entities: our brains on the one hand; and our conscious selves on the other." The brain is a precious "instrument," a "lifelong servant and companion," providing "lines of communication from and to the material world," but *we* are not *it*. An act of will, as Eccles sees it, is an everyday case of psychokinesis, of mind moving bits of matter. The precise "liaison brain," he thinks, is the supplementary motor area (SMA) at the top of the brain. Here, he says, is where the mind whispers to nerve cells, where free will activates the machine.

Avowed dualism like Eccles's is rare in modern brain science, and his critics, who include just about everybody, tend to regard the SMA as a warmed-over pineal gland, not much more scientific than flying-saucer cults or ancient astronauts. But even in the land of dose-response curves and "tight experimental controls," we found many who had taken the road of reductionism and met a dead end. We met scientists who quoted the *Bhagavad-Gita*, Carlos Castaneda, Plato, Aristotle, St. John of the Cross, and

The Tibetan Book of the Dead. We interviewed a biological psychiatrist who has embraced charismatic, speaking-in-tongues Christianity; a sleep researcher-turned-phenomenologist who thinks the outside world may be an unverified dream; a no-nonsense M.D. who has empirical evidence of life after death. At the heart of the physicochemical machinery of thought some scientists find the Tao.

Metaphysics Inside a Porsche 911

SO WHAT IF neurons fire in all-or-none code, if obscure chemicals called Substance P and somatostatin live in our heads, if cells in the visual system respond to dots or edges? Why should you care about neuroscience?

First, because by the year 2000, some of the following breakthroughs will have improved the quality of life, maybe even yours:

· A cure for mental illness, perhaps even a schizophrenia vaccine.

· An antidote to senile dementia (Alzheimer's disease), Parkinson's disease, Huntington's chorea, multiple sclerosis, epilepsy, and many neurological illnesses. Not long ago patients with Parkinson's disease inevitably became frozen, lifeless statues—until a drug called L-Dopa, modeled on a natural brain chemical, came along. Better drugs for epilepsy are being brewed in vitro: Pharmacologists now know how to turn these electrical storms on and off at will in slices of brain tissue. Twenty years from now Alzheimer's and other now-hopeless diseases will probably be treatable, too.

· Nerve-regeneration techniques and/or miniaturized computers linked to nerve fibers to free paraplegics from their wheelchairs. The deaf will hear (indeed, some already *are* hearing) and the "eyes" of the blind will be opened with computer implants that mimic neurons in the brain's auditory and visual areas.

· "Brain transplants" (actually grafts of specific regions of brain tissue) to treat Parkinson's disease, diabetes insipidus, and Alzheimer's disease, as well as to rejuvenate the aging brain. (By the year 2000, many of us may be interested.)

· Superspecialized drugs for everything from writer's block, memory loss, and existential ennui to antisocial tendencies and food binging. All these wonder drugs will be clones of natural chemicals in your brain.

· An advanced EEG biofeedback technology that will make present "alpha-wave" machines look like Model Ts. With such an apparatus you will become smarter by consciously "reprogramming" your internal software. Stroke victims will regain their former faculties. Our species might even evolve into angels, or at least supermen and superwomen.

· Cures for dyslexia, hyperactivity, learning disabilities, autism, alco-holism, panic attacks, and phobias—all of which used to be considered "psychological" but are now known to be biological disorders. Your pharmacy will probably stock an effective antisuicide pill and maybe a pill that transforms street thugs into student-council presidents.

· And much, much more.

But there is another, less pragmatic reason to care about neuroscience. As Bishop Berkeley pointed out, the whole world is inside your brain. Vernon Mountcastle, who won the prestigious Lasker Award in 1983 for his work on the somatosensory (tactile) system, observed in a 1975 article: "Each of us lives within the universe—the prison—of his own brain. Projecting from it are millions of fragile sensory nerve fibers, in groups, uniquely adapted to sample the energetic states of the world about us: heat, light, force, and chemical compositions. That is all we ever know directly: all else is logical inference."

How do we even know there's a world beyond the mind? We don't, said Berkeley's protégé David Hume. The whole universe is an unverifiable mirage. Most of us, of course, assume we live in a material world, complete with cathedrals, Moog synthesizers, Porsche 911s, and people who buy them. And neuroscientists would be the last to disagree. But try this thought experiment:

You and your friend George decide to take a ride in his new Porsche 911. You both perceive its color as racing green (though whether George's racing green is the same as your racing green is a question only angels can answer), and you'd probably agree on its exterior dimensions and number of forward gears. But once under way, there might well be two distinct experiences of Porscheness. At about 120 miles per hour on the interstate, for instance, George experiences euphoria, an exhilaration verging on the erotic. You, on the other hand, are in a state of stark, white-knuckled fear. Your visual experience would differ, too. George, who has done some amateur racing, sees the road and oncoming traffic almost in slow motion, down to every flaw in the pavement and every erratic movement on the part of other drivers. But to your eyes (or rather, to your visual cortex), the landscape streams by like a video game gone amok, the telephone poles compacted into the stereotypical picket fence. While in his mind's eye George sees the road just around the bend and mentally rehearses upcoming shift points and braking techniques, your imagination conjures up the local burn ward and your out-of-date will.

So which is the real world, yours or George's? If you're smart, you'll object that we changed the rules in midstream. We started with objective reality—colors, physical dimensions—and switched to the subjective—terror, euphoria, imagination. According to the principles of the Brain Age, however, both areas are now part of the knowable universe. Terror equals (theoretically, anyway) a certain concentration of neurochemicals, a certain electrocognitive pattern, and so on.

So let's take another imaginary drive, this time in a futuristic Porsche outfitted by the major brain-research laboratories. As you zip down the interstate, you and George will be having your brains scanned by positron emission tomography (PET). Electrodes will be mapping your brains' electrical activity, while portable spinal taps (ugh) will be collecting neurochemical metabolites. These things, of course, can't be done at present in a moving vehicle or in real time on a continuous basis, and obviously there would be legal and ethical problems. But they are theoretically "do-able."

What the tests would reveal, no doubt, is that you and George are experiencing not just two different states of mind but two different states of *brain*. George would exhibit the brain chemistry of euphoria, perhaps manifested by an abundance of endorphins, while your brain might be swimming with norepinephrine (noradrenaline), the "fight or flight" chemical. Brain scans might show that you were processing the visual experience of the interstate with the right, "emotional" brain hemisphere, while George's left, "analytical" hemisphere would be aglow.

Now, let's deliver the readouts, graphs, metabolite counts, and computer-enhanced scans to a panel of eminent neuroscientists. Even after months of careful scrutiny, it is doubtful that any of them would suddenly announce, "Gee, it looks like two dudes doing about a hundred and twenty on the interstate between Binghamton and Scranton—in a Porsche 911, from the looks of these serotonin curves."

The point is that the neuroscientists would not deduce a common experience from the data. They would have to conclude that, at the moment in question, you and George were living in two different worlds. Not two states of mind but two quantifiably different objective realities.

This makes for a big metaphysical headache, if you are a reductionist, monistic neuroscientist. You reject dualism, the notion that there is anything in the universe but matter. There is one world, you aver, and one world only. You certainly can't stomach the Berkeley/Hume doctrine that there is no objective reality, only mindstuff. Yet your hard data would indicate that either there are at least two worlds (i.e., the outer world of Porsches and the inner world of riding in one) or no universe at all, except that created in each individual brain. No doubt there's an objective universe out there, but how would a brain scientist prove it?

And what happens to good old cause and effect, the cornerstone of science? Any high-school physics student can tell you why pressing on the accelerator of any car will allow more fuel into the engine, which will cause the pistons to pump faster, which will turn the crankshaft faster, which will propel the vehicle down the road at a higher velocity. But stick two brains in the automobile, and no neuroscientist can predict what will happen to either of them at any given speed. Or why.

This issue doesn't just affect philosophers. It affects anyone who has ever tried to share his or her personal reality with another human being. For many people on the planet, a church or temple accoutred with the usual icons, stained glass, and appropriate music creates a holy, or altered, state of consciousness that, not surprisingly, the faithful wish to share with their children and other loved ones. Sometimes this state can be transmitted. Often it can't, no matter how closely the would-be proselyte follows the liturgy. Similarly, who can predict what will cause certain political leanings, moral standards, or sexual bliss in a person? The brain seems to have a life of its own.

The Journey Ahead

> If the brain was so simple we could understand it, we would be so simple that we couldn't.
> —LYALL WATSON

OUR TRAJECTORY through the world of the brain seemingly goes from the "hard" to the increasingly "soft." We'll start with the nuts and bolts of anatomy and neurochemistry, progress to the neurobiology of behavior, madness, violence, memory, and end up in the mind-altered hinterlands of hallucinations, dreams, and mysticism. But appearances sometimes deceive. Some of the rigorous researchers we'll first meet hunched over immunofluorescent assays in the first chapters will turn up again speculating about "God in the Brain" in Chapter 13. Just because the Modern Language Association and the American Association for the Advancement of Science don't hold joint annual meetings doesn't necessarily mean that neuroreceptors and William Blake belong to separate universes. We'll find that the "doors of perception" have many curious keys.

We might as well admit right now that we did not manage to solve the mind/brain problem. After our journey from the gritty realm of cells and chemicals to the never-never lands of hallucinations and out-of-body experiences, we still don't know whether 10^{11} wet cells make a soul. We find ourselves, like Dorothy after her adventures in Oz, back in Kansas where we started. It is, however, a *changed* Kansas.

THE
HARDWARE
OF
CONSCIOUSNESS

2

Crown of Creation

What a piece of work is a man! how noble in reason! how infinite in faculty! in form and moving how express and admirable! in action how like an angel! in apprehension how like a god! the beauty of the world, the paragon of animals! And yet, to me, what is this quintessence of dust?
—WILLIAM SHAKESPEARE, *Hamlet*

You are the crown of creation.
—The Jefferson Airplane

THE SMALL mushroomlike organ mounted on the Cryo/Cut machine is a rat brain: soft, milky white, with a little stem at its base. The rotary blade slices it into wafer-thin sections onto a plate. Miles Herkenham picks up a slice and, with a jeweler's precision, wipes it onto a glass slide. It leaves a little gray smudge, which when stained and placed under a microscope will become a delicate pointillist painting.

"Want to see a human brain?" he asks. The first human brain we see turns out to be a bag of frozen, whey-colored cubes stored in an ice-cream freezer. "Human brains are huge," says Herkenham. "You cut them into cubes with a giant rotating blade that butchers use. We call it Punk Science. We were all walking around in gloves and lab coats and safety glasses saying, 'We'd better not get any slow viruses.' "

The label on the freezer wrap reads "U.P." "What's U.P.?" we ask.

"Oh, that stands for Ultimate Person," says the thirty-five-year-old neuroanatomist. "We name all our brains. We have U.S.M.—Ultimate Squirrel Monkey—and U.S.M. Two . . ." A human brain is a precious commodity in the lab, and Herkenham and his colleagues at the National Institute of Mental Health (NIMH) are making autoradiographic pictures of these frozen brains, mapping the patterns of their receptors. Receptors are the sites in the brain where such drugs as Valium, morphine, and LSD—as well as the brain's natural chemicals—stick, and their distribution can tell Herkenham a lot about whether this particular brain was diseased or well.

"This guy had Parkinson's disease," says Herkenham, holding up a slide. "All his doparnine receptors were down."

Between one hundred thousand and forty thousand years ago, a brain exactly like yours and mine appeared on Earth. It would lead a pretty scrappy, hand-to-mouth existence for the next several thousand years, but somehow its cells were wired so that it could ponder the fate of its soul, the future of its grandchildren, and the movements of the planets. Unlike any other clump of protoplasm on Earth, it knew it would die. Somehow a million years of random mutations had built a biocomputer complex enough to write *Hamlet*, split the atom, build Notre Dame, invent Boolean algebra, and meditate on the curvature of space-time. For the human brain is, among other things, an information machine, but one so fancy that by comparison the most sophisticated man-made computer to date is a gibbering idiot—or more precisely, an idiot-savant.

For all this, the brain is the size of a grapefruit, split down the middle and wrinkled on the outside like an overgrown walnut. This soft, Jello-like organ can be weighed, dissected, viewed under a microscope, analyzed, and probed with electrodes. It obeys all the known laws of the physical universe, including those of electromagnetism, hydrodynamics, and particle physics.

The brain Herkenham was talking about happened to have Parkinson's disease, but he could just as easily have been describing a schizophrenic brain. Diagnosing hallucinations, melancholia, memory loss, or even dys-

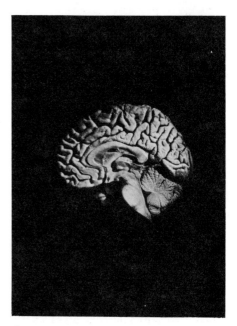

A cutaway view of a real human brain. (*Manfred Kage/Peter Arnold, Inc.*)

lexia in a clump of wet cells doesn't surprise anymore. This is routine business in the Brain Age. And though scientists may not stain brain sections to reveal signs of hope, charity, creativity, or the self, it is a central faith of the Brain Age that all of these attributes are also products of the grayish-pink organ in our skulls.

The *idea* isn't new. If the brain were a machine, one would naturally long to find the valves or switches that controlled walking, dreaming, and writing sonnets. Descartes would have tried, had he the tools; during the French Revolution some of his compatriots did examine freshly guillotined heads for signs of the soul. Sigmund Freud, trained in neurology, never doubted that the id, ego, and superego were fundamentally electromechanical phenomena. Readers of the posthumously published "Project for a Scientific Psychology" (1895) can find the father of psychoanalysis soberly discussing psychic processes as the net result of "material particles"—in other words, neurons (which had just been discovered). Much of his psychoanalytic vocabulary is borrowed from turn-of-the-century neurophysiological and neuroanatomical models. In the original German the obscure

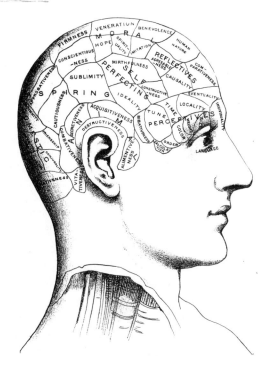

Phrenology chart: In the eighteenth century Franz Joseph Gall tried to read personality traits from the contours of a person's skull. Today scientists search for the secrets of human nature inside the brain. (*The Bettmann Archive*)

concept of *cathexis* is something akin to "local potential." And "nervous excitation" to Freud meant a "quantity of current flowing through a system of neurons."

But the wiring was simply too forbidding in 1895 or even 1920, so Freud dropped "The Project" and talked to the brain with words instead.

One scientist bent on deciphering the brain machine was the eighteenth-century anatomist Franz Joseph Gall. He was convinced that the brain housed the mind, and that particular brain regions contained particular mental faculties, thirty-five in all. But because a live, working brain was as inaccessible in those days as Antarctica, Gall's anatomy resulted in the pseudoscience of phrenology. With a psychologist friend, he drew maps of the human head, divided into districts like the arrondissements of Paris, and to each zone he assigned a faculty, such as "language," "hope," "acquisitiveness," "sublimity," "conjugality," "friendship," and "mirthfulness." He traveled to prisons, asylums, hospitals, and schools to study how bumps on the skull reflected personality—a shiftless character, a prodigious memory, a propensity for murder, or a strong maternal instinct. Today no one but the occasional crank believes in reading skull bumps, yet Gall's quest for a precise correspondence between mind and brain was thoroughly modern. Like Gall, today's leading brain scientists are working to localize the soul's attributes in 1400 grams of matter.

Harvard's David H. Hubel, who helped decipher the brain's visual code, expressed the modern neuroscientific dream thus in a 1979 article in *Scientific American*:

If Copernicus pointed out that the earth is not the center of the universe and Galileo saw stars and planets but not angels in the sky, if Darwin showed that man is related to all other living organisms, if Einstein introduced new notions of time and space and of mass and energy, if Watson and Crick showed that biological inheritance can be explained in physical and chemical terms, then in this sequence of *eliminations of the supernatural* the main thing science seems to be left with is the brain, and whether or not it is something more than a machine of vast and magnificent complexity.

The italics are ours. Like most of the brain connoisseurs, Hubel equates the nonmachinelike with the "supernatural" and ghostly and hopes to eliminate it from the rational universe. In 1975 Hubel and his colleague Torsten Wiesel won the Nobel Prize for demystifying one part of the machine. By planting tiny electrodes in the brains of cats and monkeys, they were able to explain how specialized cells in the visual system decipher messages from the optic nerve. This was no mean feat, and it laid one old ghost to rest: the *homunculus*, or "little man," that early brain watchers imagined sat inside the brain looking out through the window of the eyes.

But is this great exorcism complete? Has brain science explained how nerve cells can hope, pity, or formulate a syllogism?

Like children taking apart an old radio to see where the music comes from, in this chapter we'll examine the parts of the brain machine to find the source of thoughts, words, movements, emotions—if not "hope" and "mirthfulness." In short: How does this particular piece of matter generate a mind?

The Electrical Brain

THE BRAIN is a little saline pool that acts as a conductor, and it runs on electricity. When a neurologist pastes electrodes to the surface of your scalp and takes an electroencephalogram (EEG), he or she is picking up some of your brain's background electrical chatter. Every thought, every twitch of your finger, is an electrical event, or a series of electrical events. All the information that reaches you from the world—from the pattern of light and shadow that composes a face to the voice of the anchorman on the news—gets translated into a sequence of electrical pulses, the nervous system's *lingua franca*.

Once it was thought that the brain was a continuous mush, but at the turn of the century, the great Spanish anatomist Santiago Ramón y Cajal colored brain tissue with a Golgi stain (invented by Camillo Golgi, who shared the Nobel Prize for physiology and medicine with Ramón y Cajal in 1906) and saw individual *neurons*, or brain cells, darkly silhouetted

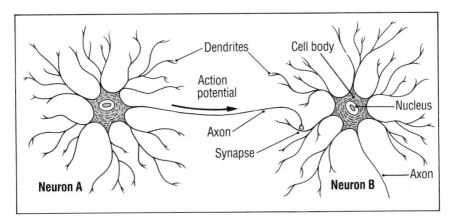

FIGURE 1   The neuron, or nerve cell, is the basic communication unit of the human brain. This simplified drawing shows one nerve cell sending an electrical signal down its axon to a dendrite of a second nerve cell. The signal is received at the synapse, a tiny gap between the membranes of the two neurons.

against a rose-colored background. Each neuron was indeed a separate unit, and there was a little gap, called the *synaptic cleft*, about one millionth of an inch wide, between one neuron and another. Ramón y Cajal made meticulous pen-and-ink drawings of the different varieties he saw—ornate "chandelier cells," star-shaped "stellate" neurons, "basket cells," and "pyramidal cells" with their wispy, tendrillike branches. In Figure 1, you can see a drawing of a typical neuron, with its *cell body*, its *axon*, and its delicately branching *dendrites*.

The axon is the cell's output side. An electrical pulse called an *action potential* travels down this long autobahn at somewhere between one and two hundred miles per hour. (Note that the brain is much slower than some of its creations, such as jet planes and computers.) Mental life may be full of ambiguities but the action potential is an all-or-none affair; a cell either fires or doesn't fire. (The *frequency*—the number of pulses—is the variable element in the code.) At the cell's receiving end are the dendrites with their multiple branches and tiny twiglets known as *dendritic spines*, all along the surface of which are the *synapses* where it receives inputs from other cells.

The electrical brain inspired a famous turn-of-the-century neuroscientist, Sir Charles Sherrington, to envision an "enchanted loom" that "weaves a dissolving pattern, always a meaningful pattern, though never an abiding one; a shifting harmony of subpatterns." The patterns shift and dissolve because the electrical events that link neurons are short-lived. Perhaps this is why so many of our thoughts are fleeting.

All information processing in the brain consists of neurons talking to one another. (The brain also has numerous *glial cells*—ten for every neuron—which form a scaffolding for the neurons. They don't fire action potentials and are not thought to play a role in information processing. However, there have been recent reports of electrical activity in glial cells, which if confirmed could multiply the brain's information units tenfold.) There are at least 10 billion, perhaps as many as 100 billion, neurons in your head (nobody knows *exactly* how many), and each of them makes between 5,000 and 50,000 contacts with its neighbors. Even using the most conservative estimate of 10^{10} (10 billion) cells, with 10^4 (10 thousand) connections each, we end up with 10^{14} (100 trillion) synaptic connections in all, which means:

· You have more "bits" in your head than any computer so far dreamed of. The number strains the mind like one of those ancient Buddhist hyperboles about counting grains of sand along the banks of a thousand Ganges. As one neurologist we spoke with put it, "Ten billion neurons,

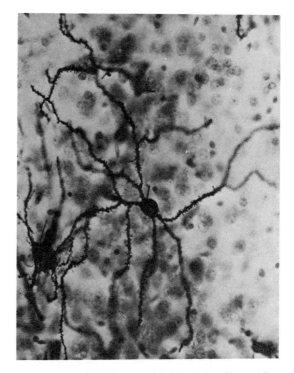

Stained and viewed under a microscope, nerve cells resemble brambles. Emanating from the cell body are long *dendrites*, each of which in turn branches off into smaller projections called *dendritic spines*. Multiple *synapses*, the sites where the neuron receives impulses, are located along the dendrites as well as the cell body. (*Courtesy of Dr. Miles Herkenham, NIMH*)

ten-to-the-fourteenth different connections—hell, you can do anything with that. That's more than enough to contain a 'soul.' "

· From the photograph at the bottom of page 33, you can see that the brain is an electrical engineer's nightmare. If you were a neurophysiologist patiently recording the firings of single neurons, as many neurophysiologists do, would you ever explain consciousness? Could a thousand neurophysiologists working a thousand years complete a "wiring diagram" of the entire human brain?

The neuron is not just a simple switch or diode either. It is a whole microworld with tiny channels in its walls for sodium and potassium ions that alternately polarize and depolarize the cell and make it fire. But if we want a coherent picture of how a brain works, we'll need to move up from the level of neurons to the level of large collections of neurons. So let's take a look at the brain's parts.

Neuroanatomy for Novices

WHEN THE FIRST ANATOMISTS cut up brains and looked inside, they took their lines of demarcation from the ridges (*gyri*) and valleys (*sulci*) on the wrinkled surface. Below the surface they found shapes and structures that reminded them of bridges, sea horses, almonds, and other everyday objects. They named the brain's parts accordingly, as if free-associating from Rorschach blots, and that's why neuroanatomy is full of Greek and Latin words for bridge (*pons*), sea horse (*hippocampus*), almond (*amygdala*), and bark (*cortex*). Don't be intimidated by the terms. They're no more difficult than the fanciful names that Vasco da Gama or Ponce de León bestowed on the mountains, rivers, and bays of the New World.

The brain consists of three basic parts: hindbrain, midbrain, and forebrain. The hindbrain includes the cerebellum and the lower brain stem. The midbrain contains some sensory relay areas in the upper brain stem. The forebrain contains all the rest, including the cerebral hemispheres and their outer covering called the cortex; the limbic system; and the structures of the diencephalon—thalamus, hypothalamus, and so on.

A many-layered spherical organ, the brain is often likened to an onion, and our tour will begin at its core and progress outward. In a sense we'll be retracing evolution, for the brain, as it evolved in innumerable generations of reptiles, mammals, primates, and early human beings, sprouted new additions over and around the old ones. (Figure 2 will help you find your way around, although there's no perfect way to depict a three-dimensional sphere in two dimensions. Textbook artists commonly carve the brain at one of three angles and show different slices, or "sections," or else make some of its parts diaphanous, like Caspar the Friendly Ghost in the comic books.)

The spinal cord meets the brain at the stalklike *brain stem*, a grand thoroughfare for sensory and motor signals. The brain stem's business includes such basics as breathing, heartbeat, sleeping, and waking. When we discuss matters like consciousness, bear in mind that, on a primitive level, the brain stem contains the on/off switch. One of its parts, the *reticular activating system*, a long tract of fibers running to the thalamus, is an all-important sentinel that keeps the brain "awake" even while you're asleep. Within another region, the *pons*, are the controls for dreaming and waking; one of its subregions, the *locus coeruleus*, sends long axons all the way to the cortex. If something interesting or threatening happens to an animal, the cells in its locus coeruleus fire excitedly (except during dreams, when they don't fire at all). In some way the locus coeruleus may tell the brain when to pay attention. Later in this chapter you'll meet the brain stem and its subdivisions as the "reptilian brain."

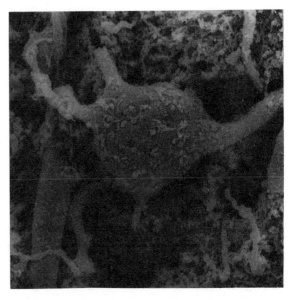

A small neuron of the cortex, magnified 5,000 times by a scanning electron microscope. Two dendrites have been broken off during processing. Note the synaptic terminals on the surface of the cell body. A small blood vessel is in the background. (*Courtesy of Dr. Arnold Scheibel, UCLA*)

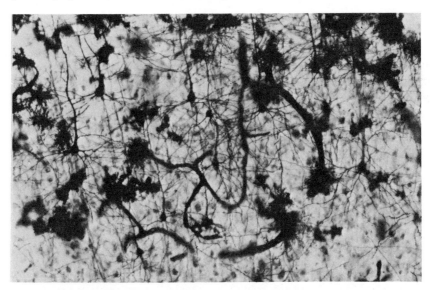

The human cerebral cortex is an enchanted forest of interconnected neurons. Here, the cells have been treated with a Golgi stain, a method that stains only about one neuron in a hundred. (The gray smudges are unstained nerve cells.) You can see the dendrites and some of the axons that compose the complex "wiring" of the cortex. Magnified about 300 times. (*Courtesy of Dr. Arnold Scheibel, UCLA*)

THE HUMAN BRAIN

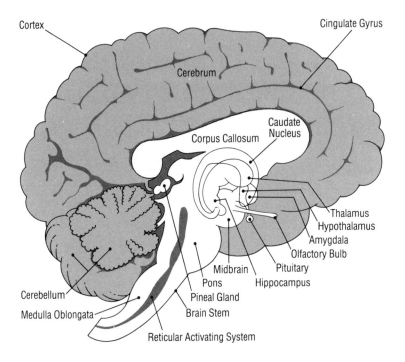

FIGURE 2 This schematic, cutaway view shows some of the important structures of the human brain. Note that the largest area is the cerebrum, the wrinkled outer covering of which is called the cortex. This spectacular enlargement of the cerebrum distinguishes human beings from other animals. Deep in the cerebrum is the limbic system, a connected ring of structures that regulates emotions and drives. The limbic system includes the hippocampus, amygdala, and cingulate gyrus, as well as several other structures, such as the septum and mammillary bodies, not depicted here. The hypothalamus, thalamus, and caudate nucleus, though not considered part of the limbic system proper, are also part of the visceral core brain. Within the brain stem is the reticular activating system, a diffuse net of cells regulating attention and wakefulness. We should note that neuroanatomy is not a cut-and-dried affair, as there is still much debate over the boundaries of many areas; for example, scientists are not in total agreement about which structures constitute the limbic system.

Attached to the brain stem at the very back of the skull is the *cerebellum* (or "little brain"). Wrinkled, folded, and lobed like a miniature cerebrum, it suggests a cauliflower or a leafy tree of life, depending on what angle it is viewed from. Its job is to process input from the muscles, joints, and tendons, control posture and equilibrium, and coordinate movement. According to recent research by New York University's Rudolfo Llinas, the cerebellum acts more like a brake than a motor, containing movement within certain boundaries. Imagine trying to thread a needle with your arms flailing wildly. That would be life without a cerebellum.

Above the brain stem we come to the oldest, innermost layer of the forebrain, the *diencephalon*. Dominating this region is the *thalamus* ("inner chamber"). In the brain the thalamus acts as O'Hare Airport. No signal from the eyes, ears, or other sensory organ can reach the cortex without passing through it. One of its districts, the *lateral geniculate nucleus*, is a relay station for signals passing from the retina to the visual area of the cortex; another, the *medial geniculate nucleus*, relays signals from the ears; and so on.

Right under the thalamus, the *hypothalamus* ("under the thalamus") perches atop the brain stem. It may be the size of a thimble and weigh no more than an ounce, but the hypothalamus acts as an all-powerful liaison between brain and body. From it hangs the pea-size *pituitary*, once considered the "master gland." Then scientists discovered that the pituitary's orders actually came from above, from the hypothalamus. Over a twenty-year period, Roger Guillemin, of the Salk Institute in La Jolla, California, bought six million sheep brains, at forty cents apiece, to hunt for the elusive hypothalamic hormones that signal the pituitary to release its hormones, while Andrew Schally, at Tulane University in New Orleans, was deep in mashed pig brain for the same reason. The search was successful, and in 1977, the two men with Dr. Rosalyn Yalow shared the Nobel Prize for demonstrating that the brain—ergo, the emotions—speaks to the glands via the hypothalamus—a discovery with enormous implications for psychosomatic medicine.

The hypothalamus has other jobs, too. It regulates the "internal milieu," blood pressure, body temperature and contains appetite control centers. Damage to one part of the hypothalamus will cause animals to stop eating, while lesions in a neighboring area will induce them to gorge themselves to death like characters in the film *La Grande Bouffe*. And the hypothalamus, like the nearby limbic system, forms part of the brain's emotional apparatus. Electrical stimulation there can send animals (or humans) into paroxysms of rage or fear.

The mystery organ of the diencephalon is the *pineal gland*, which Descartes imagined as the meeting place of body and soul. The latest news is that the pineal gland acts as an internal clock. Its light-sensitive cells help synchronize sleep-and-waking and other biological cycles with the light-and-dark cycles of the outside world.

Now on our journey from the core of the brain outward, we come to a connected ring of structures, holding the olfactory bulb (the smell organ) in the center like a mounted jewel. This is the *limbic* ("bordering") *system*, as it was named in 1952 by a farsighted Yale neuroscientist named Paul MacLean. This certainly is a more respectable term than *rhinencephalon*, or "smell brain," as this region used to be known. Then superthin electrodes and careful surgical expeditions made it feasible to map this *terra incognita* in the brains of experimental animals (and, in a few cases, in sick human beings), and suddenly scientists knew where emotions were housed. When stimulated with a mild electrical current, specific limbic sites triggered sudden rage, joy, or fear. At first it almost looked as if demons, trolls, and angels inhabited the S-shaped *hippocampus* (or "seahorse"), the *amygdala* ("almond"), the breast-shaped *mammillary bodies*, the ridged girdle of the *cingulate gyrus*, and the other parts of the limbic system. The picture of emotions occupying localized compartments would have gratified Gall, but it didn't turn out to be quite so neat. Stimulating one part of the amygdala would stir up rage one day, fear another; another piece of the organ seemed to be a pleasure spot. Often it was hard to predict what a given bit of tissue would unleash. In addition to its emotional jobs, the hippocampus also apparently consolidates or stores memories. The amygdala has perceptual and memory functions, too. There are probably no cells in the limbic system that are hard-wired to do one thing (like generate anger) and nothing else. Sorry, Gall.

The limbic system is located in the depths of the *cerebrum*, the newest part of the brain. Here evolution added all the gadgetry that distinguishes man from the lizard, so it is not surprising that in humans the cerebrum is an overfed giant. Two-thirds of our brain mass consists of the twin cerebral hemispheres draped imperiously around all the other parts. The first thing you notice about the cerebrum is that it is split into *hemispheres* that are like two separate brains. Everything in the right side has a mirror image on the left (or nearly so; the symmetry isn't perfect), so you have two frontal lobes, two temporal lobes, two parietal lobes, two occipital lobes, two amygdalae, two hippocampi, et cetera. And the brain is a looking-glass world in another sense. The left hemisphere moves the right side of the body; the right hemisphere controls the body's left. The visual world is also split down the middle and crisscrossed, with our left visual field traveling to the brain's right half and the right visual field to the left. *Why two of everything?* Did nature design a backup in case of damage? And why the left-right reversal? No one knows. This is one of the brain's mysteries, which will occupy us a good deal in Chapter 8.

Covering the cerebrum is the wrinkled crust of the *cortex*, sometimes called the *neocortex*, to emphasize its evolutionary newness. A redundantly folded sheet of tissue about three millimeters thick, the human cortex would cover about one and a half square feet if unfurled. The cortex made its first significant appearance in mammals. In humans it has mushroomed into a vast "thinking cap" that wraps over and around the rest of the brain. At least 70 percent of the neurons in the human central nervous system is in the cortex.

No snake, as far as we know, has ever planned for the future, worried, or solved a differential equation, because snakes don't possess a cortex. Dogs, cats, and mice all have one, and they are capable of learning from experience, mastering mazes, and anticipating reward or punishment. But the cortex of lower mammals is paltry compared to ours. You and I do much of our living in this overgrown, convoluted thinking cap. As David Hubel and Torsten Wiesel put it, "A mouse without a cortex appears fairly normal, at least to casual inspection; a man without a cortex is almost a vegetable, speechless, sightless, senseless." If we are the crown of creation, we owe it to our cortex.

Unlike the lower structures we've talked about, the cortex *looks* the same all over, a lumpen porridge. Even under a microscope it's hard to find a pattern in the tangled thicket of cells and dendrites. Which fibers go where? Do certain cell types do certain things? Is this furrowed surface really all of one piece, or are some areas designed to "do" one thing, like move the big toe, but not another?

Parts of the cortex are superbly specialized, as we'll see later in this chapter. First we'll describe its grossest lines of demarcation, the four *lobes*. Like rivers and mountain chains forming the borders of nations, ridges and indentations, called gyri and sulci, mark the boundaries of each region of the cortex.

Geography of the Cortex The *occipital lobe*, at the back of the head, contains the primary visual area. A stroke or a wound in this area will cause blindness, or at least wipe out a portion of the visual field, depending on the extent of the injury. In fact, bullet and missile wounds during the First and Second World Wars taught neurologists a lot about the visual "map" contained in this part of the brain.

The *temporal lobes*, right above the ear on either side of the head, make intimate connections with the limbic brain below. People with damaged temporal lobes can't file experiences into long-term memory. Stimulating this lobe with electricity triggers strange emotions out of context, weird reveries, and sensations of *déjà vu* (an inexplicable sense of familiarity) and *jamais-vu* (when the familiar seems alien). Temporal-lobe epilepsy is full of similar psychic oddities. There is a primary auditory

GEOGRAPHY OF THE CORTEX

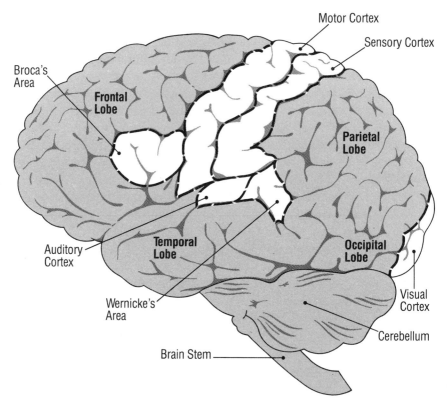

FIGURE 3 The human cortex is divided into four lobes: the frontal, parietal, temporal, and occipital, each of which is duplicated on either side of the brain. This drawing represents the left hemisphere, which in right-handed people contains regions specialized for language, including Broca's area and Wernicke's area. In addition, there are other parts of the cortex that govern specific functions, including the primary visual, auditory, sensory (tactile), and motor areas.

processing area in the temporal lobes, and visual messages, already processed in the occipital lobe, are sent here for more abstract kinds of processing.

The *parietal lobes* arch over the roof of the brain from ear to ear. In 1870 a pair of German scientists removed the skull of a dog and stimulated its exposed cortex with a weak electrical current. In one part of the cortex, the electrode activated different parts of the dog: a leg, then a paw, then the head. This was the first hint that the brain contained a schematic map of the body. We now know there are two different topographic maps inscribed on the surface of the parietal lobes, one motor and one somato-sensory (tactile). As with the brain's visual map, the details have been sketched in by observing human tragedies, including those caused by wars, strokes, and tumors. A lesion in one small region of the cortex might paralyze one leg; a bullet hole in another area may deaden a hand or one side of the face. Charting correlations between the site of brain injury and the resulting defect, neurologists discovered that every inch of the body was represented in an organized manner in the cortex.

As you can see from Figure 4, the brain's image of the body is distorted: a "homunculus" with outsize lips, tongue, hands, thumbs, and genitals. The map is distorted in scale like a Mercator projection because super-sensitive bodily parts or those requiring extreme motor finesse occupy more cortical space. For example, an inch of finger projects to a wider area of the brain than an inch of chest, presumably because deft, discriminating digits became important to primates or tool-using early hominids.

The *frontal lobes* occupy the front of the brain behind the forehead. What they do may be illustrated best by the sad saga of one Phineas Gage, who lost his. In 1848, when he was a twenty-five-year-old foreman, an explosion at a Vermont construction site drove an enormous iron rod through Gage's skull. To the amazement of his fellow workers, the impaled man sat up and spoke coherently within minutes. After a local doctor operated to remove the rod, the patient recovered, and physicians marveled at his apparent normality. But appearances were deceiving. The hole in his frontal cortex shattered Gage's personality. From a shrewd, competent, and level-headed businessman, he degenerated into a fickle, foul-mouthed, irresponsible drifter who couldn't hold a job. Phineas Gage, his friends lamented, was "no longer Gage."

Maybe later neurosurgeons should have paid more attention to the Phineas Gage case. Instead, in 1935 a Portuguese psychiatrist named Egas Moniz performed a bold new operation to relieve many forms of mental illness, including aggression and hyperemotional states. Called the *pre-frontal lobotomy*, it became extremely popular in the United States, where over forty thousand people were turned into zombies during the 1940s and early 1950s. With a surgical pick and mallet, a surgeon—or even, appall-ingly, a nonsurgeon—would simply bore into the patient's frontal cortex, then twist the pick, cutting the nerve fibers running from the prefrontal cortex (at the extreme front of the frontal lobes) to the rest of the brain. As part of a project dubbed Operation Icepick, surgeon Walter Freeman, the Hernando Cortez of the frontal lobe, once lobotomized twenty-five women inmates at a West Virginia mental hospital in a single day. It was

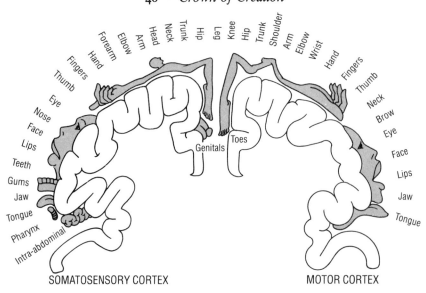

SOMATOSENSORY CORTEX   MOTOR CORTEX

FIGURE 4   How does your brain picture your body? Which parts of your body take up the most space in your cortex? The answer can be found in the two distorted homunculi (*homunculus* means "little man") shown above. On the surface of the cortex are two different body maps: the somatosensory cortex and the motor cortex. The somatosensory cortex receives touch messages from all parts of the body, while the motor cortex controls movement. Note the attention paid to the head and face in both cortices compared with the trunk, for instance. Note also how the hands, especially the thumb, assume special importance in the motor cortex. In reality, no two brains would have exactly the same cortical "maps." A surgeon or jeweler, for example, might have an even greater portion of the cortex devoted to the fingers. (After Penfield)

Freeman who performed the first lobotomy in the U.S., on September 14, 1936, at George Washington University Hospital in Washington, D.C. The patient was a sixty-three-year-old woman known as "Mrs. A. H.," whom Freeman characterized as "a typically insecure, rigid, emotional, claustro-phenic individual" and "a past master at bitching [who] really led her husband a dog's life." After the surgery Mrs. A. H.'s anxiety abated some-what, though Freeman observed on a visit to her home that she was still "shrewish and demanding with her husband."

When Egas Moniz was awarded a Nobel Prize in medicine in 1949, *The New York Times* pronounced the honor "fitting" and added: "Surgeons now think no more of operating on the brain than they do of removing an appendix. [Moniz and his co-laureates] taught us to look with less awe on the brain. It is just a big organ with very difficult and complicated functions to perform and no more sacred than the liver."

If there is anything sacred about a human being, it is surely his brain—*especially*, perhaps, the frontal lobes. Without an intact frontal cortex, a human being may appear normal at first glance, but hang out with him for a while and you notice he's emotionally shallow, distractable, listless, apathetic, and so insensitive to social contexts that he may belch with abandon at dinner parties. He may have memory gaps; he lacks foresight; his inner world is not what it used to be. A patient with a frontal lobe lesion becomes so distracted by irrelevant stimuli that he cannot carry out complex actions, according to the late distinguished Russian neuropsychologist A. R. Luria. An "assigned programme" of behavior is replaced by "uncontrollable floods of inert stereotypes," he noted. "One such patient, for instance, when asked to light a candle, struck a match correctly but instead of putting it to the candle . . . he put the candle in his mouth and started to 'smoke'

At least forty thousand lobotomies were performed in the United States during the 1940s and 1950s. One of the victims was the movie actress Frances Farmer (above), who was lobotomized by Dr. Walter Freeman himself in 1948, during one of his icepick crusades, at Western State Hospital in Washington State. Afterward, the ill-fated star, whose rebelliousness had resisted insulin shock, electroshock, and hydrotherapy, "drifted off into the oblivion of surgically induced mediocrity," in the words of David Shutts, author of *Lobotomy: Resort to the Knife*. Her lobotomy goes unmentioned in Dr. Freeman's memoirs. (*The Bettmann Archive*)

it like a cigarette." Others, chronicled in Luria's book *The Working Brain* (1973), can't make sense of simple drawings.

A patient with a frontal lobe lesion is shown the picture of a man who has fallen through the ice. People are running towards him in an attempt to save his life. On the ice, near the hole, is a notice "danger." In the background of the picture are the walls of a town and a church. . . . Instead of analysing the picture [the patient] sees the notice "danger" and immediately concludes: "the zoo" or "high-voltage cables" or "infected area." Having seen the policeman running to save the drowning man, he immediately exclaims: "war," while the walls of the town with the church prompt the explanation "the Kremlin." Analysis of the picture in this case is replaced by elementary guesswork, and organized intellectual activity is impossible.

"The stream of happenings is not segmented and so runs together in a present which is forever, without past or future," notes Stanford neuro-psychologist Karl Pribram, an early opponent of lobotomy, in his book *Languages of the Brain*. "The organism becomes completely . . . at the mercy of his momentary states, instead of an actor on them."

During the heyday of lobotomies, Pribram, then at Yale, argued that the frontal cortex was not some vestigial appendix to be cut as a psychiatric panacea and that its intimate nerve connections with the limbic system must be important. "I was almost kicked out of Yale for saying things like that," he recalls.

It was a case of neuroscientific hubris. Physiologists had noted that mild electrical stimulation of the frontal lobes didn't seem to *do* anything—no muscles jerked, no lights flashed in the brain, no strange sensations were evoked, as was the case with the other lobes. So they thought the frontal cortex didn't do anything much. Because lobotomy patients' IQ scores, as measured by the Stanford-Binet test, didn't usually drop after the operation, doctors pronounced these people unimpaired. When it comes to measuring the brain's most subtle and fragile products, our yardsticks (electrodes, IQ tests) are crude.

What the frontal lobes "control" is something like awareness, or self-awareness, which is hard to quantify. Consider: The frontal cortex of rats is minute. In cats it occupies a paltry 3.5 percent of the cortex. In chimpanzees the figure has risen to 17 percent. But in Homo sapiens it's a whopping 29 percent. The ratio of frontal cortex to the rest of the cortex may be one index of evolutionary advancement. Do these lobes govern some essential feature of humanness, or even godliness, as some scientists have suggested? "If God speaks to man, if man speaks to God," neuroscientist Candace Pert tells us, "it would be through the frontal lobes, which is the part of the brain that has undergone the most recent evolutionary expansion."

Paul MacLean, for one, considers the frontal lobes the "heart" of the cortex. He observes, "In the progress from Neanderthal to Cro-Magnon man, one sees the forehead develop from a low brow to a high brow. Underneath that heightened brow is the prefrontal cortex. . . . The prefrontal cortex is the only part of the neocortex that looks inward to the inside world. Clinically, there is evidence that the prefrontal cortex by looking inward, so to speak, obtains the gut feeling required for identifying with another individual." In other words, empathy.

The Triune Brain

WHEN FREUD looked beneath the smooth veneer of modern man, he discovered a much more ancient, more primitive self within. The father of psychoanalysis saw himself as a psychic archeologist unearthing "mental antiquities" that dated back to infancy, on the one hand, and to a remote ancestral past, on the other. Humans may have evolved to frock coats and monocles, Freud reasoned, but in some way all of prehistory was preserved in the unconscious.

Freud gave us a tripartite self, composed of id, ego, and superego, but Paul MacLean gave us something more concrete: the "triune brain." (See Figure 5.) To MacLean, who today directs the Laboratory of Brain Evolution and Behavior in Poolesville, Maryland, the Homo sapiens brain is a folded-up record of our evolutionary past. Like an archeological site, like Heinrich Schliemann's multi-leveled Troy, its older "civilizations" are buried under the new, so that in deeper layers of the brain one uncovers relics of the dinosaur age. According to MacLean, human beings possess an atavistic reptile brain and a paleomammalian (old mammalian) brain under the folds of the civilized neocortex. These three brains in one operate like "three interconnected biological computers, [each] with its own special intelligence, its own subjectivity, its own sense of time and space and its own memory."

The distinctly human portion, of course, is the neocortex, "the mother of invention and father of abstract thought," as MacLean sees it. Foresight, hindsight, and insight are some of its products. It reasons, plans, worries, writes memos and sonnets, invents steam engines and drip-dry fabrics, and programs artificial brains called computers. Through its centers for vision, hearing, and bodily sensations, we traffic with the external world.

The "old mammalian brain" resides in the limbic system, the headquarters of the emotions. A throwback to mice, rabbits, and cats, the limbic system is hooked on survival, the preservation of self and the species, and its behavior revolves around the "Four F's": feeding, fighting, fleeing, and sexual behavior (as one neurobiological joke goes). "One of the pe-

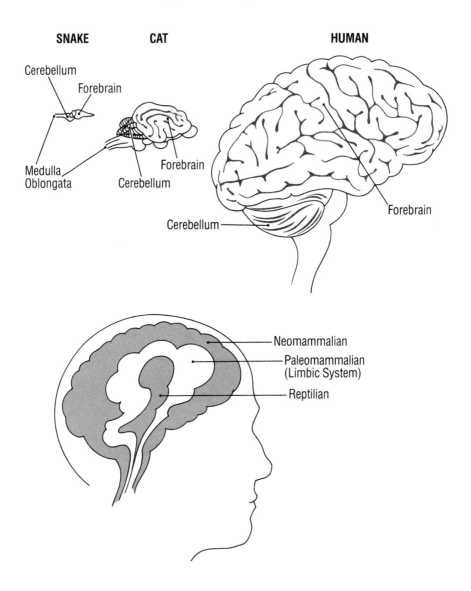

SNAKE   CAT   HUMAN

Cerebellum

Forebrain

Medulla Oblongata

Forebrain

Cerebellum

Forebrain

Cerebellum

Neomammalian

Paleomammalian (Limbic System)

Reptilian

FIGURE 5 The dramatic evolution of the forebrain (cerebrum), from reptiles to lower mammals to human beings, is shown in the first three drawings. The fourth drawing at bottom depicts the "triune brain," as described by Paul MacLean, which schematically illustrates how all three brains coexist today in the human brain. Our brain, says MacLean, is not a pristine and original creation. Rather, it contains within it vestiges of its entire evolutionary past. As the brain evolved, it added new structures around the older, primitive ones, so that "reptilian" and "paleo-mammalian" behavior routines still lurk in our heads.

culiar characteristics of the emotions," MacLean observes, "is that they are not neutral: Emotions are either agreeable or disagreeable." We mammals are built so as to feel pleasure when we behave in ways that enhance our self-preservation or that of the species, and pain when our survival needs are thwarted. Pain and pleasure are the limbic system's yin and yang, and it judges all experiences accordingly.

Finally, the old reptile brain in the brain stem and its surrounding structures, MacLean says, lives like a troll under a bridge in a Scandinavian fairy tale. The R-complex, as it is called, contains many of the same "archaic behavioral programs" that motivate snakes and lizards. Rigid, obsessive, compulsive, ritualistic, and paranoid, it is "filled with ancestral lore and ancestral memories." Being so "hard-wired," it is doomed to repeat the past over and over again. The old reptile brain doesn't profit much from experience.

The Dragons of NIMH

ON A HOT, humid July day, we rent a car in Washington and drive out to Poolesville. The green, rolling Maryland countryside ripples under the heat while cattle graze in suspended animation beyond white picket fences. At the Laboratory of Brain Evolution and Biology, the NIMH's rural outpost and animal farm, a changing guard of creatures acts out the scenarios dictated by the lower brains. A few years ago alligators, sunk in reptilian dreamtime, filled the ponds. ("We had to wait for the cold weather [when the animals are safely sluggish] to move them," our guide tells us.) Lizards, performing their ancient, obsessive ceremonies in the small, glassed-in jungle of a terrarium, have been MacLean's chief source of reptilian lore. Turkeys strut and ruffle ceremonious feathers in the yard, while, inside the building, squirrel monkeys fly about their cages like hyperkinetic wind-up toys. There are also Siberian hamsters, including a writhing pile of pink, fetal-looking newborns. The rats next door inhabit a spacious cage under the all-seeing eye of a computer that monitors their grooming, eating, sleeping, fighting, and social status. This rat colony once inspired a novel, *The Rats of NIMH*, and an animated film. And it's been the subject of a fifteen-year experiment, which continues like a long-running soap opera that transcends the memory (or life span) of its individual characters.

The father of the triune brain, a seventyish man whose eyes gleam with curiosity behind his glasses, is in the library preparing a slide show for us. First he shows us a plastic model of a human brain, holding it like an enchanted globe as he speaks of the virtues of handling brains. A real brain, he points out, "feels much like a ripe avocado." It is, in a word, soft, and MacLean likes to remind people that "the cold, hard facts of science, like the firm pavement underfoot, are the products of a soft brain."

"The people I feel sorry for are physicists, because they don't have the advantage of taking out a brain and handling it," he tells us. "They're working with infinite temperatures, infinite mass, the Big Bang . . . And the speeds they've assigned these things, using the speed of light as a yardstick! . . . But maybe it's an illusion, because it's all being interpreted by the brain, which is just soft mush imprisoned in this bony shell. The brain does everything. It's not your eyes that are looking at me—it's not eyeball to eyeball—it's brain to brain. As far as we can see, it's all just mush."

MacLean offers us half his sandwich, and stories pour out of him like a Homeric hero at a feast. When Carl Sagan came to interview him for his book *The Dragons of Eden*, MacLean gave him his first brain to hold, a rabbit brain. "Nothing can compare with holding a brain in your hands," MacLean tells us. "Every angle you slice it, you see something different. My pharmacologist friends don't understand this. They just grind it up and throw chemicals at it."

He switches on the projector and we watch small lizards dart among the leaves of a terrarium, changing from brown to green and back again to match the background. One freezes like a statue, bobbing its head repetitively. Two rivals face off. They inflate their chests, puff out their neck ruffs, and do push-ups—all of which, in lizard society, means, "Back off. I'm boss."

"All tetrapods—mammals, birds, reptiles—use four basic kinds of display," MacLean explains. "Signature, challenge, courtship, and submission. Without the submissive display none of us could survive." Watching the challenge pageantry of multicolored rainbow lizards, for instance, MacLean's practiced eye sees the knights of King Arthur's court. "Twice we saw dominant lizards defeated and humiliated," he remembers. "They lost their majestic colors, turned a muddy brown, became depressed, and died two weeks later."

If you watch enough lizards, it's not hard to see the reptilian underside of man. Archie Bunker's chair is like a lizard's territorial defecation post, a "signature" display. Military pageantry is reptilian. So are FBI paranoia, Rainbow Girls' rites, the corporate underling nodding his head in the presence of the boss, the corner office with its trappings of rank. The goose step and the stylized solemnity of the graduation processional remind MacLean of the weird stiltlike walk that lizards use for challenge purposes. And so on.

Later, through a one-way mirror, we watch a squirrel monkey compulsively "display" at his mirror image (which he sees as a rival monkey), spreading his thighs and thrusting his erect penis forward. This isn't a sexual gesture, but a monkey's way of greeting a newcomer. Reptilian displays must live on in mammal brains, in the R-complex, MacLean figured. To test his hypothesis, he performed systematic brain surgery on some of his monkeys several years ago: When he destroyed the globus pallidus in the brain stem, a monkey no longer gesticulated at his reflection in the mirror. MacLean concluded that the archaic reptile brain was responsible for this display.

"Ruffling feathers, hair standing on end," he muses aloud. "How did these primitive brains learn to use this way of looking fierce to fend off a rival? How did that stupid brain ever dream up something like that? You can't answer these questions. Nature is full of tricks, a magician.

"Physiologists spend their lives trying to figure out how we see perfect images," he adds. "But no one inquires into how we see partial representations, archetypes. A turkey walks across the yard, some little thing sets him off, and he starts copulating *in vacuo*. In aggressive encounters, squirrel monkeys use penile displays as a threat, but it's only a symbol."

So are the all-seeing eye, the cross, the star of David, red stoplights, the hammer and sickle, McDonald's golden arches, fetishes, fads, fashions, designer jeans, the fins on a Cadillac, neon dancing girls at Las Vegas. Like our bestial ancestors, humans are wired up to respond to archetypes, to "partial representations." Our brains take the part for the whole, seeing snakes, mothers, and honeymoon hotels in Rorschach inkblots. "Look at our artifacts, the cave paintings," says MacLean. "The eye is everywhere, the genitals are everywhere. The part stands for the whole. Maybe psychoanalysis is built on that principle."

Writing about the triune brain in *The Ghost in the Machine*, Arthur Koestler joked that when an analysand lies down on a psychiatrist's couch, an alligator and a horse lie down with the man. According to MacLean, what we need is a "paleopsychology," a reptilian-paleomammalian psychology to go with our two lower brains. The three mentalities inside us are dissociated and often in conflict. Below the cortical mantle the ancient rites of submission and dominance, sexual courtship, greeting, nesting, hoarding, marking territory, kowtowing to the leader, and ganging up on newcomers persist. "People wonder why so many human beings are paranoid. Well, we have this basically reptilian brain. Everybody has to be paranoid. If you weren't a little paranoid, you wouldn't survive a minute. Whenever I cross the street I'm a little paranoid, looking over my shoulder, this way and that." He swivels his head rapidly, right to left, left to right, like a paranoid lizard. "And, you know, scientists are paranoid," he adds. "It helps to have a paranoid delusional system to organize your research.

"I think of a patient named L. R., an epileptic," he continues, on the subject of paranoia. "She had these big bolts of lightning coming off the base of the brain—the only place we were seeing a spike—and during this time she had the feeling that God was punishing her for overeating. If you have a good neocortex working for you, you try to explain your paranoid feelings and persuade other people. You go out and start a religion and recruit followers. Some paranoids are very persuasive."

A few years ago, MacLean and his co-workers wondered what a hamster without a cortex would be like. So they surgically destroyed the cortex of baby hamsters on the day after birth—and got entirely normal hamsters. Because animals without a cortex could still play and nurse and care for their young, MacLean traced these distinctively mammalian traits to the limbic system, the paleomammalian brain. "But," he tells us, "if you also destroy the cingulate gyrus, the newest part of the limbic system, the *animals don't play.*

"It has become clear to me recently that the cingulate gyrus contains the three behaviors we identify with mammals and *not* with reptiles: nursing and maternal care, play, and audiovocal communication. I've looked at the lizard brain myself, and it has no counterpart of the cingulate gyrus. I think this is sort of revolutionary. But most people don't share my excitement. They say, 'What the hell, all animals play. All animals take care of their young.' This is not correct. From the standpoint of human evolution, one can't imagine anything much more important than this original family situation developing and the things that go along with family—vocalization and play. Maybe play is a way of promoting harmony in the nest so the little ones don't bite each other and get themselves all scratched up."

While the neocortex, with its sensory equipment, surveys the outer world, the limbic system takes its cues from within, MacLean thinks. It has a loose grip on reality. In the 1940s MacLean became fascinated with the "limbic storms" suffered by patients with temporal-lobe epilepsy. "During seizures," he recalls, "they'd have this Eureka feeling all out of context—feelings of revelation, that this is the truth, the absolute truth, and nothing but the truth." All on its own, without the reality check of the neocortex, the limbic system seemed to produce sensations of déjà-vu or jamais-vu, sudden memories, waking dreams, messages from God, even religious conversions.

"You know what bugs me most about the brain?" MacLean says suddenly. "It's that the limbic system, this primitive brain that can neither read nor write, provides us with the feeling of what is real, true, and important. And this disturbs me, because this inarticulate brain sits like a jury and tells this glorified computer up there, the neocortex, 'Yes, you can believe this.' This is fine if it happens to be a bit of food or if it happens to be someone I'm courting—'Yes, it's a female, or yes, it's a male.' But if it's saying, 'Yes, it's a good idea. Go out and peddle this one,' how can we believe anything? Logically I've never been able to see around this impasse. As long as I'm alive and breathing and have a brain to think with, I will never forgive the Creator for keeping me in this state of ignorance.

"And now here's the new version of the Faust story," he says, grinning like a kid who knows a good joke. "Our lineage goes back two hundred fifty million years—that is, to the age of the therapsids, the 'mammal-like reptiles' that are our remote kin. That's ten million human generations, or as I sometimes say, forty million presidential libraries. It's a long time. Anyway, the devil says to Faust, 'If I tell you the secret of the universe at the end of another two hundred fifty million years, would you go along with the bargain?' Faust says, 'Yes.' So two hundred fifty million years pass, and then the devil comes back and explains everything. Faust says, 'I don't understand.' The devil says, 'How would you expect to understand? Your brain hasn't developed a bit in two hundred fifty million years.' 'Oh, no,' says Faust. 'I forgot to ask about that when we made the bargain.' "

The Hard-Wired Brain

"GIVE ME the baby and my world to bring it up in . . ." declared John B. Watson, "and I'll make it climb and use its hands. . . . I'll make it a thief, a gunman, or a dope fiend. The possibility of shaping in any direction is almost endless." To the behaviorists a newborn human brain was a *tabula rasa* (the term comes from John Locke) on which experience could write any kind of text.

"One textbook in psychology," MacLean notes, "begins by saying, 'All human behavior is learned.' Well, if all human behavior is learned, why is it that in spite of all our intelligence and culturally determined behavior, we continue to do all the ordinary things that animals do?" The triune brain, with its hard-wired programs from the bestial past, is MacLean's answer.

Simple organisms are rather like automata, with most of their behavior "wired in" from birth. The dances of bees are stereotyped, as is a frog's response to the silhouette of a bug, or any buglike shape, moving across its visual field. Lizards automatically display their neck ruffs and do push-ups at a shadowgram of a lizard, MacLean discovered. Even chicks, duck-lings, and goslings are genetically programmed to follow the first moving object they see after hatching, as the eminent Austrian ethologist Konrad

Lorenz discovered in the 1930s, when newly hatched goslings followed him everywhere like bewitched lovers. This was called "imprinting." Since then hundreds of experiments have proved that baby birds will imprint on duck decoys, boxes, colored lights, milk bottles, and toilet floats, as well as famous scientists.

In the 1930s Roger Sperry, then at the University of Chicago, rotated a salamander's eyes, disconnecting the nerve fibers from the eye to the optic tectum in the brain and reconnecting them in such a way as to turn the creature's visual field upside down. After the operation the salamander acted as if it saw an inverted world. When an object moved upward it followed it by moving its eyes downward. Its brain never adjusted. Sperry's experiments showed that a salamander or a frog will stick out its tongue in the wrong direction forever until it starves to death for lack of edible insects.

Mammalian brains are more flexible. Because mammalian nervous tissue doesn't regenerate like an amphibian's, you couldn't do the rotated-eye experiment on humans even if you wanted to. But an enterprising turn-of-the-century psychologist, G. M. Stratton, made himself a pair of distorting goggles that reversed up and down and left and right. At first he could scarcely get around in his topsy-turvy world, but after several days his brain adapted and his surroundings looked upright and normal again.

If humans are less robotlike than salamanders or ducks, it's not because we have *no* wired-in behaviors. In fact, we have quite a few. What makes the difference is the *ratio* of "unwired" to wired-in gray matter, because neurons that are not committed at birth to a set function, like discerning insect shapes or moving the tongue, are available for learning, for modification. Virtually all the cells in an amphibian or reptile brain directly process sensory information (input) or control movement (output), but in humans a great gray area—about three-fourths of the cortex—lies between sensory input and motor output, called the *association areas*. These include the frontal lobes and parts of the temporal, parietal, and occipital lobes. "The human cortex spends most of its time talking to itself," says Miles Herkenham. "It's astounding. When you look at where the fibers go, you'd be hard put to figure out how it even communicates with the rest of the body. It might as well be plucked out to live by itself."

If we're seeking the neural basis of consciousness, we might look to the ghostly zone between input and output. After all, the association areas of primitive mammals are negligible, while those of the evolutionarily recent species, like primates, are vastly expanded. This exponential increase in the number of cells and their interconnections created animals with near-infinite bits, near-infinite "choices," in their brains. But at what precise point in evolution did consciousness, or the inward-looking faculty we call self-consciousness, arise?

Are Animals Conscious?

DOES LASSIE really know what's going on, or is it the dog biscuits off-screen? Descartes saw animals as machines, but machines that could do many things on their own, such as breathing and digesting food, without the help of an immortal soul. The soul was a thinking thing, and only man needed one. This view is echoed, albeit in less theological terms, by Sir John Eccles: "Even when we come to the apparently intelligent actions of higher animals with their remarkable abilities to learn and remember," Eccles writes in a 1974 essay, "I have not found any reason to go beyond the purely mechanistic neurophysiology in explaining their brain performances, which of course was the position of Descartes." To this C. Wade Savage, of the University of Minnesota, retorts: "Then why go beyond the purely mechanistic neurophysiology in explaining the performance of *humans*?" Why, in short, should human behavior—but not animal behavior—require a soul? In his essay "An Old Ghost in a New Body," Savage writes:

We tend to regard a subject's description of what his situation is . . . as the only test of whether he is conscious. And since animals cannot provide such descriptions we conclude that they are not conscious, not self-conscious. (Eccles, at least, seems to reach the conclusion in this manner.) But consider. If a dog is brought home from a long stay in the hospital, and immediately proceeds to search for familiar objects and places, then he knows what his situation is, and is conscious. If the dog is surprised in the act of eating a steak waiting to be broiled, and slinks away with his head down and his tail between his legs, then he knows what he is doing and is concious. So if consciousness requires a soul, dogs (some of them, at least) have souls.

Indeed, we'd be hard put to draw a line through the evolutionary scale and declare that right here, at point X, consciousness emerged. A pigeon is taught to peck at a button of a certain color for a food reward. Is the bird an unthinking stimulus-response machine, or is it formulating a primitive theory of cause and effect ("If I peck here, grain will appear.")? Rockefeller University biologist Donald Griffin, the author of a recent book, *Animal Thinking*, argues that such simple mental processes are "hallmarks of conscious awareness." Some animals plan, make choices, adapt to new situations, cooperate, count, ratiocinate. Lions in Kenya hunt cooperatively, using strategies like human warriors; ravens count to seven, as evidenced by their ability to select from a group of covered pots one with seven marks on the lid. And then there are all the smart chimps who figure in the neuropsychology texts. When Karl Pribram taught a colony of chimpanzees at Stanford's Center for Advanced Studies to trade poker chips in exchange for food, the animals went beyond the experiment, developing a primitive economic system, hoarding chips as if they were securities certificates and trading them among themselves.

"To what extent," we ask Pribram, above whose desk, a pensive, baleful-eyed monkey gazes down from a framed oil portrait, "are nonhuman primates and other higher mammals capable of self-consciousness—an awareness of self as distinct from the outside world?"

"Well, we've tried to test this," he tells us. "The usual test is the mirror test. You paint the animal's forehead and place him in front of a mirror, and if he tries to rub the paint off his forehead, you know he's aware that he's seeing his own image. The major apes—gorillas, chimpanzees, and orangutans—do this, but the minor apes, such as gibbons, don't. It's an interesting cutoff point."

His soft voice trails off and then resumes. "I'm worried about the test, though, because gibbons, who fail it, are very, very socially aware. I also sometimes get the feeling that my dog feels guilt, that he may be self-conscious."

"Yet," we ask, "you seem to see a quantum leap between chimpanzee and human intelligence; is our intelligence so unique?"

"Of course it is!" says Pribram. "How many chimpanzees are sitting across from each other, interviewing each other, recording the interview on tape, and transcribing it into a manuscript? I'm tempted to say that humans are as different from nonhuman primates as mammals are from other vertebrates. We're not unique in possessing intelligence, but our kind of intelligence is very, very special."

Talking Apes

"Beasts abstract not."
—JOHN LOCKE

"Baby in my drink."
—WASHOE (observing a doll floating in her water)

THERE ARE those who consider consciousness an exclusively human attribute, perhaps a by-product of a soul. In Eccles's view, not only are animals devoid of it but so is the nonverbal half of the human brain. "We can regard the minor hemisphere," he writes in his 1974 essay, "as having the status of a very superior animal's brain. It displays intelligent reactions and primitive learning responses . . . but it gives no conscious experience to the subject." Eccles is not alone in equating conscious experience with the ability to state, "I am conscious."

The Swiss psychologist Jean Piaget saw children under the age of seven or eight as preconscious, and Julian Jaynes, a maverick Princeton professor, has theorized that the Greeks of Homer's time did not have consciousness as we know it. In *The Origin of Consciousness in the Breakdown of the Bicameral Mind*, Jaynes asserts that until about 2000 B.C., Homo sapiens lived inside a two-chambered brain, with little connection between the two cerebral hemispheres. Ancient man was incapable of introspection, says Jaynes, and mistook his own internal messages (emanating from the mute right hemisphere) for the voices of gods—gray-eyed Athena consoling Achilles, Aphrodite and her fateful love spells, and so on. As you can see, "consciousness" is a fuzzier term than, say, "excitatory postsynaptic potentials."

Discussions of human specialness usually center on the gift of speech: our faculty for using signs and symbols to stand for things and then to construct abstract or imaginary worlds beyond the here and now. But is man the only talking animal? The question became less abstract in 1966, when an infant chimpanzee named Washoe moved into a secondhand house trailer in a backyard near Reno and began lessons in American Sign Language (ASL), the sign language of the deaf. Besides learning to eat with a fork and spoon, drink from a cup, use the toilet, wash dishes, and appreciate the local Dairy Queen, the world's first "talking chimpanzee" acquired a working vocabulary of 132 signs under the tutelage of her human foster parents, University of Nevada psychologists Beatrix and R. Allen Gardner. She also strung signs together into telegraphic two- and three-word sentences, uttered *bon mots* like "Baby in my drink," coined neologisms (watching a swan splash into a pond, she combined the signs *water* and *bird* to exclaim, "Waterbird!"), and imparted the gift of speech to an adopted infant chimp named Loulis.

Washoe and the other "talking" apes who followed have done much to refute Locke's pronouncement. They evidently understand the concept of class (that is, that bananas and apples fall into the class of fruit; that the sign *cow* refers to any cow, not a specific cow). They employ words like *potty* and *dirty* as a form of name-calling, thus demonstrating a feeling for metaphor. At the University of Pennsylvania a chimp named Sarah, using colored tokens for words, reportedly grasps the concepts of "same" and "different," as well as the conditional relationship expressed in English as "if . . . then"—in other words, simple logic. At Stanford a female gorilla named Koko has learned to lie, swear, joke, pun, and produce metaphors, similes, and three-word sentences in sign language, according to her trainer, Penny Patterson. A sample of gorilla wit:

KOKO Do food.
HUMAN TRAINER: Do where? In your mouth?
KOKO: Nose?
HUMAN: Nose?
KOKO: Fake mouth.
HUMAN: Where's your fake mouth?
KOKO: Nose.

Having opened a window onto nonhuman consciousness, we discover a mental landscape resembling our own. We find that other primates, at least, are capable of elementary logic, jokes, banter, deliberate misinformation, cajoling, deep sorrow, rich communication. But is it language?

Many people view signing apes as nothing more than animals begging for food, sophisticated versions of conditioned rats in Skinner boxes. But in 1984 a simian cinema verité experiment by Roger Fouts, who took over Project Washoe in its fourth year, showed that (1) chimps do converse among themselves when no humans are present, and (2) they don't talk about food all that much. In Fouts's videotapes of the private signed discussions of Washoe, now a dowager of nineteen, and four younger chimps, play and social interaction were the dominant topics, with signs for "chase," "tickle," "groom," and so on far outnumbering the idiom of eating.

The verbal apes' most formidable critic is MIT linguist Noam Chomsky, to whom the essence of language is syntax (grammar) not semantics (meaning). Chomsky and his brethren assert that the telegraphic, grammatically impoverished apetalk is not real language, for it lacks the rich syntactic structures that permit humans to construct an infinite number of meaningful sentences from a finite number of units.

"Baloney!" Allen Gardner retorts. "Imagine trying to ask directions on the street with just grammar and no semantics. Obviously the survival value of language must be in communicating information. That's semantics.

"A medieval philosopher like Chomsky," he tells us, "says there is this Great Divide between man and beast. You know, the reason they tried to burn Galileo at the stake was that he said the Earth was not the center of the universe. It's the same idea."

Talking animals—outside of Aesop, anyway—seem to stir up a deep metaphysical unease. But even if we concede that lower primates can talk and reason, Homo sapiens would be no less special. What other species has Cray computers, hand-held calculators, lunar launch vehicles, Teflon pans, the *Encyclopedia Britannica*, the AFL-CIO, the Supreme Court, the Tokyo subway system, the Louvre, and *Paradise Lost*?

The Wood Where Things Have No Names

She was rambling on in this way when she reached the wood: It looked very cool and shady. "Well, at any rate it's a great comfort," she said as she stepped under the trees, "after being so hot, to get into the—into the—*what*?" she went on, rather surprised at not being able to think of the word. "I mean to get under the—under the—under *this*, you know!" putting her hand on the trunk of the tree. "What *does* this call itself, I wonder? I do believe it's got no name—why, to be sure it hasn't!"
—LEWIS CARROLL,
Through the Looking Glass

IN THE "wood in which things have no names," Alice might have been wandering in the silent forests of prehistory or in the phantasmagoric dawn of Gabriel García Márquez's novel *One Hundred Years of Solitude*, when "the world was so recent that many things still lacked names, and in order to indicate them it was necessary to point." Genesis tells us that God delegated to Adam the job of naming all the creatures of Eden. Trees, birds, fawns, and the other objects of the universe don't possess God-given names. Names are pragmatic products of a human brain, which needs labels to get around. Consider Alice's earlier conversation with the Gnat:

"Of course they [the insects] answer to their names?" the Gnat remarked carelessly.
"I never knew them to do it."
"What's the use of their having names," the Gnat said, "if they won't answer to them?"
"No use to *them*," said Alice; "but it's useful to the people that name them, I suppose. If not, why do things have names at all?"

The wood where things have no names might also be a metaphor for the aphasias, or language disorders. The misfortunes of a nineteenth-century French aphasic first revealed the existence of a speech center in the brain. Because the idea smacked of Gall's phrenology, many scientists were skeptical when the Parisian doctor Pierre-Paul Broca announced his findings at a meeting of the Paris Anthropological Society in 1861. But history has proved him right. The aphasic Frenchman, known in the literature as "Tan" because *tan* was the only word he could say, had suffered a stroke to his left cerebral hemisphere. After Tan's death, Broca did an autopsy and uncovered a lesion near the facial area of the motor cortex, the region that now bears his name. (See *Broca's area* in Figure 3.)

"If you ask a Broca's aphasic how he spent the Easter holidays," observes UCLA's Eran Zaidel, a prominent "split-brain" researcher, "he may answer something like this: 'Uh, uh, Easter . . . ho, ho, holiday, like . . . eat turkey . . . many lights . . . people . . . very good.' " His speech is labored, halting, telegraphic, but not without sense. Strangely he may sing fluently and beautifully, though his writing suffers from the same defects as his spoken discourse.

"Oh yes, we have done it, could be different but nevertheless done. Go, go, gone, and however successful, it still fails. I wish indeed, good morning." That, says Zaidel, is the way a *Wernicke's aphasic* would respond to a query about his holidays. The site of injury here is Wernicke's area in the left temporal lobe (named after the German neurologist Carl Wernicke), and the result is fluent but nonsensical, semantically flawed speech. The problem is one of meaning, not articulation, and a Wernicke's aphasic can't understand what other people say to him either. Yet he often remains blissfully unaware that anything is wrong. Analyzing the defects of stroke victims, Carl Wernicke constructed a model of how the brain produces language, which still holds up. The underlying sense of a statement arises in Wernicke's area, whence it travels to Broca's area. There a detailed vocalization "program" is formed and then transferred to the nearby motor cortex, which activates the muscles of the mouth, lips, tongue, larynx, and so on.

A third variety of aphasia, *anomia*, or *anomic aphasia*, follows injury to the temporal-parietal area. The anomic patient literally can't find the words, written or spoken. "For example," says Zaidel, "if you point to a fork and ask the patient to name it, he may respond with, 'It's a, ah, ahh . . . (eating motions). It's a spoon. No, no, I mean it's a . . . You eat with it, a, ha, I can say it.' You ask him then, 'Is it a knife?' And he will say immediately, 'No, no.' And if you cue him by starting, 'Use your knife and . . . ,' he will often be able to complete it, 'Fork.' Here the disorder is one of reference—of the relation between words and the things in the world that they stand for." Like Alice stranded in the wood where things have no names.

Thus some parts of the human cortex *do* house particular faculties, in an almost phrenological fashion. Wipe out a particular group of cells, and language goes. (Actually, it's not quite so simple, for the speechless hemisphere is not entirely nonverbal, as we'll see. But in principle we can trace language to localized centers.) And there are other cortical areas that govern a narrow range of behavior. Monkeys missing a small region of the frontal lobes can no longer choose an object from a pair after a certain delay. People shorn of parts of the temporal lobe can't retain memories.

Then there's an intriguing neurological problem called *prosopagnosia*, the inability to recognize faces.

"In the normal individual," noted the late Dr. Norman Geschwind of Harvard in "Specialization of the Human Brain" (1977) in *Scientific American*, "the ability to identify people from their faces is itself quite remarkable. At a glance one can make out a person from facial features alone, even though the features may have changed substantially over the years or may be presented in a highly distorted form, as in a caricature. In a patient with prosopagnosia this talent for association is abolished." The prosopagnosia victim can read, name objects, and recognize familiar voices, but faced with a photograph of his sister or his sister in the flesh, he can't name her. This defect apparently results from damage to the underside of both occipital lobes, extending forward to the inner surface of the temporal lobe. "The implication," added Geschwind, "is that some neural network within this region is specialized for the rapid and reliable recognition of human faces." A useful ability for a social animal like man, who must store the images of hundreds, perhaps thousands, of friends, relatives, business associates, enemies, political figures, and celebrities in his memory bank.

Alas for Franz Joseph Gall, there are no "mirthfulness," "friendship," and "acquisitiveness" centers in the cortex. Most higher functions involve many parts of the brain working in concert. We can see, however, that the behaviorists are wrong: the human cerebrum is *not* a blank slate. Millions of years of evolution have outfitted it with some specialized equipment, inborn "programs" for surviving on this particular planet. Every human infant is the end product of a long line of ancestors who experienced the world in a certain way and whose brains were molded by those experiences. "In one sense," Jacob Bronowski reflects, in *The Identity of Man*, "the brain is more like a man-made machine than is the rest of the body."

Universal Grammar

IF ITS BRAIN were a tabula rasa, a child should be capable of learning any language, even Martian or Alpha-Centaurian if it happened to be raised by extraterrestrials. No one really questioned that dictum until an iconoclastic linguist named Noam Chomsky started preaching a radical new doctrine in the mid–1950s. We owe our gift of speech, Chomsky declared, to a genetically programmed "language organ" in the brain. And evolution has shaped this organ so that it is capable of learning only those tongues that fall within a narrow band of possibilities. Comanche, Urdu, English, Serbo-Croation, and every other language spoken on the Earth conform to a "universal grammar" in our heads, says Chomsky. If they did not, we couldn't understand them.

"If a Martian landed from outer space and spoke a language that violated universal grammar," Chomsky told an *Omni* magazine interviewer, "we simply would not be able to learn that language the way that we learn a human language like English or Swahili. We would have to approach the alien's language slowly and laboriously—the way that scientists study physics. . . . We're designed by nature for English, Chinese, and every other possible human language, but we're not designed to learn perfectly usable languages that violate universal grammar."

The clues came from the mouths of babes. If language learning were a matter of mimicry and conditioning, as the behaviorists claimed, how could children learn to talk in the first place? Every natural language contains an infinite number of sentences, yet the number of sentences actually pronounced in a child's hearing during the learning phase may be quite small. Nonetheless, by the age of four, the average child utters any number of completely original, grammatically correct sentences. The only possible explanation, in Chomsky's view, is that the "deep structure" of language is inborn. Only the "surface structure," which varies from language to language, is learned.

What sort of linguistic know-how is built in? "Take the sentence 'John believes he is intelligent,' " Chomsky told *Omni*. "Okay, we all know that *he* can refer either to John or someone else; so the sentence is ambiguous. . . . In contrast, consider the sentence, 'John believes him to be intelligent.' Here the pronoun *him* can't refer to John, it can refer only to someone else. Now, did anyone teach us this peculiarity about English pronouns when we were children? . . . Nevertheless, everybody knows it—knows it without experience, without training, and at quite an early age."

B. F. Skinner, the grand old man of behaviorism, has insisted that humans are hard-wired by nature to see and hear but that experience supplies just about everything else. "This view can't possibly be correct," Chomsky retorts. Language learning is a little like puberty or aging, a genetically programmed event in the life of an organism. Of course, a person needn't be exposed to puberty in order to experience it, whereas a child does pick up the tongue of his parents or caretakers. Chomsky doesn't claim that language is *entirely* inborn or that you have brain cells that encode knowledge of the Greek pluperfect subjunctive or the proper declension of *Gesellschaft*.

"The language organ," he explains, "interacts with early experience and matures into the grammar of the language that the child speaks. If a human being grows up in Philadelphia, as I did, his brain will encode knowledge of the Philadelphia dialect of English. If that brain had grown up in Tokyo, it would have encoded the Tokyo dialect of Japanese. The brain's different linguistic experience—English versus Japanese—would modify the language organ's structure."

The Finite Brain

IF CHOMSKY is right, and humans could not understand Martians—or angels or gods—if they spoke to us, other experiences must be off-limits to our species, too. "We like and understand Beethoven because we are humans, with a particular, genetically determined mental constitution," Chomsky suggests, "but that same human nature also means there are other conceivable forms of esthetic expression that will be totally meaningless for us." Perhaps whole realms of knowledge lie beyond the wavelengths our brains can decode. Perhaps genetic barriers keep us from solving certain intellectual problems, appreciating certain kinds of beauty, or conceiving a nonhuman kind of science.

"We often lose sight of the fact that the brains we carry in our heads are not the last word in nervous systems," muses Georgetown University neurophysiologist Daniel Robinson, in *The Enlightened Machine*. As the "bug detectors" in a frog's brain program it to interpret the universe in terms of bugs and nonbugs, our brains may likewise be limited by a finite set of preconceptions. "The frog fixes himself in the weeded pond, a creature with perhaps one idea," Robinson writes. "The arrangement of neural elements in his retina is such that, no matter what the real world is or does, the only 'truth' is that black convexity moving across his eye. . . . What are our universals? Are there 'truths' all around us that our neurons cannot process? Are the truths we've found more an expression of the peculiarities of our neurophysiology than a reflection of the way the world behaves?"

When human physicists, peering into the heart of matter, "see" charmed quarks, left-handed quarks, positrons, neutrinos, antiprotons, are they seeing the basic building blocks of the universe or the projections of their own brains? Despite the modern *unlock your infinite creative potential* philosophy, brains have their limitations. On the other hand . . .

Why Evolution Did Not End in 100,000 B.C.

ACCORDING TO anthropologists, the human cerebrum evolved to its present form some forty thousand years ago in the cranium of Cro-Magnon. Even Neanderthal man, who hunted and foraged a hundred thousand years ago, had a brain as large as ours, packaged in a long skull with a sloping brow. Thus the spectacular enlargement of the cortex from early mammals to apes to early hominids ends around 100,000 B.C. It wasn't until 15,000 B.C., however, that ancient humans painted vivid, lifelike horses and bulls on cave walls. No cities appeared on earth until 5,000 B.C. Not until the fourth century B.C. did man devise a form of writing (the first texts were Sumerian bills of lading and other mundane documents), thereby finding a way to store knowledge outside the brain. This time lag suggests that brain size and cell count don't necessarily tell the whole story.

Why did nature rest on its laurels in the early Paleolithic era instead of fabricating ever newer and better thought organs? There are theories that the girth of the female pelvis limits cranial size such that were our brains any bigger, human females could not deliver their babies. However, the hard-wired equipment that biological evolution bequeathed us is only part of the story. Yours is *not* a Stone Age brain, because brains, unlike other bodily organs, undergo a secondary evolution that occurs after birth.

From the brain came words and symbols, social systems, myths, symphonies, histories, churches, atlases, encyclopedias, the seven o'clock news, and op art—in a word, culture—and, once created, these brain products transformed the brain. It's hard to imagine a human being untouched by human culture. Unfortunately we don't have to imagine. In 1970 a thirteen-year-old girl named Genie was discovered chained to an infant's potty-chair in a fetid, darkened room in Los Angeles. Since she was twenty months old, her psychotic father had kept her there, chained to the potty-chair or to a crib, seldom spoken to, punished when she uttered any sound, and fed only baby food. At the time she was brought to the Children's Hospital in Los Angeles, Genie couldn't stand erect, speak, or chew food. Eventually she did learn to walk, dress herself, eat solid foods with a knife, fork, and spoon, draw pictures, and do many other things. UCLA linguists even taught her to talk, though imperfectly, thereby proving that people can acquire language even after the "critical period" for speech is long past. (The famous "wild boy" of France, isolated from human contact until the age of twelve, reportedly remained mute.) In any case, the moral is that a human brain deprived of human society doesn't develop beyond a subhuman state.

British neuroscientist-author Steven Rose writes in *The Conscious Brain*, "Our cranial capacity or cell number may not be so different from the early Homo sapiens, but our environments—our forms of society—are very different and hence so too is our consciousness—which also means that so too are our brain states; the connectivity, if nothing else, of the brains of twentieth-century humans cannot be identified with that which characterized our ancestors." Rose is absolutely right: Our brains are changed by the way we use them.

Making Our Own Brain Maps

Man is nothing else but what he makes of himself. Such is the first principle of existentialism. . . . Man is at the start a plan which is aware of itself, rather than a patch of moss, a piece of garbage, or a cauliflower; nothing exists prior to this plan; there is nothing in heaven; man will be what he will have planned to be.

—JEAN-PAUL SARTRE, *Existentialism and Human Existence*, 1957

"THE BRAIN is not a machine in which every element has a genetically assigned role; it is not a digital computer in which all the decisions have been made," Michael Merzenich, of the University of California at San Francisco (UCSF), tells us. "Anatomy lays down a crude topographic map of the body on the surface of the cortex, which is fixed and immutable in early life. But the *fine-grained* map is not fixed. Experience sketches in all the details, altering the map continually throughout life."

And that, in short, is why I am I and you are you.

Merzenich isn't just philosophizing. With UCSF colleague Michael Stryker, he has been methodically sticking microelectrodes into the brains of squirrel and owl monkeys to find out how the brain arranges its internal maps. Merzenich and Stryker concentrated on a patch of the somatosensory cortex that receives touch information from the hand. By recording the firing of single cells in response to stimulation of a fingertip, a point on the palm, and so on, they traced a continuous topographic map of the hand on the brain surface. Each animal they studied had an individual brain map, differing in size and other details.

When one or more fingers were amputated, the maps shifted. Over a period of weeks sensory inputs from the remaining fingers moved into the missing digit's zone, enhancing the sensitivity of the surviving fingers. When the median nerve of the hand was severed and allowed to regenerate, the cortical map resembled a Picasso hand, with its thumb represented in at least six disconnected places. Yet sensitivity tests indicated that, to the monkey, the thumb "felt" relatively normal. "Apparently," says Merzenich, "an ordered map in the brain is not absolutely necessary to recognize familiar objects."

In another experiment the UCSF cartographers trained a monkey to push a lever with its finger several thousand times a day and then surveyed the small, four-and-a-half-square-millimeter area of cortex corresponding to that finger. Sure enough, the map in the brain had been reorganized by use, proving that experience dramatically alters cortical geography. If this is true of monkeys, says Merzenich, it would be all the more true of human beings. A jeweler polishes the tiny, luminous facets of a gem under a magnifying glass. An eye surgeon makes microscopic stitches on a patient's cornea. Their brains come to reflect their skills. Every individual on earth has a different brain map.

"Here's how I look at it," says Merzenich. "Phase one of brain organization is when the anatomy is set down, and that isn't alterable beyond a critical period, early in development. Then there is phase two, beginning in childhood and extending into adult life, when the *functional* connections between neurons are made. This process has hardly been studied until now.

"We think the cells of the cortex are wired up anatomically to receive inputs from a very wide zone," he explains. "There are thousands of alternate ways in which any part of the skin surface—arm, hand, leg, et cetera—could be represented in the brain. Only *one* of the ways is selected, however, for cells respond to only a fraction of their input. So a neuron might receive input from half the hand, say, but only respond to a small zone on the tip of the finger. Yet under certain circumstances—like a stroke—the map can still be modified. The cell could learn to respond to stimulation on another finger or somewhere on the palm. But not on the big toe—anatomy strictly limits how far things can change."

Merzenich thinks the same rules apply to motor maps, auditory maps, *all* neural maps. Only more so: "The zones we study are the most tightly connected, with the least potential for alteration," he says. "We think when you get into the cortical zones where we really live—where we perform recognition and categorization of things—the input is spread over a wider field and experience can probably modify it more."

Neurons, in short, compete in a Darwinian manner for space in the brain, much as species compete for an ecological niche. At least that's the theory of Rockefeller University's Gerald Edelman, a Nobel Prize-winning microbiologist-turned-neuroscientist. "The brain, in its workings, is a selective system, more like evolution itself than like computation," he told *The New Yorker*. "We are part of that complex web of natural selection which has itself evolved a selective machinery called our brain. In each of us there lies . . . a second evolutionary path during a lifetime: it unites culture with a marvelous tissue in which the hope of our survival lies."

"Our results fit Edelman's predictions," says Merzenich. "It makes sense to look at it as a selection process." Compared with the tidy, compartmentalized, either/or efficiency of computers, Mother Nature is messy, a slattern. But, according to Edelman and Merzenich, this unruly Darwinian game of chance and adaptation among nerve cells is the basis of your freedom. Your genes don't predestine you to be a surfer, a dreamer, a world-class chess player, a Mercedes mechanic, a Folies Bergères girl, a drill-bit salesman, or Jean-Paul Sartre. Your accumulated thoughts and actions weave your neurons into the unique tapestry of your mind.

Is it possible to tamper with the course of the second evolution?

"Now I want you to consider some possibilities that might sound a bit weird," Merzenich tells us. "First, imagine what would happen if the map were unstable and could be altered rapidly. If it changed too fast, you might get errors of association. The primary sensory maps might be out of phase with the brain's other maps, and the consequence might be schizophrenia. Now take the opposite situation, in which the map is superstable and scarcely affected by experience. You can probably imagine what the resulting mental disease might be."

"Senility?" we guess.

"Right. Or maybe depression. So there's an enormous potential for treating mental illnesses by making the maps either more or less plastic. You might fool the brain into giving the area affected by a stroke more space in the brain. Drugs that made the brain more plastic might speed up the learning of new skills or rejuvenate elderly brains.

"We know that amphetamine withdrawal, for example, destabilizes the map. We can tell from recordings that the cell's receptive field—what input it responds to—changes quickly. But the question is, how much can you speed up the changes before you create disorder in the internal map? Or say you wanted to *stabilize* the map. Since I'm interested in humans, I'm thinking of purely psychological methods that could do it. Perhaps you could stabilize the brain of a schizophrenic by creating a superstable environment."

Educated Rats

ONCE UPON A TIME there were some rats who lived in a laboratory in Montreal, Canada. One day a famous behavioral psychologist, Donald O. Hebb, took some of the rats home with him and raised them as pets. These rats became very smart. They could find their way through mazes, even complicated ones, much better than the other rats, who stayed behind in the humdrum, solitary cages of the lab.

Much later, in the 1960s, a group of University of California at Berkeley scientists, headed by Mark Rosenzweig, elaborated the allegory of the smart and dull rats. They raised littermates either in an "enriched environment" (communal cages full of running wheels and toys, where the rats

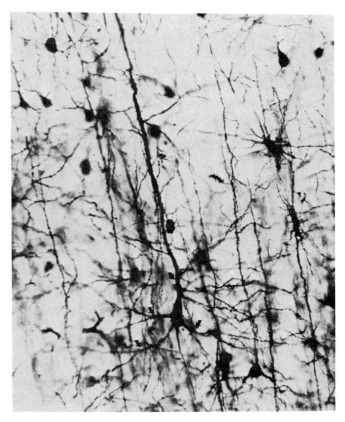

This micrograph shows the visual cortex of a rat raised in an "enriched" environment. According to William Greenough, its dendrites (arrows) are 20 percent more extended—and thus richer in synapses—than those of rats raised in individual laboratory cages. (*Courtesy of William T. Greenough, University of Illinois*)

were also handled and petted by their caretakers) or an "impoverished" one (individual cages with low sensory stimulation). Then they took out the rats' brains, weighed and measured them, and reported that the enriched group had a thicker cerebral cortex. Few scientists believed these reports at first. How on earth could the social environment physically change the brain?

One early believer was psychologist William Greenough, of the University of Illinois. In the early 1970s he replicated the Berkeley results and more. He raised one group of rats in isolation in standard laboratory cages, a second group in a "social situation" with two animals per cage, and a third in a luxurious cage stocked with Mattel toys and homemade metal-and-wooden playthings. Later, staining the brain tissue with a Golgi stain and carefully tracing the branching dendrites of single neurons under a microscope, Greenough found that the stimulated rats had more dendritic branches. (The differences between social rats and isolates weren't striking.) If dendritic branching sounds like dull stuff, recall that the multiple synapses along the dendrite are the neuron's receiving stations. More dendrites presumably mean more synapses and more connections.

"And more information, in a very important sense!" Greenough points out. "The rat is not just a little passive critter that stares out at the room. He flies all over the cage and has a great time, and the experience modifies his brain. Experienced organisms have brains with more connections between nerve cells. Our assumption is that these connections are storing information. More synapses mean more behavioral repertoires, a wider array of responses, more choices. The question is, how specific is the information stored in the dendritic connections? Could particular memories be stored in this way?

"I'll tell you what I think," he continues. "People think memory is a unique thing, but I see memory as an extension of development. At first the developing brain uses experience to get its basic wiring laid down. Later on it uses similar mechanisms—dendritic growth, the formation of new synapses—to store information in the pattern of nerve-cell connections. That's the idea we're working on right now."

When you learn the word *boulangerie* or plug into a computer network with Pascal, a new text is actually etched into your cerebral "wiring"— and it all happens with astonishing speed. There is evidence that new synapses form in ten to fifteen seconds or less, according to Greenough. "It's mind-blowing," he comments. Nobody knows if old synapses are erased at a corresponding rate since, in Greenough's words, "we don't know how to measure that; we don't know what to look for." But obviously your brain is being continually remodeled by what you put into it.

Scientists have known for years that young brains are more malleable than old ones and that there are "critical periods" early in an organism's life when experience is particularly influential. If newborn kittens are sequestered in a room whose walls are covered with either horizontal or vertical stripes, their brains are shaped accordingly. Afterward the "horizontal cats" walk right into chair legs, as if unable to see verticality, while the "vertical cats" cannot leap from one horizontal surface to another.

Laborious experiments by Hubel and Weisel have demonstrated that the visual cortex has nerve cells that are selectively tuned to lines and edges of a particular orientation. Such electrode studies soon revealed that the vertical felines had fewer horizontal detectors in their brains and that the cats raised among horizontal bars had scant vertical-detector cells. Kittens who grow up in a "planetarium" environment of bright spots against a dark background develop lots of spot detectors and few line detectors. So the brain's reality is fixed by its early experiences—which might account for the psychoanalytic verity that infantile traumas lead to neuroses or psychoses later in life. Not surprisingly the subjects of the first enrichment studies were very young rats, because an old brain, naturally, could not be taught new tricks. Or so everybody thought.

Recently, however, Greenough and his colleagues tried their stuff on mature rats. They selected a group of sixty-day-old young adults (the equivalent of human college students) and another of 450-day-old, middle-aged rodents and subjected them to either enrichment or isolation. The results? "With the young adults," Greenough tells us, "we did get results, though they were less striking than in baby rats. Their brains didn't grow many new dendritic branches, but enrichment did *extend* the terminal spines. When we looked at the middle-aged animals, on the other hand, we were amazed. Enrichment had very dramatic effects on their brains, just as dramatic as in very young rats. We don't know why. Maybe in stimulating the middle-aged brain you're heading off a decline.

"If there's a message, it's that the brain is dynamic throughout life. The old view was that the neural architecture was fixed at birth or certainly at maturity. We saw the brain as static because we were looking at micrographs of dead tissue where nothing ever moves. Only in the last five years have neuroscientists become aware of the incredible structural plasticity of the brain."

Even elderly brains, Greenough says, need stimulation. Especially elderly brains, perhaps. "People have compared old people in nursing homes to the population still waiting to get in," he tells us. "And there's a whopping difference in IQ. By the time you've been in a home six months, your IQ has already plummeted. Nursing homes are badly designed; they starve the brain of experience."

The brain does not live on glucose alone. Cultivation feeds it. Isolation kills it. And maybe, just maybe, the experiments we've heard about can help us with an old conundrum.

Can Hope Fire a Neuron?

QUESTION: How can a thought, which has no mass, no electrical charge, no velocity, no material properties at all, act upon a physical organ, the brain?

MATERIALIST ANSWER: It can't. Have you ever tried to slice bread with your will? Well, it's just as silly to imagine that thoughts can slip through a brain-cell membrane and invade the nucleus or can jump up and down on the axon to make it fire. Mental phenomena, being immaterial by definition, don't affect physical objects.

REDUCTIONIST ANSWER: Thoughts, schmoughts. All your thoughts are *really* just electrochemical blips in nervous tissue. Because "mental states" are ghostly by-products of brain events, mere figments, there's no need to worry about how the two might interact.

DUALIST-INTERACTIONIST ANSWER: As surely as there are tables and rocks, there are desires, beliefs, perceptions, worries, dreams, regrets, memories, and pains in the universe. Mental states are real, even if you can't see, touch, or taste them, and they do influence our brains.

But how? Since Descartes, the interactionist dilemma has been something like this: If a thought affects us, it must *do something* to neural tissue, but something incorporeal can't possibly make a dent in something physical. Or can it?

If experience can change the brain's architecture, if play or a rich social life can grow dendrites, maybe something like hope can redirect the traffic of nerve signals in your head. This notion is disturbing only if we imagine the mental and material as two separate substances. You live in a mental universe as well as a physical universe of chairs, tables, electrons, trees, and planets. The sentence you're reading exists as a pattern of black marks on a white page and as a thought in the author's head, a thought in your head, a thought in your friend's head if you tell him or her about it, and so on. Then, again, we might imagine the thought in your brain as a flow of sodium and potassium ions through a cell wall or something. So the thought may take material form or not, but do you commute back and forth between two separate worlds, a mental world and a physical world?

In this chapter we've viewed the brain as a remarkable biomachine designed by evolution for eating, mating, distinguishing friends from foes and males from females, recognizing faces, marking territory, manipulating symbols, anticipating the future, and a thousand great and small tasks. The human brain, we've seen, undergoes a second sort of evolution during its lifetime. Rather than a fully programmed computer, it is an "open" system, an ongoing dialogue with the environment—which includes newspapers, radio telescopes, billboards, music, Paul MacLean's triune-brain theory, Noam Chomsky's linguistics, and other man-made things. In the next chapter we'll see how brain chemistry fits into this scheme.

3

The Chemical Brain

I think chemicals will soon rule the mind of man.
. . . I am a witch with a mania for making extracts
from the fruits of strange bushes [and will soon
be] sending a specially nourished pigeon to take
a crap in the tea of the President of the United
States when he's in the Rose Garden of the White
House and we'll control the world.
—ARNOLD MANDELL, M.D., *Coming of*
Middle Age: A Journey

He seemed surprised. "You *found* the American
Dream?" he said. "In *this* town?"
I nodded. "We're sitting on the main nerve
right now," I said.
—HUNTER THOMPSON, *Fear and*
Loathing in Las Vegas

SCENE from the National Institute of Mental Health, April 1982: Two
brown rhesus monkeys sit in plastic restraining chairs, with IV tubes
dripping saline into the thigh of one and a mysterious fluid into his
partner. A quarter of an hour later, while the first monkey still sits around
nonchalantly, eating and drinking, the second monkey starts to squirm and
wring his hands. Within minutes he looks like a scene out of *The Exorcist*,
screeching, howling, writhing, clawing at his fur, pounding his chair, uri-
nating, and defecating. The monitors show that his heart is racing, his
blood pressure has soared to dangerous levels, and his adrenaline level is
ten times higher than normal.

The monkey's demon is anxiety. But this anxiety has nothing to do with
unresolved Oedipal complexes, existential anguish, or any of the neurotic
impedimenta of Woody Allen films. This is *angst* in a test tube. It came
from an obscure-sounding compound called B-CCE, which NIMH scientists Steven Paul and Phil Skolnick hoped might lead them to the "brain's
own Valium." A natural Valium, or benzodiazepine, has been a Holy Grail
for pharmacologists since 1977, when receptors for the antianxiety agent
were first discovered in brain tissue. Why would our brains have special
binding sites for a Hoffman-La Roche drug unless something like Valium

already existed there? That question, at any rate, beckoned Paul and Skolnick a few years ago.

Apologizing for the bloodstains on his corduroy pants—"It's probably mouse brain"—Skolnick tells us the B-CCE story over the clatter of metal trays in the cafeteria. We're in Building 10 of the NIMH, one of the temples of the new faith. "Back in 1977," he tells us, "Steve and I were just sitting in the lab one day, cutting up rat hypothalami under magnifying scopes—they're just tiny. And Steve said, 'Did you see that paper in *Nature* about the Valium receptor?' I said, 'Yeah, technically, it looks good, but it must be bullshit. There's no Valium in the brain. Why would there be receptors for Valium?'

"He said, 'Right.' So then we were cutting, and suddenly Steve looked up and threw his glasses down. We dropped the experiment we were doing right then—that was the last experiment we ever did on hypothalami. We called up Paul Marangos, who's a biochemist, and went down to the slaughterhouse, got some cow brains, and started looking around for an endogenous Valium."

Endogenous is shorthand for "originating within the organism" (the opposite of *exogenous*), and an endogenous Valium is still to be found. In 1981 a Danish scientist seeking this modern-day elixir boiled a thousand liters of human urine and extracted a mysterious compound called B-CCE. Alas, B-CCE turned out to be a red herring, a by-product of the extraction procedure, not a natural Valium. In tests on rats it appeared to have little affinity for the Valium receptor. But when Paul, Skolnick, and others tested the compound on *monkeys*, they discovered that B-CCE did bind to the Valium receptor—with dramatic results. Instead of a miracle tranquility drug, however, it was just the opposite: an *anti-Valium*.

"From the looks of it, a large dose is like being pushed out of an airplane without a parachute," Skolnick tells us. "I mean, the monkey is just sitting there and a minute later he's scared shitless. It's bottled fear! We got increases in heart rate, blood pressure, and stress hormones like cortisol, so it seems to be a good model of stress. When we first saw it we couldn't believe it. After lunch we switched the monkeys and gave B-CCE to the animal that got saline before, and it happened all over again. Then we knew we were on to something.

"Of course, we can't ask the animal, 'How are you feeling?' But a physician in Germany recently gave a derivative of B-CCE to humans, and their descriptions were of classic free-floating anxiety: 'The walls are closing in! I just want to get out of here!' One guy got so anxious he tried to run out of the room."

Like a sorcerer's abracadabra, formulas like B-CCE are portals to a powerful new knowledge. The recent discoveries in neurochemistry have been likened to the splitting of the atom, perhaps because, until very recently, the puzzle box of the brain was locked up tight. Analysts probed it with talk, while the behaviorists focused on input (stimuli) and output (observed behavior) and wrote off the shadowy, in-between realm of moods, emotions, subjectivity, awareness, and the other unmeasurables.

Then, in the late 1960s and 1970s, came a series of startling neurochemical breakthroughs. "We have these complex human emotions, which we have always believed were of the soul," muses biological psychiatrist Philip Berger, of Stanford. "Analytic psychiatrists of the 1950s said you could never have an antianxiety drug because anxiety was too fundamental, too complicated; it was existential *angst*. But one of the best definitions of anxiety is *that emotion that five milligrams of Valium makes better.*"

Would Hoffman-La Roche have given *The Metamorphosis* an upbeat ending? Turned Sören Kierkegaard into a regular guy? Some say the new alchemists have found the doorways to the self. At any rate, they've turned up some fifty-odd brain chemicals that seem to make us happy or sad, sexy, schizophrenic, suicidal, or obsessed. They know the molecular structure of some of these chemicals and the genes that contain their blueprint. They know the enzymes that make and destroy them. They have discovered microscopic keyholes in the brain called receptors that could open the whole Pandora's box.

"Behavior isn't such a mysterious thing," says NIMH's Candace Pert, one of the trailblazers of the pharmacologic revolution. "I think it emanates from microcircuits of electrons flowing from neuron to neuron.

"What we're working on now," she explains, "is connecting up neurochemistry, the brain's 'juices,' with circuit diagrams of the brain. Circuit diagrams are what neuroanatomists have been concerned with for years: the interconnections of cells, the wiring. Now we're learning which neural pathways secrete endorphins [our natural opiates] and which secrete other neurojuices.

"There's no doubt in my mind that one day—and I don't think it's all that far away—we'll be able to make a color-coded wiring diagram of the brain. A color-coded map, with blue for one neurochemical, red for another, and so on. We'll be able to describe the brain in mathematical, physical, neurochemical, and electrical terms, with all the rigor of a differential equation."

If Pert's prophecy comes true, it will mean more than a new generation of mind drugs modeled on the brain's natural ones, though the advent of such tailor-made chemicals will certainly alter the inner landscape. It could also redefine man, creating a world where romantic love is traced to a few

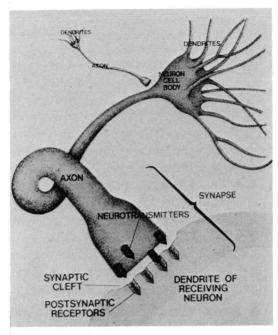

Nerve cells communicate by means of chemical messengers, or *neurotransmitters*. When a neurotransmitter molecule seeps across the microscopic gap of the *synaptic cleft*, it locks on to a specially shaped receptor on the postsynaptic cell. This is how our brains transmit the signals that process information, regulate emotions, and keep us alive. (*Courtesy of Henry N. Wagner, Jr., Johns Hopkins University*)

nanomoles of "Aphroditine," perhaps, and where ten milligrams of "Fraternitonin" could transform a brooding misanthrope into a back-slapping Rotarian; where all your personality traits—your love of Strauss waltzes, your preference for tall, willowy redheads or dark, black-eyed men, your tendency to vote a straight Republican ticket—are explained as a subtle mix of a few brain juices. What then? Who would you be?

God at the Synapse

ALL THE TOOLS of the pharmacologic revolution work at the miniature anatomy of the synapse, where neurons communicate. In the last chapter we said that neurons send signals in the form of electrical pulses, or action potentials, of varying frequencies, but that's not the whole story. When an action potential arrives at the synapse, it triggers the secretion of a chemical messenger, called a *neurotransmitter*. In the 1950s the British neuroscientist Sir Bernard Katz discovered that transmitters are released in little packets, or quanta, that seep across the gap to bind to the next cell. By adding up all the electrochemical messages that reach it during a certain interval, the cell on the receiving end "decides" whether to fire an impulse down *its* axon. (There is subtraction involved, too, for synapses can say no as well as yes. Some neurochemicals are inhibitory instead of excitatory.)

But all manner of things can happen to a neurotransmitter molecule during its hazardous 0.3 to 1.0 millisecond passage across the synaptic cleft. It can be broken down in the gap before it reaches the other side, in which case no signal is transmitted. One of the enzymes that is supposed to break it down afterward might not work, in which case the transmitter floods the synapse and neighboring cells. So here, at the meeting place between cells, is where all our mind drugs act—alcohol, LSD, sleeping pills, morphine, caffeine, tranquilizers, marijuana, antidepressants—though we've only recently figured out how. For hundreds of years human beings have unknowingly been using plant products that are neurotransmitter lookalikes, drugs that resemble our natural chemicals and interact with their receptors.

For a drug or a natural transmitter to have an effect, it must fit into a specially tailored receptor on the postsynaptic cell. This is usually described as a "lock-and-key arrangement," but in reality the receptor is a three-dimensional protein molecule on the cell membrane that changes its shape when a neurotransmitter locks onto it. When a chemical couples with a receptor, a neuron may fire or be dampened, a muscle cell may contract, a gland cell may secrete a hormone. Pain, sex, memory, mood states, and mental illness are all products of the interaction of chemicals and receptors.

If the brain were just electrical, if its only language were the binary code of the action potential, we might really be deterministic, computerlike machines. But the chemical brain is more slippery. "Introduce a gap between synapses, a junction with room for uncertainty," writes Steven Rose, "and the . . . brain becomes less certain, more probabilistic." At each synapse the impulse can either be duplicated exactly, reduced, increased, or delayed. Different signals may be added, subtracted, mutiplied, divided, transformed. Maybe all this uncertainty makes for a subtle, fluid, and unpredictable mental life.

The synapse itself is an object of reverence to some. Eccles has theorized that these gaps of uncertainty leave room for free will and the "self-conscious mind" to intervene. Ultimately, his scenario can be pictured as a "God of the synapse" reaching down from time to time and tampering with the mechanism ever so slightly—just enough to make a neuron fire, perhaps. For Candace Pert the junction between nerve cells is a liaison between the new pharmacology and Freudian theory. "We think repression occurs at the synapse," she says. "Freud was right about the unconscious. In studying the way the brain processes information, we've learned that much never reaches consciousness. As input from the senses percolates up to higher levels of the nervous system, it gets processed at each stage. Some is discarded; some is passed on to higher brain regions. There's a filtering, a selection, based on emotional meaning, past experience, and so on."

Windows on the Brain

IN ORDER to see mind chemicals at work you need windows into the brain's interior. One new high-tech vista on the working brain is *glucose mapping*, the joint brainchild of Martin Reivich of the University of Pennsylvania and an NIMH team led by Louis Sokoloff. Since sugar (glucose) fuels the brain machine, the rate of glucose metabolism region by region should be an accurate index of neural activity. First, the brain mappers inject a radioactive isotope of glucose (deoxyglucose–2) into an animal's bloodstream, along with a drug, if they're doing a pharmacological study. Then, after sacrificing the animal, they do autoradiography. They freeze its brain, cut it into paper-thin sections, and lay each slice onto radiation-sensitive film (just like the badges worn by workers who handle radioactive materials, which is where Sokoloff got the idea in the first place). A detailed metabolic record of the brain results, a pattern of light and shade revealing active or inactive neurons. From the radiation densities, a computer constructs a multicolored map, which can be stored and displayed on a video screen for a scientist to rescan and "zoom in" on details with the flick of a joystick. (Glucose mapping is the basis of PET, or positron emission tomography, about which more is in the next chapter.)

The miracles of glucose metabolism can be illustrated by one story. It took Hubel and Wiesel twenty years of laborious trial-and-error recordings from electrodes in individual nerve cells to map the brain's visual cortex. When an animal saw a vertical line, for example, the scientists found active and inactive neurons lined up in distinct "orientation columns" on the cortex. And by covering first one eye and then the other, they traced the now-famous *ocular dominance columns*, the alternating bands of input from right and left visual fields. "The deoxyglucose method can do that in one shot," says Carolyn Smith, who is part of the Sokoloff team. "These are pictures taken from the striate [visual] cortex of a rhesus monkey. One of his eyes was patched. See how the bands of active neurons and inactive neurons alternate across the cortex? Each is four hundred microns [a micron is one-millionth of a meter] wide, about like the ocular dominance columns. We published this picture around the same time Hubel and Wiesel published their work. Not being visual physiologists, we didn't know what they were. We went around asking everyone at NIMH, 'What could these be?' "

"Electrophysiological recording techniques rely on many electrodes, implanted sequentially in an animal's brain, to build a picture of the working mechanism inside," Louis Sokoloff explains. "These methods are time-consuming and usually require recordings from many animals. . . . By contrast, glucose mapping provides a fairly quick snapshot of the whole brain in a single animal. . . . It is like obtaining immediately a photograph of a person's face, rather than assembling, as detectives sometimes must, a painstakingly obtained composite image based on many individual observations."

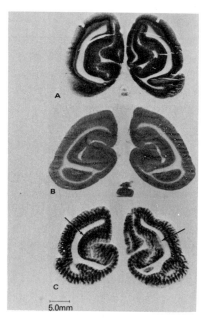

The primary visual area, or *striate cortex*, of a macaque monkey was mapped with radioactive glucose. (The left hemisphere is on the left; the right hemisphere, on the right.) The top autoradiograph (A) was taken when the animal had both eyes open; the dark shade stands for high metabolic activity. In the middle picture (B), both eyes were covered and the visual system was inactive, hence the lighter color.

The bottom autoradiograph (C) shows the activity in the visual area when only *one* of the monkey's eyes was covered. The pattern of dark and light stripes represents the input to the brain from the open and closed eyes respectively. Each stripe is about 0.3 to 0.4 millimeters wide, exactly the width of the *ocular dominance columns* Nobelists David Hubel and Torsten Wiesel had mapped out in the striate cortex. (*Courtesy of C. Kennedy, M. H. Des Rosiers, O. Sakurada, M. Shinohara, M. Reivich, J. W. Jehle, and L. Sokoloff,* Proc Natl Academy Sci, *USA 73-(11): 4230-4234, 1976*)

"With the deoxyglucose method," says Smith, "you can do studies in a conscious, behaving animal with an intact nervous system. You can give a drug—morphine, amphetamine, LSD, PCP [the street drug angel dust], or ketamine [a potent cousin of PCP]—to an animal, and see the relationship between behavior and the metabolic map in the brain."

The Impossible Dream

AS SCIENTISTS began to unscramble the brain's chemical codes, a wonderful dream took shape: Everything would soon be explained. Fear, despair, hope, and madness would turn out to have simple neurochemical equations. *Norepinephrine*, or noradrenaline, the "fight or flight" chemical, was responsible for motivation, learning, motor activity, and excitement. The inhibitory transmitter *serotonin* caused sleep and sometimes depression. Or, alternately, depression involved too little norepinephrine, mania too much. And it looked as if the brain transmitter *dopamine* was the key to two terrible illnesses, schizophrenia and Parkinson's disease.

A historic accident in 1952 launched a whole new psychiatry. In a French asylum some raving, back-ward schizophrenics became miraculously calm when they were given an antihistamine drug called *chlorpromazine*. Since chlorpromazine reduced the level of dopamine in the brain, it looked, *mirabile dictu*, as if schizophrenia was simply the result of excess brain dopamine. Chemists avidly synthesized a new class of dopamine-lowering drugs (Thorazine, Haldol, and so on), thereby ending the era of straitjackets and padded cells. But while these drugs alleviated some symptoms, they did not *cure* schizophrenia. Nor is there a "magic bullet" for depression, mania, paranoia, or garden-variety neurosis.

In 1960 a *deficiency* of dopamine in certain brain pathways was found to be responsible for the shaking limbs, shuffling steps, rigid musculature, and blank, masklike stare of Parkinson's disease. A dopamine precursor called *levodopa* (L-dopa) was developed in 1967, and patients who had been mute, immobile zombies for years suddenly began walking and talking, like statues sprung to life. Some of these "awakenings" are chronicled by neurologist Oliver Sacks in his extraordinary book *Awakenings*. Most of his patients were survivors of a 1917–1928 pandemic of sleeping sickness (*encephalitis lethargica*) who later developed a severe, Parkinsonian "postencephalitic syndrome." Sunk in a "decades-long sleep," a Black Hole-like "implosion" of being, many of these patients had been, in Sacks's words, "ontologically dead."

Like mythological returnees from the realm of death, the awakened ones brought back amazing tales. Some had remained transfixed in the exact moment in 1926 or 1928 when they were first stricken. Others told of being entombed in an inert body, a "prison with windows but no doors," in one patient's words.

L-dopa was not an undiluted magic potion, however. After a brief halcyon period, it typically unleashed a new chamber of horrors—grotesque hallucinations, delirium, murderous furies, compulsive growling, gnashing of teeth, involuntary movements, delusions, tics, compulsive cursing, to name just a few of the "side effects." Sacks tells of patients seesawing erratically between two pathological poles—the rigid, withdrawn "imploded" state of Parkinsonism and an "exploded" psychotic state. Moral? To Sacks it is the "utter inadequacy of mechanical medicine, the utter inadequacy of a mechanical world view." As we shall see, the brain is not a simple machine that can be repaired by adding X grams of a single chemical.

Eventually the naive 1950s and 1960s picture of one transmitter causing one behavior, or even three or four distinct behaviors, yielded to the realization that sadness, dreams, or the compulsion to snack endlessly on Fritos involves a complex ballet of scores of neurotransmitters, precursor enzymes, metabolizing enzymes, and the newly discovered "brain hormones" called neuropeptides. It was a rude shock at first. When today's grand old men were in school, the textbooks named a sole neurotransmitter, acetylcholine. In the 1950s there were two. Even a decade ago, there seemed to be no more than six: acetylcholine, norepinephrine, dopamine, serotonin, and the amino acids glycine and GABA (gamma-aminobutyric acid).

Now we know the brain is a Tower of Babel of some fifty known languages and hundreds of unknown idioms. "There are easily a hundred, probably two hundred, neurotransmitters, every one of them as interesting as the old ones," says master pharmacologist Solomon Snyder, of Johns Hopkins University. "Yet all the psychiatric drugs we use today act through the three or four transmitter systems we've known about for twenty years." That too is about to change.

The Age of the Receptor

THE PAPER that launched it, "Opiate Receptor: Demonstration in Nervous Tissue," by Candace B. Pert and Solomon H. Snyder, was published in *Science* on March 9, 1973. Pert and Snyder wrote, "We report here a direct demonstration of opiate receptor binding, its localization in nervous tissue, and a close parallel between the pharmacological potency of opiates and their affinity for receptor binding." In the gray, Latinate prose of scientific journals, they were announcing that they'd found the brain's opiate receptor, the site on the cell surface where morphine works its peculiar magic. Several big-name scientists at several universities had been racing toward the then-mythical opiate receptor (which most people believed in, but no one had seen), but the person who got there first was an unknown, twenty-five-year-old graduate student named Candace Pert, then working under Snyder at Johns Hopkins.

Pert's recipe: Take radioactively tagged naloxone (a morphine blocker that binds to the same receptors) and put it in a culture of homogenized mouse brain, filter it, and then count the radioactivity with a scintillation counter, a sort of computerized Geiger counter. That will show how much naloxone has stuck to the brain. Now take opiates—methadone, morphine, et cetera—and toss them into the mouse-brain mixture. Then add hot naloxone and see how much binds. Pert found, to her delight, that if she added an opiate first, little naloxone bound to the brain sites. The clear message was that the opiates had plugged up the receptors. But if she added a *nonopiate*—phenobarbital, atropine, serotonin, norepinephrine, or histamine—naloxone bound just as before. That meant that these receptors were custom-made for opiates.

Why would God design a special receptor for the product of a poppy plant? The answer lurking in the neuroscientific collective unconscious after 1973 was, *of course*, there must be a natural morphine in the brain! And indeed there was. The first natural opiate was discovered by a pair of Scottish scientists, John Hughes and Hans Kosterlitz, in 1975. It was a short, five-amino-acid protein chain they dubbed an *enkephalin* ("in the head"). All of a sudden the field got hot, and naturally occurring opiates of all shapes and sizes cropped up, like fragments of a lost legend.

In 1975 Stanford's Avram Goldstein extracted an opiate substance from fresh cow pituitary that was *not* enkephalin. A year later, C. H. Li and David Chung at the University of California at San Francisco announced the discovery of *beta-endorphin*, 31 amino acids long (the first five matched the five amino acids in enkephalin), and it turned out to be none other than Goldstein's mystery chemical.

Other researchers, meanwhile, were isolating and sequencing alpha-endorphin and gamma-endorphin, and then, in 1979, Goldstein turned up a *dynorphin*, basically a long enkephalin, with some extra amino acids on its tail. By 1984 there were long dynorphins and short dynorphins, various enkephalins and endorphins, a whole menagerie of brain opiates. And there were more varieties of opiate receptors—called mu–1, mu–2, delta, kappa, sigma, and so on—than you want to hear about. The name that stuck was *endorphin*, shorthand for "endogenous morphine," to describe all our natural opiates.

It was blue-ribbon science and few doubted that there was a Nobel Prize in it somewhere down the line. But for whom? In 1978 the Lasker Award for Basic Medical Research, commonly a stepping-stone to the Nobel, was awarded to Solomon Snyder, John Hughes, and Hans Kosterlitz. The conspicuous absence was that of Candace Pert. Why was she excluded when hers was the first name on the opiate receptor paper, as is standard practice for the primary researcher? Scientists we spoke to pointed out that it is traditional for tenured scientists to get credit for the work of underlings and bottle washers. But John Hughes was a graduate student, too. Who picks the Lasker winners anyway? The department chiefs and senior scientists in the field do, and they are undeniably part of a men's club. "The basic female position in science," as Pert once put it, "is postdoc for life, a perennial research associate." Pert's exclusion, many people thought, had a lot to do with gender.

In the custom of women and other scientific *üntermenschen*, Pert was expected to hold her tongue. "Be a good girl," one of her superiors at NIMH advised at the time. If anyone was *not* cut out for a shrinking violet role, though, it was Candace Pert. She turned down her invitation to the Lasker Award luncheon (which she considered a crumb tossed in her direction) with an eloquent letter of protest. "I was not about to sit through a luncheon and be patted on the head," she explained. One thing led to another, and the Lasker dirty linen was aired in the editorial pages of *Science*, even (horror of horrors) in the popular press. Pert became a *cause célèbre*, which is not necessarily a good thing if you work at the NIMH.

"I'm sick of being asked about the Lasker Award controversy," Pert told us at our first meeting in April 1981. "I mean, I don't just want to be known as this grumbling lady scientist. The opiate receptor turns out to be just one of dozens of different receptors in the brain, which can be detected by the same technique I developed. Now I'm looking for the angel dust receptor, where PCP binds. There's also the 'Hoffman-La Roche' receptor, the binding site for Valium."

If Pert was anxious to change the subject, if she seemed a bit paranoid about being quoted, it was because the Lasker affair had already taken its toll. She had been introduced at scientific meetings as "Candace Pert, the Scarlet Lady of Neuroscience." She worried about being a *persona non grata*, about losing her job. "Sol is a brilliant and wonderful teacher," she said of her former mentor. "I have nothing but the fondest feelings for him."

If the archetype of the scientist is a logical, sexless android with the unwholesome lunar pallor that comes of long hours of communing with dose-response curves and rat-brain homogenates, Candace Pert embodies a new archetype. The stereotypical scientist speaks a language as void of passion or ego as Cobol, a tongue in which the personal pronoun *I*, or even the more impersonal *we*, disappears into a droning, anonymous passive voice: *Inescapable foot shock (60–Hz sine waves, 3–mA constant current) was delivered through a scrambler to the grid floor of a Plexiglas grid.* Or: *Cerebral spinal fluid obtained by lumbar puncture from schizophrenics has been found to differ from that of control subjects when opiate-receptor-binding substances were measured.*

Pert, on the other hand, has been known to give talks entitled "From Molecules to Mysticism." She notices unorthodox connections between radiation counters and scientists' libidos ("As one bachelor scientist joked, 'Nothing beats sex on the counter, especially when the data's good.' "), and one of her experimental goals is "my copulating-hamster experiment," a receptor-density map of sexual pleasure. She is as warm, passionate, voluble, high-spirited, and audacious as the generic technician-nerd is cold-blooded, introverted, tight-lipped, and methodical. But that image is, of course, a myth.

"People find the stereotype comforting, but it is a lie," Pert wrote in an essay in 1984. "Scientists are as emotional, perhaps more emotional

Candace B. Pert, in her lab at the NIMH. Her discovery of the opiate receptor in 1973 launched the "Age of the Receptor" and set the stage for the endorphins, the brain's natural opiates. (*Courtesy of* ADAMHA *News Photo*)

than most people." If they did not fall madly in love with wild, unproven ideas, she observed, scientists would be defeated by the tedious precision of experimentation—"100 cells or 1,000 cells? 10 minutes or 30 minutes? If just one step out of 63 is performed incorrectly, the numbers flowing out the radiation counter can be totally meaningless. . . . As human beings on the planet, scientists display the usual *neuropeptidergic* biorhythms that somehow create our moods." In other words, substances like endorphins rule the emotions of scientists no less than those of flamenco dancers.

Our Own Natural Opiates

IF THE FOUNTAIN OF YOUTH or the alchemical philosopher's stone had materialized in somebody's lab, it might not have stirred up as much excitement as endorphins. Endorphins are simply natural brain chemicals with a molecular structure similar to morphine and other opiates. In other words, while we have been infusing our bodies for centuries—sometimes illegally—with opium, heroin, morphine, and other narcotics, our brains have been routinely making these drugs all along. We tend to think that heroin addicts live in an artificial land of vapors, while the rest of us experience a "real world" unclouded by chemicals. The truth is that there is no such thing as a chemical-free reality. The greatest manufacturer and user of drugs is the human brain. And each of us is subtly altering our brain chemistry—and our reality—all the time.

Just as you'd expect, endorphins are potent natural painkillers. Biochemists have been busily testing various endorphin fragments and receptors *in vitro* in search of an ideal morphine without side effects. There's now evidence that internal opiates are the secret behind three mysterious forms of analgesia: acupuncture, electrical brain stimulation, and the placebo effect. This is a "fact to give dualistic philosophers pause," as endorphin pioneer John Liebeskind of UCLA put it. If the placebo effect—by definition "all in the mind"—can be turned off by naloxone, an endorphin-blocking drug, the boundary between mind and body becomes a bit blurry, doesn't it?

Beyond that, these "promiscuous chemicals," as University of Michigan researcher Stanley Watson dubs endorphins, seem to play a role in everything from anorexia nervosa to Zen. Long-distance runners, "compulsive" ones especially, have been found to have elevated beta-endorphin levels, as do some anorexics, meditators, and schizophrenics. (Are all these folks hooked on natural opiates?) The opiate blocker naloxone curbs some schizophrenic hallucinations, wakes up hibernating hamsters, promotes rodent sexual activity, revives people from traumatic shock, and sobers up drunk animals and human beings. So endorphins appear to have a hand in such diverse phenomena as psychosis, hibernation, celibacy, shock, and the buzz that follows two glasses of champagne.

They may also be involved in the peculiar altered state caused by floating in the sensory void of an "isolation tank." Heavy drinkers have high levels of beta-endorphin in their blood and lower-than-normal levels in their spinal fluid, an anomaly that leads pharmacologist Kenneth Blum, of the University of Texas–San Antonio, to theorize that some alcoholics take to the bottle to compensate for an innate endorphin deficiency.

At Bowling Green State University in Ohio, baby guinea pigs, puppies, and chicks that had been separated from their mothers stopped their crying ("distress vocalizations") when they received low doses of endorphins. "It was almost as if opiates were neurochemically equivalent to the presence of mother," reports researcher Jaak Panksepp. He adds that low doses of morphine make juvenile rats antisocial, much like human heroin addicts. "Perhaps," he reflects, "brain opiate systems can create feelings of belonging, so people who are lonely and isolated can use narcotics as a substitute for interpersonal bonds." The orphaned-animal experiment also gave him ideas about autism, some of the earliest symptoms of which "include a lack of crying, a failure to cling to parents, and a generally low need for social companionship." Could this mystifying mental illness be the work of excess endorphins? If so, says Panksepp, "we would expect the child to respond less to those social acts that normally provide comfort: the soothing voice, the gentle touch, the comfort of being rocked."

Screening Reality

JULY 1983. NIMH's Building 10 is full of ideograms of the new age. "*Hazardous Materials*," signs warn. "DO NOT USE RADIOACTIVE MATERIALS IN THIS CENTRIFUGE." Rat cages rattle past on trolleys. Metal lockers, centrifuges, and freezers full of frozen brains line the olive-drab corridors. In Candace Pert's laboratory a rat autopsy is in progress. Tiny organs float like Japanese paper flowers in a glass of fluid. "We're going to prove that the mind controls immunity," a young man in a lab coat tells us. "These rats were injected with an endotoxin, and we want to see the effects on the peptides. You're not an antivivesectionist, are you? Okay, that white thing is the brain. The pink things floating on top are the lungs. The big red thing is the spleen."

Pert pokes her head out and motions us into her cubicle. Her desk is a morass of papers with small clearings for file baskets marked "Cancer," "Feeding," "Sex." The walls are covered with fantasy posters, a child's drawing signed "Vanessa," and vividly colored autoradiographic pictures

Miles Herkenham, who collaborated with Candace Pert to map the opiate receptors in the brain. (*Courtesy of Milo Olin, NIMH*)

of opiate receptors. Just as Babylonian astronomers climbed their ziggurats and scanned the night sky for signs of God's order, Pert looked for a coded message from the universe in these constellations of receptors glowing green, blue, and yellow against a dark background. But to see the receptors this clearly she had to team up with Miles Herkenham. "When Miles was a post doc at MIT in the seventies, working under Walle Nauta [considered by many to be the greatest living neuroanatomist], he was mapping cortical projections, and he noticed these islands—empty spaces. One day in the library he happened to read my paper on autoradiographic mapping of opiate receptors, and he said, 'My God, it looks like her patches fit my holes. Isn't that weird.' "

After he finished his fellowship, Herkenham came to work at the NIMH, but it was two years before he knew Candace Pert was in the building next door. When he did, he phoned her and invited her to a seminar he was giving. "My first impression was, 'What kind of a guy wears so much turquoise jewelry?' " Pert recalls. "Then I noticed the exquisite beauty of his material. I said to him, 'All our autoradiography is ugly compared to this!' " Pert had been shopping for a neuroanatomist, as it happened, and she asked Herkenham if he'd join her in working on a new technique for visualizing receptors. "Miles said, 'I'd love to, because I want to know if your patches fit my holes.' "

A year later Pert and Herkenham had their method down. They could remove a rat brain, freeze it, and then slice it finely with a cryostat. After thawing each slice onto a glass slide, they incubated it in a radioactive opiate (morphine with a tritium tag). Then they rinsed the slice and counted how much hot morphine stuck. "Then you can put the sections in a cassette and do autoradiography on them with tritium-sensitive film," Pert explains. "Or you can dip them in radiosensitive emulsions and see the receptors that way. It's much better than just mashing up the brain. You can do different things on adjacent sections and compare patterns in the same brain."

The receptors, illumined like miniature galaxies in the autoradiographic photographs, seemed to tell a story. "As an anatomist," says Herkenham, "I could tell immediately that opiates given to the cortex would do certain things." Behind his desk is a row of little boxes, "from my previous life as a tract tracer," each containing a rat brain. "I was electrically stimulating rat brains—manipulating the arousal mechanisms—to make them learn faster. Then I traced the anatomical pathways where the stimulation worked." The mystery of the "islands" he spotted then was solved by the receptor maps. "It was karmic," says Pert. "The two pictures fit perfectly, like a mosaic. His [neuronal] projections were sparing the patches of opiate receptors." Herkenham explains, "If you compare the two maps, you could surmise that the pathway uses an opiatelike substance as a transmitter."

Pert pondered the receptor patterns as if they were the soul's hieroglyphics. She noticed that certain parts of the brain, like the limbic system and various sensory-processing stations, were crowded with them. "If you follow the 'wire' from the senses up into higher processing areas, at every way station you find a dense collection of opiate receptors." She also noted the following facts: There were two basic classes of morphine-related opiate receptors, the so-called mu-1 and mu-2. The primitive Type 2 receptor is found in fruit flies and even in single-celled organisms, but the more evolved Type 1, which changes its three-dimensional shape to fit the occasion, appears only in vertebrates and is distributed unevenly. "We sliced up monkey brains," she says, "and we found that the Type Two receptor, the fruit fly kind, was distributed evenly all over the brain. But the Type One receptors formed a gradient. Areas of the brain that have undergone recent evolutionary expansion are chock-full of these malleable, Type One opiate receptors.

"I have a fantasy about what this means. As raw information from the universe, from the outside world, percolates up to higher levels of consciousness, it gets filtered at several stages. The natural opiates act as a

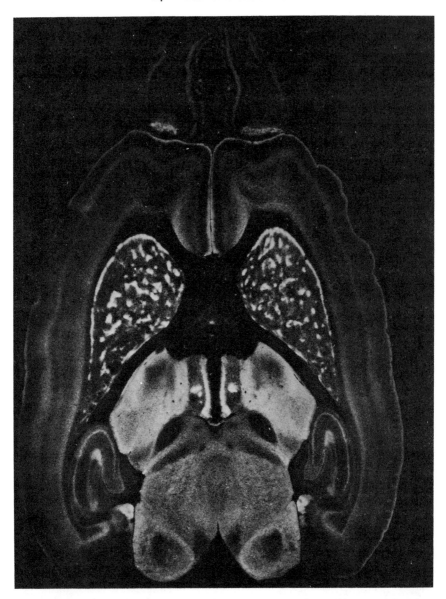

The Face of Pleasure: Herkenham and Pert's autoradiographic map of opiate receptors (above) may be the only neuroscientific event ever immortalized on a T-shirt. (Designed by Pert's sister, an artist, it bears the slogan, "The Face of Pleasure.") The receptors, labeled with a radioactive opiate drug, show up in this section of rat brain as shades of gray and white against a black background. The complex pattern of receptor density and distribution provides hints about the way the brain "filters" reality. (*Courtesy of Dr. Miles Herkenham and Dr. Candace B. Pert, NIMH*)

filtering mechanism. The more advanced the animal, the more the sensory input is processed, and the more Type One receptors it has. Some recent evolutionary event made the opiate receptor more flexible so that it is capable of change, modification, inhibitory control. We're not fruit flies."

"Opiates," Miles Herkenham tells us, "can affect the incoming signal at many levels. In a single-celled organism they communicate to the cell what the outside environment is like. With us, it's not just what we sense, but how we interpret what we sense."

"You screen reality," Pert proposes. "Through the endorphin system your brain decides what stimuli to pay attention to. Every creature has its own window on the universe. Nobody knows what the world really looks like, as philosophers like Bishop Berkeley and David Hume observed. Everybody's version is different."

Music, Endorphins, and the Idealist Philosophers

FOR MOST OF US the boundary between "inside" and "outside" seems clearcut. Outside is a world of objects, nature, other creatures; inside is a private kingdom of thoughts, dreams, desires, and memories, enclosed in the hard casement of the skull. When someone confuses the two, mistaking his own thoughts for the orders of KGB agents, we label him schizophrenic. If we look deep into the perverse complexity of the nervous system, however, we learn that internal and external realities aren't so easy to distinguish.

In 1977 Avram Goldstein posed an odd question to a motley group of Stanford medical and music students and employees at his Hormone Research Laboratory. Did they ever, when moved by their favorite music, experience thrills or tingles, a prickly feeling at the back of the neck or along the spine? Some said, yes, music did affect them that way. Whereupon Goldstein picked ten volunteers and put them in darkened, sound-proof booths with headphones. Each time the wistful strains of Mahler or the shrieking wah-wah guitar solos of Jimi Hendrix (or whatever the subject's favorite musical passage was) sent shivers down their spines, the subjects indicated so with hand signals. Between sessions Goldstein gave them shots of either saline (a placebo) or the endorphin-blocker naloxone. It was a double-blind study; neither the subjects nor the experimenters knew who got what. After nineteen separate tests, the pharmacologist reported that a third of the listeners experienced fewer and less intense thrills after naloxone. The implication: The sublime tingles of musical appreciation had something to do with endorphins.

Brain Age Mind/Body Quiz

1. The thrills of musical pleasure come from
   a. the music.
   b. a thirty-one-amino-acid protein molecule in the listener's head.
   c. the placebo effect.
   d. the Jupiter effect.
   e. all of the above.
2. I got the blues because
   a. my baby left me for another guy/gal.
   b. I'm a Cancer with Pisces rising.
   c. my mojo's workin' but it just won't work on you.
   d. I see no viable solution to the problems that beset our modern age.
   e. I suffer from a dysfunction in my opiatergic system, and my neuropharmacologist is on vacation.
   f. Since my baby left me, my endorphins just don't seem to work the same.
3. A tree falls in the forest as the sun sets over a beautiful emerald bay. Someone is there to witness all this, but this observer has just been given an injection of naloxone along with the experimental compound "anhedonizine," which inhibits the release of twenty endogenous pleasure chemicals.
   a. Did the tree fall? yes/no
   b. Did the sun set? yes/no
   c. Was the sunset breathtaking? yes/no
   d. Would Berkeley and Hume have found modern neuropharmacology interesting? yes/no
4. Write an essay describing the relationship between Monet's water lilies and the endogenous opiate system.

The Brain's Yin and Yang

"ENDORPHINS are part of the brain's internal reward system," explains Larry Stein, chairman of the pharmacology department at the University of California at Irvine, who knows as much as anyone about the chemistry of reward and punishment. Laboratory rats, given the chance, will self-administer endorphins to the point of exhaustion, just like human junkies. But you don't need a glass pipette dripping endorphins directly into your cerebral ventricles. The basic

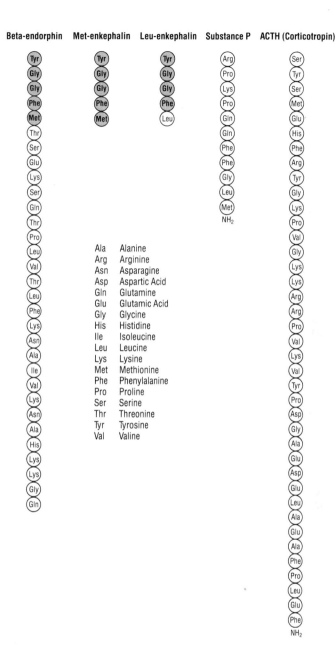

Beta-endorphin   Met-enkephalin   Leu-enkephalin   Substance P   ACTH (Corticotropin)

Ala	Alanine	
Arg	Arginine	
Asn	Asparagine	
Asp	Aspartic Acid	
Gln	Glutamine	
Glu	Glutamic Acid	
Gly	Glycine	
His	Histidine	
Ile	Isoleucine	
Leu	Leucine	
Lys	Lysine	
Met	Methionine	
Phe	Phenylalanine	
Pro	Proline	
Ser	Serine	
Thr	Threonine	
Tyr	Tyrosine	
Val	Valine	

FIGURE 6   This drawing shows the structure of some of the neuropeptides. These newly discovered "brain hormones," of which the endorphins are the brightest celebrities, regulate everything from emotions and hunger to sex, sleep, and pain. They are basically short chains of amino acids (alanine, arginine, asparagine, etc.), the building blocks of life. Note that beta-endorphin contains within it the five amino acids composing met-enkephalin and the first four amino acids of leu-enkephalin. Many of the natural opiates are fragments of other, larger molecules.

idea is that such things as eating, isolation-tanking, listening to the *St. Cecilia Mass*, repeating a mantra, and—who knows?—maybe praying, seeing a beautiful sunset, or listening to a politician's spiel about America's greatness somehow release your "reward" neurochemicals, "reinforcing" that experience with a general sense of well-being.

"The brain is just a little box with emotions packed into it," says Candace Pert. "And we're starting to understand that emotions have biochemical correlates. When human beings engage in various activities, it seems that neurojuices are released that are associated with either pain or pleasure. And the endorphins are very pleasurable."

Endorphin is only one member of an extended family of brain chemicals called the *neuropeptides*. Like proteins, peptides are linked chains of amino acids. Mostly known by acronyms, they sound about as scintillating as the labels on a circuit board—ACTH, alpha-MSH, TRH, VIP, CRF, CCK, Substance P, vasopressin, Factor S, oxytocin, bombesin, angiotensin, and so on—but they have revolutionized neurochemistry. If you know your endocrinology, you'll recognize many of them as hormones. ACTH, or adrenocorticotropic hormone, is a pituitary hormone that travels to the adrenal glands lying atop the kidneys, and in the brain it is broken down into two active fragments, MSH and beta-endorphin. Vasopressin is an antidiuretic hormone. TRH (thyropin releasing hormone) and CRF (corticotropin releasing factor) are hypothalamic hormones that trigger the release of pituitary hormones. VIP (vasoactive intestinal peptide) and Substance P were discovered in the gastrointestinal tract long before either Candace Pert or Miles Herkenham, to name just two, were born.

When, in the mid–1970s, neuropeptides started showing up in the brain, manufactured by neurons instead of glands, everyone wondered what exactly they did there. Were they neurotransmitters? What kinds of information processing did they perform? No one is quite sure yet. Scientists conjecture that instead of carrying a discrete signal across a synapse as classical transmitters do, the peptides perform fine-tuning, perhaps by acting as co-transmitters and influencing the release of other transmitters. If neurotransmitters are on/off switches, the peptides act more like dimmers.

Their global effects seem to be a throwback to the ancient Greek "humors," the bodily fluids that were said to make one melancholy, phlegmatic, or merry. Mood, memory, pain, pleasure, sex, hunger, satiety, sleep, stress, aging, mental illness, and well-being are all influenced by these "brain hormones." A few examples: Vasopressin, an antidiuretic hormone in the body, appears to act as a memory drug in the brain, as does a fragment of MSH/ACTH. Vasopressin levels in the blood fluctuate erratically in victims of anorexia nervosa, according to NIMH researcher Philip Gold. Maybe, he theorizes, the "indelibly coded ideas" and "obsession with thinness" that mark this wasting disease have something to do with this memory-solidifying peptide. A fraction of ACTH has been found to make withdrawn rats, as well as mentally retarded and elderly humans, more sociable.

As a hormone, CCK, or cholecystokinin, regulates gallbladder contraction and gut motility; in the central nervous system it seems to push the satiety button (which makes it one candidate for a natural diet drug). The newly discovered Factor S brings deep, slow-wave sleep. Don't confuse it with Substance P, which brings pain (the *P* in the name actually stands for *powder*), the blocking of which could be the basis for a brand-new painkiller. As for somatostatin, its metabolism is disturbed in many diseases, including schizophrenia, depression, Parkinson's disease, Huntington's chorea ("Woody Guthrie disease"), and Alzheimer's disease.

CRF, which as a hypothalamic hormone tells the pituitary to release ACTH, acts as a stress chemical (and maybe as an appetite suppressant) in the brain. At the Salk Institute in La Jolla, California, researcher George Koob placed rats in a brightly lit square box with a metal-grid floor. After nervously circling the box's shadowed periphery for a while—"It's like arriving early at a party in Southern California, when all the guests are hugging the walls," Koob commented—the animals began to make cautious forays into the illumined center. When they were given injections of CRF, however, the rats grew so uptight they never ventured into the open at all. "In the brain," Koob concludes, "CRF increases stressfulness. It could be an anti-Valium-like effect." One wonders: Will pathologically shy or introverted humans someday take anti-CRF pills—or something similar— to attend a New Year's Eve party or deliver a speech to the Shriners' convention?

"The body has been very smart," says peptide researcher Stanley Watson. "It uses the same active protein materials over and over again, as hormones in the body and as something more like neurotransmitters in the brain. The specific function comes from where something is or how it's connected to something else. It's like a telephone system. We all use the same instruments and we work out specific connections. The wiring confers much of the brain's specificity."

Chemical Emotion
Even insects express anger, terror, jealousy or love by their stridulation.
—CHARLES DARWIN

It is the cocktail hour, and a sticky, *dolce far niente* dusk falls over the outdoor barbecues, swing sets, and automatic sprinkler systems of suburban Bethesda. "I just gave this talk at NIMH called the 'Biochemistry of Emotion,' " says Candace Pert, settling into a splayed chaise longue in her backyard. The household's homey disarray reminds us of illustrations of the woman-who-lived-in-a-shoe-and-had-so-many-children-she-didn't-know-what-to-do in the Mother Goose rhymes. "It's really wild. All the peptides are about *emotion* . . . What's the matter, Brandon? Can't you find your pocket?" Sixteen-month-old Brandon Pert, who was born at home with a midwife in attendance, is tugging at the sides of his OshKosh playsuit, his face crumpling into a tragedy mask. His mother guides his hand, along with the stick it's clutching, into a pocket. "Pock-et," Brandon repeats, enraptured.

"For something as important as emotion," says Pert, "you might think God or evolution stumbled on certain chemical combinations that worked well and that these would be kept. They are. We've measured opiate receptors in everything from fruit fly heads to human brains. Even uni-cellular organisms have peptides. Opiates induce eating in protozoa, just as in human beings."

"Do you think even cockroaches feel some sort of emotion," we ask, "or is that just anthropomorphism?"

"They have to, because they have chemicals that put them in the mood to mate and chemicals that make them run away when they're about to be killed. That's what emotions are usually about—sex and violence, pain and pleasure. Even bacteria have a little hierarchy of primitive likes and dislikes. They're programmed to migrate toward or away from a chemo-tactic substance; they're little robots that go for sugar at all costs and away from salt.

"If you were designing a robot vehicle to walk into the future and survive, as God was when he designed human beings, you'd wire it up so that behavior that ensured the survival of the self or the species—like sex and eating—would be naturally reinforcing. Behavior is controlled by the anticipation of pain or pleasure, punishment or reward. And that has to be coded in the brain."

If there are traces of operant conditioning, reinforcement, and such in Pert's worldview, it may be the legacy of the psychology books that led her to the brain in the first place. This was in the mid-1960s, when her psychologist husband Agu Pert (from whom she is now separated) was a graduate student in learning theory at Bryn Mawr College in Pennsylvania, and Candace Pert was a "nineteen-year-old college dropout with a baby." With a temperamental style somewhere between hyperactive and hypo-manic, Pert was ill-suited to domesticity in a cheerless basement apartment in a building where the elderly tenants complained about the toys left outside. Starved for stimuli, she read voraciously: first, all the back issues of *Playboy* in her husband's collection; then *The Feminine Mystique* and some Ayn Rand; finally, all her husband's psychology textbooks. This heady mixture of psychology, proto-feminism, and enlightened selfishness had the effect of propelling Pert back to college to study the biological basis of behavior. The rest, as they say, is history.

"I remember leaving for school the first day and looking back at my son, still in diapers, with the babysitter. And I thought 'My God, what am I doing, leaving my son for someone else to take care of?' My mother was always there while we were growing up, baking cakes and cookies, like the mother on 'Leave it to Beaver.' But then I thought, never in human history have women done nothing but lie around all day and take care of children. In agrarian societies women are out in the fields with their babies."

Evan Pert, now seventeen, had a model behaviorist babyhood, but the next child, Vanessa, seemed to anticipate the antibehaviorist wave in psychology. "When we were first married we believed in John Watson," Pert recalls. "We believed a child was a tabula rasa. I can remember our son crying and my husband saying, 'Is he diapered? Is he fed? Well, then everything is all right; don't go in.' We waited outside the door, and he soon fell asleep. 'Aha,' we thought, 'We did it. Brilliant, rational twentieth-century parents, using behavioral principles.' Then nine years later we had our little girl and she wouldn't stop crying. She slept with us until she was five years old. . . . I think we were ignorant not to give credit to the innate talents and uniqueness of the creature we're permitted to raise."

Vanessa emerges from the back door, "Did my mom tell you about the fire in our house?" she asks. "It was in the kitchen. My brother was making tea and he turned the wrong burner on, and there was this pot that we made tortillas in last night that had grease in it, and it caught on fire." Dragging a large stick as a talisman, Brandon runs over to his sister like an advertisement for behavioral conditioning. She picks him up and lugs him around the yard as if he were an oversize doll. All the while, Candace Pert seems to operate on four or five channels at once, carrying on a running conversation with us about Substance P, while simultaneously fielding questions about lost tennis shoes and planning what to make for dinner (two guests are expected that night).

"There is a reciprocal relationship between the natural opiates and Substance P, the pain peptide," she tells us. "Both tend to be found in the same places in the brain and the spinal cord, and they do opposite things. When there's painful stimulation of the nerve fibers in the spinal cord, Substance P is released, and there's hard evidence that opiates *suppress* Substance P. They're yin and yang.

"What I want to know is how this works at higher levels of the nervous system. Like, there are tons of Substance P receptors in the septum, in the limbic system. When you stimulate the septum with electrodes, you get what is known as *septal rage*—cats hiss and scratch and go crazy. Substance P probably has something to do with that. But what does Substance P do in the cortex? Everything we know about it says it's released in response to painful stimuli, but what is pain—or pleasure—when it is coming in from the visual system or the auditory system?"

This dichotomy of good and bad, heaven and hell, within us has a medieval ring, as if the central nervous system were one big morality play. Perhaps our religious cosmologies, our good angels and bad angels, are only rococo projections of our internal reward/punishment system. Perhaps the polarities we find in the universe—mind/body, electron/positron, matter/antimatter—are not so much facts of nature as of the human brain. Listening to Pert, we have disquieting visions of the Book of Life written in cryptic chemical formulas and of ourselves as programmed creatures in a vast existential T-maze, migrating blindly toward food pellets and away from foot shocks. Are we so robotlike?

"We humans are stuck with some hard-wired circuitry," says Pert. "But we have the ability to intellectually transcend our petty programming by choosing good, loving thoughts over nasty, violent ones."

Or perhaps we can transmute base consciousness into gold with a psychopharmacologic philosopher's stone.

Redesigning the Brain

A pity I don't have an interpreter. Psychedeli must be from psychedelicatessen. And the theoapotheteria on Sixth Avenue has to be a theological apothecary bookstore, judging from the items on display. Aisles and aisles of absolventina, theopathine, genuflix, orisol. An enormous place; organ music in the background while you shop. All the faiths are represented too—there's christendine and antichristendine, ormuzal, arymanol, anabaptiban, methadone, brahmax, supralapsarian suppositories, and zoroaspics, quaker oats, yogart, mishnameal, and apocryphal dip. Pills, tablets, syrups, elixirs, powders, gums—they even have lollipops for the children. Many of the boxes come with haloes. At first I was skeptical, but accepted this innovation when after taking four algebrine capsules I suddenly found myself perfectly at home in higher mathematics, and without the least exertion on my part.

—STANISLAW LEM,
The Futurological Congress

LEM'S MYTHICAL, mind-altered promised land offers edible books, psychotropic groceries, and drugs for all occasions. Euphoril, Optamitizine,

Ecstasine, Felicitine, for instance, and their antidotes Dementium and Furiol. Amnesol to forget, Vigilax to stay alert, Equaniminine for the troubled soul, Credendium to make oneself credible, Authentium to create "synthetic recollections of things that never happened." Not to mention Freudos, Quanderil, Morbidine, and a hundred other psychoactive pills, lozenges, teas, suppositories, and philtres. As man learns that all of reality, all of the universe, is within his brain, the pharmacopoeia becomes his church, his university, his utopia.

"For all perception is but a change in the concentration of hydrogen ions on the surface of brain cells," a mind engineer tells the book's protagonist. "Seeing me, you actually experience a disturbance in the sodium potassium equilibrium across your neuron membranes. So all we have to do is send a few well-chosen molecules down into these cortical mitochondria, activate the right neurohumoral-transmission effector sites, and your fondest dreams come true."

If there are Authentiums, Credendiums, and Freudos in our future, it is the in vitro people who will make them. They're the biochemists and pharmacologists who throw radioactively tagged drugs into liquefied animal brains and observe how they stick to the receptor molecules. Who can redesign your brain by changing its codes. Who will create the perfect antidote for pain, depression, ennui, phobias, writer's block, addictions, nameless dreads, compulsive eating, or unrequited love.

"With our in vitro tehnology," says NIMH biochemist Paul Marangos, "we can develop 'magic bullets,' drugs that go right to the desired receptors and bypass the others. That means they won't have a lot of side effects. All the barbiturates, antidepressants, and tranquilizers we use today were devised twenty years ago to treat worms in dogs or something. When we throw them into various assays, they affect *everything*, all the transmitter systems.

"Any psychiatrist will tell you," he adds, "that ECT—electroconvulsive [shock] therapy—is as reliable as any of our present antidepressants. And look what you're doing with ECT! You're just scrambling all the circuits and letting them find their way back together again. That about sums up our pharmacological sophistication up to now."

Enter designer drugs. "All our old drugs were discovered through one accident after another," says Solomon Snyder, "and after we already had the drugs we went back and figured out how they worked. Now we have the molecular tools to design a whole new line of drugs. We can identify the enzymes that make transmitters and the enzymes that degrade them and make a drug to inhibit one of those enzymes. And we can sculpt agents around specific receptors."

About two dozen types of receptors have been identified so far, including one for the street drug PCP (angel dust), and another three hundred may still be incognito. Among other things, the receptors provide a precise and speedy measure of the potency of test drugs. "You don't have to screen a drug in twenty-five big rats anymore," says Snyder. "It used to take all day to test one drug." Now up to a thousand different tests can be run on a single rat brain. A hundred trial drugs can be screened in a day.

An End to Anxiety "THE SECRET OF NIMH: Right Before Your Eyes and Beyond Your Wildest Dreams" reads the movie poster above Steven Paul's desk, like an emblem of the new *zeitgeist*. "God or whoever created the Valium receptor," he tells us, "created it so that it has different binding sites, some that bind agonists, some that bind antagonists. [An agonist is a drug that mimics the action of a neurotransmitter; an antagonist blocks the action of a neurotransmitter.] That means we can produce a partial agonist, a drug that sits in the middle of the spectrum. A Valium that produces tranquility without sedation and maybe has a metabolite to wake you up the next day."

The "anti-Valium," B-CCE, is part of the quest. But is the mental state it induces the same as real-life anxiety? To find out, Paul and his co-workers deliberately made lab monkeys anxious by staring at them from close range, touching their feet, and doing other things that lower primates find stressful. Some of the animals reacted by nervously smacking their lips, scratching themselves, and swiveling their heads; others freaked out and screamed. And however a given monkey responded to real stress, it reacted the same way to a dose of B-CCE.

Paul and Skolnick think there's a message for psychosomatic medicine in the B-CCE experiments, a likely model for how a bad day at the office translates into ulcers, hypertension, heart disease, maybe even cancer. Given that emotional stress (B-CCE–induced or otherwise) can wreak such physiological havoc—speeding up the heart, raising blood pressure to dangerous levels, and flooding the body with "stress hormones" like cortisol, ACTH, and adrenaline—it's easy to see how a mental state can make a person sick or well. "I'm going around proselytizing to the drug companies," says Skolnick. "You could give B-CCE to animals chronically and see if they develop ulcers, cardiovascular disease, or cancer." And who knows? Maybe an anti–B-CCE could prevent stress diseases.

"Is there a natural Valium in the brain, or an anti-Valium, or both?" he wonders. "Is the receptor an on switch, an off switch, or an on/off switch? We don't know. Some people say that you don't need a natural Valium, but what are these sites doing there then?"

America's best-loved prescription drug was discovered serendipitously, long before anyone knew about receptors. The Czech chemist who synthesized Valium in the 1930s had no idea what he'd conjured up. Some twenty-five years later, after the chemist had fled to the United States and found a job with Hoffman-La Roche, he decided to throw out the dusty bottle on his shelf. First, though, he decided to test the compound . . . and today Valium accounts for 40 percent of Hoffman-La Roche's $1.4 billion budget. But now that the benzodiazepine (Valium) receptor has been found, a Valium without the side effects of addiction and drowsiness is the goal.

American Cyanamid scientists are tinkering with a compound called TZP that sticks only to one subclass of benzodiazepine receptor, producing mellowness without fatigue. At Saint Elizabeth's Hospital in Washington, D.C., biochemists have unearthed a mysterious new neuropeptide they've baptized DBI, or diazepam (Valium) binding inhibitor. It is not the long-awaited natural tranquilizer but just the opposite, a natural anxiety agent that, paradoxically, displaces both Valium and B-CCE at the receptor. Perhaps a mirror-image chemical to DBI will turn out to be the hoped-for "clean Valium." In the year 1991 there may be not one but three or four "Equaniminines," all modeled on our brain's own molecules.

Perfect Sleep and Perfect Wakefulness

IF YOU WANT a safe, no-side-effects sleeping pill, this is for you. Or perhaps you'd like a drug with the wake-up power of a hundred cups of espresso but without the jitters. In either case, you might be interested in one of the brain's own chemicals, *adenosine*, a sort of natural anticaffeine. Or, more precisely, caffeine is an antiadenosine. "What adenosine does, basically, is shut off firing in a large number of different neurons. It puts you to sleep," says Paul Marangos, one of the explorers of the adenosine receptor. "Caffeine, which is a purine with a chemical structure similar to adenosine, 'shuts off' the adenosine receptor and wakes you up."

Only a couple of years ago did Marangos and his peers learn to measure adenosine receptors. To do so, they had to make good analogues, adenosinelike compounds that stick to the receptor but aren't rapidly broken down in the brain like adenosine. Now they can say definitively that caffeine wakes you up by plugging up this receptor. "And the thing that excites me," says Marangos, "is that the adenosine receptor is turned off by caffeine levels well within the range of what's in your head when you drink a cup of coffee. That's a very specific effect."

Marangos wanted to know what *chronic* caffeine consumption did to the brain. So he fed mice the equivalent of four to eight cups of coffee daily for forty days and measured the adenosine receptors. Their brains adapted to the chronic adenosine blockade, it turned out, by sprouting many new receptors. "Chronic caffeine consumption makes the adenosine system hyperactive," says Marangos. "That's probably why you get abnormal drowsiness, headaches, and caffeine craving." Maybe those Sanka-brand commercials have a point, after all.

"We have mechanisms in our own central nervous system for sedation or arousal—the fight-or-flight response," he tells us. "Those are the two ends of the spectrum. And we have various compounds in our brains that fall somewhere on this spectrum. Maybe we'll find that hyperactive children have an endogenous antiadenosine or something. Maybe depressives and manic-depressives have some sort of disturbance of the adenosine system."

As future drugs go, adenosine analogues look marvelously utilitarian. Solomon Snyder and his co-workers have created something in a test tube that is *ten thousand times* more potent than caffeine in blocking the receptor. Tomorrow's cram drug, the night watchman's dream? And on the soporific side: "The beauty of the adenosine analogues we're working with," says Marangos, "is that *exquisitely* low doses, around a tenth of a milligram per kilo, put the animals to sleep. They're orders of magnitude more potent than the barbiturates or Valium.

"Barbiturates are dirty. The only way barbiturate sleep resembles real sleep is that the person doesn't respond when you talk to him. I've been trying to get the pharmaceutical houses to look at adenosine—it shouldn't be difficult, it's a naturally occurring compound—but that's like trying to move the Rock of Gibraltar. They start making money on one drug and they don't want to see another one for five years, when the patent runs out. But I think you could design a safe, clean sleeping pill around the adenosine system."

Memory Drugs

IT'S AN ANCIENT DREAM: a pill to make you smarter, to fix the dates of the Tudor kings in your memory (at least until the final exam), or to rejuvenate a muddled, aging brain. Perhaps vasopressin will turn out to be it. This neuropeptide has been found to triple the memory span of mice, and one of its analogues, DDAVP, has helped normal volunteers and victims of Alzheimer's disease (senile dementia) memorize lists of objects. "We think that DDAVP helps the brain code and 'chunk' information more efficiently," says NIMH memory researcher Herbert Weingartner.

Or maybe we should pin our hopes on MSH/ACTH 4–10, a fragment of the larger ACTH molecule. In tests at Boston University Medical Center, it enhanced the attention span and concentration of young and aged alike. Norepinephrine has long been associated with memory and learning (which explains why amphetamines and cocaine, which increase norepinephrine levels, are classic cram drugs), and enkephalins have improved maze running in rats. Could there be so many memory chemicals in the brain?

"We remember best the things that excite us," says psychobiologist James McGaugh, of the University of California at Irvine. "Arousal causes all these chemical cocktails—norepinephrine, adrenaline, enkephalin, vasopressin, ACTH—to spritz out. We think these chemicals are memory 'fixatives.' They may work directly at the brain, but I think they exert most of their effects indirectly, through the peripheral nervous system. When you are excited or shocked or stressed, they signal the brain, 'This is important—keep this.' "

For alcoholic memory blackouts, there's zimelidine, an antidepressant that selectively increases brain serotonin. Herbert Weingartner and his NIMH co-workers gave it to a dozen young men, who then proceeded to drink the equivalent of six cocktails. After the subjects had sobered up, they could recall their inebriated exploits in lucid, embarrassing detail (unlike the controls, whose recollections were hazy).

A cure for senility? One bright hope is the neurotransmitter acetylcholine, which "greases" the memory circuits of the hippocampus. Alzheimer's disease, a progressive, irreversible dementia that afflicts at least two million Americans, involves a drastic loss of acetylcholine neurons. A drug called scopolamine, which blocks the acetylcholine receptors, actually made normal twenty-year-olds temporarily demented. "Their immediate memory was markedly impaired," reports neurologist David Drachman, of the University of Massachusetts. "Scopolamine radically interferes with the ability to store new information." If that's the case, then acetylcholine or a close facsimile should *sharpen* the mind, right? With this idea in mind, several groups of researchers have been giving physostigmine, an acetylcholine look-alike, to senile patients. Others have been trying choline, a natural building block of actylcholine found in many foods. Small improvements have been noted, but there's still no surefire antisenility drug.

In Quest of a Perfect Painkiller

MORPHINE dulls pain, but it also lowers blood pressure, alters consciousness, and causes respiratory depression, addiction, and constipation. With the discovery of natural opiates and their receptors came a great treasure hunt for a no-side-effects painkiller. Part of the quest revolves around the six known (and twenty or so possible) opiate-receptor subtypes. If the mu–1 receptor, say, mediated analgesia but not constipation and respiratory depression, then a drug tailored to this receptor—and not the others, the mu–2, kappa, sigma, and delta opiate receptors—would be a miracle morphine minus two troublesome side effects. "We've developed compounds that block receptor-mediated analgesia in animals with no change in respiratory depression," says endorphin researcher Gavril Pasternak of Sloan-Kettering Institute for Cancer Research in New York. "So there's good evidence that different receptors mediate at least two separate opiate effects. In England they have a new drug that quite selectively binds to the mu–1 sites and causes little respiratory depression. Maybe it's the first of a new class of drugs."

There's more than one way to make a superpainkiller. "Every neuroactive peptide," says Solomon Snyder, "is made by cleaving a big precursor molecule. Multiple copies of enkephalins, which are chains of five amino acids, are trapped in large precursor proteins with hundreds of amino acids. To get the active segments out of the precursor requires two enzymatic steps. A first enzyme cleaves to the right side of the active amino-acid sequence, and then a second enzyme gets rid of the last amino acid on the other end. Well, Lloyd Fricker in our lab has identified an enzyme that looks like God made it just for enkephalin. It removes the last amino acid to make the active fragment. And now we have a very potent drug for inhibiting this enzyme.

"What would this drug do? If you block enkephalin, would you get pain? Would you bring someone out of traumatic shock—as naloxone does? Would it be an appetite suppressant like the opiate antagonists? We don't know yet.

"But if you know the principle, and if there are enzymes that are specific for each neurotransmitter or hormonal peptide, you're in Fat City. You can design specific drugs to inhibit these enzymes. They would be extremely potent, with few side effects."

Meditation Pills, Diet Pills, Aphrodisiacs

· Some of the new customized drugs have semimystical properties. A couple of adenosine compounds, EHNA and LPIA, have put NIMH rats into a paradoxical state of "quiet wakefulness," perhaps the animal equivalent of a yogi's trance. Though the rats became very still and looked "zonked," their EEG's showed uncommon alertness. "We may have hit on an altered state of animal consciouness," says NIMH's Wallace Mendelson. A meditation pill? "If it does happen," says Mendelson, "it will be in the next five years."

For years scientists had noticed that lab animals eat less when given naltrexone, an opiate blocker like naloxone. Could this be the diet pill of the future? "It certainly seems to work on people," says Allen Levine, who with John Morely has been testing it on patients at the Veterans Administration Medical Center in Minneapolis. Their first success occurred with an obese, brain-damaged patient who ate uncontrollably until an opiate antagonist quashed the urge. "Naltrexone is not addictive," adds Levine, "and it may not have any serious side effects, except that people may feel a little manic." You might also want to eschew it if you're in pain, if you're a heroin addict (it causes instant withdrawal), or if you're a member of a celibate order. That's right: Naltrexone is also an aphrodisiac, if its effects on the sex drive of lab animals are any indication.

Speaking of aphrodisiacs, consider the hypothalamic peptide LHRH, sometimes called LRH (the full name is luteinizing-hormone-releasing-hormone). After it was sequenced in the early 1970s, researchers injected it into rats and watched them assume the characteristic back-arching mating posture called *lordosis*. Was LHRH the brain's own Spanish fly? Some people said so. In his book *Mood Control*, author Gene Bylinski even prophesied acts of collective sexual sabotage based on this putative aphrodisiac:

One can easily visualize one country waging a secret sex subversion war on another by slipping LRH antagonists into drinking water or food to reduce the desire to procreate so that eventually the population of the enemy country would be reduced in a deliberate zero growth population control. Conversely, LRH or its analogues could be employed to create havoc, with citizens' minds fixed on procreation and nothing else.

Don't worry about your municipal reservoirs yet. Despite scattered reports a few years back that LHRH could renew sagging middle-aged libidos, it hasn't proved to be God's gift to the bedroom. It has also been tested on infertile women, for good reason, since it signals the pituitary to release two critical reproductive hormones, LH and FSH. But, again, no magic bullet. In a recent *Psychology Today* interview, Floyd Bloom tells why:

When LRH was first discovered, they said, "Ah ha! This is the key to infertility problems." They said, "Let's make a super LRH. We can get females to ovulate whenever we want them to." But what did they find? It didn't work that way.

. . . It lasted too long. When the brain talks to the pituitary, it speaks in short little messages. The new super LRH screams forever. The cells quit responding. . . . It's like the little boy who kept crying wolf, until nobody paid attention to him anymore.

· But why stick to banal diet pills, sedatives, and aphrodisiacs? By the year 2000 you may be reengineering your brain in ways you've never dreamed of. Phil Skolnick thinks the yin/yang principle of the nervous system could give us a whole cornucopia of futuristic mind drugs. "B-CCE is a mirror image of Valium," he says. "One causes anxiety; the other blocks it. Valium is an anticonvulsant; B-CCE causes seizures. Valium causes sedation; B-CCE activation. Valium causes muscle relaxation; B-CCE causes muscle tension. And if you can do that with one system, you should be able to do it with others. Why not? We could make drugs we've never dreamed of. An antimorphine—what would that do? An anti-Substance P. An anti-CCK. Every drug we know of might have a mirror image."

By the year 2000 there may be drugs that slow the perception of time or accelerate it so that root canal surgery passes more quickly; drugs that eliminate the need for sleep, exorcise guilt, or erase traumatic memories; drugs that selectively amplify certain senses, increase empathy, or make familiar things (such as a spouse of thirty-five years) seem novel. Music appreciation drugs; color perception drugs; introspection drugs; party drugs; mystical drugs; stream-of-consciousness drugs. Apollonian drugs, Dionysian drugs, neoclassical drugs, and surrealist drugs; drugs to dispel obsessions or re-create the state of early childhood. Perhaps if we rewrote the chemical codes in our brain, we'd experience a world resembling a painting by René Magritte, or the beneficent nature of Wordsworth's poems, or the witches of Puritan Salem. Perhaps the new alchemists will create a pill that brings about the immediate experience of eternal life, like the fabled *soma* of the *Rig-Veda*.

Food for Thought? IF YOU BELIEVE Richard Wurtman, an MIT neuroendocrinologist, the next breed of antidepressants, mood regulators, sleeping potions, and memory drugs could come from the refrigerator. No sprouts-and-Brewer's-yeast philosopher, Wurtman has accumulated solid biochemical evidence that your neurotransmitter levels (some of them, anyway) are set by what you eat. Acetylcholine is made from choline, found in eggs, liver, and soybeans. Tyrosine and tryptophan, amino acids found in proteins, are the building blocks of norepinephrine and serotonin, respectively.

"It remains peculiar to me," Wurtman told *Science News*, "that the brain should have evolved in such a way that it is subject to having its function and chemistry depend on whether you had lunch and what you ate. I would not have designed the brain that way myself."

Depression and mania, sleep and vigilance, as well as the minor peaks and valleys of our everyday moods, are orchestrated by these chemical messengers. How nice if we could take tryptophan in warm milk for serenity or sleep, say, or tyrosine to take the edge off the blues. Alas, you'll probably have to wait a few years for *The Complete Psychobiological Gourmet*, because the transformation of food into mind chemicals is a tricky affair, involving, among other things, a competition among some twenty-two amino acids for passage to the brain. But a few recent forays into food therapy are worth mentioning.

In Wurtman's laboratory the same dose of tyrosine lowered blood pressure in hypertensive rats and raised it in hypotensive ones, suggesting that this humble amino acid could be tomorrow's blood pressure drug. At Massachusetts General Hospital, psychiatrist Alan Gelenberg has been using tyrosine as an antidepressant. Meanwhile back at MIT, Wurtman and nutritionist Judith Wurtman, working on the theory that a serotonin imbalance causes unnatural carbohydrate craving, gave a serotonin-boosting drug (flenfluramine) to a group of overeaters. Many reportedly felt less compulsion to snack. Several research teams continue to test lecithin (a source of choline) as a remedy for memory loss and senile dementia, so far with only modest success.

"From Molecules to Mysticism"

ONE OF THE THINGS that in vitro people do is hunt for natural versions of psychoactive drugs. Since PCP, a/k/a angel dust, binds to special brain receptors, a lot of people think it must have a counterpart in our brains. And if the putative natural angel dust ever materializes, it may explain something about paranoid schizophrenia, an illness that bears a striking resemblance to a PCP freak-out.

In a talk called "From Molecules to Mysticism," Candace Pert spoke of rats specially trained to recognize the peculiar altered state of PCP. "When the rat feels angel dust in its brain, it pushes the left lever. When it thinks it has received a saline injection, it pushes the lever on the right," she says. Day after day scientists tested promising angel dust analogues in rats *and* in test tubes. And guess what? "The correlation between the rat's 'subjective' report and the ability of a compound to displace hot PCP from brain slices in a test tube was very high. So we have a handle on the molecules mediating this altered state!"

Ditto for opiates. "We can take a bunch of morphine analogues—

morphine, codeine, Darvon—each of which has a different analgesic potency in animals," she adds, "and look at how well they bind to the receptor in vitro. And we get a perfect parallel between the two. We can leap from a rigorous study of molecules—their three-dimensional structure—to behavior. Opiates are about pleasure, or else why would opium wars have been fought over them? And now we have the total sequences for three different natural opiates. We know the molecular structure of pleasure."

The Electric Kool-Aid Multicolored Soup

Picture the brain as a bubbling chemical pool of continually changing colors. Think of the colors as feelings—feelings released from floating gland bags. White is for euphoria and hope. Black is for depression, despair. Red is alertness, attacking, escaping, protecting, and mating. Yellow is afraid of red. Blue stills the racket from outside. Alcohol brings great bursts of red at first, then retreats to yellow. Librium and Valium shut off the yellow at first, but they make the valve leak. A drug can bring any of these colors on command. The taste of the soup is the average of all the ingredients influencing other ingredients.

—ARNOLD MANDELL, from an interview in *Omni*, November 1980

As SUBATOMIC PHYSICISTS break matter down into finer and finer (and more ethereal) particles, neuroscientists seek the building blocks of behavior in increasingly smaller units of the brain, in the structure of receptor molecules, in the microscopic ion channels in the membrane of a neuron, in enzyme reaction rates, and so on. But it is not at all clear that hope or paranoia will be found in a neuron or a subcomponent of a neuron. Indeed, there is a growing school of thought within neuroscience that large systems—for example, big ensembles of neurons or a whole brain—generate "emergent properties" that are not present in the individual pieces. No matter how many neurons you impale, you won't see the collective "dance."

One articulate spokesman for this point of view is Arnold Mandell, a brilliant and unorthodox biological psychiatrist at the University of California at San Diego. If his picture of the brain in the preceding quote has more the flavor of Arthur Rimbaud's "The Vowels" than of *Proceedings of the National Academy of Sciences,* it is not just because he is in communion with spirits less turgid than the usual techno-muses (though he is) or that he doesn't know anything about enzyme rates (which he does). His "soup" metaphor emphasizes an important feature of the brain: indeterminacy. The pharmacologic revolution described in this chapter, the march toward Pert's rigorous "color-coded wiring diagram" of behavior, is tacitly based on a mechanistic model of the brain, on what Mandell calls the "plumber's approach." The plumber's approach says that if you take *x* billion cells, each of which is chemically coded and "hard-wired" to about fifty thousand other cells, and decipher all the chemical codes and trace all the connections—if you plumb all the gritty details of the "plumbing"—you'll eventually get a sort of electrician's diagram of thought, memory, love, paranoia, or desire. Mandell says flatly, "You can't get there that way.

"The deep error in the machine, switchboard, and computer metaphors is that nothing happens until you *do* something," he tells us when we visit him at the University of California at San Diego, a campus sprawled over wild, bleached hills on the edge of the ocean, lacking in the austere right angles and perfect diagonals of most modern campuses. "It's the Newtonian view that you have to push the ball to make it move. But much of nature, including this complex compression of bonded electrochemical jelly, the brain, moves all by itself."

Mandell's brain is fluid, uncertain, probabilistic; it's a place where a million things happen at once. Love, obsession, or depression alters sodium and potassium levels all over the organ, he notes; it changes "how food tastes, whether music seems pretty, how a person walks . . . his dreams, his body temperature, his appetite, whether he asks for a raise or a vacation—stuff like this." Therefore no drug can work like a simple replacement cog in a machine or a precise colored circuit in a wiring diagram. It is more like a seasoning in a soup. "Drugs change the taste of the soup," he told *Omni*. "But it is complicated. It's like what happens when your mother-in-law moves in with you. You make adjustments, which lead to other adjustments. There is no one simple 'mother-in-law effect.' "

As he talks to us, Mandell is drawing rough geometric designs on his blackboard: a vicious circle called a "limit cycle," a squiggle of little waves, a wild abstract-expressionist scrawl to signify something called a "chaotic attractor." His conversation is laden with references to "topological space-time images of many dimensions," "phase spaces," and "low-dimensional attractors," as well as to Freud and Jung, borderline personality disorders, hallucinations, and dreams. What are these arcane mathematical objects doing in a psychiatrist's office? What strange tongue is Mandell speaking? The answer is "chaos," a new field of mathematical physics that Mandell (along with a handful of other brain scientists) believes not only applies to the brain but is the best model for its operations. According to this doctrine, brains can never be predicted or explained "with all the rigor of a differential equation," as Candace Pert had put it, because like many other parts of nature they are inherently chaotic. Yet this very "chaos" is the basis of the brain's higher-level order, of personality, character, creativity, even human societies. More about this later; for now it's worth noting simply that the brain is not a machine or at least not any machine we know of.

The human mind makes maps and models in order to tame complexity. Sophisticated theologians may conceive of the supreme deity as a transpersonal force and still pray to a Sunday-school God with a beard and halo. In the same way scientists may work with stick-and-ball models of molecules instead of swirling clouds of electrons, which is what molecules really are. Neuroscientists need simplified navigation charts to help guide them through the dense jungle of the human nervous system, the most complex collection of matter in the universe. It is often useful to visualize the brain as a telephone exchange, or to imagine a hard mechanical brain composed of locks, keys, opiate "gates," circuits, switches, and wires. A real brain, however, has no locks or keys but wet protein molecules that move and change shape continually like the god Proteus. And consciousness does not really conform to a wiring diagram.

"Up until recently," says Candace Pert, "I've visualized the brain in Newtonian terms. I've pictured the neurochemicals and their receptors as hard, little locks, keys, and balls, like the drawings in textbooks. But now I see the brain in terms of quantum mechanics—as a vibrating energy field, with all these balls, locks, and keys just being ways to perturb the field.

"I remember studying physics in college and getting a glimmer of what 'reality' is. I was just vibrating on the brink of experiencing everything as matter and energy. But you quickly return to your everyday consciousness. You can write equations about Reality, with a capital R, but you think in Newtonian mechanical terms.

"I've stopped seeing the brain as the end of the line. The brain is just a receiver, an amplifier, a little wet minireceiver for collective reality. We make maps, but we should never confuse the map with the territory."

4

Madness . . . and Other Windows
on the Brain

Enormous herds of naked souls I saw,
lamenting till their eyes were burned of tears;
they seemed condemned by an unequal law,
for some were stretched supine upon the ground,
some squatted with their arms about themselves,
and others without pause roamed round and round.
—DANTE, *The Inferno*

W E'RE at the Lourdes of modern medicine, a zone of state-of-the-art miracles. The automatic glass doors open soundlessly, and paraplegics with wire antennae pasted to their heads glide through in wheelchairs. In the cafeteria bald children with prematurely wise eyes and the gray mien of chemotherapy sip chocolate milk. In the elevators, day after day, one meets the zombie stare of Alzheimer's disease, the shuffling walk and masklike gaze of Parkinson's disease, the Hieronymus Bosch look of schizophrenia. Building 10 of the National Institutes of Health has half-jokingly been called a "research laboratory with beds," and certainly this enormous brick edifice houses an unusual marriage of basic science and clinical treatment. Most of the patients here are also subjects of some sort.

The schizophrenics on the south corridor of the fourth floor, for instance, are part of a double-blind study that obliges them to spend a month on a neuroleptic (antipsychotic) drug followed by a month off all medication. For the shaky times there are cold packs, gurneys with restraining straps, and an "isolation room," a cubicle with a bare linoleum floor and a mattress.

On a quiet weekday afternoon we follow psychiatrist David Pickar, who oversees the schizophrenia ward, on his rounds. Despite the kindergarten-bright, primary colors, the floral curtains, the cozy furniture, and the upright piano, the dayroom has the inanimate quality of a model family room in a budget furniture store. It is like looking into the alien, glassed-in world of an aquarium, where everything seems magnified, distorted. An overweight woman with the eyes of a numbed, captive animal slowly circles the room. A dark, painfully thin young man (who turns out to be the son of a foreign ambassador) is curled in a semifetal position on the sofa. A young man with hanging shirt tails and a bad facial tic walks over to Pickar.

"Hello, Dr. Pickar. Can I shake your hand?" Like an actor out of synch with his role, his gestures and inflections are awkward, jerky, off-key.

"How are you doing?" Pickar asks warmly. "Do you feel fidgety?"

"I don't know what that means."

Pickar explains, and Tony says he feels okay. "Are you going to be a patient here?" he asks us.

The blood and spinal fluid of these patients will end up in glass beakers downstairs—little vials of delirium, madness, darkness, in which some of the nation's finest scientists will hunt for abnormal levels of transmitter metabolites, brain enzymes, neuropeptides, hormones. "On one patient," Pickar tells us, "I may get seventy to eighty measures from cerebrospinal fluid or plasma. That technology wasn't around five to ten years ago. But we still *can't get to the organ.* If you're a basic scientist, you kill the animal, you look at the brain, you see a defect. Unfortunately there are no animal models of schizophrenia, for things like the holding of false beliefs and the perception of unreality. Maybe it's a human disease. So we're like the men in Plato's cave. We study shadows—CAT scans, PET scans, plasma metabolites.

"My real interest is doctoring, caring for patients. Dealing with the cortex of a schizophrenic is an unbelievable thing. It's alien, yet there are these existential moments when you know a patient well and you can peek into that world. It's an abyss, empty and exhilarating."

Beyond the Id and the Ego

How CAN YOU SEE into a human brain? There are three principal avenues, the first and oldest of which is the scientific study of madness. For Freud, breakdowns in the usual ego mechanisms—slips of the tongue, obsessions, phobias, dreams—were clues to the darker corners of the psyche. Neurologists historically have mapped the operations of different regions of the cortex with the help of tumors, strokes, and epileptic seizures. If you want to know how a normal brain works, a broken one can teach you a lot.

In this chapter we'll take a close look at schizophrenia, the most disabling and incurable of the mental illnesses, and examine the clues this disease offers toward understanding the brain's processes. We'll also look at the brain through two relatively new high-tech windows: PET (positron emission tomography) scans and the computerized study of brain waves.

There's no doubt that brain doctoring in the 1980s has more the aura of Los Alamos or Silicon Valley than of Freud. Rather than with the netherworld of the libido, modern brain science is concerned with solid matter, things that can be seen, heard, felt, and measured. Brain scientists perform blood tests for anorexia, phobias, obsessions, compulsions, and double identity. They search for a gene for dyslexia and a gene for melancholy. Perhaps even a virus or an antibody that may distort the "doors of perception" of a schizophrenic.

These doctors wield elaborate machines: sophisticated computer systems that extract the subtle EEG signals corresponding to thoughts (or at least thought shadows) from the sea of electrical noise in the brain. Computerized electroencephalography that can single out a child at risk for developing schizophrenia or detect an "Aha!" response in the shape of a certain V-shaped wave that appears three hundred milliseconds after a stimulus. The names of some of the new brain-imaging equipment could have come out of a "Star Trek" episode: brain electrical activity mapping (BEAM); computerized axial tomography (CAT) scanners; nuclear magnetic resonance (NMR); and positron emission tomography (PET). PET scans, in fact, are based on the Star-Trekkian principle of tiny collisions between matter and antimatter, a feat that requires a cyclotron on the premises. The result is an "X ray" of the brain's metabolic activity in luminous technicolor hues. Such devices not only provide remarkably clear pictures of epilepsy, dementia, strokes, tumors, Parkinson's disease, and other organic ailments, but they're also showing that much "psychological" illness has a biological basis.

Candace Pert's vision of a psychiatric consultation in the year 1990 involves a PET scanner and an inventory of neuroreceptors:

You'll go in for a total receptor workup with a PET scan. The doctor will drop in a highly selective drug with a radioactive isotope to "light up" your receptors and get a nice three-dimensional map of your brain. You'll see the distribution of the different receptors—all the ones we know of and some we haven't discovered yet. You'll see which areas are okay and which need fine-tuning. The computer will store receptor densities for each neurotransmitter on a separate floppy disk. Then maybe you'll be given a customized dose of, say, ten different drugs that will straighten things out.

There's this incredible shame about mental illness. But the brain is just another organ. It's just a machine, and a machine can go wrong. One neurochemically coded system might have a kink in it.

A decade ago photographing receptors inside a living human brain would have sounded about as feasible as building a shopping mall on Uranus, and when Pert first articulated her fantasy (in 1982) it hadn't actually been done yet. A year later scientists at Johns Hopkins began using a PET scanner to trace the radioactively lit trails of dopamine receptors in human heads. "The explosion of knowledge in brain science is equal to our ability to probe outer space," says Michael Phelps, the inventor of the PET scan. "We have the techniques now to probe the inner space of the body."

But how far have we come in our understanding of the exact relation between brain and psyche? Is there a crimson whorl on a PET scan signifying delusions of persecution? An electrical pattern for paranoia? Can our fancy machines give us a readout of a person's state of consciousness, level of anxiety, religious beliefs? Can they mend a shattered mind? Let's start with a look at schizophrenia.

A Visit to the Underworld

APPROXIMATELY one percent of the population suffers from schizophrenia, the most baffling and tragic of the psychiatric illnesses. The nineteenth century knew it as dementia praecox, or "dementia of youth," since it struck in adolescence or early youth (rarely after age thirty), and seemed to inevitably progress toward mental deterioration. The term *schizophrenia* was coined early in this century by the Swiss psychiatrist Eugen Bleuler, who thought that psychic fragmentation was the trademark of the illness. "I call dementia praecox 'schizophrenia' because . . . the splitting of the different psychic functions is one of its most important characteristics."

The litany of schizophrenic symptoms reads like a guidebook to the underworld. Most patients suffer from hallucinations, delusions, and "thought disorders," a category that includes impaired logic, jumbled thinking, bizarre ideas, and "loose" associations. They may sound like beat poets out of control, employing skewed semantics, neologisms, stream-of-consciousness ramblings, punning, echolalia (parroting), and "word salads." E. Fuller Torrey, a psychiatrist at St. Elizabeths Hospital in Washington, D.C., once quizzed a hundred schizophrenic patients on the meaning of the proverb "People who live in glass houses shouldn't throw stones." Only a third were able to supply the standard explanation; all the others gave extravagant, overly literal, or highly personalized translations:

Because if they did they'd break the environment.

People should always keep their decency about their living arrangements. I remember living in a glass house but all I did was wave.

People who live in glass houses shouldn't forget people who live in stone houses and shouldn't throw glass.

The inner life of a schizophrenic is pervaded by suffocating fears, morbid guilt, nameless dreads, and grotesque fantasies. At the same time, he or she may exhibit "flat affect" (emotional blunting), a symptom that many observers believe is the core of the illness. "I have two patients in whom I am unable to elicit *any* emotion whatsoever," reports Torrey in his book *Surviving Schizophrenia: A Family Manual.* "They are polite, at times stubborn, but never happy or sad. It is uncannily like interacting with a robot. One of these patients set fire to his house and then sat down placidly to watch TV. When it was called to his attention that the house was on fire, he got up calmly and went outside. Clearly the brain damage in these cases has seriously affected the centers mediating emotional response."

Like the hypersensitive princess in "The Princess and the Pea," a schizophrenic's senses are overly acute or distorted. He cannot concentrate. Reality is a blinding glare, a cacophony of sounds, an overwhelming swarm of messages that his brain can't process in the normal way. Norma MacDonald, an articulate Canadian psychiatric nurse who returned from an acute schizophrenic episode and wrote about it in the *Canadian Medical Association Journal* in 1960, described the terrain thus:

The walk of a stranger on the street could be a "sign" to me which I must interpret. Every face in the windows of a passing streetcar would be engraved on my mind, all of them concentrating on me and trying to pass me some sort of message. . . . I had very little ability to sort the relevant from the irrelevant. The filter had broken down.

"Schizophrenics don't do well at cocktail parties," says Torrey (who himself has a schizophrenic sister). "They simply can't process all the incoming stimuli. So they withdraw. The limbic sensory-processing equipment isn't doing a good job. In order to communicate at all, the schizophrenic has to use the simplest mechanisms in the brain—the 'reptilian brain,' in the Paul MacLean sense. It's like having your leg crippled from polio and trying to walk as best you can."

"From early on," says Allan F. Mirsky, chief of NIMH's Laboratory of Psychology and Psychopathology, "schizophrenics find it difficult to distinguish between signal and noise and to assign levels of importance to various classes of stimuli. Everything becomes important; nothing is trivial."

Add to this a distorted sense of self, a feeling of personal unreality, often coupled with a distorted body image. Much as Gregor Samsa woke up to find himself in the body of a huge cockroach, in Kafka's *Metamorphosis*, a schizophrenic may see his body transforming into a beast or a statue, becoming invisible, or leading an alarming life of its own.

I saw myself in different bodies. . . . The night nurse came in and sat under the shaded lamp in the quiet ward. I recognized her as me, and I watched for some time quite fascinated; I had never had an outside view of myself before. In the morning several of the patients having breakfast were me. I recognized them by the way they held their knives and forks. —A schizophrenic patient quoted in *Surviving Schizophrenia* (Torrey)

"The crisis of identity is shattering," Solomon Snyder writes in *Biological Aspects of Mental Disorder*, "and it confronts them with basic existential questions such as, Who am I? What is the meaning of life? What is reality? [R. D.] Laing has not been the only writer to speculate that schizophrenics, in their grandiose ideation, are reporting back from a world of deeper emotional reality than we enter in ordinary life."

I hadn't read anything to do with, er—with—ideas of transmog—migration of souls or whatever you call it, transmog—transmig—reincarnation. But I had a feeling at times of an enormous journey . . . a fantastic journey. . . .

I wasn't just living on the—the moving moment, the present, but I was moving and living in a—in another time dimension added to the time situation in which I am now. . . .—A schizophrenic quoted in *The Politics of Experience* (1967) by R. D. Laing.

Sometimes the ego's breakdown can be a break*through*, Laing proposed. After all, Eastern religions view the ego as an illusion, a dream, a film of *maya*, and the egoless state as supreme enlightenment. "The 'ego' is the instrument for living in *this* world," Laing wrote. "If the 'ego' is broken up or destroyed . . . then the person may be exposed to other worlds, 'real' in different ways from the more familiar territory of dreams, imagination, perception and fantasy." Others have seen in the schizophrenic descent a psychic parallel to the mythological hero's or shaman's journey. But if it is a voyage to other planes of existence, schizophrenia is seldom a pleasant Caribbean cruise.

What Causes Schizophrenia?

FREUD'S HIGH THEATER of oral fixations and dream symbols was built on the ruminations of anxiety-neurotics, hysterics, and obsessive-compulsives, not schizophrenics. When he did analyze a paranoid schizophrenic, a man known to him only through another analyst's memoirs, he diagnosed a "conflict over unconscious homosexuality" and an inverted Oedipal complex. For the most part, though, he seems to have considered schizophrenics unsuitable for talking therapy. Some of his protégés were bolder and proffered theories about the etiology of schizophrenia ranging from "the unceasing terror and tension of the fetal night" to various unpleasant events during the oral, genital, and Oedipal periods of development.

But European psychiatry never really abandoned the idea that the brain, not the misty psyche, was the problematic organ. In America it was a different story. Throughout the 1940s and 1950s, schizophrenia was laid at the doorstep of mothers who were domineering and rejecting, or fussy and overprotective, and inadequate, passive, harsh, or distant fathers.

By the late 1950s the "schizophrenogenic," or schizophrenia-causing, family replaced the evil Schizophrenogenic Mother, and the psychotic was seen as the victim of familial "double binds" (heads-I-win, tails-you-lose situations), "marital skews," and "pseudomutuality" (a sort of false family closeness). Meanwhile, the "antipsychiatrists," notably R. D. Laing and Thomas Szasz, were proclaiming that schizophrenics were merely society's scapegoats, twentieth-century witches and heretics, and that their "illness" might be a sane response to an insane family, a rational response to an irrational world.

Modern, post-Bedlam psychiatry took pains to separate schizophrenia from organic brain disorders. Bleuler set the tone by asserting that "in contrast to the organic psychoses, we find in schizophrenia . . . that sensation, memory, consciousness, and motility are not directly disturbed." While the organic dementias were marked by intellectual deficits and structural changes in the brain, according to this school of thought, schizophrenia involved a physically normal brain and a basically unimpaired intellect.

Today, as researchers take a closer look at schizophrenic brains (thanks, in part, to the new machines), the boundary between the organic and psychological is fast vanishing. "The brains of people who have schizophrenia," Torrey states flatly, "are different from the brains of people who do not have the disease."

Dopamine Disease

THE MODERN AGE of biological psychiatry began with the serendipitous discovery in the 1950s that a drug, chlorpromazine, made schizophrenics a lot better. In the early 1960s it was determined that chlorpromazine worked on the brain by reducing the amount of a certain transmitter, dopamine. Scientists had also noticed that amphetamine, a notorious *psychotomimetic* (psychosis mimicker), which exacerbates the symptoms of schizophrenia, *raises* dopamine levels.

Out of this evidence came the dopamine hypothesis, which was to dominate schizophrenia research for the next two decades. In its first and simplest form it stated: "Too much dopamine in the brain causes schizophrenia. Ergo, reducing dopamine levels cures schizophrenia." Unfortunately, it didn't turn out that simple.

The dopamine-lowering drugs used to treat schizophrenia, drugs like Thorazine, Haldol, and Mellaril, don't *cure* it at all. "Antipsychotic drugs merely help suppress troubling ideas," reports schizophrenia researcher Steven Matthysse, of McLean Hospital in Belmont, Massachusetts. "Patients will say, 'The aliens are smaller; they're talking softer,' or 'The FBI is still bugging my telephone, but you can't worry about that.' But the drugs do nothing for the emotional and interpersonal defects." Thus arose the dopamine hypothesis, revised version: "Schizophrenia is the result of a dopamine imbalance complicated by multiple disturbances in other neurochemical systems."

In search of the precise biochemical equation, scientists methodically sift through schizophrenic serum samples for DBH, a dopamine breakdown product; PEA (phenylethylalamine), an amphetaminelike compound long suspected of being an internal toxin; the norepinephrine metabolite MHPG; the serotonin metabolite 5–HIAA; enzymes such as monoamine oxidase (MAO); endorphins and enkephalins; hormones such as cortisol and vasopressin; and more compounds than you want to hear about.

No chemical so far has proved to be *the* answer, and the prevailing view is that schizophrenia is a neurochemical jigsaw puzzle composed of many interlocking pieces, some of which haven't yet been identified.

Although schizophrenics *do* seem to suffer from alterations in dopamine transmission, Torrey tells us: "My friends still can't tell me how the dopamine system got this way." If you're looking for the cause, or in medspeak, the *etiology*, dopamine hasn't led there yet. Says Fritz Henn, chairman of the psychiatry department of the State University of New York at Stony Brook, "My own feeling is that it's not the cause. I think the dopamine system just acts as a big amplifier for all sensory input. The drugs work by just knocking the sensitivity out of the system. But what is disordered is the input itself."

Where's the Damage?

WHEN A PATIENT suffers from an organic brain disorder, sooner or later doctors uncover a plaque, a lesion, a tumor, a "neurofibrillary tangle," a region of scar tissue. Why, then, does the brain damage of schizophrenia (if it *is* a case of brain damage) elude X rays, CAT scans, and high-powered microscopes? Why are there no plaques or lesions to account for the delusion of being a Joan of Arc?

While the "schizophrenic lesion" remains to be found, a few subtle

The neurons of the hippocampus in a normal human brain (above) and in the schizophrenic (below), magnified 150 times. The schizophrenic cells are more disorganized and tend to point in all directions. Is this why schizophrenics interpret the world so differently from the rest of us? (*Courtesy of Joyce Kovelman and Dr. Arnold Scheibel*)

signs of physical damage have lately come to light. In postmortem brain tissue, Joyce Kovelman and Arnold Scheibel of UCLA's Brain Research Institute spotted a weird cellular "disarray" in the schizophrenic brains (and not in the matched controls). The pyramid-shaped cells of the hippocampus, normally arranged in an orderly manner, were grossly misaligned. Some of them were rotated ninety degrees out of their proper position. Some of the dendrites were upside down. Might this result in a mix-up of electrical signals—and symptoms such as hallucinations and delusions of persecution? Scheibel, a well-respected anatomist and psychiatrist, thinks so, and speculates that the damage stems from a genetic defect or a viral infection in the womb.

When neurologist Janice Stevens aimed her microscope at schizophrenic brains, refrigerated at −70 degrees centigrade for as long as forty years at St. Elizabeth's Hospital's "brain bank," she saw signs of cell loss, calcification, and *gliosis* (old scarring), especially in the limbic system. "Gliosis is actually an old finding," she tells us. "People pooh-poohed it for years. There was such an emphasis on bad mothers that the idea of a progressive, organic disease was ignored." She, too, is thinking in terms of an old viral infection.

The first CAT scans gave the schizophrenic brain a clean bill of health, but the new, high-resolution scans tell another tale. They reveal that a significant minority of schizophrenics (about a third) have visible enlargement of the cerebral sulci or of the ventricles, the lakes of spinal fluid surrounding the gray matter. The ventricles' gain, it appears, is the brain's loss. "We think ventricular enlargement reflects some loss of brain mass, some cerebral atrophy," says psychiatrist Daniel Weinberger of NIMH and St. Elizabeth's Hospital, whose expertise in these matters was summoned to the witness stand at the 1982 trial of would-be Presidential assassin John Hinckley. (Hinckley's CAT scan showed enlarged sulci.) "It's not a specific finding. You also find enlarged ventricles in Alzheimer's victims, in cancer patients undergoing chemotherapy, and other diseases. Now that we have evidence there's something going on in the brain of a schizophrenic, we've got to go back and look at the brain."

Weinberger thinks the place to look is the third ventricle, forming the perimeter of the limbic region. He tells us, "Every study that looked at the third ventricle, except one, has found abnormalities. If any part of the brain should be abnormal in schizophrenia, it's this limbic forebrain. Electrodes in this area produce schizophrenialike phenomena, such as 'forced thinking,' bodily illusions, fear, ineffable cosmological experiences, paranoia. If the connections between the limbic forebrain and the frontal lobe are disordered, you've lost one of the highest integrative systems in the brain."

What do enlarged ventricles, loss of gray matter, gliosis, signify? Says Weinberger, "Something has happened or is happening to the brain. It might be a virus, an autoimmune disease, an inherited defect, prenatal damage, a neurotoxin, or a multitude of things. I don't think there's just one cause of schizophrenia. I think it's a manifestation of old—probably in utero—damage to the limbic-cortical circuitry. I say it's old damage, because there's no evidence that it's progressive.

"Schizophrenics with enlarged ventricles are different from schizophrenics with normal CAT scans. They have a history of being introverted, asocial, and peculiar as kids—even before they got sick. They have more of the deficit symptoms: flat affect, amotivation, poverty of thought, withdrawal, emptiness, poor insight. They have what we call soft neurological

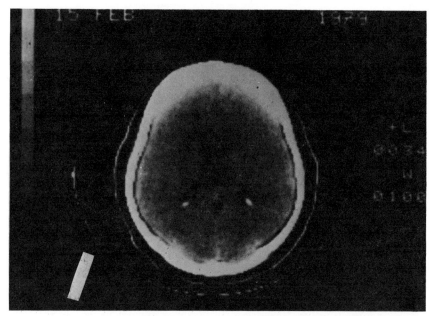

A CAT scan of a brain with normal cerebral ventricles. (*Courtesy of Daniel R. Weinberger, M.D., Chief, Section on Clinical Neuropsychiatry, NIMH*)

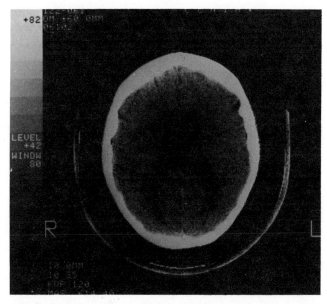

A CAT scan of a schizophrenic brain with enlarged cerebral ventricles. More than a third of all schizophrenics appear to have lost brain tissue, perhaps as a result of a prenatal virus or some other disease process. (*Courtesy of Daniel R. Weinberger, M.D., Chief, Section on Clinical Neuropsychiatry, NIMH*)

signs, symptoms of subtle neurological damage. Their prognosis is worse, and they're less likely to get better on drugs.''

The Search for the Schizovirus

THE FINDING to which Weinberger referred was first reported by psychiatrists Timothy J. Crow and Eve Johnstone, of Northwick Park Hospital in Harrow, England, who had systematically CAT-scanned some fifteen hundred patients. Crow has also isolated from the spinal fluid of some schizophrenics (about a third of those tested) a "viruslike agent" that had marked cytopathic, or "cell-killing," effects in a culture. Since the putative virus also turned up in the spinal fluid of some patients with depressive psychoses, Huntington's chorea, and other illnesses, Crow doesn't claim it's a schizophrenia virus per se. "It is possible that a number of different agents are being detected," he reports in a 1981 article. "Our studies are based on the hypothesis that schizophrenia might be either an unusual response to some commonly occurring virus or the result of infection with some as yet unidentified agent."

"Ten years ago," confides Torrey, another acolyte of the viral hypothesis, "my friends all made fun of the 'schizovirus.' That started to change when Carleton Gajdusek got the Nobel Prize and people realized that kuru was a viable model for a chronic central nervous system illness. When I talked to Gajdusek in 1973, he said, 'Where have you guys been for the past twenty years?' " In 1963 Gajdusek tracked kuru, a deadly disease confined to New Guinea tribes with a penchant for cannibalism, to a "slow virus" transmitted, in this case, from the brains of the dead to the living who ate them. The fact that the virus lies dormant in the body like an unexploded bomb for twenty years before flaring up and destroying the brain and nervous system interests Torrey and his colleagues. Is schizophrenia the result of a similar hard-to-detect slow virus?

Torrey has spent ten years diligently collecting spinal fluid from three hundred schizophrenics and seventy normal controls, including himself. "It's just like looking for any other virus," he says. "You take the antigen [the viral agent], put it in the spinal fluid, and look for an antibody." A third of the schizophrenic spinal-fluid samples he tested had elevated levels of antibodies to cytomegalovirus (CMV), a member of the herpes family, which can attack brain tissue. "It suggests," he tells us, "that something in the brains of these people reacts strangely to CMV. We're not prepared to say CMV *causes* schizophrenia. It's a notoriously opportunistic infection, and it may be secondary to another virus or an immunological disorder.

"We know this virus has a predilection for the limbic system. Just as the rabies virus likes certain kinds of cells, and herpes zoster [the shingles virus] likes the spinal cord, CMV goes for the limbic system. It also likes the inner parts of the auditory tract, which might explain why schizophrenic hallucinations—unlike drug hallucinations—are primarily auditory."

The viral-theorists also cite statistics showing that schizophrenics have a greater-than-average likelihood of being born between January and March and of becoming psychotic between June and August. Unless you believe in malefic astrological influences, the seasonal pattern suggests something flulike. And while schizophrenia is obviously genetic in part, genes don't explain everything. A monozygotic (identical) twin of a schizophrenic runs a 50 percent risk of developing the illness, yet, since monozygotic twins are genetically identical, you'd expect a 100 percent rate if genes were all-powerful. And if twins *live together* at the time one of them develops schizophrenia, Crow reported recently in the journal *Lancet*, the other twin's risk is higher, especially in the first six months. "These findings suggest either that both twins are exposed to an [infectious] agent at the same time," he states, "or that such an agent is passed from twin to twin."

Is schizophrenia contagious? On a recent sabbatical in western Ireland, Torrey found strange pockets of schizophrenia in certain towns. Crow tells of an epidemiological study of a large Moscow housing complex: When the families moved into the brand-new dwellings, one building had one or two schizophrenic residents and the other two buildings had none. Virtually no families moved away, and none moved in, and a decade or so later, the first building had a rash of new cases of schizophrenia, five times as many as in the neighboring buildings. "If that's true," says Fritz Henn who has high praise for Crow's research, "it has enormous implications. Then people who are doctors, nurses, and orderlies in state hospitals over a period of time ought to have a higher incidence of schizophrenia. And that study could be done. We may go out to Long Island, where there are many mental hospitals, and get records from the 1950s on people who worked there for over ten years."

"But where's the *pathology*?" asks Pickar, who is putting *his* money on refinements of the dopamine hypothesis. "In multiple sclerosis you see plaques in the brain. There's nothing like that in schizophrenia. In fact, the majority of schizophrenic brains look entirely normal on a CAT scan. If schizophrenia is a virus it sure isn't like any virus we understand."

"Why you don't see plaque formation in schizophrenia I can't tell you," Torrey replies. "I can tell you that we know that viruses can get into brain cells and change their chemistry, and there is no way to see any difference under a microscope."

In a court of law, the "schizovirus" would rest on circumstantial evidence, nothing to hang the defendant on, certainly. Yet in a field lacking eyewitnesses and smoking guns, it's worth listening to the forensic lab's analysis of fibers at the crime scene.

The Autoimmune Theory of Schizophrenia

BACK IN THE MID–1950s Robert Heath, chairman of the psychiatry department at Tulane Medical Center in New Orleans, found a mysterious protein in the blood serum of schizophrenics, which he baptized *taraxein* (from the Greek for "madness"). After experimenting with monkeys to make sure the procedure was safe, Heath injected the taraxein fraction into nonpsychotic prisoner-volunteers (using a comparable serum fraction from normal people for controls). Like characters in a mad-scientist horror movie—and, as matter of fact, these experiments were filmed, like a kind of neuropsychiatric *film noir*—the men who received the taraxein injections were plunged into instant psychosis. "Some hallucinated and had delusions and thought disorders," Heath recalls. "Some became severely anxious and paranoid. Some were withdrawn and catatonic. An hour or so later, they went back to being entirely normal." What was this protein with the power to turn men mad?

In the mid-1960s, Heath announced that taraxein was actually an immunoglobulin, an antibody to brain tissue. He reached this conclusion thus: He injected sheep with tissue from different parts of the brain, waited for their bodies to produce antibodies to the brain, harvested the antibodies, and injected them systematically into monkeys. These monkeys became "psychotic" when they were injected with antibodies to *septal* tissue, a fact that had a special meaning for Heath. Having spent a decade and a half tuning into abnormal, seizurelike electrical activity in the brains of dozens of chronic schizophrenics (see Chapter 5), he had become convinced that damage to the septal area, deep in the limbic system, was the trademark of the illness. Now he suggested that schizophrenics' immune systems mistake their own brain tissue (specifically the septal region) for a foreign invader and attack it. Heath maintains, "It makes a lot of sense to think that schizophrenia is an autoimmune process, like lupus erythematosus, myasthenia gravis ["Aristotle Onassis disease"], or Hashimoto's thyroiditis. In Hashimoto's disease the body makes antibodies that attack thyroid tissue; in schizophrenia the antibody would be to brain tissue."

The psychiatric mainstream in 1967, however, was still basking in the warm glow of the dopamine hypothesis, and Heath's methodology was judged less than impeccable. When other scientists failed to replicate his results, no lesser luminary than Harvard's Seymour Kety ("Mr. Schizophrenia," as one scientist referred to him) wrote a scathing review of his work. Heath retorts that one team *did* replicate his findings ("No one ever mentioned this"), but taraxein seemed doomed to the status of a semibizarre footnote in the book of biological psychiatry.

But times change, and the autoimmune theory is making a small comeback—in Candace Pert's laboratory, among others. Pert's original idea was to take antibodies from mental patients and drop them into special binding assays to see whether they attacked, say, the dopamine receptors. "It didn't work," she says. "I happened to have four receptor assays, and there are more than fifty brain receptors, and I didn't hit the right one. So basically, we decided, don't worry about which receptor it is. First look for antibodies that bind to brain, then we'll figure out the receptor."

We look over her shoulder at the milky liquid that was once the brain of a twenty-one-year-old accident victim. ("He was six-foot-two," says Pert. "He must have been handsome.") This is the culture in which Pert and colleague Lynn DeLisi, a psychiatrist, will test putative antibodies from psychiatric patients. While we are visiting, DeLisi rushes in like someone who has just received a telegram from the president. "I saw her!" she tells Pert. "I saw the patient! In the dental clinic. She's a thirty-six-year-old bipolar [manic-depressive] woman." DeLisi has been screening sample after sample of serum from mental patients. First, their blood is run through a machine that filters out the antibodies and puts the blood, *sans* antibodies, back in the patient (this is known as plasmapherisis). Then the antibody fraction goes into the brain mixture.

"Yesterday," Pert explains, "we were running a bunch of patients, and everything was like six or seven thousand [a binding count]. This one patient was thirteen thousand, which is off the charts.

"So every day we can look at her symptoms, collect blood, and figure out where the antibody binds. Who knows? Maybe after plasmapherisis she'll get better. Maybe she has antibodies to five different receptors, and on the days she's more paranoid her angel dust receptors are being titillated, and on the days she's depressed and suffering, her Substance P receptors are being attacked."

By the time Pert and DeLisi published their data (in January 1985), they were able to report that psychotic serum was more apt to "attack" brain tissue than normal serum was—or at least that 18 percent of their mental patients had a higher binding count than any of the normal controls. "A few years ago," Pert tells us, "an insulin-resistant form of diabetes was discovered, in which the body makes antibodies to the insulin receptors. Why shouldn't there be antibodies to brain receptors? What's so special about the brain?"

Windows on the Brain

BUT THE BRAIN *is* special, so special that nature has sequestered it from the outside world with a stone-hard skull and from the rest of the body with the *blood-brain barrier,* membranes that filter and restrict the chemical traffic between the bloodstream and the central nervous system. A living brain is a cloistered princess in a tower, all but unreachable except through messengers and go-betweens.

"Let the biologists go as far as they can," Freud wrote, "and let us go as far as we can. One day the two will meet." As a young physician, he carried out some very respectable research on the nerves of crayfish, crabs, and lampreys. If he chose to dissect dreams, fantasies, and phallic symbols instead, it was not because he thought the mind was made of diaphanous stuff. It was because the neurobiology of his day had no windows on the organ of thought. That is no longer quite the case.

In 1978 at Brookhaven National Laboratory in Suffolk County, New York, Alfred Wolf, chairman of the department of chemistry, and his co-workers PET-scanned two schizophrenic men who communed with unearthly voices. "One heard voices telling him he was God," Wolf recalls, "and the other guy thought he was the devil. We had them here on the same day, and they kept arguing with each other." God and the Prince of Darkness, it turned out, shared the same brain pathology, as did every chronic schizophrenic ever scanned at Brookhaven (they number more than fifty by now). On the color-coded display, the frontal lobes—the putative locus of such faculties as insight, foresight, and empathy—glowed bluish green, which meant abnormally low metabolic activity.

"It was very exciting," says Wolf, "because it was the first demonstration of a clear abnormality in a schizophrenic brain. And *all* the schizophrenics we scanned had it. Of course, they were all chronic schizophrenics with dementia-praecox–type symptoms."

Positron emission tomography was born in 1973 at Washington University in St. Louis, where a scientific team led by Michael E. Phelps sawed a hole in the center of an old wooden table, fastened radiation detectors around it, and strapped a dog to the platform. The first images were, in the recollections of one team member, "funny, squiggly blurs." The resolution would improve, and some would consider the pictures as much a conquest as the out-of-focus televised shots of Neil Armstrong alighting on the pockmarked surface of the Sea of Tranquillity: They were the first interior views of a conscious, working brain.

Says NIMH's Louis Sokoloff, one of the scientific godfathers of PET, "In the past the only time you got inside a living brain was when the animal or human being was anesthetized. But when you anesthetize the brain you're changing the very things you want to study. We have had methods—such as cerebral blood-flow studies—available for years to look at the operation of the brain as a whole. But unlike most other tissues of the body, the brain has different parts reserved for specific functions. Now we can see inside each part of the organ."

PET owes something to Sokoloff's metabolic mapping method. The brain's activity is calculated from the rate at which it burns glucose—or oxygen, or theoretically anything else that brain cells absorb. But instead of removing a brain and cutting it up, as in autoradiography, a PET scanner "slices" the brain mathematically. This takes it out of the lab-animal realm and into the human sphere (the radiation involved is equivalent to ten chest X rays, far less than a GI series). The patient lies on a padded tray with his head in a ring of radiation detectors that will record his brain activity. He receives an injection of glucose tagged with a radioactive isotope, which "lights up" the brain cells that absorb it.

First a cyclotron makes the isotope, usually fluorine–18. Because fluorine–18 has a half-life of only 110 minutes, it must quickly journey from the cyclotron (sometimes in a neighboring state) to the patient's veins. Oxygen-15, with a half-life of fifteen minutes, is even more fleeting. A chemist who handles these substances must have some of the qualities of a short-order cook and some of a magician. Once the radioactive mixture gets into the patient, it rapidly decays, emitting positrons, positively charged electrons. They collide with the negatively charged electrons in the surrounding tissue. Matter meets antimatter, and the particles annihilate each other, leaving a brief burst of gamma rays. From these the scanner reconstructs the amount of radiation in a cross section of brain, or any other part of the body, for that matter. A computer translates the gradients into a vivid video display, where the inner world appears in luminous shades from cool indigo (low activity) to crimson (high activity) like a strange new planet full of wonders.

Phelps (now at UCLA) holds up a slide that shows two different images of one man's brain. The one made by a CAT scan portrays the folds and furrows of an apparently normal brain; the other, the product of a PET scan, is black as a moonless night in Hades. What was wrong with the patient? "He'd been dead for eight months," replies Phelps. Anatomically sound as it may have been, this brain was "at an all-time biochemical low," as Phelps puts it, and this little parable sums up the difference between the two techniques. A CAT scan is essentially a fancy X-ray machine that photographs a sequence of computerized slices of the body's solid structures. It is like an aerial photograph of a freeway system without the traffic, which is superb for many medical purposes but not for monitoring ongoing chemical processes.

"The brain is a chemical organ," says PET practitioner John Mazziotta of UCLA, a neurologist. "It does no physical work at all. All its work is electrical or chemical, and the electrical work can be traced back to the chemical. So what ways do we have to look at brain chemistry?

"One way is to draw blood or spinal fluid and hunt for chemicals, but that's pretty remote from the brain. We can biopsy the brain and look at the chemistry, or we can look at the brain after death, but those things aren't very good either. We understand the brain's gross anatomy quite well, but the anatomy looks the same whether you're doing something or not doing anything. And chemical changes are the earliest signs of diseases. Anatomical changes come after the fact, if at all."

Biochemical Mapping Expeditions

THE FIRST BRAINSCAPES were seductive. They made such nice illustrations that they were immediately picked up by airline in-flight magazines, and Phelps's pictures of the human brain "watching," "listening," "thinking," and "remembering" even hang in the Oval Office. The layman got the impression that the priests of PET had captured the soul in technicolor, that they were on the verge of photographing a "memory center," an actual hallucination, or the internal equivalent of the "flashbulb" of inspiration. What can a PET scan really "see"?

PET measures *activity*, not static structures. That means that a researcher might watch his neural "pleasure centers" glow as he eats his favorite food, as one PET pioneer did. Or ponder the metabolic portrait of a memory decaying in time, as Thomas Chase, chief of experimental therapeutics at the National Institute of Neurological and Communicative Disorders and Strokes (NINCDS) is doing. Some of the cortical mapping studies, as they're called, have an almost phrenological ring. Says Chase, "We're asking, where do you think; where do you remember? We've mapped out language. We know where reading, writing, and naming are in the brain."

One might also try to map information processing in the specialized tissue of the cortex. At UCLA's glittering, state-of-the-art PET empire, Michael Phelps and colleague John Mazziotta scanned volunteers' brains as they listened to music or Sherlock Holmes stories. When right-handed people heard the stories, their left hemispheres lit up more than the right—though contrary to popular right brain/left brain lore, the right hemisphere doesn't exactly turn off when faced with words. When the task was to compare musical chords, the right half of the brain was more metabolically active. In most people, that is: Three subjects appeared to process music primarily in the (analytical, verbal) left hemisphere. "One was a professional musician," says Mazziotta. "The other two were computer-science graduate students who said they made frequency histograms in their minds or imagined dots on paper whose height reflected the frequency of the notes."

At the National Institute on Aging, in Bethesda, Maryland, a woman with glaucous, faraway eyes lies with her head in the "doughnut hole" of the scanner. For several months she has had trouble finding the words for objects and connecting her grandchildren with their names. In the past her

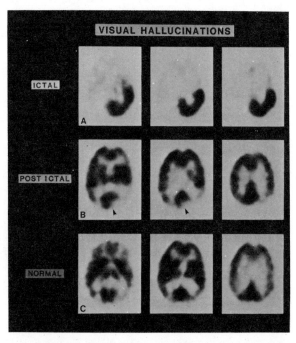

These PET scans reveal the changing brain states of an epileptic patient at UCLA. Those in the top row (A) were made during a seizure, as the patient hallucinated and then lost consciousness. The brain showed dramatically increased activity (dark color) in the right occipital (visual) and temporal lobes and decreased activity (light color) in the rest of the brain. The scans in row B were made after a month of seizures: The low activity in the right visual cortex (arrows) corresponds to the patient's blindness in the left visual field at that time. After drug therapy had kept the patient seizure-free for a year, the PET scan (row C) showed normal activity. CAT scans, in contrast, were the same for every state. (*M. E. Phelps, J. C. Mazziotta, J. Engel, Jr., UCLA School of Medicine*)

problems would have been shrugged off as garden-variety "senility" or "old age," but the PET scan shows a dark crescent of depressed activity on the roof of her brain, a pattern that Dr. Ranjin Duara, formerly of the National Institute on Aging and now at the University of Miami, has come to recognize as the signature of Alzheimer's disease. In the disease's early stages, when a CAT scan detects no abnormality, PET reveals that the patient's parietal and temporal lobes are burning fuel at a sluggish rate. In severe Alzheimer's, when the patient has forgotten everything but a few isolated pieces of the distant past, the "shadow" can be seen spreading over the entire brain. "The whole brain is down, by about ninety percent," says Duara. "It looks like it's hardly turning over."

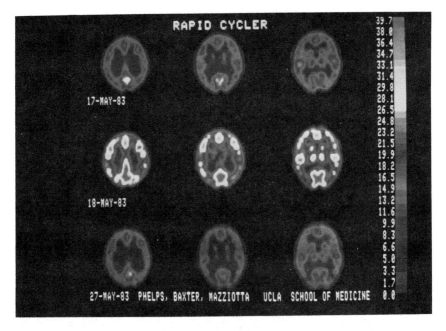

PET scans can also mirror the seesawing moods of a "rapidly cycling" manic-depressive. On May 17 and May 27, when this patient was depressed, PET scans (top and bottom rows) showed a global decrease in glucose utilization. On May 18, at the peak of a "hypomanic" cycle, the same patient's brain (middle row) showed a 40 percent increase in glucose utilization. (*L. Baxter, M. E. Phelps, J. C. Mazziotta, UCLA School of Medicine*)

Says Chase of NINCDS, "Alzheimer's disease has been considered a diffuse degenerative disease of the cerebral cortex. PET says that's not true. In the early stages we see a *localized* disorder, of the parietal association cortex primarily, which integrates information from the eyes, ears, and the peripheral sense of organs. There are names for the defects: *aphasia*— when you can't find the words; *agnosia*—you don't recognize familiar faces; *apraxia*—you can't carry out skilled movements. A housewife with Alzheimer's can no longer set the table. She can carry out all the movements, but give her a knife, a fork, and a spoon, and ask her to set the table, and she gets confused. In my opinion, the memory loss is really secondary to this jumbled-up picture of the world.

"This was never known before, because we could never see the early stages of the disease. There's a lot of pathology by the time you get to an autopsy—the brain is shrinking up, there are neurofibrillary tangles and plaques. But you're studying end-stage disease, all the garbage. We don't know yet what causes Alzheimer's, but the PET scan has taken it out of the mystery zone and shown that it's a single disease, a comprehensible disease."

Among other things, PET is a medical dream machine. It can pick out hidden tumors, subtle stroke damage, epilepsy, and draw a revealing biochemical portrait of such neurological diseases as Huntington's chorea ("Woody Guthrie disease"), Korsakoff's syndrome (alcoholic dementia), Parkinson's disease. But what about brain disorders in which there's no visible damage at all—no plaques, no tangles, no scar tissue, no lesions?

Neurological annals tell of a certain nineteenth-century Marquise of Dampierre, normally a model of aristocratic decorum, who at times was prone to barking like a dog and screaming obscene epithets. A half-century later, the Marquise's embarrassing malady would become known as Tourette's syndrome, after the French doctor, Georges Gilles de la Tourette, who diagnosed it. Yet anatomical studies of the brain have never uncovered anything to account for the bizarre vocal tics, grunts, and outbursts of *coprolalia*, or foul language.

"You could hold the brain in your hand or look at it under a microscope and still not see anything," says Chase. Just recently, however, PET scans *did* detect something wrong. "The abnormalities are in the speech areas of the cortex," Chase reports. "Coprolalia is associated with the premotor speech areas representing the mouth. This is still very preliminary, but it tells us where to look to find out what is wrong."

Some otherwise normal people are subject to attacks of panic out of the blue, a condition now known as panic disorder. They might be bending over the frozen-food section in the supermarket, or working their way through the reception line at a wedding, or driving the Bonneville down Elm Street, when they're gripped by an overwhelming fear, a sense of imminent catastrophe. The sympathetic nervous system goes into over-drive, causing hyperventilation, cold sweats, rapid heartbeat, nausea, and other extreme stress reactions.

Fearful of having an attack in public, the victim may avoid going out, and the panic disorder may evolve into *agoraphobia*, or "fear of the mar-ketplace." For some reason—and the reason, as current thinking goes, is more biological than psychological—the body's inborn fight-or-flight mech-anism, designed by nature for things like fleeing man-eating tigers, is trig-gered by such innocuous stimuli as the check-out line at Safeway.

Several years ago psychiatrists at Washington University discovered that many panic-disorder patients are supersensitive to blood lactate (one of the body's metabolic by-products) and that an IV drip of sodium lactate could trigger instant panic in these susceptible people. Washington Uni-versity neurologist Marcus Raichle, one of the country's most respected PET experts, was intrigued by the fact that panic disorder was such a well-defined condition it could even be induced in the lab. In 1984 he collected a group of patients who had panic attacks, PET-scanned them in a resting state, and then injected them with sodium lactate. All the subjects who went into a suffocating, white-knuckled fear upon being given sodium lactate showed the same pattern on the PET scan. "The abnormality was in the middle part of the temporal lobe," says Raichle. "There was a marked asymmetry between the right and left hemispheres. What does this have to do with the autonomic-visceral response to a frightening stimulus? Well, this area is a kind of intersection for sensory information going to and from the hippocampus in the limbic system. You could speculate that in panic disorder this part of the brain misinterprets incoming information and executes an inappropriate emotional response."

Of the twenty normal "controls," a lone subject had a metabolic pattern like that of the panic-disorder patients. The scientists called her up only to learn that she, too, had a history of panic disorder. "She came in, we did a lactate infusion, and it was positive as heck," says Raichle. It was probably the neatest correlation to date between a "mental" disorder and a pattern on a PET scan.

The mystery that doctors most hope PET will illuminate, of course, is the biology of the major mental illnesses: schizophrenia, depression, manic-depressive illnesses. Can PET spot the ever-elusive "schizophrenic lesion"?

Alas, most of the cognoscenti we interviewed were skeptical about the dim schizophrenic frontal lobes reported at Brookhaven and a few other centers. "It's all rubbish," said Duara. Sokoloff adds, "I have a feeling we're going to have to look inside the limbic system to get the answers to schizophrenia, and for that we need better machines, with a higher resolution."

NYU psychiatrist Jonathan Brody, who oversees the clinical side of Brookhaven's PET operation, staunchly defends the center's results. "We've now done this in some fifty subjects, and we're not worried about whether it's going to hold up. It's a question of how you define your patient population. In acute schizophrenics, in first-break patients, in patients with predominantly 'positive' symptoms [hallucinations and so on, as opposed to the dementialike 'deficit' symptoms], we don't see it. We're talking about chronic schizophrenics, who have been ill for five years or more."

At this Cro-Magnon stage in PET's evolution—when, we discovered, even the figures for a given scanner's resolution in millimeters vary widely depending on whom you talk to—the schizophrenia picture is still unclear. Depression so far eludes the scanner. There is some preliminary evidence from UCLA that "bipolar" depression (manic-depressive illness) has a distinct biochemical fingerprint: markedly reduced metabolism over the whole brain. (See photograph on page 124.) But many researchers think the Rosetta stone for the mental illnesses will be the brain's repertoire of chemical receptors.

Receptors in Living Color

"THE KEY to mental illness is probably the waxing and waning of receptors," says Candace Pert. "We now know receptors fluctuate constantly. Sometimes the actual number of receptors increases or decreases; sometimes the way the receptor is coupled to the membrane changes." Pert proposes that manic-depressives may oscillate between numb despair and wild elation to the rhythm of their waxing and waning dopamine receptors. The best remedy today for this illness is the drug lithium, which stabilizes the dopamine receptors. But the autoradiographic maps of receptors you read about in the last chapter were made from animal brains that had been killed, frozen, sliced, and thaw-mounted. No one had actually spied a neuroreceptor in a living human being until, on May 25, 1983, Henry N. Wagner, director of nuclear medicine at Johns Hopkins, PET-scanned his own dopamine receptors.

A powerful antischizophrenic drug, methyl-spiperone (which binds to the dopamine receptors), was coupled to a radioactive isotope. Dr. Wagner was injected with the compound, and less than an hour later the scanner "photographed" his dopamine receptors. They were especially dense in two areas of the *basal ganglia*, the *caudate nucleus* and *putamen* (as turned

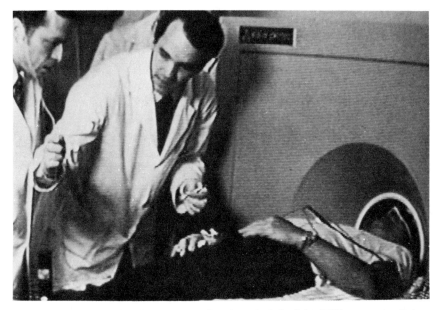

Dr. Henry Wagner's head enters the "doughnut hole" of the PET scanner at Johns Hopkins Hospital, as pharmacologist Solomon Snyder (left) and radiologist J. James Frost observe. Wagner has been injected with a radioactive form of an opiate drug, carfentanil. By measuring where the labeled opiate binds, the scanner will "photograph" Wagner's opiate receptors—the first opiate receptors ever seen in a working human brain. (*Courtesy of Henry N. Wagner, Jr., Johns Hopkins University*)

out to be the case in all the fifty-odd human brains scanned over the next year).

Wagner tells us, "The neurotransmitters basically bring us the information from the outside world, and the receptors determine how we respond." If that's so, then the elderly respond differently than the young, and men differently than women, to the messages of dopamine. Having scanned fifty normal men and women, Wagner et al. determined that dopamine receptors decline dramatically with age, especially in men. Between the ages of twenty and seventy, the male brain loses roughly 40 percent of its dopamine receptors—the sharpest drop occurs between the ages of twenty and about thirty-five—whereas the female organ loses about 25 percent. Nobody's sure what this means yet, but according to Wagner, it does "show that important changes occur in receptors, and that they're big enough to measure by PET scanning. Dopamine has to do with psychomotor coordination. You can draw your own conclusion about whether older women have better coordination than older men."

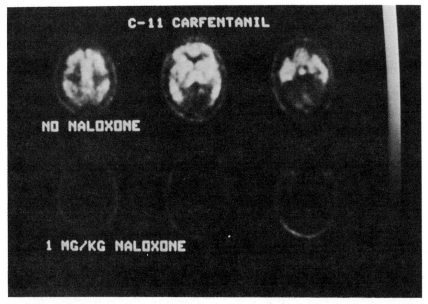

The first pictures of living human opiate receptors, from the Johns Hopkins study. The six scans represent a series of computerized cross sections of the same brain. In the top row, radioactive carfentanil (a powerful opiate) has bound to the receptors, so they appear as glowing patches. In the bottom row, an opiate blocker, naloxone, was given to plug up the receptors and prevent the radioactive drug from binding; hence the scan is dark. (*Courtesy of Henry N. Wagner, Jr., Johns Hopkins University*)

Without a vista on living brain receptors, psychiatric drug therapy up to now has been like "treating hypertensive patients without measuring their blood pressure," says Wagner. "You just go by their symptoms." Receptor imaging makes it possible to ask such questions as: What happens to the dopamine receptors in schizophrenia and Parkinson's disease, two illnesses in which dopamine transmission is impaired? How do medications—neuroleptics for schizophrenia, L-dopa for Parkinson's disease—affect the receptors? Do a schizophrenic's symptoms, his improvement or lack thereof, reflect the degree of blockage of his dopamine receptors? Can the receptor/drug interaction predict whether he will develop tardive dyskinesia, a condition of Parkinsonian-like tremors and movement problems that is a serious side effect of neuroleptics?

Exactly a year after the dopamine receptor's debut, the Hopkins PET team mapped human opiate receptors with radioactively tagged carfentanil, a narcotic eight thousand times more powerful than morphine. Their distribution was satisfyingly similar to the pattern that pharmacologist Michael

Kuhar, a member of the PET team, had observed in the monkey brain back in 1975. "It's much more dramatic," says Wagner, "when you actually see it in human beings."

In theory, any neuroreceptor can be visualized on a PET scan, provided the chemists and pharmacologists (in this case, such pros as Kuhar and Solomon Snyder) can customize a radioactively labeled chemical to fit it. A good "ligand," in the lingo. "In the pipeline" at Hopkins, according to Wagner, are hot ligands for the benzodiazepine receptor, the serotonin receptor, the histamine receptor, one type of receptor for acetylcholine, and the alpha- and beta-adrenergic receptors (where norepinephrine binds). The words may have a cryptic, inhuman ring, but these are the chemical keyholes where some of our best-loved drugs work. The ulcer drug Tagamet, the best-selling prescription drug in the United States, binds to the histamine receptors. Number two on the charts, propanolol, a medication for heart disease and high blood pressure, sits on the beta-adrenergic receptors.

Do these first receptor scans presage an era of "total receptor workups" à la Candace Pert? Will our hang-ups, our phobias, and our Oedipal complexes be stored one day in a code of optical-density gradients on a diskette? Will our mental states be diagnosed and treated according to the shifting distribution patterns of fifty-odd neuroreceptors? Probably not in the near future.

PET-scanning receptors may *not* be the answer to everything from melancholy to Parkinson's disease, for the simple reason that receptors themselves may not turn out to be the answer. There is still no hard evidence that the dopamine receptor is the main act in schizophrenia, despite the fact that the drugs work there. (So far, in the handful of patients scanned, the team at Hopkins hasn't found striking differences between schizophrenics and normal controls—though the dopamine receptors of Huntington's disease victims *were* abnormal.) Perhaps we are waiting for Godot.

Furthermore, when working with a sliced-up animal brain, scientists have ways of washing out the extraneous "junk" before making autoradiographic pictures of the labeled receptors. Obviously one can't do that with a PET section. The "junk" must be screened out mathematically, and that requires a good model of the biochemical process being measured. "The deoxyglucose method," Sokoloff explains, "was based on a biochemical mode of the behavior of glucose and deoxyglucose. You knew what you had to measure, the conditions under which you had to measure it, and how to take the numbers you got and calculate radio-glucose metabolism. The model for ligand binding is just not very convincing yet."

Besides, PET scans aren't cheap. UCLA's brand-new ECAT III, the state-of-the-art model, will cost more than two million dollars, not including the price of a cyclotron, plus a squad of nuclear scientists, neurologists, psychiatrsts, pharmacologists, chemists, biophysicists, biostatisticians, engineers, radiation scientists, computer scientists, and the like to run the operation.

Learning the Brain's Alphabet

THERE IS a temptation to look at PET scans as if they were dioramas at the state fair, as if the brain really contained gold nebulae and indigo seas. The video displays stand for numbers expressing radiation counts, which in turn are figured into a complex mathematical formula for glucose uptake. PET's inventors have *chosen* light blue, for instance, to represent low glucose uptake and red for high activity. It could have been the other way around. The brain, of course, does not actually glow in such pretty colors.

We may have unlocked the little black box, but in a rather indirect fashion. "At first," says Raichle, "there was a leap to exotic things like listening to stories in Hungarian, listening to Beethoven sonatas. And what you got was a whole lot of changes *everywhere* in the brain. Now we aren't trying to find the seat of the soul on the first pass." Instead Raichle is working on such austere stuff as the response of the visual cortex to a light flashed at different frequencies. (It is most metabolically active when the frequency is around eight cycles per second, if you want to know.) The nonscientific eye might perceive "little old compulsive neurologists looking at the small details and missing the big picture," but the task of fathoming a new language necessarily begins with the alphabet.

As archeologists patiently catalog potsherds in order to reconstruct a long-lost empire, Raichle et al. hope to work up to the big stuff, like thinking, decision making, volition. "When a hand moves," he says, "some neurons fire in the motor cortex. That's no big deal. We can see that. What I'd like to know is what happened *before* your hand moved. I happen to be a musician—I play the oboe and the piano—and I'd love to know what is going on in the brain as one sits down to play the piano. How is this unbelievably complex motor act programmed? When you learn a new piece of music, you laboriously work through it, but eventually you're not sitting there thinking notes anymore; you're thinking whole bars and measures, whole concepts, and the fingers are just whirring along. It would be wonderful to understand how this encoding occurs."

The UCLA center has actually made a small foray into the differences between conscious and unconscious processing. They scanned people performing a novel motor task (tapping the fingers of the right hand in a certain sequence) and then had them carry out an old familiar "over-learned" task (writing their names). During the finger-tapping exercise regions of the motor cortex lit up, while signing one's name activated another part of the brain, the basal ganglia, deep in the forebrain.

"Writing your name," Mazziotta theorizes, "is an automatic process. You can probably program those areas to do the task at a subconscious level." As it happens, Huntington's disease destroys the basal ganglia—as a "hole" on a PET-scan map shows—yet Huntington's patients can still sign their checks. PET suggested how: Mazziotta reports, "The pattern in those patients is all in the cortex, as in a novel task. And when you watch them do it, they write very slowly, very deliberately, as if it were not automatic. This may support the idea of programmability—that when you lose a function, you revert to more primitive strategies for getting the job done." Now Mazziotta and his colleagues are training right-handed people to sign their names left-handed, scanning them before and after the learning process.

Will PET scans provide the long-sought flowchart of information processing in the brain? "When I was growing up," says Chase, "I had an encyclopedia that showed the brain as a big telephone system. This room was for this, and that room was for that, and these women operators were sitting at the switchboard connecting everything. But the brain is much more complicated and plastic than that. If I ask you, 'Why does a board float in water?'—a question that involves some understanding of physics and a lot of cognitive skill—half your brain will light up. The idea of a center for memory may be quite naive, too."

We ask him if PET scans will prove once and for all that the mind is in the brain? "No," he says. "There's always going to be another box within every box you open. It's sort of like the atom. Every time you find another particle, you find it's not the ultimate particle but rather is made up of other, smaller particles."

Charting the Electrical Brain

Messages from the universe arrive addressed no more specifically than "To Whom It May Concern." Scientists open those that concern them.
—NORBERT WIENER

LIMITED as it is to recording processes of several minutes to several hours, PET is a lot slower than the speed of thought. The electrical activity of the brain, in contrast, can be measured in "real time," in milliseconds. So if you're interested in high-tech mind reading—even, perhaps, in the Madame Zodiac sense—it's logical to look to the frontiers of electroencepha-

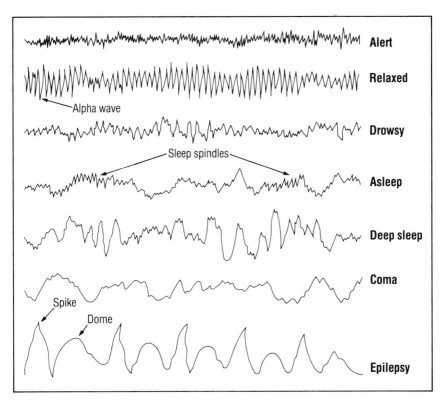

FIGURE 7 EEG recordings from the scalp of human beings can indicate different states of consciousness. Fast, low-amplitude "beta" waves correspond to alertness, while the "alpha" waves accompanying relaxation are slower and larger. During light sleep there are bursts of waves called sleep spindles; deep sleep is characterized by large slow waves. In coma the EEG is markedly slow and irregular. Epileptic brain waves have a telltale "spike and dome" pattern.

lography (EEG), the science of brain waves. Indeed, rumors are rampant in this field. We heard that a San Francisco EEG lab was building a "thought machine" with science-fiction–like capabilities; that the CIA was using or was about to use a brain wave called the P300 for intracerebral espionage; that computers existed that were capable of recognizing the neuroelectric patterns corresponding to the word *dog*. The reality turned out to be less sensational and more complicated.

The voltage fluctuations on your scalp, as you probably know, can be picked up by electrodes, amplified, and traced as seismographlike ripples on a polygraph. The amplitude (voltage) and frequency of these "brain waves" can convey valuable information about your state of consciousness: whether you're in deep sleep or dreaming; whether you're drowsy, relaxed, or alert. To a neurologist they can signify an epileptic seizure or serious brain damage. But a simple EEG recording can't decode anything as mercurial as a thought. To separate the subtle brain waves signifying acts of cognition from the random noise on the scalp requires some mathematical sleight of hand.

With the advent of high-speed computers in the mid–1960s, a whole academic industry sprang up around something called the *evoked potential* or *event-related potential* (ERP), which only a computer can see. The ERP represents the brain's response to a specific stimulus or event. To hear it over the ongoing electrical din, you must present a stimulus—a click, a flash of light, a tone, a word, an electrical shock—to a person over and over again and record his EEGs. After many repetitions, a computer performs "signal averaging": It averages all the recordings and cancels out the background noise to extract the waveform that is an ERP, "a faint whisper in the polyneural roar of the EEG," in the words of ERP expert Emanuel Donchin.

Throughout the 1960s and 1970s scientists studied these little peaks and valleys in the EEG record as palmists ponder heart lines and mounts of Venus, and mapped their amplitude (height), "latency" (time of appearance), and their distribution over the scalp. They named them and linked them to "expectancy" or "selective attention," "readiness" or "the detection of novelty." The "expectancy wave" was a large, ramp-shaped negative potential that seemed to appear over the cortex when a person expected something to happen. It also occurred a fraction of a second before someone initiated a voluntary movement, inspiring some talk (notably by Sir John Eccles) about the electrophysiology of free will. A negative wave appearing about 120 milliseconds after a stimulus was baptized the N120 and became an index of "selective attention." (When one is told to pay attention to a tone and ignore a light flash, the N120 gets larger.) There was an N200, an N400 (the newest ERP), and the perennially fascinating P300.

Anatomy of the "AHA Wave"

THE P300 is a jagged ravine in the EEG record (positive waves are downward slopes; negative waves sweep upward) approximately 300 milliseconds after the brain is confronted with surprise, novelty, or the unexpected. In the muted universe of the EEG laboratory, a P300 emerges when a high tone (a "beep") follows a series of low tones ("boops") or a female name crops up after a slew of male names. The rarer the event, the larger the wave, or, in the lingo, the P300's amplitude is "inversely related to subjective probability." A robust P300 also occurs when an expected event does *not* happen— when, say, you present a person with a series of light flashes and omit one.

The *éminence grise* of the P300 wave is Emanuel Donchin. At his well-equipped EEG kingdom, the Cognitive Psychophysiology Laboratory of the University of Illinois, a young woman tries to "buy a used car" from a computer. Woman and machine haggle like vendors at an Oriental ba-zaar, making offers, counteroffers, and concessions, until the transaction is completed. The computer is programmed to shift between two different strategies, a "mean" one, in which it grants few of the player's concessions, and a "generous" one, in which it grants 80 percent. All the while, a pair of electrodes monitor the player's EEGs and a video camera records her facial expressions every 500 milliseconds. Was there a correlation between a smile and a waveform on the scalp? Donchin wondered. After all, he points out, what psychophysiologists are supposedly after are "psycho-physical correlates" of behavior, and a smile is a kind of behavior.

The answer was no. There was no smile/P300 correlation, no frown/P300 correlation, no facial expression/P300 correlation. Does that invalidate the P300? On the contrary, according to Donchin. Though the woman's face remained impassive, the electrodes picked up a P300 wave whenever the computer changed from mean to generous, or vice-versa. "Something in-side the cranium is activated, reliably, whenever the computer switches strategy, and is manifested on the scalp by the P300," he observes. Perhaps an ERP is a better index of cognition than a smile.

Charting P300s and other computer-averaged waveforms, electrophy-siologists try to deduce how signals travel from the eyes, ears, and skin surface to the cortex during split-second time windows. "*When* the P300 occurs is important," says Connie Duncan-Johnson, of the NIMH. "If it takes you longer to evaluate a stimulus, encode it, access memory, and figure out what it is, the P300 occurs later. That is called latency, and it can vary between 300 and 800 milliseconds." And, of course, the wave's amplitude, or height, is important. People with "perfect pitch," unlike the musically ungifted, produce a small P300 or none at all when their brains process tones—at least in a University of Illinois experiment that called for subjects to name the octave number and pitch of a series of tones. Why? "My theory," says Donchin, "is that the P300 represents an updating of a model of the environment in working memory." Since people with perfect pitch "have access to a set of internal standards" for tones, he theorizes, they don't need to update their auditory working memory when-ever a rare tone pops up.

Other researchers are using the P300 (and other ERPs) to probe information-processing problems in autism, schizophrenia, amnesia, learning disabilities, and other syndromes. At the NIMH, Duncan-Johnson found that schizophrenics produce weak P300s in response to auditory signals, though their brains appear to react normally to visual stimuli. Psychologist David Friedman of the New York State Psychiatric Institute analyzed the EEGs of children of schizophrenic parents and found that these "high-risk" kids had deficient P300s. Researchers at the State University of New York's Downstate Medical Center reported in *Science* that they'd turned up flattened brain waves in both chronic alcoholics and *sons* of alcoholics (average age twelve). Since the aberrant P300 wave evidently shows up long before the onset of alcoholism, psychiatrist Henri Begleiter and his colleagues suspect it's an inherited trait. Could the P300 be a genetic marker, an early-warning sign of inborn information-processing deficits? If so, perhaps brain-wave analysis could weed out the genetically vulnerable from the rank and file. Perhaps doctors could even intervene and *modify* these "prepsychotic" or "prealchoholic" EEGs while the organ of thought is still malleable.

Why Is the Department of Defense Watching?

AT THE UNIVERSITY OF ILLINOIS, college students wired with scalp electrodes track flying targets on a video screen while simultaneously counting the "beeps" (and ignoring the more frequent "boops") they hear over earphones. During a simple beep/boop drill, big P300 waves are recorded, but when simulated air-traffic-controller duty is assigned, the P300s shrink. "The more difficult the primary task," says Donchin, "the smaller the wave associated with the beep/boop task." Experiments like these told Donchin that in addition to measuring cerebral surprise, the P300 wave could gauge mental workload. "It can tell how difficult the task is, how much attention the person is paying, how many mental resources he has available, whether his attention is divided."

Should this seem remote from the real world, you might like to know that the military has a keen interest in the slopes of computer-averaged brain waves. Donchin's lab (among others) has been funded for over a decade by the air force and various Department of Defense (DOD) agencies. "The original fantasy of the DOD agency that started funding us," he explains, "was the Firefox fantasy, where you put a pilot in the cockpit of a fighter plane and monitor his brain waves, and if he stops paying attention, the system wakes him up or takes over." The Firefox fantasy has not panned out. "While it's possible, it's not really useful at this time," says Donchin, "because no one designs planes that can use this kind of information."

If the P300, the "surprise wave," could be packaged, no doubt a lot of people would wish to buy it, including professional negotiators, poker players, advertising and market-research firms, and the intelligence community. It has been said that the P300 could measure "leadership potential" and "decision-making ability" in military officers. That it could make a more accurate lie detector (for ERPs are a lot closer to the source of behavior, the brain, than are the galvanic skin responses that present polygraph machines measure). Some even speculated that the ebb and flow of these waves could expose the thoughts of uncooperative prisoners of war or hostile foreign agents. Alongside its abiding interest in clairvoyants, "remote viewing," and other parapsychological phenomena, the CIA reportedly keeps tabs on EEG research.

Under the headline TECHNOLOGY COULD LET BOSSES READ MINDS, the *Washington Post* proclaimed (on June 3, 1984) that "researchers in both academia and industry say it is now possible to envision a marketable product that could instantaneously assess whether employees are concentrating on their jobs by analyzing their brains as they work." The main tool of industrial Big Brother was to be the P300 wave. To this assertion, Donchin replies: "We can indeed monitor mentation using the ERP. Furthermore . . . the ERPs provide a unique opportunity to monitor nonconscious mentation. Yet I believe it is not possible, and I believe it will never be possible, to use the ERP to 'read minds' in the popular, Friday night horror movie sense of the phrase."

Why not? According to Donchin, "the language with which the ERPs speak is arcane." It is not a fixed code, but one in which the variables—rising and falling amplitudes, short and long latencies—mean different things in different contexts. Hence, he maintains, "it is unlikely that it would be possible to attach a machine that would yield a simple, universal . . . number that can be used by an office manager . . ." to nab daydreaming employees or anybody else. Whew! Inviolate for now, the ultimate sanctuary of the mind.

Biocybernetic Dreams   THERE ARE fantasies, too, of direct brain-machine links that bypass the body and its senses; of missiles and robots controlled by brain waves; of computers endowed with the ability to decipher and store the complex waveforms that constitute a person's thoughts. There is even a fantasy of a form of personal immortality (or perhaps reincarnation) based on the idea that the "software" of a brain could be copied and then survive the death of the bodily "hardware."

"I have my mind taped every six months, just to be safe. After all, the tape is *you*—your individual software, or a program, including memory store. Everything that makes *you*," says a character in Justin Leiber's science fiction tale *Beyond Rejection*. Once duplicated, the millions of channels of inputs and outputs that constitute you could live on forever in the transistorized bowels of a computer, be implanted into a new body, or both. This would create some serious identity crises, of course, some of which are explored by the Tufts University philosopher Daniel C. Dennett in a yarn called "Where Am I?" (from *The Mind's I* by Daniel C. Dennett and Douglas Hofstadter): "The prospect of two Dennetts was abhorrent to me, largely for social reasons. I didn't want to be my own rival for the affections of my wife, nor did I like the prospect of two Dennetts sharing my modest professor's salary."

Naturally, no computer in the world is capable of storing the software of the human brain. Even if the artificial intelligence czars of MIT, Stanford, and Carnegie Mellon could one day create such a machine, the silicon "spare brain" fantasy still has flaws. To maintain the twin-selves dilemma of Dennett's story, the spare brain's activity has to be totally synchronous with the original. But a real brain, which is continually being reshaped by "inputs" from the environment, would soon cease to resemble the copy. And the notion of mind as "software" and brain as "hardware" (a popular analogy in cognitive science) is an imperfect description of our thought organ, in which the "hardware"—for example, synapses—is modifiable and inseparable from the "software." Indeed, Dennett and the other authors of spare-brain stories are aware of these problems.

Adverbs in the Brain

MOST OF the mind-reading scenarios assume that the EEG is a "language," like English or Swahili, which could one day be translated by an appliance that acts rather like a simultaneous interpreter at the United Nations. That brain waves are coded messages capable of being stored by computers or transmitted to distant rockets. Or, at the very least, that there is a close and real correlation between verbal language and neural language.

As it happens, a late-occurring wave called the N400 is related to language. The brainchild of Marta Kutas and Steven Hillyard of the University of California at San Diego, it is the most recently discovered ERP. When a person reads a sentence with an unexpected, incongruous, or nonsensical ending, Kutas and Hillyard discovered, a large negative brain wave appears

400 milliseconds later. DON'T TOUCH THE WET . . . flashes across on the fluorescent-green terminal. If the next word is PAINT, there's no N400. But if the word DOG appears instead, a large N400 is recorded from the reader's scalp. This electrical pattern, Kutas and Hillyard propose, reflects "the 'reprocessing' or 'second look' that occurs when people seek to extract meaning from senseless sentences." The more improbable or out of context the terminal word, the larger the N400 wave. The sentence HE TOOK A SIP FROM THE WATERFALL evokes a moderate N400, according to Kutas and Hillyard, while the more bizarre HE TOOK A SIP FROM THE TRANSMITTER elicits a very strong one. (Violations of grammar that don't involve "semantic incongruity" do *not* elicit N400 waves.) The discoverers of the N400 think their waveform has clinical promise as a tool for evaluating reading impairments and language disorders.

At UCLA, psychologists Warren Brown and James Marsh explored other relations between evoked potentials and language. In their studies, the word *fire* in the sentence "Ready, aim, fire" elicited a different P300 wave from *fire* in the context of "Sit by the fire." The brain evidently discriminated between the noun form and the verb form of a homophone. Later, fancier experiments demonstrated that various different uses of *rows/rose* and *rights/rites/writes* were associated with markedly different brain waves. Brown even traveled to Zurich and ran a similar experiment in Swiss-German, using noun and verb forms of *fliege* ("fly"), with identical results.

But how far can this kind of thing go? Is there a characteristic waveform corresponding to the word *cauliflower*? Could EEG machines provide a "readout" of nouns, verbs, and adverbs inside a person's head? "No way," says Marsh. "If we could do that, we'd be a natural resource; we'd be behind barbed wire. It's highly unlikely that anything as general as an ERP component is going to reflect something as specific as lexical meaning." Instead, Marsh and others think ERPs reflect broad linguistic categories, something like Noam Chomsky's "deep structures." Psychologist Robert Chapman of the University of Rochester found that words with similar connotations elicited similar brain waves: Words with "good" connotations, like *beauty*, triggered one sort of electrical response; "bad" words like *crime* another. Because these category/brain-wave correlations were consistent across different subjects, Chapman theorizes that there may be a universal language in the brain expressed in the EEG.

"Of course," says Marsh, "the ERP is quite crude. Nobody even knows where a P300 wave is generated. Some say it's the hippocampus. Some say the parietal cortex. It probably involves a lot of different structures."

Beyond the P300   EVOKED POTENTIALS are recorded from the scalp, after all, which is a bit like trying to figure out how a computer works by putting a microphone on top of the console. Not everyone is convinced that the N120 and the P300 are the alpha and omega of brain research. Certainly Alan Gevins, the thirty-eight-year-old director and chief scientist of EEG Systems Laboratory in San Francisco, is not. "Okay," he says, "whenever anything is novel, odd, or important to you, some population of neurons somewhere in the brain fires in synchrony. You get a couple of bumps, including a P300. It's a very robust phenomenon; it's unquestionably there. But what does it mean? People say it's measuring 'stimulus set selection,' 'controlled processing capacity,' the 'updating of working memory,' or other abstruse, highfalutin constructs. I just see that someone put two or three electrodes on the scalp and asked the subject to tell the difference between a beep and a boop—something that really wouldn't be called a higher brain function by anyone on the street. Maybe I'm being kind of harsh on these people, but that's my role in the field. Basically, I think they're just being lazy. They spend their time devising occasionally ingenious variations on the same two or three basic experiments, but how much can they hope to learn when they're using antiquated, twenty-five-year-old recording and analysis technologies to study what may be the universe's most complicated physical system?

"Researchers often get quite deluded. People have claimed to measure specific EEG patterns for different words, for instance. A man at SRI [Stanford Research Institute] made this claim a couple of years ago, and he was supported by someone in government. The bottom line was that his 'brain measures' were contaminated by face and scalp muscle tension—and his work was disregarded.

"It's a humbling experience to see what's actually involved in recording these things. . . . If the person blinks his eyes, or grits his teeth, or raises his eyebrows just slightly, you should see what happens to the raw tracing on the polygraph. The way the person moves his tongue inside his mouth can contaminate the brain potentials. I've learned that it's very difficult to pull out a signal from the brain that has to do with a higher brain function when you're working on the scalp. So I'm a real conservative guy."

So obsessive-compulsive is the EEG Systems Laboratory about "contaminants," so austere and methodologically pure are its experiments, that the work here has the texture of high-tech Zen. And like a Zen proverb, the results resist easy translation into ordinary language. The subjects play a video game in which they line up an arrow with a target by pressing a "pressure-sensitive transducer" with an index finger, or, seeing a number on the screen, they depress the bar with a force proportional to its magnitude. The aim is to isolate a discrete atom of perception from all other neuroelectric events. "I look at very, very simple tasks," says Gevins. "When you see a number, how is that information communicated to your finger, which moves a half second later? What is the difference between seeing a number and hearing a number? I control everything else to the hilt to make sure only one variable is varying." The time windows through which Gevins et al. view the working brain seem infinitesimal to us, but by electrophysiological standards, they've expanded to centuries. "We're building up gradually," he says. "In our last generation of experiments in 1980 to 1983 we analyzed about a second's worth of activity surrounding a stimulus, and now we're looking at about five seconds. Besides measuring the effects of the stimulus, we're looking at a person's anticipation of a stimulus, his response, and the updating that occurs when he gets feedback."

The results? No flashy little "Aha waves" or anything suitable for glossy pictures in airline magazines. To the nonscientist the electrocognitive maps made by Gevins et al. might as well be Linear B. "Any behavior, even something as simple as seeing a number and pushing a finger, or seeing two lines and figuring out how far apart they are," says Gevins, "seems to involve the coordinated effort of a lot of different areas all over the brain." Subtle landmarks come into view; the computer painstakingly plots the shifting dance of correlations among wave shapes in different parts of the brain; the data are expressed in "correlation diagrams," otherworldly and abstruse as the Feynman diagrams in particle physics. You and I and the producers of TV specials might wish that the brain were more like a telephone system or an electrican's wiring diagram, but if it were, would you be you?

The Brain's Native Language

"PSYCHOLOGISTS tend to think the brain thinks in English," Gevins tells us. "But who knows what language the brain thinks in? The native language of the brain may be as far away from English as the machine language of a computer is from LISP [a sophisticated programming language, invented by Stanford AI expert John McCarthy]. There's probably more of a gap, actually." The equivalent of the machine language of the brain, in Gevins's view, is "very complex electromagnetic field configurations, with very fine modulations in amplitude, frequency, wave shape, and spatial distribution."

A working definition of "selective attention" alone can't decode these esoteric electromagnetic emanations, so the EEG Systems Lab houses an unusual interdisciplinary crew. Among its (mostly young, mostly hip) senior scientists are a particle physicist, an electrical engineer with a specialty in electromagnetic wave propagation, a neurophysiologist, a cognitive psychologist, a signal-processing expert with a background in decoding human speech, and several computer whiz kids. Gevins himself is equally comfortable in neurophysiology, engineering and computer science, and cognitive psychology. What are all these high-tech types doing around the brain?

"We're working on building an advanced electromagnetic recording and analysis device, with many, many channels," Gevins tells us. The first step was a sophisticated, custom-designed software system called ADIEEG, with state-of-the-art signal-processing and pattern recognition capability. "You can't just go out and buy a packaged program to do brain-wave analysis," says Gevins. "It's not like a spread-sheet program, a frequency analysis program, or even a standard set of statistical programs." And rather than presuming to read the brain with a couple of electrodes, the EEG Systems Lab equips its subjects with a space-age-looking helmet bristling with fifty or sixty of them. ("CAT and PET scans use about 500 sensors, after all. It's absurd to think you can sample the brain's intricate electromagnetic field by putting an electrode or two on the scalp.") The result is a dense rain forest of data.

"Recording from just one person with sixty channels, we may get a hundred million bytes of data," says Gevins. "In one experiment we might have ten subjects, so there's a billion bytes. That's about one hundred thousand times more data than you get in a typical average evoked-potential experiment. What do you do with that? To put a billion bytes of data through a complicated analysis with fifteen or twenty steps and come out with the right answer at the end is a very neat trick."

Certainly, the eye—or brain—alone can't keep track of the swarm of variables. Nor can the crude "signal averaging" used in evoked-potential research, a technique that Gevins dismisses as World War II vintage. What's needed is more sensitive signal processing, and that's what's at the core of the EEG Systems Lab's software. Signal processing is a whole field within electrical engineering, with entire journals devoted to it. It's used to restore Caruso recordings, to detect the movement of Russian troops from spy satellites, to decode human speech, and to find oil. "What it comes down to is how small a signal you can resolve buried in what amount of background noise, how far away you can see a penny," says Gevins.

And that, in a nutshell, is the reality behind the fabled "thought machine" at EEG Systems Lab.

The Impossibility of Mind Reading

IF ANYONE could create a brain-eavesdropping device, the EEG Systems Lab could. And it can't, even if it wanted to. Gevins even objects to using terms like "decoding" in connection with the dynamic, probabilistic processes of the brain. "I've been asked a bunch of times, Is there a code in the brain for the word *dog*?" he says. "I think people have seen too many spy movies. First of all, the brain probably doesn't work that way. It isn't a deterministic machine with an invariant code; it's statistical, probabilistic. And if the brain *did* work that way, I can't imagine the kind of instrument you'd need to resolve it. If there *were* unchanging codes for the word *dog*, there would be hundreds of them, corresponding to all your different associations with *dog*. And they might be scattered all over the brain. Do you know how many billions of bits of information would be required *each second* to pick out something like that? And the number of contaminants that would interfere with it?"

How about correlations between brain waves and semantics? "The results are in the wrong place," he says. "Differences have been found over Broca's area [traditionally associated with the physical production of speech] when people were *listening* to words. The differences should have been over Wernicke's area. I also have to ask, What is happening in a person's mind when he hears the same word or phrase over and over? *He rows the boat . . . He rows the boat . . . He rows the boat.* After a while, it doesn't have any linguistic meaning.

"As for all this stuff that gets into the *National Enquirer*—you know, CIA MAKES NEW MIND CONTROL DEVICE—people get awfully paranoid about this, because it concerns the mind and the spirit, the last resort of privacy. But it's pretty farfetched. Not that people won't try it, but it won't work. A person can just grit his teeth, and the whole thing is screwed up. Television works much better for mind control than EEG techniques."

If the mega-thinking-cap in the works at Gevins's lab won't read or control minds, what *will* it do? Well, if this group succeeds in mapping out the major nodes of the brain's electrical communication system, a number of things become possible, according to Gevins. Doctors could spot the defects in electrical transmission that are probably the first signs of senility. One might more clearly identify and understand the information-processing malfunctions in learning disabilities, attention disorders, memory deficits, and many neuromuscular and psychiatric diseases. Using a new science of attention-regulation, hyperactive children could learn to focus and control their attention spans. Brain-damaged people might learn to deliberately "reprogram" their own software. "Right now we don't know what happens when the brain is recovering from a stroke," says Gevins. "It's an electrical problem, and we have no way to measure that. If we could, recovery could happen a lot more quickly."

Beyond that, Gevins is thinking about hastening the evolution of the species. "I hope we're not limited to being gorillas with big forebrains trying to amass as many bananas as possible. If there's a key to our future evolution it must have to do with using the 'software' of the brain to its full capacity. A major difference between a person we call sharp and one we call dumb is the ability to focus or expand the mind's view at will—narrowing it for prolonged concentration, or expanding it to encompass the relationships between many parts of a complex system. Those are the processes I want to understand."

But expeditions into the electrocognitive jungle have brought humility. "As scientists we sometimes get very arrogant about all our fancy toys," he tells us. "But we're like cavemen when it comes to understanding anything fundamental about the relationship between the mind and the brain. If you try to imagine what astronomy was like before the invention of the telescope or microbiology before the microscope . . . well, that's where we are in brain science."

5

Electrical Heavens and Hells

> The premise of the book was this: Life was an experiment by the Creator of the Universe, Who wanted to test a new sort of creature He was thinking of introducing into the Universe. It was a creature with the ability to make up its own mind. All the other creatures were full-programmed robots.
>
> —KURT VONNEGUT,
> *Breakfast of Champions*

IN THE WINTER OF 1963, in Cordoba, Spain, an event occurred that was surely modern neuroscience's most flamboyant hour. As reporters and other spectators watched spellbound, a Spanish-born physiologist named José Delgado stepped into a bull ring armed with many of the colorful accoutrements of bullfighting—plus a little neurotechnological secret that El Cordobès could never have imagined. Delgado waved his red matador's cape at a fierce-looking bull, and the bull charged in the usual manner. All of a sudden, however, the animal stopped dead in its tracks, literally skidding in the dust a few feet from the unorthodox matador. As the world soon learned, Delgado had mastered his bull by remote control, pushing a button on his belt that radioed a signal to an electrode buried deep in the animal's brain.

At Yale University in the 1950s, Delgado and his co-workers had perfected a method of implanting standard thin-wire electrodes in specific brain regions and linking them to something called a stimoceiver. The stimoceiver, which was anchored to the skull with dental cement, could transmit messages to and from the brain by radiotelemetry—sending spontaneously produced EEGs to a distant machine for analysis or, alternately, delivering measured amounts of current to selected bits of gray matter. All the time this was happening, their laboratory animals could go about business as usual: eating, sleeping, courting, or defending their territory, unencumbered but for the funny electronic boxes on their heads. In the case of the bull, the exposed tip of the electrode tapped into an area in the core brain called the caudate nucleus, and electrical stimulation there apparently meant "Whoa" or "Calm down." It is difficult to read a bull's thoughts, of course, and therein lies one of the problems of animal research.

Delgado was not the first practitioner of electrical stimulation of the brain, nor is he the last word on the subject. Other scientists in other laboratories have performed feats of electronic conjury just as important, if less showy. The brain's natural language is electrical, of course, and so it is not surprising that a small current delivered through an electrode could profoundly affect behavior. By altering the polarization across cell membranes, electricity in effect changes the neural code, the signals that neurons send to other neurons, and thus ensues a whole chain of minute electrical events that may culminate in rage, paralyzing fear, a strange ritual of walking in circles, or any number of behaviors.

The father of electrical brain stimulation was a Swiss Nobel Prize–winning physiologist named Walter Hess. In the 1930s Hess put electrodes in cats' brains—specifically, in the hypothalamus, a master control center for basic drives and visceral functions in the brain's core—and turned on the juice, and his cats flew into a hissing, clawing rage. Or, at least, Hess said they did. Other scientists scoffed and claimed that the cats' actions were purely mechanical. It wasn't until the 1950s that Hess was proved right.

In the early 1950s the advent of needle-thin microelectrodes allowed scientists to probe the neural circuitry of awake, behaving animals for the first time without unduly damaging their brains. New instruments that controlled the placement of the electrodes according to precise coordinates also helped transform what had been crude, hit-or-miss brain raids into well-planned expeditions. Still later, modern digital computers would bring order to chaos, digesting and organizing the morass of EEG readouts that these studies generated. Piece by piece, a vast *terra incognita* within the skull was mapped: notably, the once-inaccessible territory below the cortex that scientists of the 1930s and 1940s had ignorantly dubbed the rhinencephalon or "smell brain." Thanks to a handful of brain-stimulation pioneers—most prominently a team of scientists at Yale and another at the Montreal Neurological Institute—we now know the old, primitive smell brain as the crucial emotional circuitry of the limbic system.

The cortex may reason with the subtlety of angels or Platonic philosophers, but if there is a Freudian id in our brain it is surely in the limbic system. In 1953 a young American named James Olds, working at the Montreal Neurological Institute, made one of the great serendipitous discoveries of our age. Having sunk his electrodes into the hypothalamus of a white laboratory rat, he stimulated it every time it wandered into a certain corner of its cage. Since stimulation of the hypothalamus is highly unpleasant, Olds expected the rat to avoid that corner like the plague, but the animal reacted to stimulation by developing a compulsive *fondness* for that part of the cage. A postmortem look at its brain showed why: The electrode wasn't in the hypothalamus at all, but in a mysterious area just above it called the *septum*. This was the "pleasure center" that Olds and colleague Peter Milner would eventually make a household word.

Olds went on to explore the topography of this intracranial Pleasureland throughout the next decade, and he soon found it was a complex pathway, or in his terms, "a river of reward," rather than a distinct "center." Eventually, the researcher would eschew the word *pleasure* in his scientific writings, for he had begun to wonder whether the compulsive behavior of electrode-stimulated animals always signified euphoria. The rat, of course, cannot tell us whether we've hit upon nirvana-in-the-brain or something more like a neural itch.

Soon after their startling adventure with the white rat, Olds and Milner hit upon the idea of letting the animals stimulate themselves, by pushing a lever that activated the electrodes in their heads. These "self-stimulating" rats were soon neglecting the mundane pleasures of food, water, and sex for the superior joy of direct intracranial stimulation. Some would push the magic button thousands of times until they passed out from exhaustion or hunger. The rats also learned to master complex mazes and braved swimming across dangerous moats motivated only by this neuroelectric reward. In the lingo of behaviorism, self-stimulation was "reinforcing."

But life in the behavioral psychology lab deals in punishment as well as reward, negative as well as positive reinforcement. When some parts of the limbic system and nearby areas were stimulated, rats attacked their cage mates in a frenzy; monkeys bared their teeth and struck out at imaginary objects; cats hissed and their fur bristled. When the current was sent to still another region, cats shrank in terror from the very mice they would ordinarily devour. For the scientists who first experimented with controlled brain stimulation it was like viewing a series of invisible dramas, enacted all out of context—like the imaginary Napoleons and Marie Antoinettes who fill state mental hospitals. If fear, rage, sorrow, joy, or longing are actually *contained* in certain collections of neurons, as the self-stimulation studies seemed to show, does that mean our emotions are only phantoms? Which is real: the smile of our beloved or the discharge of cells in our "pleasure center"? Maybe we'd do just as well to live entirely inside our skulls and dispense with the outer world altogether.

These are the sorts of imponderables that have preoccupied philosophers, and suddenly practical-minded scientists were looking them square in the face. Delgado, for one, could not ignore the thorny philosophical and social issues raised by his adventures with ESB (electrical stimulation of the brain). He has even written a remarkable book, *Physical Control of the Mind: Toward a Psychocivilized Society*, in which he wrestles with such weighty matters as free will, the physical location of the self, and the mind/body dilemma. But like a sixteenth-century conquistador dreaming of taming exotic wildernesses, he heralds the coming conquest of the mind as if *control* were the issue:

We may wonder whether man's still ingrained conceptions about the untouchable self are not reminiscent of the ancient belief that it was completely beyond human power to alter omnipotent nature. We are at the beginning of a new ideological, technological revolution in which the objectives are not physical power and control of the environment, but direct intervention into the fate of man himself.

Natural evolution is sluggish, measured in eons rather than decades, Delgado laments, but the emergence of self-consciousness on the scene opens the possibility that "evolution may some day be directed by man." Can we rewire our circuits and control our propensity for murder or mayhem? Design a better brain for our species? Delgado thinks so, though he admits that brain scientists are handling a potentially dangerous toy.

"Is it feasible to induce a robotlike performance in animals and men by pushing the buttons of a cerebral radio stimulator?" he wonders in the pages of his book. "Could drives, desires, and thoughts be placed under the artificial command of electronics? Can personality be influenced by ESB? Can the mind be physically controlled?"

If it did nothing else, his public toreador act made the dark fantasy of electronic mind control eerily real to millions. And Delgado's lesser known ESB experiments do the same. Consider the case of Ali, the bad-tempered, irascible boss of a monkey colony in Delgado's Yale laboratory. In the complex social hierarchy of monkeys, we may catch glimpses of our own antics, and Ali's fall from power is now recorded in the neuroscientific literature much as a conquered Roman emperor figures in the history books. Radio stimulation of his caudate nucleus was Ali's downfall. It made him so docile that he no longer engaged in the ritual hostile displays that had kept the troop in his grip, and he even allowed himself to be caught and handled by his human caretakers. After a while the control lever to his brain was mounted on the wall of the cage so that every time it was pressed, it delivered five seconds of stimulation to his brain. A resourceful monkey named Elisa, in a flash of simian logic, learned that pressing the lever rendered Ali harmless.

"When Ali threatened her," Delgado recalls, "it was repeatedly observed that Elisa responded by lever pressing. Her attitude of looking straight at the boss was highly significant because a submissive monkey would not dare to do so, for fear of immediate retaliation. . . . She was responsible for maintaining the peaceful coexistence within the colony." Could human dictators be so easily toppled?

Then there was Rose. Ordinarily a model monkey mother, according to Delgado, she lost all maternal instinct when her midbrain was radio-stimulated. For ten minutes she'd fly into a rage, biting herself compulsively and ignoring the pathetic distress calls of her infant, Roo. Finally, Roo was forced to seek solace with an adoptive mother.

Of course, it is the human beings who have walked about the wards with electrodes in their brains who tell the most eloquent stories. Our fears of mind control naturally center around the control of human minds by other humans. Very few theologians worry about whether a cat's free will is violated by a five-milliampere current to its thalamus. And, of course, only humans can say what it is they feel. When a cat's fur stands on end, the scientist can never be entirely sure whether his electrodes have triggered a rage response or merely hit some fur-standing-on-end neurons. (As a matter of fact, many investigators think that cats and other animals are capable of something called "sham rage," which consists of all the motor responses without the corresponding emotional state.) When the same area is stimulated in a human being, however, he may report, as one of Delgado's patients did: "It's rather like the feeling of just having been missed by a car and leaping back to the curb and [saying] Br-r-r-r."

The humans who have been treated with ESB include severe epileptics, patients with intractable physical pain, and other severely ill people. Delgado's patients were mainly epileptics who suffered from several seizures a day.

"J. P." was a twenty-year-old woman who suffered from temporal-lobe seizures as well as inexplicable outbursts of violence. She had once stabbed a nurse in the chest with a pair of scissors during one of these rage attacks, but at other times she was no more homicidal than the average schoolmarm. We meet her in the following scenario with Delgado:

A 1.2 milliampere excitation of this point [the right amygdala] was applied while she was playing the guitar and singing with enthusiasm and skill. At the seventh second of stimulation she threw the guitar away and in a fit of rage launched an attack against the wall and then paced around the floor for several minutes, after which she gradually quieted down and recovered her usual cheerfulness.

Stimulating other parts of the brain triggered a bizarre sequence of movements similar to the empty circling, stalking, or head-turning rituals of stimulated animals. When Delgado stimulated a particular region, one man turned around slowly, moving his head from side to side, exactly as though he were searching for something. The stimulation was repeated six times, with the same result each time. The patient's actions had the mechanical purposelessness of a programmed robot.

In *Breakfast of Champions*, a book full of tragicomic ruminations on the mechanistic behavior of Homo sapiens, Kurt Vonnegut recalls a similar vignette from his own boyhood:

The syphilitic man was thinking hard there, at the Crossroads of America, about how to get his legs to step off the curb and carry him across Washington Street. He shuddered gently, as though he had a small motor which was idling inside. Here was his problem: his brains, where the instructions to his legs originated, were being eaten alive by corkscrews. The wires which had to carry the instructions weren't insulated anymore, or were eaten clear through. Switches along the way were welded open or shut.

This man looked like an old, old man, although he might have been only thirty years old. He thought and thought, and then he kicked two times like a chorus girl.

He certainly looked like a machine to me when I was a boy.

Yet we are dealing with human beings, and something in the human brain must crave meaning, for Delgado's patient consistently offered reasonable explanations. "When asked, 'What are you doing?' the answers were 'I am looking for my slippers,' 'I heard a noise,' 'I am restless, and I was looking under the bed.' " Delgado couldn't decide whether the electrodes had evoked a vivid hallucination or a meaningless motor routine that the patient tried to justify after the fact.

The list goes on and on. Tiny electrical currents on the frontal-temporal region brought on hallucinations, illusions, and sensations of déjà-vu. Frontal-lobe stimulation made tactiturn patients chatty and responsive. One woman even felt moved to kiss the doctor's hands and utter seductive and endearing phrases. Stimulation of the caudate nucleus—remember the bull and Ali, the deposed monkey boss?—provoked feelings of sudden, inexplicable dread. But what is most unsettling is that Delgado's patients apparently accepted these dramatic changes of mood or behavior "as natural manifestations of their own personality and not as artificial results of the tests."

We humans walk around believing that we are set apart from those with hooves, claws, and fur by virtue of our special self-consciousness and our free will. But ESB experiments reveal that our species can be as puppetlike as the next and that electrodes may, at least under some circumstances, override our will. Do we even know where our thoughts come from? Delgado observes, somewhat smugly, that his research is bound to gnaw at our pride. Not only did we have to learn from Copernicus that we aren't situated at the epicenter of the universe and from Darwin that our forefathers swung from trees, but now: "The analysis of mental activities in the context of brain physiology indicates that our own self, our ego, is not so unique or even independent as Freud pointed out many years ago."

Actually Delgado is only partly right. The notion of an autonomous ego was hardly sacrosanct before ESB—or even before Freud. What were Aphrodite, the Furies, or the Cretan Minotaur but projections of psychic elements man can neither govern nor fathom?

And when it comes to "mind control," what is "mind" and what constitutes "control"?

When your family doctor makes your leg jerk forward with a tap at the knee, we do not say he is manipulating your mind, even though no act of will can make your leg sit still. Is eliciting a series of strange movements—or perhaps even a rapid mood change—with a brain electrode so different? Well, it *is* different. It is different because motivation is not a property of muscle groups or peripheral ganglia but of neurons. If you could control a person's motivation, you'd certainly be knocking at the doors of his selfhood. But can the electrode gang do that?

For all his neurovisionary zeal, Delgado admits that his craft is still crude and the results of ESB are quite unpredictable in humans. There are also many things that ESB can never do. For instance, you can forget any fantasies of ESB-trained pets fetching your slippers or turning on your television set. Or of electrodes that will turn any untutored human into a brain surgeon or an Olympic-class skier. "Much of the brain participates in learning and a monotonous train of pulses applied to a limited pool of neurons cannot be expected to mimic its complexity," Delgado writes. "The acquisition of a new skill is theoretically and practically beyond the possibilities of electrical stimulation."

Electrical pulses can't simulate personal identity, language, or culture either. "Memories can be recalled, emotions awakened, and conversations speeded by ESB," says Delgado, "but the patients always express themselves according to their background and experience."

Imagine that a Dr. X has placed electrodes into the brain of Patient Y, who happens to have a homicidal disposition. And that Dr. X's futuristic EEG machine can match each of Patient Y's actions with a distinct pattern of brain waves. Now say that a certain pattern of firing occurs just before Patient Y commits a murder and that the omniscient Dr. X can be *absolutely sure* that this slice of the EEG record reads "ready to murder." He's still left with some unsolved problems. Even if he could record the firing of every neuron individually, he still wouldn't know the *reason* for the murder. There's only one way to know that, and that is to ask Patient Y.

An iconoclastic scientist named Robert G. Heath has done something very much like that.

> It's true, though:
> how strange are the back streets
> of Pain City . . .
> —RAINER MARIA RILKE,
> *Duino Elegies*

A sick-sweet scent of mildew hangs over the French Quarter in New Orleans, and the bodies of last night's pleasure seekers lie in doorways like limp, unstrung puppets. On the day we arrive here, the *Times-Picayune* reports that police from St. John the Baptist Parish are still looking for a murder suspect known as the "swamp rat of the bayou" near Lake Pont-chartrain. The hunted man, a mental patient deranged by an old blow to the head, has been hiding out in that dense, primordial bog for eight days, enduring lightning storms, moonless nights, mosquitoes, and torrential rains. No one, least of all the posse that is pursuing him, can figure out how he survives.

If New Orleans is a city with an overripe id, it is also home to Tulane University Medical School and its unique department of neurology and psychiatry. We have an appointment with its sixty-eight-year-old chairman emeritus, Dr. Heath, a scientist well acquainted with the back streets of the id. A modern high-rise a few blocks from the French Quarter houses the operating rooms where, in 1950, Heath first put depth electrodes into the brain of a human mental patient. Now silver haired and nominally retired, Heath looks rather like one of those semimythical television doctors who will drive fifty miles just to dispense a little down-home wisdom to a troubled patient.

Before Olds turned up the pleasure center in rats, Heath found it in the human organ. His electrodes charted the circuitry of pain, too, in some of the illest brains in Louisiana. It was the first time electrodes had been used inside human brain tissue (except very briefly during epileptic oper-ations just to guide neurosurgeons around the homogeneous macaroni of the cortex), and so Heath's operations were controversial, to say the least.

In the years from 1950 to 1952, he implanted brain electrodes in twenty-six patients. Some of them suffered from incurable epilepsy, intractable physical pain, Parkinson's disease, and other medical conditions, but most came out of the dimly lit back wards of the state mental hospitals. With dental burr-drills, Heath and his co-workers drilled through the patients' skulls, guided the electrodes carefully into specific sites, and then left them there, at first for a few days, later for years at a time. The result was a chronicle of the electrical activity of a conscious human brain—while its owner talked, reminisced about his childhood, flew into a rage, wept, or hallucinated.

On Heath's desk we notice a pottery ashtray decorated with odd wavy hieroglyphics. "Oh, a friend made that for me. That's the schizophrenic spike-and-slow-wave," he says. Sure enough, on closer inspection, the glyphs are EEGs. "We found, you see, that psychotics have this abnormal spike in the septal region, a key site in the pleasure system."

He peels back the wrinkled outer cortex from a varicolored plastic model brain to show us the parts that dominate this saga of pain and pleasure. Septum, amygdala, hippocampus, thalamus. Even the names sound like creatures out of a medieval bestiary. "By implanting electrodes and taking recordings from these deep-lying areas," he explains, "we were able to localize the brain's pleasure and pain systems. We'd interview a patient about pleasant subjects and see the pleasure system firing. If we had a patient who flew into a rage attack, as many psychotics did, we'd find the 'punishment' system firing." The pleasure system includes the septal area and part of the almond-shaped amygdala; the other half of the amygdala, the hippocampus, the thalamus, and the tegmentum (in the midbrain) constitute the punishment system.

Interestingly, the septal spike that Heath spotted in psychotics' brain waves did *not* turn up in the EEGs of the patients who were being treated for epilepsy, intractable pain, or Parkinson's disease. Whenever a mental patient flew into a violent rage or turned into a catatonic zombie, the EEG was almost certain to display the telltale sawtooth pattern. If the patient got well, the spike disappeared. Abnormal electrical activity in the septal area, Heath became convinced, meant that something was terribly wrong with the psychotic brain's "pleasure system."

"The *primary* symptom of schizophrenia isn't hallucinations or delusions," he tells us. "It's a defect in the pleasure response. Schizophrenics have a predominance of painful emotions. They function in an almost continuous state of fear or rage, fight or flight, because they don't have the pleasure to neutralize it."

The psychiatric term is *anhedonia*, Greek for joylessness. (*Anhedonia* was the working title of one of Woody Allen's most successful films; later the name was changed to *Annie Hall*.) "Schizophrenics will often say, 'I just don't feel pleasure. I don't know what it is,' " Heath adds. "If you talk to schizophrenics about falling in love, they don't fully understand it. They've read books. They know how you're supposed to act and they copy what other people do. But they don't have the qualitative feeling."

It turned out that electrical stimulation of the pleasure system automatically turned off the punishment system—what Heath calls the "aversive system"—and vice-versa. And so Heath tried to cure mental illness with direct electrical stimulation of the pleasure neurons. "If we stimulated their pleasure systems, violent psychotics stopped having rage attacks," he says. "We even stimulated the septal area in people suffering from intractable cancer or arthritis pain and we were able to turn off the pain. All of this makes sense: When you're feeling pleasure, you don't feel angry, and when you're in a rage you certainly can't feel pleasure." By stimulating the septal pleasure area, he could make homicidal manias, suicide attempts, depressions, or delusions go away—sometimes for a long time. And this treatment, curiously, also worked for epilepsy.

"At first we thought one stimulation would reverse the psychotic process," he remembers. "In the old days we could only leave the electrodes in for a few days. One of our first patients was a hopelessly psychotic young gal. She was catatonic and wouldn't eat, and her life was in danger. We stimulated her septal area and she stayed well for four years. We thought at first we had cured her." But the patient eventually suffered a relapse.

As it turned out, it took more than a few pulses of current to exorcise madness. Heath had to devise safer electrodes that could be left in the brain for years so that a patient could be restimulated at intervals. Then, in 1976, the "most violent patient in the state"—a mildly retarded young man who had to be tied to his bed because of his savage outbursts—received Dr. Heath's first brain pacemaker.

The pacemaker is an array of tiny battery-powered electrodes that delivers five minutes of stimulation every ten minutes to the cerebellum, at the very back of the brain. Its power source, a battery pack about the size of a deck of playing cards, could fit neatly in the patient's pocket. (Later it was miniaturized to matchbook proportions and implanted in the recipient's abdomen; it requires recharging every five years.) The cerebellum, Heath learned, is a better entryway to the brain's emotional circuitry. Stimulating a precise half-inch of its cauliflowerlike surface automatically fires the pleasure area and inhibits the rage centers, and so it was no longer necessary to invade the limbic areas farther forward in the brain.

The first pacemaker patient soon stopped trying to slash himself and his caretakers and went home from the hospital. All was well, for a while. Then the man inexplicably went on a rampage and attempted to murder his parents. Before he was subdued, he had severely wounded his next-door neighbor and narrowly missed being shot by the sheriff. Heath's X rays quickly spotted the problem: broken wires between the pacemaker and the power source. Once the wires were reattached, the rage attacks waned again. The young man is now in vocational rehabilitation and doing well.

In 1974 a pretty, intelligent twenty-one-year-old librarian was shot in the head during a holdup. After an operation that removed much of her frontal lobes, she had frequent seizures, was barely conversant, and had to be fed through a tube because she stopped eating. By the end of the next year she was in a continual frenzy. She lashed out at anyone within range and once tried to stab her father. She screamed whenever she was touched and complained of constant, excruciating pain all over her body. Her brain pacemaker was installed in November 1976, and, magically, the rage episodes subsided. She started eating; her memory improved; and her doctors began describing her personality as "pleasant," even "sparkling."

Another patient, a severely depressed former physicist, was troubled by voices that commanded him to choke his wife. When he got one of Dr. Heath's pacemakers in 1977, the infernal voices vanished, along with his perennial gloom. He and his wife began to visit relatives and dine together in restaurants for the first time in years. But *his* wires eventually broke, and once again his wife was threatened with strangulation. When the gadgetry was mended, so was the man's psyche.

Ironically, the many technical snafus that plagued the pacemaker gave Heath the perfect controls for his experiments. If Patient A behaves like a model citizen as long as his batteries work, only to run amok like a psychopath in a low-budget horror film when, *unbeknownst to him*, the machinery breaks, it's probably not a placebo effect. Even so, the cerebellar pacemaker is not a psychiatric cure-all. By Heath's estimates, about half of the seventy-odd patients have been substantially rehabilitated—no mean feat, given that pacemaker recipients come from the ranks of the "incurable"—but others have never emerged from their private hells. For some reason, depressives and patients prone to uncontrollable violence have benefited most; chronic schizophrenics the least.

Fortunately for posterity, Heath and his colleagues filmed many of their bold journeys into the human emotional apparatus. In a windowless cubicle crammed full of film reels, he shows us movies of some of the early stimulation sessions. They're starkly real. We feel like high-tech voyeurs to the raw and primal scenes inside the human brain.

In the first film, a woman of indeterminate age lies on a narrow cot, a giant bandage covering her skull. At the start of the film she seems locked inside some private vortex of despair. Her face is as blank as her white hospital gown and her voice is a remote, tired monotone.

"Sixty pulses," says a disembodied voice. It belongs to the technician in the next room, who is sending a current to the electrode inside the woman's head. The patient, inside her soundproof cubicle, does not hear him.

Suddenly she smiles. "Why are you smiling?" asks Dr. Heath, sitting by her bedside.

"I don't know. . . . Are you doing something to me? [Giggles] I don't usually sit around and laugh at nothing. I must be laughing at something."

"One hundred forty," says the offscreen technician.

The patient giggles again, transformed from a stone-faced zombie into a little girl with a secret joke. "What in the hell are you doing?" she asks. "You must be hitting some goody place."

The "goody place" is the septal pleasure center, which the unseen technician is stimulating with an electrical current. "She was a mean one," Heath muses. "She was hospitalized for years for a schizoaffective illness. . . . This film was made in 1969, and the treatment has held on her—she's doing well."

Blue whorls of marijuana smoke float through the air of the next film Heath shows us. The patient, a young man with a mustache, looks agitated as a traumatized laboratory animal at the outset. Glumly he confides to Dr. Heath, "To tell you the truth, I really couldn't feel good if I tried." An official-sounding voice-over informs us that he's also prone to "rageful paranoid ideation."

Since this film has a split screen, we can watch the patient on one side, and the spidery script of his EEGs on the other. At first, there are sharp spikes on the line labeled SEPTUM. Then, after ten minutes or so, a dreamy smile passes over the patient's face, and he lapses into stream-of-consciousness nostalgia:

T. J. had the best grass. . . . We'd sit around in his living room like a couple of little children. It's like a birdhouse and it overlooks the expressway [laughs]. . . . That's really funny; it's the other way around: The expressway overlooks us!

He told me a lot of tall tales from sea . . . said they grow real good grass in Indonesia. [Giggles] It's too much—I'm about to start singing that song, 'Those Were the Days, My Friend . . .' before we got busted and came down from that wave, down to a more earthlike level. . . . Things were really enchanting. We were like a couple of children that live on the same block.

"There—see the big delta wave appearing in the septal region," Heath tells us. Sure enough, large, languorous waves are now coming from the lead to the septal electrode. "There's almost an exact correlation," he adds. "When he gets a rush of good feeling, the record shows large-amplitude waves in the pleasure system." (As an intriguing footnote, the same electrical pattern crops up when the young man merely *remembers* past highs. Are memory and reality electrochemically indistinguishable?)

Drugs affect our pain and pleasure circuits by blocking or enhancing the natural chemicals that course through them. But the ticket to the brain's Shangri-La isn't so easily purchased. While marijuana does excite the septal area temporarily, Heath tells us, its *long-term* effects are in the opposite direction—depression, apathy, withdrawal. The same is true of cocaine, heroin, and all the other street drugs.

Along with the depth electrodes, Heath's team would often surgically implant a sort of tube, called a canula, through which they could deliver precise amounts of a chemical directly into the brain. Oriental sacred texts (and Aldous Huxley's *Brave New World*) mention a legendary bliss drug called *soma*, the food of the Himalayan gods. The real-life version might be acetylcholine, a natural chemical transmitter. When the Tulane researchers injected acetylcholine into a patient's septal area, "vigorous activity" showed up on the septal EEG, and the patient usually reported intense pleasure—including multiple sexual orgasms lasting as long as thirty minutes.

"I can show you a film of one of the recordings," Heath offers, fishing through some of the reels on the shelves. We half expect a neurologic peep show, but the film he digs out is the raw EEG record of a woman patient, who was being treated for epilepsy, under the influence of acetylcholine. A flat, clinical voice-over accompanies the staticky march of brain waves across the screen:

Now we're coming to the start of the changes. . . . It's in the form of a fast spindle, about eighteen per second . . . first in the dorsal right anterior septal, then it spreads to the other septal leads. . . . This is still correlated with the same clinical findings of intense pleasure and particularly of a sexual nature. . . .

A half hour after the acetylcholine injection, the patient is still having orgasms. Heath points at an ominous-looking scrawl on the EEG and notes, "See, it looks almost like the spike-and-dome pattern of epileptic seizure. It's a very explosive activity."

The flip side of joy is pain. The next film shows a patient having his "aversive system" stimulated. His face twists suddenly into a terrible grimace. One eye turns out and his features contort as though in the spasm of a horrible science-fiction metamorphosis. "It's knocking me out . . . I just want to claw. . . ." he says, gasping like a tortured beast. "I'll kill you. . . . I'll kill you, Dr. Lawrence."

Some might see Robert Heath as a sort of modern-day Virgil of the brain's underworld. To others he's an almost Strangelovian figure. When he first showed his movies to an assemblage of psychiatrists, neurologists, and other scientists, some were outraged. Murmurs of medical hubris, mind control, and unsafe human experimentation circulated—in large part because of the film we just saw. But what looks like a scene from the Spanish Inquisition, Heath assures us, is no more than electrical stimulation of the rage/fear circuits. Unfortunately, the audience, back in 1952, misread it.

"They thought we were hurting him," he tells us. "But we *weren't* hurting him. We were stimulating a site in the tegmentum in the midbrain, and all of sudden he wanted to kill. He would have, too, if he hadn't been tied down. . . . He started remembering a time when he lost his temper— when his shirts weren't ironed right and he wanted to kill his sister. That showed us we'd activated the same circuit that was fired by his spontaneous rage attacks."

It is hard to envision Robert Heath as a cold-blooded experimentalist. We'd seen his compassionate, almost courtly bedside manner on film. We'd watched him put freaked-out paranoids at ease and coax intimate confidences out of sullen, mumbling shantytown depressives. There may be a bit of the old-fashioned country doctor in Robert Heath—who is, as a matter of fact, a country doctor's son. When Heath was fourteen, his father arranged for him to to see an autopsy, not realizing that the body being carved up in the icy light of the morgue was his son's former scoutmaster. "I'll never forget the horror of that," Heath remembers. "Here was a man I'd known and liked, and they were cutting him up and cracking jokes. I always try to tell my students not to forget the human side of medicine."

There was another force working against Heath in the early 1950s. The American romance with Sigmund Freud was in full flower, and schizophrenia was being blamed on schizophrenogenic ("schizophrenia-causing") mothers, oral fixations, and other incorporeal demons. To insist, as Heath did, that mental illness was a *biological* disease was highly suspect; to propose to erase all those deep, dark traumata with a few pulses of electricity was heresy. Today, of course, it's hard to find an informed researcher who *doesn't* consider schizophrenia a biological process.

Dr. Heath's movies are disturbing nonetheless. It is one thing to contemplate, in the opaque prose of science-journal articles, the "continuous spindling, most pronounced in amygdala leads of an epileptic patient during an episode of profound anxiety and irritability," another to see stark terror in grainy, home-movie black and white.

Man makes the best experimental animal because he can tell us what is happening in his enormous, complicated cerebrum. But how much does he really know? José Delgado's patients came up with pseudo-explanations for their behavior. Did Heath's patients accept their electro-transformations as normal mood changes? What did the man whose terrible metamorphosis we just witnessed on film think about his sudden murderous fury?

"As soon as we turned off the current he went back to normal," Heath recalls. "We asked him why he had wanted to kill Dr. Lawrence [not his real name], and he said he had nothing against Dr. Lawrence; he was just there. He's like a psychotic person on the street who lashes out at whoever is around."

What exactly sets you or me apart from the average psychotic on the street then? Can stimulation of the rage/fear circuits override our genteel Judaeo-Christian superegos? Or is the superego—or whatever we call the internal censor that keeps us from uttering dark curses at innocent passersby—an electrochemical phantom as well?

"No, your ethics are not an illusion," Heath says. "But how are they set up? You're taught, Thou shalt not kill. I'm sure you've had rage attacks when you felt like killing someone. Why don't you kill? Because you're too damned scared!

"As a child your parents are the authority figures who will punish you. Later it gets internalized as God or whatever. But all moral learning is ultimately based on the pain and pleasure circuitry in your brain—on your internal reward and punishment system."

As for mind control, Heath insists that it is "impossible to control another mind." He's probably right, if by mind control we mean demonic scientists or overzealous CIA agents with their fingers on the control buttons of innocent citizens' pain/pleasure circuits. The fact is that the only brains to be outfitted with electrodes or pacemakers are decidedly abnormal ones. No one knows whether a low-voltage current to *your* rage/fear centers would turn *you* into a homicidal maniac. (If it did, imagine the courtroom dramas of the future: "Ladies and gentlemen of the jury, my client is not responsible for his actions. The EEG record will demonstrate that at the time of the crime his rage circuits were misfiring. . . .")

Heath's experiments raise questions that, so far, lie unresolved. Who is the real Patient X? The guy who wanted to murder Dr. Lawrence just because he was there, or the poststimulation persona, who politely apologized for his outburst? If you say, "Well, of course, his *real self* is the person he is when his brain is not being stimulated—the nonviolent one," think again. According to Heath, Mr. X was subject to spontaneous storms of rage, and electrical stimulation instantly triggered the memory of the day when he wanted to kill his sister because she'd put too much starch in his shirts. Of course, he refrained from actually killing her, but some people *do* kill their sisters (or try to stab their parents, or choke their wives) over trifles. In the next chapter, we'll look further at the brain circuitry for violence. For now, let's say that "free will" is a more complicated issue than Thomas Aquinas or the architects of British common law could have imagined.

That evening we dine with Heath in an elegant restaurant converted from a nineteenth-century bordello. Afterward he gives us a tour in his small, beat-up yellow Volkswagen. Driving past the impassive, self-contained antebellum mansions of the Garden District, we turn abruptly into the gaudy nightworld of the French Quarter. On Rampart Street our guide points to the row of houses where nineteenth-century gentlemen kept their octoroon mistresses and explains the intricate legal contracts that governed these liaisons. The subject turns to pleasure.

Heath tells us that some of his patients were given "self-stimulators" similar to the ones used by Olds's rats. Whenever he felt the urge, the patient could push any of three or four buttons on the self-stimulator hooked to his belt. Each button was connected to an electrode implanted in a different part of his brain, and the device kept track of the number of times he stimulated each site.

Heath tells of one patient who felt impelled to stimulate his septal region about 1,500 times an hour. He happened to be a schizophrenic homosexual who wanted to change his sexual preference. As an experiment, Heath gave the man stag films to watch while he pushed his pleasure-center hotline, and the result was a new interest in female companionship. After clearing things with the state attorney general, the enterprising Tulane doctors went out and hired a "lady of the evening," as Heath delicately puts it, for their ardent patient.

"We paid her fifty dollars," Heath recalls. "I told her it might be a little weird, but the room would be completely blacked out with curtains. In the next room we had the instruments for recording his brain waves, and he had enough lead wire running into the electrodes in his brain so he could move around freely. We stimulated him a few times, the young lady was cooperative, and it was a very successful experience." This conversion was only temporary, however.

On Bourbon Street, Heath parks the car, and we thread our way among tourists in Bermuda shorts gazing raptly into bottomless/topless nightclubs. Rowdy disco music mingles with Dixieland jazz; delicate grillwork French balconies overlook souvenir shops hawking T-shirts with off-color slogans. Drunks lie down and sing spirituals to the plump yellow moon.

We ask Heath if human beings are as compulsive about pleasure as the rats of Olds's laboratory that self-stimulated until they passed out. "No," he tells us. "People don't self-stimulate constantly—as long as they're feeling good. Only when they're depressed does the stimulation trigger a big response.

"There are so many factors that play into a human being's pleasure response: your experience, your memory system, sensory cues . . . ," he muses, as we stop to hear a mellow saxophone solo floating out of Preservation Hall. "I remember seeing that guy from Harvard who used drugs—Timothy Leary—on television. He was asked whether drugs were a bad influence on young kids, and he said, 'This is nothing. In a few years kids are going to be demanding septal electrodes.'

"But it doesn't work that way."

It isn't very flattering to see ourselves as robotlike creatures programmed with a persistent delusion of "free will," among other follies. Zap a particular slice of the amygdala (or wave a certain tricolor flag) and we'll jump to our feet and recite the Pledge of Allegiance. But is that the whole story? Obviously not. Some parts of our brains—for instance, the limbic structures that interpret all our experience in a simple binary code of pain and pleasure—may be rather robotlike at times. As an experiment, watch exactly what you do every morning from the moment your alarm clock goes off until, say, your midmorning coffee break. Then ask yourself whether a meticulous observer from another galaxy might mistakenly conclude you were a preprogrammed entity. On the other hand, human behavior is extremely unpredictable over the long run, as even the ESB subjects proved. (What else would you expect from a creature with ten billion neurons, and 10^{14} interconnections, in its head?) Here is how Kurt Vonnegut, in another passage from *Breakfast of Champions*, summed things up:

His situation, insofar as he was a machine, was complex, tragic, and laughable. But the sacred part of him, his awareness, remained an unwavering band of light.

And this book is being written by a meat machine in cooperation with a machine made of metal and plastic. . . . And at the core of the writing meat machine is an unwavering band of light.

At the core of each person who reads this book is a band of unwavering light.

6

Caligula's Brain:
The Neurobiology of Violence

You dozed and watched the night revealing
The thousand sordid images
Of which your soul was composed.
—T. S. ELIOT, "Preludes"

EVER SINCE Cain put fatal dents in Abel's skull, Homo sapiens has been a pretty deadly creature. After a hundred thousand years of evolution, we have not only failed to eradicate violence, we have developed it into a global fixation. Some of the best minds of our species have dedicated themselves to building the A-bomb, then the H-bomb, and today particle-beam weapons. This obsession with violence all starts, of course, in the brain—from that first punch to a sibling's nose to the final turning of the nuclear key in a Minuteman missile silo. But consider the following neurofantasy:

Man finally gains control over the violence center in his head. Around the middle of the twentieth century, electrodes in certain limbic centers are found to pacify wild bulls and wilder humans. But because it is neither ethical nor feasible to put brain electrodes into every man, woman, and child on the planet, the leading neuroscientists of the 1990s begin diligently mapping the chemistry of aggression, identifying and labeling the sixty-five different neurojuices that control our baser instincts. By 2030 a chemical assay called the Bio-Aggression Index is administered to all schoolchildren. Those with scores above the mean begin a preventive program of brain-wave–biofeedback therapy and the new wonder drugs Pacifizine and Inhibitol. By century's end most of the prisons are empty mausoleums and *war* has become a quaint, obsolete term like *troubadour*.

Is this fantasy possible?

Why There Will Never Be an Antiwar Pill

AT FIRST GLANCE it looked as if scientists in the Netherlands had found it: an honest-to-goodness antiaggression drug. Called DU 27716, it was an experimental compound that dramatically curbed certain kinds of rodent hostility. Among mice it's customary to attack any strange mouse introduced into the cage; but a male mouse treated with DU 27716 absolutely won't do so. It's easy enough to turn an animal into a pacifist by simply tranquilizing it, of course, but DU 27716–treated mice are perfectly alert. Interestingly, too, the compound erases *offensive* hostility while leaving the defensive artillery intact: Mice on DU 27716 will fight back when attacked.

If there ever was a promising aggression antidote, it would seem to be DU 27716. The problem is that its effects on mice don't necessarily predict what it might do to Homo sapiens. Even rats, which belong to the same genus as mice (different species), react a little differently to DU 27716: They still attack newcomers, albeit less often. And there are other, more formidable barriers to a peace pill.

One man smashes another over the head with a broken beer bottle during a bar brawl. Another man plays with scenarios of "mutual assured destruction" in the Pentagon's computer room. These are both acts of violence in many people's books, but in what misty never-never land would a single chemical compound turn both off? For all we know, the men with their fingers on the launch code of those sleek, computerized Cruise missiles might be the very sort of people *least* inclined to bar brawls. (Consider, for example, the vocabulary such folks use—for example, *Peacekeeper* missiles—to avoid the outward taint of violence. The Lawrence Livermore National Laboratories, a leading bomb lab, recently held a seminar entitled "Upgrading Lethality" for highly civilized physicists who would probably have shied away from a seminar on "How to Kill a Lot of People.")

Even among lower mammals, aggression is a many-splendored thing. At Yale in the 1960s, a cat (with electrodes in its hypothalamus) was put into a cage with a rat. Turning on the current sometimes transformed the animal into a fierce, spiky-furred Halloween cat. It would hiss and claw and attack the rat, but it wouldn't actually bite it. At other times hypothalamic stimulation triggered a very different attack mode, which the human observers dubbed "quiet biting," in which the cat coolly captured and bit its prey with no sign of emotion. The scientists reported that they had identified two completely distinct forms of feline aggression, one full of melodrama and ritual display ("affective aggression"), the other, a housecat version of the normal, cool, predatory behavior of the big jungle cats. If that's the case with cats, we can hardly expect to trace wife beating, imperial poisonings, the Hundred Years' War, and the Manson family killings to a single cause.

A Power Parable   Like the creatures in *Aesop's Fables*, research animals sometimes expose our own foibles in caricature, and a group of vervet monkeys might serve as a parable of power. Three centuries ago the slave ships trafficking between West Africa and the Caribbean also brought over vervet monkeys for sale as house pets to the island gentry. Their descendants now roam wild through the lush, humid hills of St. Kitts—except for those whose social life is being monitored (and manipulated) within the wire enclosures of research facilities in St. Kitts and faraway California.

UCLA psychiatrist Michael McGuire became an authority on monkey politics more by serendipity than design. "I originally planned to be in the monkey business for about six months and then get back to humans," he tells us. "Now it's fifteen years later." Actually McGuire has a foot in both worlds. We meet him in his office in the formidable brick high rise that is the UCLA Neuropsychiatric Institute, where the minds he contemplates belong to troubled humans. The monkeys live out in the heat and dust of the San Fernando Valley, in large, wire cages on the grounds of the Sepulveda Veterans Administration Hospital. But their social hierarchies are not so alien.

Human history is full of kings, popes, emperors, generalissimos, and upstarts. Some simian societies—baboons, chimpanzees, and squirrel monkeys, for instance—have a graduated pecking order, in which monkey A lords it over monkey B, who lords it over monkey C, and so on. A colony of vervet monkeys, in contrast, is a tiny totalitarian state with an all-powerful dictator. "The dominant male does what he wants, sits where he wants," says McGuire. "He has access to any resources, including the females. He defends the group if it's threatened; he does a lot of herding when they're traveling; he surveys the periphery of the territory to make sure there's no hanky-panky. And there are two peaks during the days when the leader goes around flexing his muscles, as it were. If you're a subordinate, then you get off the rock you're sitting on. It's not that the boss wants to sit on the rock. He never does. He just lets you know he's boss."

In the late 1970s an amazing fact emerged from the biochemical data that McGuire's colleague Michael J. Raleigh was collecting on one vervet colony. Over the next few years, McGuire diligently took blood samples from forty-five different monkey colonies, and there it was: The leader of each colony had twice as much serotonin in his blood as any of the other males. That prompted a crucial question. Was the chief simply born with more serotonin in his brain, or did his biochemistry get that way *as a result* of his social rank? To find out, McGuire took the boss out of his social group and quarantined him in a solitary cage, where his blood serotonin promptly dropped. When he was put in a cage with only females, the same thing happened. ("It seems to be male-to-male interaction stuff; it depends on a male's rank among other males.") Meanwhile, back at the colony, another male rose to power in the boss's absence and within two weeks *his* serotonin was at twice the normal level. But when the deposed monarch was restored to his throne, his serotonin rose again, while his temporary replacement's serotonin dropped back to its old subservient level. At least in monkeys, serotonin levels closely mirror the ups and downs of social status.

We muse about Napoleon's serotonin levels before and after Waterloo. McGuire laughs and gives us a more down-to-earth analogy. "I just got a call early this morning from a guy from a talk show in Australia. And his notion was that you invite a man to dinner along with his wife's ex-boyfriend, and you do a serotonin measure. . . . Yeah, I don't think humans are very different."

"How exactly does social status affect serotonin levels?" we ask McGuire.

"We don't have all the details," he replies, "but I can tell you this. We just did a study in which we put the dominant animal behind a one-way mirror, where he sees the rest of the group but they don't see him. He goes through all the displays and threats, and, of course, the subordinates don't respond. He sees the subordinates sitting where he usually sits or copulating with the females, and his serotonin goes down. So apparently it isn't enough just to flex your muscles. You have to get the response from the others. The dominant male *needs* the subordinates to kowtow to him.

"Now we're asking, Are there critical information-processing differences when an animal shifts from dominant to subordinate, or vice-versa?" he continues. "You're the department head, and then someone is brought in over you and you're demoted. It may be that the whole process of social interaction produces a *different physiological you.* Maybe you'd see the same stimulus differently. Say you're dominant and I'm subordinate. It's a hot summer day and suddenly an ice-cold Coca-Cola appears. You'll see it as yours and I'll see it as yours. I might want it, but I wouldn't doubt that it's yours."

The irony is that it is clearly McGuire who is dominant here. Not just because we're in his territory (a large, airy office with many of the trappings of rank) but because he's a man with an authoritative force field. When somebody broke into the vervet cages recently and twenty monkeys ran loose around the shopping malls and freeways of the valley, it was McGuire who took charge and issued the orders to round them up. His penetrating gaze, beneath strong shaggy eyebrows, seems to size up a situation quickly, be it the power plays masked behind bureaucratic politesse or the body language of deference. And the truth of this situation is that he's sick of journalists. Besides early-morning phone calls from Australian talk-show personalities, there have been more cute stories in newspapers and women's magazines than a scientist cares to attract. First, it cuts into McGuire's time. Also having one's name in the popular press too often smacks of *publicity,* which is a mildly dishonorable state. Anyway, McGuire has allotted us a half hour, and we sense we'd better make good use of it.

If power and prestige affect one's serotonin levels, so, it seems, does serotonin determine machismo. When McGuire gave passive males a drug that boosted their serotonin levels, they soon assumed the demeanor of power, performing a series of intelligence tests with the quiet assurance of chairmen of the board. Conversely, dominant monkeys seemed to turn submissive after they were given a serotonin-inhibiting drug—approaching the same tests in panic and trepidation.

But behind the power struggles of males is the influence of females. If you want to know who's boss—or who *will* be—*cherchez la femme.* "If you watch closely," says McGuire, "you see that the females select one male that they groom with, and they often flank him in his knock-down drag-outs with other males. Within two weeks the male favored by the females will be dominant. Now, do the females know something we don't know? Do they know who's going to become dominant? Or maybe behind every male vervet there's a female vervet. We don't know."

If, in some sense, a monkey colony is a human society in microcosm, what is the moral to the neuroscientific fable? First, McGuire would like to correct a misconception that has been circulating. "This thing has gotten out of hand," he tells us. "An Australian newspaper just ran a headline that portrayed the dominant male as a big bully who pushes everybody around. He's just the opposite, really. It's the subordinate males who are nasty and grumpy; when a male becomes dominant, all of a sudden he becomes benevolent, sweet. He sits with the females and grooms them. . . ."

"The leader is a benevolent despot, then?" we ask.

"Exactly. He's less aggressive when he's dominant. The fight is to get there, but once you're established and everybody acknowledges your power, you keep the peace."

For the boss monkeys' human counterparts, then, better look among law-and-order types. McGuire did, at a UCLA fraternity. The fraternity's officers turned out to have higher serotonin in their bloodstream than the rank-and-file members. At the University of Iowa, meanwhile, researcher Douglas Madsen tested the blood serotonin of male college students and reported that coronary-prone "Type A" personalities had higher levels. "We certainly won't find that it's *just* serotonin in dominant humans,"

McGuire cautions. "There's probably an interaction with norepinephrine—maybe it has to be high simultaneously—or with GABA, or with some other chemical we haven't even identified. But to find that serotonin is *twice as high* in the dominant males, in all of *forty-five* colonies . . . that's an astounding statistic."

The Internal Secretions of Henry Kissinger

THE LAWS of biopolitics seem to run both ways. Not only can an individual's neurochemistry affect society—we might visualize internal events inside Henry Kissinger, for instance, influencing peace negotiations in the Middle East—but the environment (power and social rank) also *changes the brain*. And that interests Lionel Tiger, the colorful anthropologist from Rutgers.

At a 1983 symposium at Rockefeller University, the author of *Men in Groups* and other ruminations on power gave a talk entitled "Social Structure and Internal Secretions," inspired in part by McGuire's monkeys. "That there is a close and real connection between social status and internal secretions," he told the audience, "should interest people studying human behavior. . . . It may be that power has an impact on internal secretions such that people who *have* power don't like to lose it, for instance." Maybe dominance is "immensely satisfying at the internal physiological level," Tiger mused, in which case Henry Kissinger's famous quip that "power is an aphrodisiac" might be literally true.

Having imagined the embodiment of the name Lionel Tiger as a powerful, stately presence, we were surprised to see an unimposing-looking man of short stature and malleable, semicomic features. The power Tiger radiates is of the hyperkinetic, stage-show magician variety—pulling conceptual rabbits out of thin air and changing them into something else before you can spot how he did the first trick.

"Around 1974," he continued, in his 78 rpm speaking style, "I said it was very likely that you'll find a physiological basis for feeling good. If depression is biological, why should there not be a neurophysiology of enjoyment? At that time, of course, I had no idea we would be discovering the endorphins." Something like optimism, he extrapolated, might be a "sociohormone," vital to the well-being of a community. Operating perhaps through the endorphins circulating in our heads, it might even affect the birth rate or attitudes toward investment.

"If you got a telegram informing you that you'd just won a Pulitzer Prize," he said, "and you monitored all your internal secretions, I'm absolutely convinced you'd find marked changes. It isn't necessary that the news be true. It's the fact that you believe it's true that counts." The same principle must operate in the collective "world of ideas," according to Tiger. A jingoistic State of the Union speech, for example, probably modifies the citizenry's "internal secretions" in one way or another.

Of course, it's unlikely that future pollsters will add serum samples to their questionnaires. Although neuroscientists are exploring links between specific internal chemicals and schizophrenia, autism, and even learning disabilities, they don't hunt for correlations between serotonin levels and the defense budget, because such phenomena are not testable. Tiger doesn't claim his theories lend themselves to the latest radioimmunoassay techniques. He simply observes that microevents inside the human brain are part and parcel of the world of ideas; that endorphin, serotonin, and enzymes X, Y, and Z are just as much the reason for wars, revolutions, and human rights manifestos as scarce natural resources or territorial disputes.

But since we're eons away from a surefire scientific solution to war, let's turn to the more tractable problem of individual violence.

What Makes Charley Run?

THE "CHARLEY" of this story is actually a composite of several real sailors, but we'll speak of him as though he were one hard-living young man, with a bad service record and a chemical glitch in his brain. Charley's troubles started long ago. As far back as grade school, his fidgety, impulsive ways and hair-trigger temper earned him a reputation as a troublemaker. By age seventeen he'd dropped out of school and was drifting from job to job (short-order cook, gas station attendant, meter reader), never sticking around any place too long. His relationships with girls were of the love-'em-and-leave-'em sort. He picked fights in bars and once beat up a traveling salesman in an all-night diner. People in his hometown were relieved when Charley packed his bags and joined the navy.

But if he was an ornery civilian, military life suited him less. For one thing, he had definite problems with authority, and his superior officers didn't appreciate being given the finger. Nor did the navy approve when Charley got drunk one night and pulled a knife on a stranger in a bar. Finally, after he took his rifle down to the railroad tracks and impetuously shot a hole through the window of a passing train, Charley was dishonorably discharged.

He was sent for observation to the National Naval Medical Hospital, in Bethesda, Maryland, where he joined a number of other troublemaking sailors and marines. After taking down the young sailor's life history and administering a few standard psychological tests, the psychiatrists there diagnosed his problem as a "borderline personality disorder." That's psychiatric shorthand for cases somewhere between sociopathy and florid psychosis—meaning that Charley suffered from occasional delusions but was not clearly psychotic. Then, in a scenario remote from the beer-soaked pool halls of his youth, Charley went on to make medical history.

Brain researchers from the nearby National Institute of Mental Health were called in to study Charley's spinal fluid and that of thirty-seven other equally maladapted servicemen for clues to what made them so hyperaggressive. What they turned up was a deficiency of serotonin, the same neurotransmitter we met earlier in the UCLA monkeys.

Because there are laws against "sacrificing" human subjects, be they graduate students or dishonorably discharged servicemen, the scientists couldn't actually measure the sailors' brain chemicals. (That's why we know so much about the chemistry of rat aggression—the brains of violent rats have consistently shown defects in serotonin transmission—and so little about man's.) But there are ways around that impasse. As serotonin is metabolized in the body, it breaks down into a chemical called 5–HIAA, which shows up in a person's blood, urine, and cerebrospinal fluid.

Reasoning that levels of spinal fluid 5–HIAA might tell them something about human aggression, two scientists from NIMH, Gerald Brown and Frederick Goodwin, entered Charley's case. Between 1978 and 1980, they analyzed the spinal fluid of thirty-eight servicemen at the naval hospital; because they worked independently of the psychiatrists who made the clinical diagnoses, they did not know beforehand which vial of milky fluid corresponded to which case history. Imagine their satisfaction when they got a near-perfect match.

The truculent servicemen not only had generally low levels of 5–HIAA, but the more violent each man's history and psychological profile, the lower his 5–HIAA. A graph of the 5–HIAA scores and "mean aggression scores" on psychological tests approached a neat inverse relationship. Since 5–HIAA in spinal fluid presumably reflects serotonin levels in the brain, the clear implication was that low brain serotonin and impulsive, aggressive behavior go hand in hand.

How does this finding fit with the UCLA monkey study? To McGuire's mind the anarchic servicemen sound a lot like his low-status vervets, who are likewise cursed with low serotonin. In these cases random aggression is not the mark of dominance, but quite the opposite. "If you drive serotonin down in the monkeys," he tells us, "you make them nasty, hostile, bitchy, crazy. It's hard to know what an antisocial monkey is, but if you equate it with stealing things and so forth, the ones who are given a serotonin downer are more that way. The dominant male follows the rules. He sets them and he also follows them. Meanwhile, the other animals are up to all kinds of things when his back is turned.

"Of course," he points out, "the advantage of animals is that you can switch them from dominant to subordinate and back again and look at the same animal in both conditions. But people—well, you get a bunch of people who have been filtered through a social system that goes back hundreds of years, and they're finally called sociopaths, for better or worse. God knows what the effects are. You certainly can't shift them around overnight."

Suicidal Brains

BROWN AND GOODWIN, meanwhile, didn't rest on their laurels. They soon turned up a second, interesting correlation: A number of their wild bunch had tried to commit suicide, some of them repeatedly. And these suicidal servicemen had lower 5–HIAA levels than their nonsuicidal peers. "If a man was very aggressive, he was likely to have low 5–HIAA," Brown explains in a voice that, like many of the voices around NIMH, has a faint, languorous trace of a southern accent. "If he was suicidal, he was also likely to have low 5–HIAA. If he was both aggressive and suicidal, he was almost sure to have abnormally low 5–HIAA."

What does it all mean? Nearly a century before serotonin or its obscure-sounding metabolite 5–HIAA was heard of, Sigmund Freud theorized that suicide was really aggression turned inward. "My work has convinced me that Freud was right," confides Brown, who is a practicing psychoanalyst as well as a neuroscientist. "Suicide and aggression have the same source in the brain." Low serotonin, Brown and his co-workers believe, is a signal of impulsiveness that may lead to violence toward others or toward one's self.

How much can you generalize from the bodily fluids of three dozen malcontent sailors? Not much, if they were an isolated case. But suddenly many pieces of an elaborate neurobiological puzzle begin to fit together.

Two years before Charley and his gang donated their spinal fluid to science, researchers in Sweden turned up an unexpected connection between low 5–HIAA and suicide. The patients in question were being hospitalized for depression, and those with the lowest 5–HIAA levels, as it happened, had tried to do away with themselves violently—using shotguns rather than sleeping pills, for instance. The story has a rather macabre sequel. The scientists separated the patients into two groups on the basis of 5–HIAA scores and followed up on them two years later. To their horror one-fourth of the low-5–HIAA people were dead, the victims of successful suicide.

Since then several different experimenters have been able to look inside the brains of suicide victims and compare them with the pickled brains of people who died of other causes. What they saw there was evidence that the serotonin receptors, the sites where the chemical binds to the brain, were unusually sparse.

One likely practical payoff from all this is a routine chemical test for suicide risk. And it's not so farfetched to envision tomorrow's psychiatrists prescribing suicide-prevention pills to the suicide-prone. "A pharmacologist at Eli Lilly," Gerald Brown tells us, "has just published an interesting study. He gave animals a new antidepressant drug that increases serotonin levels in the brain, and he also gave them tryptophan, an enzyme that is a serotonin precursor. When administered alone, the antidepressant has only short-lived effects on serotonin metabolism. But when combined with tryptophan, it enhances it for a long time.

"I don't want to raise anyone's hopes prematurely. But something like that could turn out to be an antisuicide drug."

The Case of the Missing Biochemical

OKAY, but what about aggression *toward others*? Was the violence/low 5–HIAA connection found in Charley's gang just a laboratory curio or something more fundamental? Finally, will Eli Lilly or Hoffman-LaRoche chemists design us a nice "anticrime drug" that boosts the serotonin levels of potential bad guys?

No sooner had Brown and Goodwin published their data, in mid–1982, than a Finnish-born psychiatrist named Markku Linnoila uncovered another clue in the cerebrospinal fluid of twenty-five convicted murderers. The convicts, who had been referred by the courts to the University of Helsinki's forensic psychiatry clinic, fell into two categories: psychopaths, who had committed senseless murders "totally out of the blue," and paranoid murderers, who killed their victims after lengthy premeditation. Linnoila, now at NIMH, and Matti Virkunen, of the University of Helsinki, analyzed the murderers' chemical makeup and reported that the psychopaths had strikingly lower 5–HIAA levels than either the paranoids or normal controls.

While murder's shapes are legion, psychopaths and paranoids are two very distinct classes of perpetrators, in Linnoila's opinion. The former kill violently, without rhyme or reason, and feel no remorse; the latter have well-organized delusional systems. That the two crimes have different chemical "fingerprints" suggests that biology may not be entirely out of place in the courtroom.

Meanwhile, in Sweden, the Case of the Missing Biochemical cropped up again when a group of mass murderers was found to have unusually low 5–HIAA levels. Only one of the convicts had normal levels of the metabolite, in fact, and he was not your garden-variety killer. He turned out to be a mild nursing-home attendant who had quietly performed euthanasia on two dozen aged patients in his care. The Karolinska Institute researchers seem to have stumbled on the provocative fact that Jack the Ripper's rampages and the mercy killings of a brooding stoic philosopher are not the same thing as far as the brain is concerned.

A lack of 5-HIAA in the spinal fluid is supposed to reflect a lack of serotonin in the brain; so what do we know about this neurochemical with a name like a Greek muse? "In most brain tracts," Gerald Brown informs us, "serotonin is inhibitory. And inhibition is one of the basic biological principles governing our organism. Without it, you can't regulate your biochemical pathways, and things go awry. This was the case, if you will, with our very impulsive, antisocial servicemen. Freud saw inhibition as the basis of civilization. In order to have judgment you need to pause, delay, reflect."

A caveat: Don't assume, whenever there's a correlation between biological factor X and behavior Y in a human being, that X (a missing hormone, a chemical imbalance, or whatever) *causes* Y. A little *reductio ad absurdum* will illustrate why. Suppose one social scientist compiles statistics on the average snowfall over ten winters, while another collects data on mean SAT scores during the same period. When a striking statistical correlation turns up between the two, the scientists coauthor a learned paper on "The Effects of Winter Precipitation on Academic Trends," the gist of which is that in snowy weather high-school students stay indoors and study and thus do better on standardized tests. It has an aura of plausibility, but what other, nonmeteorological factors—such as higher pay for teachers—were at work at the same time? If in lieu of SAT scores we had statistics on unmarried couples who live together, would we believe that annual snowfall had an impact on "liberalizing trends in premarital cohabitation"? Of course, conscientious researchers guard against silly correlations by doing controlled studies and screening out other factors, but the point is that *correlation is not necessarily causality.*

Now, a few dishonorably discharged sailors and murderers show signs of low serotonin, while dominant vervet monkeys have the opposite chemical portrait. What's the message here? Would we find high serotonin in the blood of Pentagon think-tankers, heads of states, and student council presidents and low serotonin in outlaws, psychopaths, and pool-hall punks? Maybe, but watch out.

For example: High serotonin, the earmark of "dominance," has sometimes been considered a marker of depression, while other studies muddy things further by suggesting that depression actually involves *low* serotonin.

Low 5–HIAA, for that matter, isn't always the mark of the psychopath, the suicide, or the dead-end kid. "We know there are normal people, who are neither suicidal nor antisocial, who have low 5–HIAA," says Brown. "Interestingly, though, we've yet to find anyone with *high* 5–HIAA who is impulsively aggressive." In the salty bouillabaisse of the brain, serotonin is only one of about two hundred seasonings.

Now imagine we did have an antiaggression drug and that it really could convert a psychopath or a feisty small-time ne'er-do-well like Charley into a sober, civic-minded Jaycee. Who should be given such a drug? What authority shall decide what is "antisocial" and what is socially acceptable behavior? Psychiatric diagnoses come in and out of fashion, after all— yesterday's "pseudoneurotic paranoid schizophrenia" being today's "borderline personality disorder." There's always a danger that the hypothetical "Pacifizine" might be used on the wrong people, just as prefrontal lobotomies were in the 1940s and 1950s.

For a grim vision of antiviolence therapy, you can refer to the moral rehabilitation of Alex the street punk in *A Clockwork Orange*. In real life, of course, "violent brains" have been the subject of some baroque neurosurgical dramas, as we shall see.

The Secrets of the Cerebellum

IN THE LAST CHAPTER we witnessed startling conversions wrought by electrical stimulation of the brain's pain and pleasure centers. We saw that Dr. Robert Heath's brain pacemaker has rescued people afflicted with "intractable behavior pathologies" from a life of padded cells and straitjackets by turning down the fear/rage switch in their heads. Now we'll return to Dr. Heath's astonishing gadget: If a continuous low-voltage electrical current applied to the cerebellum can curb homicidal outbursts, does that mean that violence is an inborn neurologic defect? And that it has nothing to do with, say, growing up in a broken home in the South Bronx with a crazy, alcoholic or drug-addicted mother?

Wrong. When it comes to producing a violent person, the brain and the social environment interact in such intricate ways that the old nature-versus-nurture debate seems rather like those hair-splitting early Christian councils about the precise proportion of humanity/divinity in Christ. The story of the cerebellum is a case in point.

The first clues came from the famous Harlow monkeys. At the University of Illinois in the 1950s and early 1960s, psychologist Harry F. Harlow performed a series of now-legendary experiments in sensory and emotional deprivation, raising infant rhesus monkeys in solitary wire cages without toys or companions. After three months even an obtuse observer couldn't miss the signs of emotional damage. The small monkeys sat forlornly in a corner of the cage rocking back and forth like autistic children. When they came of age and rejoined the colony, their social ineptness was pitiful. Unable to decipher the most rudimentary simian social signals, they could barely distinguish friend from foe, self from nonself. They recoiled in terror from the sight of their own hands and compulsively mutilated themselves. The males never learned to court or mate, while the females who became mothers neglected or abused their babies. Most important, from our perspective, these monkeys were given to outbursts of inexplicable violence.

At first the Harlow monkeys were taken as proof of the psychoanalytic dictum that bad mothering (or in this case, no mothering at all) caused schizophrenia, for the isolated monkeys looked about as "schizophrenic" as is possible for a nonhuman primate to look. But Harlow confounded the Freudians by separating rhesus infants from their mothers and raising them with age mates. These monkeys developed quite normally. What crucial sensory lack, then, was causing the "deprivation syndrome"? A former colleague of Harlow's, William A. Mason, devised an ingenious experiment in the late 1960s to find out.

Mason compared three groups of young monkeys: One group was reared in the usual way with their mothers. A second group grew up with a "movable surrogate," consisting of a motorized, swinging bleach bottle; while a third group of infants got a stationary surrogate, a bleach bottle covered with fur and fixed in place. The result? The monkeys reared with their mothers, of course, grew up normally, and the monkeys whose only solace was a fixed surrogate developed a bad case of the deprivation syndrome. The monkeys given the movable surrogate, however, surprised the psychologists by being much less screwed up. Was movement crucial to emotional development?

James W. Prescott, a developmental psychologist then working at the National Institute of Child Health and Human Development (NICHD), thought so. He managed to get hold of five of the emotionally stunted Harlow monkeys, whose weird stereotypic rocking motions reminded him of some of the institutionalized children he'd seen. Any kind of sensory deprivation must damage the growing brain's emotional systems, he figured. Noticing that an *immobile* surrogate produced such basket cases, his thoughts turned to the cerebellum, the three-lobed structure at the very back of the brain that governs movement and balance.

"At that time," he recalls, "there was very little data to support my theory that stimulation of the cerebellum might have something to do with emotions. Actually, back around 1800, Franz Joseph Gall, the father of phrenology, said the cerebellum was involved in pleasure or lack of pleasure, but he was discredited because of the phrenology stuff. . . .

"Anyway," he continues, "I thought we'd find a neuropathology in the isolation-reared animals, so I shipped them to Tulane so Bob Heath could implant them. I suggested that he put electrodes in the cerebellum as well as the limbic sites." Where other investigators had failed to find anything wrong with these sensory-deprived brains, Heath's electrodes detected a great deal amiss. There were abnormal "spike" discharges in the monkeys' limbic pain-and-pleasure areas, very like the pathological EEGs of violent human psychotics. And, to be sure, strange spikes also occurred in the cerebellum, where Heath had never thought to look before.

"The paleocerebellum, or old cerebellum, governs propioception," Heath explains. "That's the input from your muscles, joints, and tendons that lets you know what position your body is in, where you're located in three-dimensional space. It also regulates balance, your vestibular sense. Now, why do children like to be tossed in the air, hang upside down, and ride merry-go-rounds and roller coasters? Because these sensory experiences feed directly into the emotional system."

Hard evidence came from the sad-eyed Tulane lab monkeys in their little plastic restraining chairs. As electrodes in different sites of their brains recorded second-to-second electrical changes, Heath showed that bursts of activity in the paleocerebellum set off similar ones in the septum, hippocampus, and amygdala, and vice-versa. The upshot was that the cerebellum, the limbic pain/pleasure centers, and various sensory relay stations were all part of one circuit! This was not just a heretical rewriting of neuroanatomy—the textbook drawings of nerve tracts don't show cerebellar-forebrain connections—but it explained to Heath how the isolation-reared monkeys got so weird. Messages from our eyes, ears, and skin, as well as the body-sense signals processed in the paleocerebellum, stir trains of electrical impulses in the distant emotional centers, setting in motion a giant emotional-sensory feedback loop. (We all can testify to how quickly a Mozart sonata or a good massage travels to our "pleasure center.") Imagine, then, the effects of sensory isolation on an immature brain.

"We already knew from human studies," Heath tells us, "that if you're suspended in weightlessness you'll hallucinate, have delusions, and experience what is known as depersonalization." Heath sees a curious connection between body sense and sense of self in the shattered inner world of psychosis, for a psychotic's body image is distorted along with his ego. "Psychotics, you know, often say they feel unreal or don't know who they are—that's depersonalization," he says. "And typically that lack of self-awareness can be detected long before the classic symptoms of halluci-

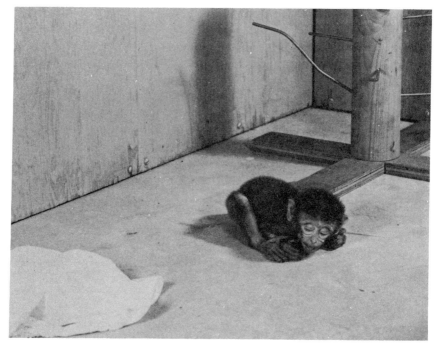

The deprivation syndrome: In a series of famous experiments performed by psychologist Harry Harlow, baby monkeys reared in isolation cringed in the corners, rocking forlornly like autistic children. They also became withdrawn, socially inept, violent, and incapable of mating. (*University of Wisconsin Primate Laboratory*)

nations and thought disorders appear." Could an impaired cerebellum or faulty cerebellar-limbic nerve connections be responsible?

Heath went on to develop the cerebellar pacemaker and implant it in the heads of violent mental patients, some of whom improved dramatically. James Prescott, meanwhile, was embarked on a course of research that would leave him jobless, without funds, and mired in bitter lawsuits against his superiors at the NICHD.

Love Versus Violence

"I'M NOW CONVINCED," says Prescott, "that the root cause of violence is deprivation of physical pleasure. When you stimulate the neurosystems that mediate pleasure, you inhibit the systems that mediate violence; it's like a seesaw."

During his fifteen-year stint at the NICHD, Prescott sought a cure for violence as religiously as other researchers hunt for a cancer cure. The bearded, gentle-voiced neuropsychologist started the NICHD's Developmental Behavioral Biology Program specifically to trace the origins of hostility in the developing brain. In particular, he wanted to answer some questions about child abuse, since abused children often grow into violent adults, and it was his single-minded crusade on these subjects that would put him on a collision course with the whole, sprawling, concrete-and-chrome Health, Education and Welfare (HEW) bureaucracy.

"A whole variety of experiments," he tells us, "have shown how plastic and changeable the mammalian brain is. You can change the function of certain brains cells by rearranging the sensory environment: Cats raised in a planetarium environment, for instance, can only see spots and dots.

"The primate brain is especially immature at birth and depends on sensory stimulation for normal growth. In cases of extreme somatosensory deprivation—that is, touch and movement—the brain systems that normally mediate pleasure don't develop at all." When that happens, the organism, whether it's an isolation-reared monkey or a child locked in a closet, tends to become violent.

Wandering away from neurohardware to test his hypothesis, Prescott asked whether child-care customs might have a bearing on a society's overall violence. "We'd expect that cultures that give infants a lot of physical affection—touching, holding, and carrying—would be less physically violent," he says, "and they are." The neuropsychologist confirmed his hunch in anthropological studies of forty-nine cultures, from the peace-loving Maoris to the martial Comanches. Theft, child abuse, and customs of "killing, torturing, or mutilating the enemy" were uncommon or even absent in the nurturing cultures. When the statistics were run through the computer, a society's ranking on the Infant Physical Affection Scale predicted its rate of "adult physical violence" in 73 percent of the cases—an accuracy rate that Prescott says would occur by chance only four times out of a thousand.

That today's love-starved baby may be tomorrow's hard-core felon, rapist, child molester, or wife beater is hardly a revolutionary proposition. But Prescott insists that the early emotional environment shapes the physical structure of a child's brain and not just the hazy contours of its ego. He can rattle off evidence that sensory deprivation during the brain's formative period harms the endorphin system (an obvious chemical pleasure pathway) and stunts the fine, filigreelike branching of the cell dendrites. All this, he says, reduces the normal two-way traffic between cerebellum and forebrain, resulting in permanently warped "pleasure circuits" *and* violent behavior. The whole pathology can actually be seen in the abnormal cerebellar "spike discharges" that Heath and his colleagues were picking up down in New Orleans in the early 1970s.

"One of the things I was trying to do, and I was blocked by my boss at NICHD, was to screen prisoners with a history of violent behavior to see if they have this spiking activity," Prescott tells us in his *sotto voce.* "Professor Bernard Saltzburg, who headed the Tulane research program, developed a computer analysis method to detect these deep brain spikes from ordinary scalp EEG recordings. I was excited because here was a possible neurodiagnostic technique for identifying impaired brain function in violent criminals. That could translate into saving lives!"

In 1978 Prescott was invited by the Federal Bureau of Prisons to give a scientific seminar on "spikes" in inmates' brain waves, and that's when his troubles started. The NICHD had a new director, Dr. Norman Kretchmer (a former president of the American Pediatric Association), who didn't share Prescott's interests, and he forbade Prescott to speak to the prison people on government time. Prescott asked permission to speak on his own time, and when he didn't get a response, he went ahead and gave the seminar during his vacation. Unfortunately, Prescott returned to his office to discover that Kretchmer had red-inked even this request.

The psychologist filed formal grievances with the NIH and HEW, charging Kretchmer with "Obstruction of Science and the National Health Interest" and other sins of official misconduct. When his jeremiads fell on deaf ears, he went public, firing off two dozen letters (on NICHD letterhead) to a potpourri of scientific associations.

On April 11, 1980, Prescott got his dismissal papers, which read: "Removal for improper use of official position and resources to promote research on 'developmental origins of violence' and 'child abuse and neglect,' subjects that are not within the mission of the NICHD as part of the programs of this institute." The agency had been spending a hefty two million a year on child-abuse research, retorts Prescott, who claims he was really fired from his $43,000-a-year job in retaliation for whistle-blowing. Why was Kretchmer so dead set against child-abuse research? "Who knows?" Prescott tells us.

During the ensuing brouhaha, the NICHD boss confided to *The Child Protection Report (CPR)*, a newsletter, that Jim Prescott sometimes did things that were "a little weird." One of those things was publishing theories on child abuse in a 1977 issue of *Hustler* magazine (which is not *Archives of General Psychiatry*, after all). Kretchmer told *CPR*'s editor and publisher William E. Howard that the graphic photos of battered children accompanying Prescott's text were designed for readers to "get off" on (a statement Kretchmer later denied after Howard published it but that Howard insists is an accurate quote).

Prescott says public service (he received no money for the article), not prurience, inspired him to proclaim his message in a skin magazine. At the same time, he's an apostle of "body pleasure" as an antidote to violence and an impassioned foe of paternalism and authoritarianism, and perhaps aspects of his antiestablishment pleasure principle did rattle some non-hedonic superegos around the NIH. For all his brilliance, Prescott occasionally sounds like a man who has spent too many hours in a hot tub.

"To experience profound states of consciousness," he explains, "you've got to have the neural equipment. Sensory experience must be integrated into higher brain centers, and that requires a cerebellar-limbic-neocortex connection." Ours is the age of violence and the quick fix, according to Prescott. Massage parlors, Forty-second Street pornography, alcohol, drugs, rape, sadomasochism, and other cheap thrills are imperfect substitutes for "genuine, integrative pleasure." Unfortunately many of us can't experience the latter, because our cultural anhedonia has stunted our neural pleasure systems.

"Our Judeo-Christian tradition is based on *denial* of the body," Prescott tells us. "Look at the ultimate message of Christianity—the crucifixion, mutilation, the agonizing death on the cross. Then you have hair shirts, self-flagellation, the whole penitential movement.

"If you read about St. Theresa's ecstasies or the hallucinations of St. John of the Cross, you'll find some very illuminating passages that reflect the damage of sensory deprivation. I think it's the same phenomenon as the isolation-reared monkeys who bit and mutilated themselves in the absence of sensory stimulation. You see it in deprived children, too."

In place of an ascetic metaphysics, Prescott endorses a sort of new-age sexual mysticism. Its priests are more likely to be priestesses, for in Prescott's view, women possess the "neurocircuitry essential to real spirituality"—that is, rich nerve connections between the cerebellum and the higher brain centers. The cerebellum, he thinks, may be responsible for the fact that female orgasms are full of floating, out-of-the-body sensations and quasi-mystical feelings of union. He did a survey on this subject a few years ago and reported that men's sexual experiences, in contrast, are usually "reflexive," knee-jerk reactions.

"You don't need a supernatural deity at all," he says, "if you belong to a physically affectionate, caring culture. We need to examine the biological basis of our metaphysics. We're violating our natural pleasure systems, then looking for a reward in heaven—which, ironically, is supposed to be a pure pleasure state."

Meanwhile, back at the establishment, Prescott's appeal to get his job back was turned down, prompting *The Child Protection Report* to write that his case was "taking on all the trappings of an old-fashioned railroading." The *Federal Employee* ran an article entitled "NIH Hatchet Job on

Distinguished Scientist." Prescott filed lawsuits against Kretchmer and the government, and several divisions of the American Psychological Association championed his cause. As for Kretchmer, he left the NICHD unceremoniously in the summer of 1981, amid rumors of other official complaints against him, and took a job as a professor of nutrition at the University of California at Berkeley.

That didn't help Jim Prescott very much. His dismissal left him stone broke, in debt to lawyers, and so stigmatized that he couldn't land another job. He had to withdraw all the money from his government pension fund to live on, and then, in his words, a "domino effect" followed, in which he lost his house and ultimately his marriage. When we last talked to him he was beginning to put the pieces back together by doing independent consulting work and trying to raise funds for the Violence Prevention Network, of which he is president. (Actor Daniel J. Travanti, star of TV's "Hill Street Blues," is national chairman of the Network.)

The Crocodile Man

Here the face of the prostrate felon slips, sharpens into a snout and withdraws its ears as a snail pulls in its horns. Between its lips the tongue, once formed for speech, thrusts out a fork.

—DANTE, *The Inferno*, Canto XXV

SUPPOSE that cerebellar spike discharges are diagnosed in the brain of an accused murderer. The defendant's lawyer summons Heath, Prescott, or other expert witnesses to explain about brain-wave spikes, rage centers, and the neurobiological origins of violence. Then he argues that his client, burdened with a grave biological defect, could not control his homicidal impulses. The jury votes to convict him of a lesser charge (manslaughter, say) or not to convict him at all.

The "diminished-capacity" defense reached its nadir, perhaps, at the murder trial of Dan White, the disgruntled San Francisco ex-supervisor who fatally shot Mayor George Moscone and supervisor/gay activist Harvey Milk in 1978. White's attorney argued that a diet of junk food had addled his client's mind. The jury must have been impressed, for White spent only three years in prison for a double homicide. Although diminished capacity is no longer a legal defense in California, the infamous "Twinkie defense" illustrates the kind of moral and legal quandaries biology-of-violence research can stir up. What degree of "brain damage" constitutes "diminished capacity" or insanity? Who is responsible for his actions, and who is not? And what "expert opinion" should we trust, given that the brain is a vast world and current diagnostic methods can only probe a few outlying hamlets?

In their book *The Crocodile Man: A Case of Brain Chemistry and Criminal Violence*, authors André Mayer and Michael Wheeler recount the real-life case of a young man they call Charles Decker. "Decker" had reportedly picked up two hitchhiking teenage girls and proceeded to beat them over the head with a stonemason's hammer. He stopped just short of killing them, and stricken with guilty second thoughts, dropped the victims off at a nearby house and turned himself in to the authorities.

Decker's father happened to be an endocrinologist, and he called up a friend, Dr. Mark Altschule, the noted Harvard Medical School diagnostician, for advice. After pondering young Decker's case—his history of sudden, uncontrollable outbursts, the fit of sudden, senseless savagery, and the abrupt remorse—Altschule found parallels in the book *Violence and the Brain*, by Harvard neurosurgeons Vernon H. Mark and Frank R. Ervin. Under Mark and Ervin's reign in the 1960s, no small number of psychotics and violent felons left Massachusetts General and Boston City Hospital with electrodes in their amygdalae (and, in some cases, Delgado-designed "stimoceivers" atop their skulls). These violent people, Mark and Ervin proclaimed, suffered from an organic brain disorder they baptized the "episodic dyscontrol syndrome."

The concept borrows heavily from Paul MacLean's triune brain theory (Chapter 2), according to which a primitive reptilian brain lurks in the deepest layers of human neural tissue like a Minotaur in a cave. Normally, Mark and Ervin theorize, our newer, more evolved "brains," the neocortex and (especially) the limbic system, keep the oldest brain under wraps. But if the limbic control apparatus goes haywire, the ancient, reflexive, unthinking reptile brain can dart out, undoing 400 million years of evolution in an instant. (*Violence and the Brain* contains drawings of a crocodile brain posed against the human organ.)

Convinced that Decker had the classic symptoms of "dyscontrol," Altschule proceeded to test him for chemical abnormalities. A glass of Tab spiked with alcohol produced what appeared to be a toxic breakdown product in the young man's blood, and this became the putative cause of his "dyscontrol." As an expert witness for the defense, Altschule managed to persuade the judge—the heavy scientific testimony was deemed too complex for a jury to follow—that a biochemical jinx provoked Decker's loss of self-control. At one point Decker's lawyer solemnly "moved his pointer from a silhouette of the human brain to a second, contrasting diagram labeled *crocodile*." The result: The modern-day Crocodile Man got a suspended sentence and six years' probation for bashing in the skulls of two young girls.

In a thoughtful review of the *Crocodile Man*, published in *The Sciences*, Ashley Montague, the anthropologist, exposes the neurological voodoo surrounding the case. He writes: "The fact is that the limbic system and the triune brain are artifacts, creations of neuroanatomists, part of what I would call 'the higher phrenology,' and nothing more. Despite its reification, the idea of three brains in one is anatomically and physiologically unsound; there is only one brain. . . ."

Montague has a point. Triune-brain aficionados sometimes speak as if the bestial ghosts of our evolutionary past could actually rear up on their furry or scaly hind legs to haunt us. While there certainly are relics of primitive brain structures within our highly developed cerebrums, human beings are *not* snakes or salamanders. The fact is that reptile behavior is more or less prewired—a salamander's brain is elegantly designed for catching flies, but remove the local insects and you have a starved salamander—whereas ours is not. We come into the world with a small repertoire of programmed behaviors and a near-infinity of choices, and you might say that choice makes a "superego" possible.

Can a biochemical anomaly erase that and toss us back to the primeval swamps? Montague thinks not, and he's probably right:

Experiments in neuropharmacology have shown clearly that dysfunctions in the chemistry of the brain can substantially affect behavior ranging from mood to murder. But this would not be taken to imply, as was done in the case of the Crocodile Man, that chemical changes alone determine a person's actions. Every human brain has a long individual history. . . . To some extent, all behavior depends on previous sensory inputs and experiences. That a reptilian brain can, on occasion, overcome the master-controlling power of the new brain I gravely doubt.

Amygdalectomy, Demonology

Now what does all this have to do with the mind/brain question?

Biological determinists assert that the mind is "in" the brain, and there's a curious tendency among the biology-of-violence people to speak as if violence were "in" the twin amygdalae (or the hypothalamus, or the brain stem, or wherever) like a resident demon. The new demonology may have hit its apogee at a prison hospital in Vacaville, California, where, in 1968, three inmates had parts of their amygdalae burned out with electrodes to exorcise their violence. (The prisoners gave their consent, but some people question whether inmates are in a position not to consent.) The man overseeing the surgery was Dr. R. R. Heimberger, of the University of Indiana, a longtime fan of amygdalectomy as a treatment for epilepsy and violence.

Amygdalectomy has been known to change vicious animals into cuddlesome Disney-like creatures, but the operations reportedly worked no such miracles in the three prisoners. Even if amygdalectomy had pacified the men, it would not have proved that violence is "in" two almond-shaped structures behind the temples. As James Olds, the late dean of the "plea-sure center," was wont to point out, there are no real centers in the brain, only complex, overlapping "pathways." The fact that lesioning, stimulat-ing, or otherwise tinkering with one of those pathways may switch on ecstasy, rage, or fear doesn't mean that the emotions actually reside in the tissue. (Having part of your liver removed might make you depressed, too, but melancholia clearly isn't "in" the liver.)

Mark and Ervin, the authors of *Violence and the Brain,* seem to locate pathological violence in the "old" amygdala, the portion we share with crocodiles (the more recently evolved half of the amygdala, according to the authors, is more civilized). And their book contains the following terse pronouncement about criminally violent "dyscontrol" victims: "Hoping to rehabilitate such a violent individual through psychotherapy or education, or to improve his character by sending him to jail or by giving him love and understanding—all these methods are irrelevant and will not work. It is the malfunction itself that must be dealt with, and only if this fact is recognized is there any chance of changing his behavior."

Mark and Ervin took that ideology a step further in a 1967 letter to the *Journal of the American Medical Association,* coauthored with Dr. William Sweet, chief of neurosurgery at Massachussetts General Hospital. Some of the people chucking rocks at police cars during the inner-city riots then sweeping the country, the neurosurgeons suggested, might be suffering from localized brain damage as well as sociopolitical malaise. "The real lesson of the urban rioting," they wrote, "is that, besides the need to study the social fabric that creates the riot atmosphere, we need intensive re-search and clinical studies of the individuals committing the violence."

In *Physical Control of the Mind,* José Delgado, too, ruminates on the neurophysiology of riots: "It would be naive to investigate the reasons for a riot by recording the intracerebral electrical activity of the participants but it would be equally wrong to ignore the fact that each participant has a brain and that determined neuronal groups are reacting to sensory inputs and are subsequently producing the behavioral expression of violence." While Delgado, at least, balks at the logistical difficulties of herding angry Watts residents into stereotaxic devices, notice that he states that "neuronal groups . . . reacting to sensory inputs" *produce* violent behavior. What is wrong with this picture?

Accustomed to turning behaviors on and off with the flick of a switch, the electrode brotherhood sometimes falls into the most unabashed sci-entific reductionism. Admittedly without neurons, chemical transmitters, and such, there would be no behavior at all. (We'll leave aside "computer intelligence" for the moment.) But to equate a mental state—or the still more complicated phenomenon of "violent behavior"—with a population of wet cells is a bold claim indeed. What Mark, Ervin, and Delgado have all done is to leap boldly back and forth between two different domains, the behavior of a whole organism (and even groups of people) and the electrical pulses of certain neurons, without acknowledging that there might be any translation difficulties. And there are.

Consider: To explain human behavior, we could look at groups of people, as sociologists do, or we could perform psychological experiments on individuals. We could also use fine-wire electrodes and tap groups of neurons or even the flickerings of single neurons. But why stop there? If you reflect on it, behavior ultimately depends on molecules in the brain and on the atoms and subatomic particles that compose them. So we might just as well say that quarks "produce" violent behavior. Of course, following elusive quarks around won't give us a scintilla of information about a psychopath's tirades, whereas the electrochemical dances occurring in his amygdala may reveal something interesting, even something clinically useful. But they won't tell us exactly what "produces" violence.

7

Memory:
From Sea Slugs to *Swann's Way*

> We, in a glance, perceive three wine glasses on
> the table; Funes saw all the shoots, clusters and
> grapes of the vine. He remembered the shapes
> of the clouds in the south at dawn on the 30th of
> April of 1882, and he could compare them in his
> recollection with the marbled grain in the design
> of a leather-bound book which he had seen only
> once, and with the lines in the spray which an oar
> raised in the Rio Negro on the eve of the battle
> of the Quebracho. . . . He could reconstruct all
> his dreams, all his fancies. Two or three times he
> had reconstructed an entire day.
>
> —JORGE LUIS BORGES,
> "Funes el Memorioso"

AN ARGENTINE YOUTH falls off his horse one day in a story by
Borges and wakes up with an eidetic memory ("photographic" in
the vernacular). That is to say, he remembers every conversation,
every sight, every sound, every word on every page in every book, the
shape of every leaf of every tree of every forest in his experience. Even
the exact configuration of the shadows at 3:15 P.M. on a certain December
day ten years ago is stored indelibly in his brain. *Everything* is.

A flawless memory turns out to be a dubious blessing, though, because
poor Irineo Funes cannot see the forest for the excruciating detail of the
trees (to say nothing of the microscopic geometry of the leaves, the grooves
in the trunk, and so on). "He was, let us not forget, almost incapable of
general, platonic ideas," Borges writes. "It was not only difficult for him
to understand that the generic term *dog* embraced so many specimens of
differing sizes and different forms; he was disturbed by the fact that a dog
at three-fourteen (seen in profile) should have the same name as the dog
at three-fifteen (seen from the front). His own face in the mirror, his own
hands, surprised him on every occasion." Funes is an *idiot savant*. His
reality is so molecular, so fine grained, that abstractions and generalizations
elude him completely.

That is how Borges imagined it. He could not have known when he wrote his story that a real Funes was living in Russia and being studied by the renowned Soviet neuropsychologist A. R. Luria. In 1968 Luria published a book called *The Mind of a Mnemonist* about "S.," a man with total recall, who could repeat entire conversations verbatim and reproduce complex nonsense formulas twenty years after the fact. Luria spent about thirty years analyzing S.'s methods, one of which was to take "memory walks" along the streets of Moscow, envisioning certain objects placed against buildings, store windows, and statues. When he wanted to recall the items, he would simply imagine the street with the memories strewn along it. But this tactic was not foolproof. "Sometimes I put a word in a dark place and have trouble seeing it as I go by," he wrote in his journal. "In one instance, the word 'box' was placed in front of a gate. Since it was dark there, I couldn't see it."

There were graver problems. Words became fused with images and took on a life of their own, rising up all out of context: "Take the word 'something' . . ." he wrote. "For me there is a dense cloud of steam that has the color of smoke." Since even the most neutral phrase would set off an endless chain of associations, S. was hard put to make sense of simple conversations. Reading was a Herculean task: "Even when I read about circumstances that are entirely new to me, if there happens to be a description, say, of a staircase," he confided, "it turns out to be the one in a house I once lived in. I start to follow it and lose the gist of what I am reading." Overwhelmed by the swarming mass of the particular, S. was as handicapped as the hypothetical Funes. He'd been a newspaper reporter, a stock market analyst, and an efficiency expert, but finally, unable to cope, he was reduced to earning a living as a sideshow memory man.

The Other Side of the Coin

NOW MEET "N. A." He's an amiable forty-five-year-old San Diego man who sports a military crewcut and whose conversation is seasoned with the slang of the late fifties. His ruling obsession is a vast collection of guns, shells, and rocks, which he loves to show off to visitors. N. A. has lived with his mother in the same house for many years, but when he tries to find his way home from woodshop at the V. A. Treatment Center, it is like looking for a strange house on a strange street in a dream. Despite an IQ of 124, he is baffled by TV programs; every time there's a commercial break he loses track of the plot.

N. A.'s affliction is called global anterograde amnesia, which in his case means he's stuck forever in 1960. Unlike the temporary amnesias that soap-opera characters so often fall prey to, his won't be magically reversed by a fresh blow to the head, because the part of N. A.'s brain that is responsible for laying down new memories is damaged beyond repair. In 1960 he was a bright young air force recuit living in a dormitory with a roommate who liked to play around with a miniature fencing foil. One day N. A. turned around at the wrong time, just as his roommate was executing a thrust. The foil entered his nostril and pierced his brain.

Though doctors may not be able help N. A. very much, the reverse is certainly untrue. The things that N. A.—and the better-known "H. M.," who lost his memory stream back in 1953 following an operation for epilepsy—can't remember and the things he *can* are clues in a complicated medical detective drama. Put yourself in N. A.'s shoes:

You have only the haziest recollection of yesterday or even of half an hour ago. You don't know whether the person you're talking to is a perfect stranger or someone you've known for years. You can't hold a job. Your social life evolves around occasional Mah-Jongg games with your mother and her friends and visits from the doctors who study your memory lapses. Although you clearly recall rebuilding the engine of an old Cadillac and driving it halfway across the country in 1958, your every moment since 1960 vanishes behind you as soon as it is lived.

"The outstanding feature of N. A.'s life-style is its constricted regularity," notes the team of University of California scientists who have been observing him for the past nine years, in a 1981 article in the *Journal of Nervous and Mental Disease.* "Only those routines learned through years of living in the same place can be performed reliably. . . . Cooking appears to place a great burden on his memory. . . . He is constantly going through his closets and cupboards, arranging things. Indeed, he seems to express obsessive concern that everything is in its right place and becomes irritated even if the telephone receiver is askew."

H. M., whose amnesia is even more severe than N. A.'s, recently told his doctors: "Every moment is like waking from a dream." Without an ongoing memory stream to connect one moment to the next, H. M. and N. A. are stranded in a perpetual, vacuous present—except that they do have their respective pasts intact. What if the past were also removed, and one had *no memories at all?* The idea is almost unthinkable because in a very important sense you *are* your memories; without them you'd be about as individual as the lobby of a Ramada Inn. Imagine that your entire memory store was surgically removed and transplanted into the brain of Joe X. Who would then be "you," your body without your personal record or Joe X? The private kingdom of our memories gives us "continuity of self," in the words of the Nobel neurophysiologist Sir John Eccles. "The self changes," he notes in *The Self and Its Brain.* "We start as children, and we grow up, we grow old. Yet the continuity of self ensures that the self remains identical, in a sense. And it remains more truly identical than the changing body."

But what is a memory? Is it actually located somewhere in your brain and, if so, where? What is the neural code for memory storage and retrieval? Are particular memories—say, the image of the house you lived in when you were eight years old—stored in particular chunks of brain tissue; in patterns of electrochemical connections (perhaps widely distributed throughout the brain); or in some other way? Are memories filed permanently, and if so, how does the brain manage to pack a lifetime of reminiscences into an organ the size of a melon? (Information theorist John von Neumann once estimated that the memories stored during the average human lifetime would amount to 2.8×10^{20} [280,000,000,000,000,000,000] bits—assuming that nothing is forgotten.)

A physiological mechanism for memory is a sort of Holy Grail in brain science, and not surprisingly. If scientists ever turn up an exact correspondence between a group of neurons and the memory of your first communion, we would be close to knowing how three pounds of wet tissue can house a mind. At the center of this quest is the engram, or "memory trace," which no one has ever seen but which a lot of people believe in.

The Elusive Engram

THE KING of the engram hunters was the venerable physiological psychologist Karl Lashley, who directed the Yerkes Laboratory of Primate Biology, then in Ocean Park, Florida, until 1956. For some twenty-five years Lashley tried to find where a particular memory trace was stored in the brains of rats. He trained his rats to run mazes and then systematically removed section after section of cortex and retested them on the same maze. Sooner or later, he thought, his scalpel would zap the piece of tissue that stored that knowledge, and he would then see a rat with zero maze-running know-how. He was bitterly disappointed. What he observed were rats with massive holes in their cortex stumbling, staggering, and hobbling but nevertheless navigating around the maze. The operations certainly interfered with their performance, but no part of the cortex seemed to matter more than another. The impairment was more or less proportional to the total amount of cortex removed, and Lashley was forced to conclude that the engram didn't reside in any place in particular. Toward the end of his life, in a rather morose paper entitled "In Search of the Engram," he reflected: "This series of experiments . . . has discovered nothing directly about the real nature of the engram. I sometimes feel, in reviewing the evidence on the localization of the memory trace, that the necessary conclusion is that learning just is not possible."

Of course, Lashley knew that learning was possible, and so he formulated a theory of "equipotentiality," according to which all parts of the cortex are equally important for storing information about mazes. The corollary: Memories are widely distributed rather than local.

Lashley's theory was a compromise—and a disappointing one at that—in the search for the memory trace. But even while Lashley was reaching his cul-de-sac, up north, one of the great breakthroughs in memory science was being made, accidentally, by a Canadian neurosurgeon.

Flashbacks in the Temporal Lobe

When one of these flashbacks was reported to me by a conscious patient, I was incredulous. . . . For example, when a mother told me she was suddenly aware, as my electrode touched the cortex, of being in the kitchen listening to the voice of her little boy who was playing outside in the yard.

—WILDER PENFIELD,
The Mystery of the Mind

DR. WILDER PENFIELD wasn't looking for engrams when he performed his historic operations at the Montreal Neurological Institute in the 1940s and 1950s; he was cautiously probing the brains of epileptics with electrodes in order to pinpoint the damaged regions. These patients had to remain conscious throughout so that their responses could guide the surgeon around the mysterious folds of the exposed cortex. If, when he touched a certain site, the patient heard buzzing sounds, Penfield would know he was in the auditory cortex; stimulating an area of the "motor strip," on the other hand, might make the left hand jerk upward like a puppet's. In this way Penfield and his colleague Herbert Jaspers sketched in many of the details (thumb, nose, left toe) of the brain's sensory and motor maps, for which later generations of neurologists would thank them. But that was workaday stuff compared with what the doctors discovered around the temporal lobes.

The late Hughlings Jackson, Penfield's mentor, had observed years earlier that epileptic discharges in the temporal lobes (behind the temples, on either side of the brain) could produce "dreamy states" or "psychical seizures": sensations of déjà-vu, odd reveries, inexplicable feelings of familiarity or strangeness, and so on. When Penfield probed this area of the brain he seemed to summon up *memories*. Actually they were more like sudden flashes of the past—a conversation in a drawing room, the ghostly voice of a child calling, the sound of cars passing outside—complete with all the emotions of the original event. It was as if the surgeon had tapped into some Freudian storage bin: One patient accused him of unleashing her "subconscious."

"It was evident at once that these were not dreams," Penfield mused in his book *The Mystery of the Mind*, written shortly before his death in the mid–1970s. "They were electrical activations of the sequential record of consciousness, a record that had been laid down during the patient's earlier experience. The patient 're-lived' all that he had been aware of in that earlier period of time as in a moving-picture 'flashback.' "

Amazed at what his electrode had conjured from a strip of gray matter, the surgeon tried to disprove the phenomenon, but it did not go away. "D. F. could hear instruments playing a melody," he reported. "I restimulated the same point thirty times (!) trying to mislead her, and dictated each response to a stenographer. Each time I re-stimulated, she heard the melody again. It began at the same place and went on from chorus to verse." In the case of another patient, Penfield placed numbered squares of paper on the surface of her exposed brain to mark each spot he stimulated. Here is a portion of the record, with the numbers matched to points on the temporal-lobe surface:

12—"Yes, I heard voices down along the river somewhere—a man's voice and a woman's voice . . . I think I saw the river."
15—"Just a tiny flash of a feeling of familiarity and a feeling that I knew everything that was going to happen in the near future."
17c—"Oh, I had the same very, very familiar memory, in an office somewhere. I could see the desks. I was there and someone was calling to me, a man leaning on the desk with a pencil in his hand." [At this point Penfield warned D. F. he was going to stimulate, but actually did nothing. Her response: "Nothing."]
18a (stimulation without warning)—"I had a little memory—a scene in a play— they were talking and I could see it—I was just seeing it in my memory."

After seeing small electrical currents miraculously produce many such *tableaux vivants*, Penfield concluded that the brain stores everything its owner has ever experienced and in its original form. After all, didn't his patients recall things of which they had no conscious recollection? And rather than being jumbled or distorted, as one might expect, the "flashbacks" seemed to play themselves out in their proper order like scenes in a movie. "Since the electrode may activate a random sample of this strip from the distant past," he reasoned, "and since the most unimportant and completely forgotten periods of time may appear in this sampling, it seems reasonable to suppose that the record is complete and that it does include all periods of each individual's waking conscious life."

It certainly looked like an engram, but where was it stored? In the tissue of the temporal cortex itself? Penfield thought so at first and accordingly renamed this area the "memory cortex." A few years later, deciding that stimulation there actually "activates a record located a distance from that cortex"—in the diencephalon, or higher brain stem, to be exact—he came to refer to the temporal cortex as the "interpretive cortex."

How to explain the apparent contradiction between Lashley's dead-end quest and the highly localized memory stores of Penfield's patients? One possibility is that memories are coded redundantly, over and over again in various parts of the cortex, so that if one "engram" is wiped out, there's a duplicate somewhere else. (The brain *is* a highly redundant organ, after all.) Or maybe memories are stored as dynamic processes spread over the whole brain, which can nonetheless be triggered from local spots (like Area 17 of the temporal cortex), much as dialing Area Code 202 plugs your telephone into part of Ma Bell's network. Or perhaps what Penfield conjured was not an engram at all.

The idea of an inviolate, if often inaccessible, memory record is pretty sacrosanct in this business. It fits nicely with the notion that truth serums, hypnosis, free-association techniques, as well as electrical brain stimulation, can uncover a lot of dusty antiques in the mental attic. Freud's dictum that "in mental life nothing which has once been formed can perish" remains a central gospel of psychoanalysis. And, of course, there is the Proustian *petite madeleine*, a little pastry in a scallop-shaped shell that launched the world's most celebrated literary flashback.

You remember the incident in *Swann's Way.* Proust, or his narrator alter ego, has a bad cold one day. His mother gives him a petite madeleine and a cup of tea, and the taste of the warm liquid mixed with crumbs sets off existential shudders, as luminous bits of the long-forgotten past float back into his mind. But the state of grace fades almost immediately, and so the narrator detaches his consciousness from the present and concentrates on making the holy moment reappear. Another sip of tea, a few more pastry crumbs, a medley of dismembered visions. Finally he identifies the source of this rapture. Many years ago, when he was a little boy, his great-aunt used to give him madeleines and lime-blossom tea, and this familiar taste is a hot line to the village of his childhood.

Immediately the old grey house upon the street . . . rose up like a little stage set to attach itself to the little pavilion opening on to the garden . . . and with the house the town, from morning to night and in all weathers, the Square where I used to run errands, the country roads we took when it was fine. And as in the game wherein the Japanese amuse themselves by filling a porcelain bowl with water and steeping in it little pieces of paper which until then are without character or form, but the moment they become wet, stretch and twist and take on color and

Marcel Proust: A scalloped pastry launched the original Proustian experience. (*The Bettmann Archive*)

distinctive shape . . . so in that moment all the flowers in our garden and in M. Swann's park, and the water-lilies on the Vivonne and the good folk of the village . . . and the whole of Combray and its surroundings, taking shape and solidity, sprang into being, town and gardens alike, from my cup of tea.

Most of us have probably experienced similar, if less literary, sensations of déjà-vu. But what if Proust's magic muffin recaptured a *phony past*?

Fake Memories THAT POSSIBILITY was raised recently by a University of Washington memory researcher who does not believe in a permanent engram. To psychologist Elizabeth Loftus, memory is not a fastidious court reporter but a bad answering service manned by frazzled or negligent operators. As an extreme example, take the case of the "Hillside Strangler" of Los Angeles.

As the police and prosecutors listened spellbound, Kenneth Bianchi confessed to murdering a string of Los Angeles–area women in 1977 and 1978 as well as two young women in Bellingham, Washington. There was a problem however. As the months dragged on, Bianchi's gruesome story kept flip-flopping. Sometimes he had complete amnesia for the killings.

At another time he said he'd strangled one victim, waitress-prostitute Yolanda Washington, in the back seat of the car while his cousin and accomplice, Angelo Buono, drove. Then he said he remembered walking into the house and seeing his partner choking the woman. At another time he told his lawyers and psychiatrists that he really wasn't sure if he had strangled any of the girls himself or if the details he "remembered" were actually gleaned from police files and interrogations. If he was not a pathological liar, Bianchi's on-again/off-again amnesia raised some weird questions. College students may forget the lists of nonsense words they're asked to memorize in psychology experiments, but was it really possible for someone to "forget" something like mass murdering?

Yes, thought Elizabeth Loftus, who was consulted on the case, it was altogether possible. "From the information we had," she tells us, "there was no way to prove whether he was lying or not. But I think you can manufacture a reality for yourself that is indistinguishable from true reality."

The thrust of Loftus's research is that anyone's memory can be tampered with and falsified after the fact like an embezzler's account ledger. Even solid citizens walk around with their heads full of fake memories. Say a person is shown a "murder suspect" with glasses and straight hair and later overhears someone mention the suspect's curly hair. The witness almost invariably "remembers" a frizzy-haired culprit (often without glasses), according to Loftus. In a series of other "eyewitness" experiments, details supplied by other people inevitably contaminated the memory. Stop signs became yield signs, barns grew up out of thin air, yellow cars turned fire-engine red. And what happens to the underlying "engram"? Loftus thinks it has vanished forever into the limbo of lost things. "It may be that the legal notion of an independent recollection is a psychological impossibility," she says.

As for hypnosis, "truth serums," polygraph tests, and all those other supposed portals to the truth: "There's no way even the most sophisticated hypnotist can tell the difference between a memory that is real and one that's created," she tells us. "If you've got a person who is hypnotized and highly suggestible and false information is implanted in his mind, it may get embedded even more strongly. One psychologist tried to use a polygraph to distinguish between real and phony memory, but it didn't work. Once someone has constructed a memory, he comes to believe it himself."

Now let us journey back to the operating room at the Montreal Neurological Institute. In a paper called "On the Permanence of Stored Information in the Human Brain," published in the *American Psychologist*, Elizabeth Loftus and her husband, Geoffrey Loftus, reexamine the Penfield record with a more jaded eye. Of 1,132 cortical-stimulation patients, they note, only forty reported "experiential flashbacks," the bulk of which consisted of disembodied voices, snatches of music, and vague thoughts. Even the more lifelike recollections, the Loftuses believe, are probably less than faithful to the original. For example, they cite one of Penfield's patients who suddenly saw herself as she had appeared in childbirth. The Loftuses point out that when a patient sees herself from the sidelines, she is more likely reconstructing the experience rather than "reliving" it. Another patient said, "I think I heard a mother calling her little boy somewhere" and said it was "somebody in the neighborhood where I live." But eighteen minutes later, when the same spot was stimulated, she said, "Yes, I hear the same familiar sounds. It seems to be a woman calling. The same lady. That was not in the neighborhood. It seemed to be at the lumberyard." She added that she had never in her life been around a lumberyard. Once again, the Loftuses conclude, this is the case of a patient reconstructing rather than reliving an experience, because it involved a location in which she had never been.

Penfield's conclusions raise other questions. If so much is recorded (*all periods of an individual's waking, conscious life*, no less!), is there any limit to what the human brain can store? If you need to recall, say, the summer of 1965, you really don't want an impeccable, second-to-second replay of June through August 1965. You need something much more distilled: perhaps a handful of "peak experiences" at the beach. *Maybe*, of course, the entire, unexpurgated record of your summer of 1965 is somewhere (dormant) in your brain cells, and it is only in the *retrieval* that you somehow fast-forward past reams of irrelevant details, but that is unlikely. If you were designing the sort of information-processing system a brain is, it would be extremely impractical to store memories permanently in their original form. You need mechanisms for transforming and recording them; for "chunking" information into categories (Baseball Games I Have Attended; Blind Dates I'd Rather Not Have Had); for performing multiple correlations very quickly (Is this cylindrical object a cup? Does this woman remind me of my ex-wife?), and so on.

Is your memory a phonograph record on which the information is stored in localized grooves to be replayed on demand? If so, it's a very bizarre record, for the songs sound different every time they're played. Computer memories *are* assigned to particular "addresses," from which they can be retrieved by typing the correct code. Computers are not supposed to have hazy recollections, add false information, embellish the facts or otherwise change the story. Human memory, in contrast, is more like the village storyteller; it doesn't passively store facts but weaves them into a good (coherent, plausible) story, which is re-created with each telling—like oral epics, the *chansons de geste*, of the Middle Ages.

So how, exactly, does your brain store memories? The principal theories follow.

Cannibal Worms

BACK IN THE 1960s memory researchers became infatuated with the master information-containing molecule, DNA—whose alphabet of nucleotide sequences spells out the shape of your nose, the whorls on your fingertips, and a lot of other things about you—and looked for an analogous code for memory. It couldn't be DNA, of course, because you don't inherit memories. But maybe memories were stored along the amino acid chains of short protein strands. Perhaps there was even a unique protein molecule for each of your recollections. The idea had a certain mystique—after all, immunologic "memory" is coded in this way, with elaborate intracellular mechanisms to distinguish between "self" and foreign tissue, familiar and unfamiliar viruses, and so on. Moreover, if it were true, one might actually *extract* the salient remembering molecules from the brain. Thus ensued a series of picturesque experiments in "memory transfer."

At the University of Michigan in Ann Arbor, a researcher named James V. McConnell worked on training the humble planarian, or flatworm. First he taught a bunch of worms to "scrunch up" at the sight of a flashing light by shocking them just after a light flashed. Then he killed them, ground up their bodies, and fed the mush to a group of untrained planaria. Sure enough, McConnell reported, the "naive" worms also had an aversion to flashing lights. Had they actually ingested a memory when they ate their buddies? McConnell said they did, but the chief of the worm runners took a lot of flak when other researchers failed to replicate his results.

In another famous memory-transfer experiment, at the University of Texas in Houston, mice were injected with purified peptides—short fragments of protein molecules, in this case, eight to fifteen amino acids long—taken from the brains of rats that had been trained to fear the dark. The peptide was dubbed *scotophobin*, Greek for "fear of darkness." The scotophobin recipients reportedly headed straight for the illumined part of a training box, which mice, being nocturnal, normally avoid.

But despite the allure of ingesting knowledge for breakfast and despite some "statistically significant" improvements on the part of some of the passive-learning animals, memory transfer fell out of fashion around the late 1960s. Nowadays most scientists have dropped the idea. For one thing, a one memory–one peptide scheme would require an awful lot of different peptides to store a human being's life story, and from what we know the brain does not have anything like that many. Besides, the cell's proteins have plenty to do without including memory coding in their job description. Most important, if intracellular proteins store memories and other higher mental functions, what does the elaborate code of connections between neurons do? That, of course, brings us to the following theory.

Much Ado at the Synapse

THE THEORY: Memories are encoded in changes in particular synapses. By altering the way one neuron speaks to another ("Fire" or "Don't Fire"), these synaptic events set up particular circuits, called *cell assemblies* or *neural nets*, that correspond to specific memories. This theory was first proposed by the Canadian psychologist Donald Hebb in 1949, and it is the reigning one today.

Here is the basic idea: When a cell is activated—for example, by a learning task with a reward at the end—its synaptic connection is strengthened. With many such strengthened synapses, you get a temporarily excited cell assembly, which is the physiological basis of *short-term memory*. Short-term memory, which lasts for a matter of hours—a couple of days, at most—thus involves transient electrochemical events at many synapses. But how do you get *long-term memory* out of this scheme?

That's trickier, but the hypothesis is that temporary electrochemical changes at the synapse can in time evolve into long-lasting *anatomical* changes. If a neuronal pathway is traversed over and over again, like a well-worn footpath, an enduring pattern is engraved. Neural messages tend to flow along familiar roads, along paths of least resistance.

This idea is curiously reminiscent of the ancient Hindu concept of *samskaras*. In *The Bhagavad-Gita for Daily Living*, Eknath Eswaran defines a *samskara* as "nothing more than a thought repeated over and over a thousand times. . . . A person with an anger samskara, for example, is prone to anger over anything. . . ." Samskaras are "engrams," ghostly traces of past experiences (which in Indian philosophy include the stored experiences of many lifetimes, perhaps back to a dim memory of being a sea anemone). As samskaras slowly accumulate in the subconscious mind like sandbanks along a river, "character" takes form.

"What we call personality," writes Eswaran, "is nothing more than a collection of samskaras. . . . On the one hand it means that there is very little freedom in what we do or even what we think. But on the other hand it means that personality is not really rigid; it too is a process. Though we think of ourselves as always the same, we are remaking ourselves every moment we think. . . ."

*Memories of a
Sea Slug*

IRONICALLY, we owe our best knowledge of the neural mechanics of memory to creatures you might have thought had no memory at all. If you dropped in on a memory seminar at the annual meeting of the Society for Neuroscience these days, you might be in for a shock. The speaker at the podium might not be discussing N. A. or H. M., or even the journeys of rodents around electrified radial mazes, but learning in the leech, the lip reflexes of a trained garden slug called *Hermissenda*, or such microcosmic matters as "Differential Classical Conditioning of a Defensive Withdrawal Reflex in *Aplysia Californica.*"

Aplysia is a brown, splotchy sea slug with a head shaped like a pig's, ears like a hare's, and the body of a tortoise without the shell. It's rather large for a slug, about the size of a human brain, and left to its own devices, *Aplysia* grazes contentedly on sea lettuce in the tide pools off the California coast. Columbia University neuroscientist Eric Kandel and his colleagues were drawn to the simple architecture of *Aplysia*'s nervous system, which consists of only about twenty thousand neurons, many of which are conveniently large enough to be seen by the naked eye. If you want to know the cellular details of learning, Kandel and company reasoned, why not study the simplest biological system that can answer your questions? In the early 1960s, therefore, this uncharismatic snail-without-a-shell was scooped up and shipped to Columbia in great quantities, and Kandel proceeded to draw a meticulous cell-by-cell wiring diagram of its nervous system.

No paragon of intellect, *Aplysia californica* is nonetheless equipped with a humble repertoire of hard-wired reflexes. If anything touches the gill on its back side, for instance, it hastily jerks it back into a little "mantle" it has for that purpose. When Kandel and his colleague James B. Schwartz tried to "teach" aplysia, they worked on modifying this inborn reflex.

First, Kandel and Schwartz squirted a jet of water on *Aplysia*'s gill over and over again. After a while the creature learned to ignore the now-familiar stimulus, and its gill-withdrawal reflex grew more lackadaisical. This is called habituation, a common learned response in humans as well as unicellular beasts. As an extreme of human habituation, consider the "Bowery-el phenomenon" described by Karl Pribram in *Languages of the Brain*: "For many years, there was an elevated railway line (the 'el') on Third Avenue in New York that made a fearful racket; when it was torn down, people who had been living in apartments along the line awakened periodically out of a sound sleep to call the police about some strange occurrence they could not properly define. The calls were made at the times the trains had formerly rumbled past. The strange occurrences were, of course, the deafening silence that had replaced the expected noise."

Sensitization is the opposite: an enhanced response to a stimulus. Habituated to the screech of metal wheels, the Bowery-el neighbors became "sensitized" to silence. If an electric shock accompanies the jet of water, *Aplysia*'s gill withdrawal becomes more vehement. Kandel and Schwartz touched the mantle on *Aplysia*'s back while simultaneously zapping its tail with electricity. After fifteen repetitions or so, the animal reacted to the gentlest prod by violently withdrawing its gill. What the Columbia invertebrate trainers were teaching the sea slug was "classical conditioning," a phenomenon immortalized by Pavlov's dogs, who would salivate at the sound of a bell once it became associated with juicy slabs of meat. It's not *The Education of Henry Adams*, but it is a modest form of learning.

And everything *Aplysia* can do, *Limax, Hermissenda*, and the homely octopus (just to name a few) can do, too. The garden slug *Limax* normally loves potatoes, but when its favorite snack is "punished" with a bitter taste, the creature soon gives spuds a wide berth. (Moreover, its sensitive lips and brain can be surgically removed and trained to respond differently to two food extracts.) The octopus can learn a number of things, including the difference between vertical and horizontal lines, and its huge, simply wired ganglia make it a living neuroanatomy lesson.

At Woods Hole Marine Biological Laboratory, in Massachusetts, Daniel Alkon put a sea slug called *Hermissenda* in one end of a glass tube, flipped on a light at the other end, and then spun the animal on a phonographlike turntable. After a few rounds of this, the trained slugs hesitated and flinched whenever the light went on instead of making a beeline for the illuminated area as uneducated slugs do. In some dim way, *Hermissenda* must remember, *Light precedes rotation*. What's more, Alkon was able to track the memory to changes in the slug's nervous system—and this paved the way for a pioneering experiment in "artificial learning." Alkon's colleague Joseph Farley, of Princeton, performed brain surgery on some untrained sea slugs. Sticking microelectrodes into individual neurons, he used electricity to induce the learning-related membrane changes. When these slugs were sewn up and placed in the training apparatus, they behaved just like their trained brethren.

Meanwhile, back at Columbia, *Aplysia* was becoming a superstar. Kandel and company found that conditioned messages such as *Gill prod means shock* could live on in the slug's memory for hours or even weeks, to judge by its responses. More to the point, the researchers were able to show exactly *where in the animal's nervous system the learning occurred*: at the synapse. The memory was stored in measurable changes in the number of neurochemical *quanta* (or packets) released from specific neurons. Habituation reduced the amount of the chemical messenger, thereby weakening the electrical signal sent to the postsynaptic cell. With sensitization, conversely, more of the chemical squirted into the gap, and a stronger message was relayed. It all made exquisite sense.

Learning the details of Kandel's work is like entering the diminutive, perfect world of a Persian miniature. With intracellular electrodes the scientist recorded the electrical potentials of the cell membrane and matched them to the number of transmitter quanta released into the synapse. Delving deeper, he determined that the amount of transmitter secreted depended on molecular events in the microscopic calcium channels of the membrane. Because the channels at the synaptic terminals are too tiny to record from directly, Kandel and colleague Mark Klein ingeniously inferred their properties from measured changes in the calcium channels of the cell body. Thus the ultimate physiological basis of habituation and sensitization was traced to the minute ebb and flow of calcium ions through semiporous tissue. Kandel did more. With an electron microscope, he showed that the physical structure of a sensitized synapse is different—at least after many, many stimulations—from a normal cell junction. Is this the lasting anatomical change believed to underlie long-term memory? Nobody is sure yet, but at long last, short-term memory has been nailed to a definite cellular mechanism—in *Aplysia californica*, anyway.

Whether the reeducation of *Aplysia* sheds any light on *your* memories— or even a laboratory rat's maze knowledge—is another matter. Certainly the invertebrate work proved beyond a shadow of a doubt that learning involves changes in nerve transmission, just as Hebb said. Kandel thinks more complex learning machines like mammals use the same basic cellular "building blocks" and that a universal "biological grammar of mentation" will one day replace the cognitive language of the psychology laboratory. In a 1979 lecture entitled "Psychotherapy and the Single Synapse" (he's a practicing psychiatrist, as well) he even reflected on synapses on the couch:

When I speak to someone and he or she listens to me, we can not only make eye contact and voice contact, but the action of the neuronal machinery in my brain is having a direct and, I hope, long-lasting effect on the neuronal machinery in his or her brain, and vice-versa. Indeed, I would argue that it is only insofar as our words produce changes in each other's brains that psychotherapeutic intervention produces changes in patients' minds.

Kandel is certainly correct about the building blocks, for nature has a habit of using the same materials—such as the endorphins that circulate through human beings and leeches alike—over and over again. And it's no doubt true that thoughts can change your brain. But if you're waiting for a unified field theory of memory, you may have to wait a long time.

Even if the ion channels of rabbits, first-graders, and presidents did behave exactly like *Aplysia*'s, those cellular details won't necessarily be the Rosetta stone of mammalian memory. We need to know other things besides. How are the synaptic changes organized into circuits? Which regions of the brain are important? Is there one kind of memory or many? What is the flow diagram of information-processing events and how does that add up to the memory of your senior prom?

The Memory Trace Found?

"WE HAVE BEEN the first to demonstrate unequivocally in a mammalian brain a memory trace that is highly localized," Stanford neurophysiologist Richard F. Thompson announced at the 1983 convention of the Society for Neuroscience. The brain Thompson was discussing belonged to a rabbit, and his lecture was entitled "The Memory Trace Found?"—a note of bravado in this understated universe where talks on "The Relationship Between Simple and Complex Spike Responses of Cerebellar Purkinje Cells Located in Identified Corticonuclear Zones" and "The Localization of β-NGF mRNA in Tissue Sections Using in Situ Hybridization" are the norm. In any case, all several hundred metal folding chairs in the auditorium were occupied.

Thompson's rabbit was put through a simple course of classical (Pavlovian) conditioning, basically, a modification of an eyelid-closing reflex. A tone sounds, immediately followed by an unpleasant puff of air to the animal's eyeball. After a few repetitions the animal squeezes its eyes shut whenever it hears the tone—its memory, of course, providing the link between the two stimuli.

That particular memory trace, Thompson reports, is actually stored in a particular cubic millimeter of brain tissue. Using surgery or chemicals to destroy a patch of neurons deep in the cerebellum, Thompson and coworker David McCormick managed to accomplish what Lashley could not: the total extinction of a learned response. After surgery the rabbit no longer closes its trained eye when it hears the tone and cannot be retrained. It's not that it can't physically shut its eyelid—it will still do so as a reflex— or that it can't hear the tone. Thompson and McCormick showed that it can. The loss, they say, is specific to the *memory* of the tone/air-puff association.

The auditorium lights dim and a green oscilloscope fills the movie screen. A white rabbit, looking just like one of the floppy bunnies in a Beatrix Potter tale, crouches nervously in a sort of metal dishtray. There's a tone and an air puff, and a little flotilla of EEGs crosses the oscilloscope screen. We see histograms of cerebellar activity "during the CS [conditioned stimulus] period." We see the white bunny hopping around the lab, pausing to nuzzle somebody's flannel pants cuffs (no motor damage after lesion).

Thompson believes that the cerebellum contains some of the hardware essential to classical conditioning, at least with "aversive" stimuli. But it is not the sole seat of rabbit memory. When the scientist complicated the lesson by putting a half-second pause between tone and air puff, his rabbits had to call on higher brain regions for assistance. A rabbit without an intact hippocampus can't learn this task, although it can master the simpler one. "We don't know exactly where the trace is stored, but it is just a matter of time," Thompson concludes.

Fragment from an Imaginary Science

These strangely disturbing eye blinks (which caused the whole phenomenal world to vanish and materialize again like an apparition in a fairy tale) were always preceded by the same dolorous tone and the same exquisite pangs of déjà-vu, as if in the brief, tenebrous passage between unconditioned stimulus and conditioned stimulus the rabbit foretasted the inevitable evil winds, the miniature siroccos that would sweep through his consciousness, stirring febrile waves on the luminous, emerald sea of the oscilloscope. Perhaps the memory was preserved, whole and uncorrupted as the corpse of a saint, cloaked in the sensual folds of the cerebellum, just as within the infinitesimal, ion-soaked membranes of *Aplysia*, traces of past associations linger for days, until the minute interstices of the synapse itself assume the same shape, like a delicately molded *pâté*, and I wondered for the first time whether one might disturb the muse of memory herself.

—A mock-Proustian view of the learned eyelid response

WOULD ANY SANE PERSON think of translating the data of the behaviorist lab into the syntax of Proust, or vice-versa? Of course not. But *why* is this a weird and impossible hybridization experiment, like cross-breeding a cow and a sea urchin? One problem, of course, is that we're dealing with two different species, namely, laboratory rabbits and turn-of-the-century French literati. The other difficulty has to do with language, and we don't mean French. In the tongue of experimental psychology, "memory" may be a simple conditioned reflex; in Proust, it's a rococo interior journey through Parisian high society, the battles of the First World War, and a hundred loves, sorrows, and disenchantments. And the fact is that your memory is much more like *Remembrance of Things Past* than it is like a stimulus/response machine. We're not suggesting that behaviorists should study Proust, only that you should guard against the reverse anthropomorphism of attributing to humans the motivations of lab animals.

Proust was not a scientist in the formal sense, but notice how, in the madeleine episode, he systematically experiments with his own senses: "I decided to make it [the state of consciousness] reappear. I retrace my thoughts to the moment at which I drank the first spoonful of tea. I rediscover the same state, illuminated with no fresh light. I ask my mind to make one further effort . . ." He frames hypotheses ("Undoubtedly what is thus palpitating in the depths of my being must be the image, the visual memory which, being linked to that taste, is trying to follow it into my conscious mind") and painstakingly tests them out. He refines his methods again and again and formulates a sophisticated theory of memory: that taste and smell, the senses to which the conscious mind pays least attention, are conduits to buried information:

But when from a long-distant past nothing subsists, after the people are dead, after the things are broken and scattered, taste and smell alone, more fragile but more enduring, more insubstantial, more persistent, more faithful, remain poised a long time, like souls, remembering, waiting, hoping, amid the ruins of all the rest; and bear unflinchingly, in the tiny and almost impalpable drop of their essence, the vast structure of recollection.

(Perhaps the reason smells are so evocative is that the olfactory nerve fibers project directly to the memory and emotion structures in the amygdala and hippocampus, whereas visual signals are filtered through several intermediate processing stations first.)

Much as Proustian memory is poorly translated into the idiom of drives and reinforcement, analogous, if less obvious, language barriers separate one scientific domain from another. Moving down the biological scale from, say, the level of social groups (where anthropologists and sociologists dwell) to organisms, to organs, to cells, to molecules, to atoms, one finds oneself in separate fiefdoms pervaded by different languages, laws, and customs. A basic canon of science is that phenomena of each level can be explained by (translated into) those of a lower level, as a chemical compound can be translated into its constituent molecules. That, in a nutshell, is reductionism, and it's not necessarily a bad word. But although color may be explained in electromagnetic terms and ultimately as a probabilistic smear of electrons, does the behavior of electrons really describe the special blue of the Sargasso Sea?

And so the slug connoisseurs sometimes have trouble conversing with the vertebrate people, who in turn may have little to say to the cognitive psychologists who know computerspeak, or to the neurologists who treat stroke patients, or to the pharmacologists who test memory chemicals in vitro. All of which makes it difficult to come up with a single definition of memory.

Kinds of Memory

JUST LIMITING our scope to humans, here's a partial list.

1. *Short-term Versus Long-term Memory.* The definition of *short-term* keeps changing, and some researchers also talk about something called "immediate memory," which is even shorter. But for simplicity's sake, think of short-term memory as something like your grocery list, and long-term memory as more like the face of your first love. Short-term human memory is said to have a storage capacity of about six or seven "chunks" of information (a chunk can be anything from a single digit to a whole thought), which is why you can remember your phone number better as 213–788–9986 than as 2137889986.

2. *Verbal and Spatial Memory.* The distinction speaks for itself. As you might guess, in most people verbal memory is linked to the left cerebral hemisphere and spatial to the right.

3. *Episodic and Semantic Memory.* Episodic, or "autobiographical," memory is the memory for particular times, places, and contexts (as in, what you did during a recent visit to Washington, D.C.). Semantic memory is context-free knowledge of facts, language, or concepts (as in "Washington, D.C. is the capital of the United States"). Episodic memory tends to go downhill with age, while semantic memory stays comparatively fresh. Some researchers believe certain of the amnesia syndromes selectively interfere with episodic memory.

4. *Procedural Memory and Declarative Memory.* This dichotomy comes from the kingdom of artificial intelligence, but it's handy for human memory, too. Procedural knowledge is "how-to" stuff, which in computers means general rules and operating procedures and in humans means knowing how to drive, swing a golf club, or repair a toaster. Declarative knowledge is made up of facts, specific items of information, such as who is President of the United States, the fact that there are nine planets in our solar system, and that you are thirty-three years old. In computers declarative knowledge is usually encoded locally, whereas procedural knowledge is, in Douglas Hofstadter's words (*Gödel Escher Bach*), "spread around in pieces, and you can't retrieve it, or key in on it. It is a global consequence of how the

program works, not a local detail." Does the same local/global distinction hold true of "biological computers"? Stay tuned.

5. *Habit Memory and Informational Memory.* This may be a restatement of number 4, with the difference that habit memory (at least in the case of some rhesus monkeys) is associated with reward. Informational memory is essentially the equivalent of declarative memory.

There are myriad other subdivisions of memory, which are a lot of Ph.D.s' bread and butter but which needn't concern you. The only other information you'll need is that the memory process is generally divided into three stages: coding, storage (or consolidation), and retrieval. The party line is that it takes hours or days for a new memory to be entered into the long-term file and that in the interim (the consolidation period) it can easily be erased. We know this because lab animals given a memory-disrupting chemical in the first few hours (or sometimes days) following a learning task forget it completely, whereas the same drug administered a bit later—after consolidation is complete—leaves the memory intact. Don't believe this. The new evidence is that consolidation may go on for *years*.

Confabulation

In 1917 a neurologist described a curious incident involving a woman who suffered from Korsakoff's syndrome, a brain disease caused by severe alcoholism that leaves its victims with an even blanker memory record than N.A.'s or H.M.'s. As if to compensate for their mnemonic bankruptcy, Korsakoff's patients are notorious for "confabulating," or making up plausible-sounding stories out of whole cloth. Anyway, as an experiment this doctor shook his patient's hand, deliberately pricking her finger with a hidden pin. The woman quickly jerked her hand away, but when queried about why she did this, she answered vaguely, "Isn't it allowed to withdraw one's hand?" Though *she* (or her conscious mind) didn't seem to know the reason for her action, some part of her brain obviously remembered.

"What is of interest," observes memory researcher Larry Squire, who recently exhumed this strange-but-true episode from the neurological archives, "is that the patient's behavior is altered by experience and that this altered behavior outlasted the patient's memory of the experience itself." What is the explanation? Do we have two different minds inside our head, one of which can know something that the other has forgotten?

Larry Squire thinks he knows the answer, and so do his colleagues at the medical school of the University of California at San Diego, who have been following N. A. around for nine years. So does an equally astute team of MIT researchers who have been keeping tabs on H. M. So does

Mortimer Mishkin, who's been surgically creating amnesic monkeys at the NIMH. But before we tell you what it is, let's take a closer look at amnesia.

Here is N. A., as seen through the eyes of Squire and colleagues Philip I. Kaushall and Dr. Mark Zetkin (in a paper called "Single Case Study: a Psychosocial Study of Chronic, Circumscribed Amnesia"):

At first meeting N. A. impresses the visitor with his normality. . . . A visitor at his house is invariably invited to inspect his collections and vacation mementos. The guns are his pride, and he wipes them carefully after each handling. "The acids in human sweat will disfigure the metal." There are model airplanes, which he has built himself, and, in his bedroom, objects by the hundreds—rocks, shells, and artifacts. "He buys on impulse like a child," his mother complains.

He will tell the visitor where he acquired things, and his discourse is lucid and intelligent. Occasionally, he hesitates, wondering when some object was acquired or perhaps whether it was bought in India or Fiji. He apologizes for forgetting your name each time. Unlike the senile patient . . . N. A. is not confused. Within a short time span, he does not repeat himself or show the same objects twice: but after the third or fourth visit, after he asks each time whether he has shown you his collections, his remarks and activities come to reveal a devastated life and an isolated mental world.

When a phone call interrupts him, N. A. loses track of whatever he was doing, and even without any interruptions, he can scarcely perform a simple sequence of steps. Although he knows "Watergate" was a political scandal that happened in either "Washington or Florida" and that some Americans were held hostage in Iran, his life since 1960 has generally been like the hazy, disappearing vapor trail of an airplane. "At one memory testing session recently," the scientists recall, "he [N. A.] repeatedly tried to recall a question that he wanted to ask. He finally searched his pockets and found a written note: 'Ask Dr. Squire if my memory is getting any better.' " It wasn't. Yet his memory of events *before* the accident is crystal clear.

Amnesia Reconsidered   EXACTLY what part of N. A.'s memory process is damaged? Is it (1) that information is improperly encoded and does not enter his memory stream; (2) that the information is filed but poorly consolidated and maintained; or (3) that the information is stored and maintained perfectly well but N. A. can't retrieve it?

Traditionally diagnosis number 3, retrieval failure, has been the theory of choice in amnesia. It would explain, for one thing, why patients with global amnesia nonetheless seem to remember some things. When recalling lists of words, for instance, many amnesics are known to make "intrusion errors"—that is, they give wrong answers that are, in fact, words from previous tests—but (here's the puzzle) *they do not remember ever having seen the words before.* From this peculiar state of affairs many memory researchers concluded that amnesics *store* memory traces but cannot get at them for some reason, though they may be able to do so under the right conditions if given the right cues.

If retrieval were the problem, however, it should affect all memories equally—yesterday, last year, and ten years ago—and as we've just seen in the case of N. A., this is not so. He has excellent access to his pre–1960 data bank. H. M. likewise retains his presurgical past intact—well, almost intact. H. M. became a neurological celebrity in 1953, when surgeons at the Montreal Neurological Institute cut out most of the hippocampus and amygdala on both sides of his brain to treat his epilepsy. The operation wiped out his ongoing memory stream and also voided about three years of memories preceding it, so that he has, in the lingo, a little retrograde amnesia on top of his global anterograde amnesia. The upshot is that his memory record dead-ends somewhere around 1950, which places him in a curious time warp. Now in his mid-fifties, H. M. is stuck with exactly the same vocabulary he had at age twenty-seven, and his days pass in a somnambulistic haze of TV, crossword puzzles, and visits from scientists. In a paper presented at the November 1983 annual meeting of the Society for Neuroscience, MIT's Suzanne Corkin supplied this doleful slice of amnesic life:

He still exhibits profound anterograde amnesia and does not know where he lives, who cares for him, or what he ate at his last meal. His guesses as to the current year range from 1958 to 1993, and when he does not stop to calculate it, he estimates his age to be 10 to 26 years less than it is. Nevertheless, he has islands of remembering, such as knowing that an astronaut is someone who travels in outer space, and that a public figure named Kennedy was assassinated, and that rock music is "that new kind of music we have." He can still draw an accurate floor plan of the house in which he lived from 1960 to 1974; moreover, he believes he still lives there.

The Forgotten Autobiography

So H. M.'s AMNESIA, having spared his early memories, can't really be a retrieval problem. Patients with alcoholic Korsakoff's syndrome, on the other hand, suffer from both anterograde *and* retrograde amnesia. Not only do they sleepwalk through the present like N. A. and H. M., but they don't remember the past very well either. That might suggest a memory-retrieval failure were it not for the fact that their retrograde forgetting has an interesting temporal gradient. The more remote the memory, the better it is preserved.

The difficulty with studying retrograde amnesia, however, is that there is no way to tell for sure what the amnesic *used* to know, unless you just happened to give him a memory test before he was stricken. Or unless you find someone who wrote an autobiography and then promptly developed Korsakoff's disease—as Patient X did. He was a respected scientist who had authored three hundred papers and five books, including his 1979 autobiography, before the tell-tale lesions of Korsakoff's showed up on his brain scan in 1981. To measure his retrograde forgetfulness, a team of Boston scientists tested Patient X on details taken from his own autobiography—facts, in other words, that he had known only a short time before. "Can you tell me about that scientific conference you went to in 1972?" they would ask him, and the former scientist would reply, as often as not, "What conference?"

The misfortunes of Patient X clarified two important details. First, Korsakoff's patients really have *forgotten* what they once knew; their retrograde amnesia can't be explained away by supposing that they'd just been absorbing less and less information as their alcoholism progressed. And secondly, their retrograde memory loss follows a distinct temporal curve. The more remote the event, the sharper their recollection of it. Patient X, for example, recognized the names of scientists who became famous before 1965, while those who hit the big leagues after 1965 were unknown to him. The reason, the memory experts think, is that more recent memories aren't yet fully consolidated and are therefore more vulnerable to loss. If this is true, it would explain how H. M.'s operation could have retroactively wiped out three years of memories; and it also suggests that consolidation goes on *much* longer than anyone dreamed—for many years, no less.

Coding and consolidation, then, *not* retrieval, is the problem in amnesia. The other revelation of these studies is that the injured brain regions themselves can't contain the memory stores, for if they did, *all* old memories would be gone. N. A. and Korsakoff's patients suffer from damage to the medial thalamus (or diencephalon). That part of the brain seems to play a role in the initial coding of information, for, according to Larry Squire, these patients' memories never get coded and filed properly. What is missing in H. M., on the other hand, is the hippocampus-amygdala region (beneath the temporal lobe). This circuit must be a consolidation station of sorts, for H. M.'s memory suffers from a "post–encoding-consolidation deficit," according to Squire. "It appears," he says, "that at the time of learning, the medial temporal region [what H. M. is lacking] establishes a relationship with memory-storage sites elsewhere in the brain, primarily in neocortex."

*Monkey See,
Monkey Forget*

IN BETHESDA, MARYLAND, sits a low, shed-like building with green paint peeling from its walls that is home to a group of amnesic monkeys. They didn't get that way by accident. If you want a flow diagram of neural information processing, you can wait for the right disease or injury to strike a human brain (and acts of God are usually pretty crude in their scope) or you can delicately tamper with a monkey's brain and see what happens, as Mortimer Mishkin, NIMH's neuropsychology chief, does. Having created a bunch of simian H. M.'s and N. A.'s—monkeys who forget an object only seconds after seeing it—Mishkin can tell you exactly where the damage is.

"Deep inside the temporal lobe we find these two very important structures, the amygdala and the hippocampus," he tells us. "We know that rats without a hippocampus can't perform in a radial maze. There is a swimming test in which they have to find an underwater perch, and they can't do that either. So we think the hippocampus is very important for localization memory. The amygdala seems to govern a different kind of associative memory. If you look at a cup, you have a fairly good idea of what it will feel like. When we train a monkey to touch an object and then choose that object from a pair just by looking at it, and then we remove its amygdala, it can't do it at all.

"If you damage *both* the amygdala and the hippocampus you produce global anterograde amnesia," he continues. "You're unable to lay down new stores, so you live from moment to moment, like H. M. You get basically the same effect if you damage the medial diencephalon, the part of the brain affected by Korsakoff's disease, for instance; you interrupt the same circuit in a different place. For an object to leave a permanent or semipermanent trace, it appears that this limbic circuit has to enter the perceptual process at a crucial point. We think it does something like give the order PRINT.

"Now, if you damage the temporal cortex itself, you take out the actual store. You can't lay down new memories, and you lose old memories too. You get dementia. One can rightly say the mind is gone."

Since Mishkin seems to have had little difficulty locating memories on the neural map, we ask him about Karl Lashley's famous failure.

"Lashley set neuropsychology back many decades when he enunciated his principle of equipotentiality," he says. "I am an out-and-out localizationist, and I suspect that every neuron in the brain is doing something different. Even the cerebral cortex, which looks like it's made up of equivalent pieces of tissue everywhere, is actually a quiltwork of different areas—

each doing its own thing and *not* doing what its neighbor is doing. It's not the bowl of porridge that equipotentiality theorists propose.

"That's not to say that a psychological function resides in a piece of tissue, which is what localizationists are charged with believing. That's not the way our nervous system is built. It's built as a connected network."

Memoryless Memory

OVER A DOZEN YEARS AGO McGill University's Brenda Milner, the chief scientist on the H. M. case, noticed that her patient had no trouble mastering the rarefied skill of drawing while watching his hands reversed in a mirror. "Just a simple motor skill," most scientists scoffed at the time. But recently Larry Squire and a graduate-student protégé, Neal Cohen (now a psychologist at MIT), took another look at such phenomena and discovered that, contrary to all logic, a person without a functioning memory stream can manage to learn and remember some things.

Today H. M. sits cross-legged on the floor playing with a puzzle called the Tower of Hanoi. Five wooden blocks with holes at the center are stacked pyramid style on one peg, and there are two empty pegs. H. M.'s task is to rebuild the pyramid in the same order on the "goal peg," while observing two rules: Move only one block at a time, and never put a bigger block on top of a smaller one. When he announces that he's stuck, the MIT scientist observing him says, "You can do it; you've done it before." In fact, he did the puzzle four times yesterday, four times the day before that, and again the day before that, each time surpassing his earlier record. "Really?" asks H. M., since for him it is always the first time. Nonetheless, he solves the Tower of Hanoi with the minimum number of moves—a perfect score.

H. M. can also recognize fragmented pictures, read mirror-reversed script and recall repeated words—becoming more adept with practice, just like any normal person, but never remembering any of the previous tests. The same is true of N. A. and other severe amnesics. Like the Korsakoff patient who recoiled from her doctor's handshake in 1917, they seem to "remember" things they do not consciously remember.

For the solution to this paradox, recall Kinds of Memory, number 4: Declarative versus Procedural, and consider them as two entirely different memory systems, or classes of knowledge, in the human brain. If you prefer, you can think of procedural knowledge as "knowing how" versus "knowing that." Whatever you call it, the message is that while amnesics don't record specific facts, events, faces, words, and so on, they can still learn certain kinds of skills, from hitting a tennis ball to assembling the

Tower of Hanoi (no mere motor skill). "We think of procedural learning, the kind of learning that is preserved in amnesia, as the tuning or adjusting of existing circuitry," Squire tells us. "Information is accessed by 'running off' particular programs, but there's no 'representation' of the specific circumstances. Some people have called it 'memory without record.' "

When Mortimer Mishkin happened on the same phenomenon in his amnesic monkeys, he called it "stimulus/response memory," or "habit," as opposed to "informational memory." A monkey minus its crucial hippocampus-amygdala circuitry cannot remember anything from one moment to the next, exactly like its human counterparts. For example, it can't remember for even a few seconds to select the right object from a pair. To Mishkin's amazement, however, the amnesic animal *can* learn and retain under special circumstances.

"If you hide a banana pellet under one of a pair of objects and let the monkey find it," he explains, "and then do the same thing again once a day, the monkey will learn to go to the right object. Yet we know it doesn't actually *remember the object*. It's very puzzling, and it led to our speculation that there are two different systems in the brain responsible for storing experience. One stores information, and the other stores stimulus-response bonds. The latter, which I call 'habit,' is a type of learning that can go on without awareness—noncognitive learning."

This discovery might even patch up the age-old rift between two camps in psychology. Do we act on the basis of ideas or stored knowledge, as the mentalists claim, or are we "conditioned" by rewarding or aversive interactions with our environment, as the behaviorists say? "*Both* are right," says Mishkin. "Our nervous system can encompass both stimulus/response learning and cognitive learning."

Consciousness Without Consciousness

"I THINK there's a phylogenetic story to all this," Larry Squire tells us. "Those of us who study mammals find it hard to associate memory with *Aplysia*, and perhaps that's because aplysia memory is more like procedural memory. The animal learns to respond, but it couldn't 'tell' you why—in a nonverbal way, of course. There's no consciousness. Maybe when you go from invertebrates to vertebrates—or maybe the cutoff point is mammals—the circuitry for declarative memory comes in, a kind of awareness."

What does that "awareness" consist of? And how to define the strange, unfathomed layers of consciousness that seem to lurk beneath the surface of conscious life? Consider, for instance, the surreal cases of "blindsight" discovered by a pair of British researchers a few years ago. (The number of oxymorons in this section gives you an idea of how paltry our introspective vocabulary is.) The scientists were working with patients who were missing the visual cortex on one side of the brain, which rendered them totally blind in the corresponding visual field. But, inexplicably, these patients were 80 to 90 percent accurate in pointing to lights and guessing different shapes—*x*'s and *o*'s, vertical and horizontal stripes—in the blind visual field.They claimed they saw nothing, however; they were just "guessing."

"When a blindsight patient sees something and tells me he can't see," says Stanford's Karl Pribram, who thinks blindsight raises interesting questions about consciousness, "that makes me think there are two levels of seeing: one that consists of instrumental behavioral responses to optical information and another that refers to subjective awareness." Coincidentally Elizabeth Warrington and Lawrence Weiskrantz, the researchers who discovered blindsight, were among the first to notice the curious "intrusion errors" that amnesics make on word lists. Whether or not blindsight and the memoryless memory of procedural knowledge have any neural machinery in common (we don't know if they do), both seem to hint at a kind of consciousness without awareness. Perhaps infant memory works along procedural/habit lines, and that's why we don't consciously remember our bassinet days. In fact, baby monkeys tested by Mortimer Mishkin seem to be born with a working stimulus/response memory but can't manage the other kind until they're about a year old, probably because the neural machinery behind declarative/fact memory takes time to mature.

Maybe there are memory circuits operating below the threshold of awareness in the odd cases of epileptic "automatism" that fill the neurological literature. Wilder Penfield, among others, was fascinated by the fact that people could be turned into "mindless automatons" by epileptic discharges around the temporal lobes. He relates the case of "A.," who had a seizure while playing the piano. After a brief pause the man went right on playing "with considerable dexterity" on automatic pilot but with no memory of the episode. And of "B.," who suffered one of these seizures while walking home. "He would continue to thread his way through busy streets on his way home," the neurosurgeon reported. "He might realize later that he had had an attack because there was a blank in his memory for a part of the journey, as from Avenue X to Street Y." Everybody in this business seems to have his or her favorite automatism story. Paul MacLean tells us about an epileptic train motorman who blacked out but nevertheless drove his train from the 125th Street station right into Grand Central, obeying all the red and green lights on the way. Karl Pribram recalls a state-hospital psychologist who remembered going to her room and falling asleep on a certain evening, but who, in fact, suffered a seizure, got dressed, went to a party, had a gay time, and returned home again—all in a somnambulistic trance.

Who is playing the piano/driving the train/attending the party while the conscious self is AWOL? "I don't know," admits Pribram. "Perhaps the 'self' is a particular code. Unless our experience is translated into that code, it stays outside our memory stream." Of course, we now know that coding is the problem in amnesia, and we know, moreover, that the coding-consolidation process can take years and years. "I think we haven't given enough attention to the fact that the brain must code and recode everything over and over again," Pribram adds. "You change. You aren't the same person you were five years ago."

Two (or More) Selves in One?

WILDER PENFIELD, interestingly enough, was one of the first scientist/philosophers to grapple with the enigma of dual consciousness. "Consider the point of view of the patient," he wrote, "when the surgeon's electrode, placed on the interpretive cortex, summons the replay of past experience. The stream of consciousness is suddenly doubled for him. He is aware of what is going on in the operating room as well as the 'flashback' from the past." Take the young South African patient who was astonished to find himself "laughing with his cousins on a farm in South Africa," while simultaneously lying on an operating table in Montreal.

In Penfield's view, there were two parallel conscious "streams" in such cases, one "driven by an electrode delivering sixty pulses per second to the cortex," the other by stimuli in the immediate environment. But did the patient ever confuse the two? No, said Penfield. He knew he was on the operating table and not in the Transvaal. Therefore, according to Penfield, the patient's mind "can only be something quite apart from the neuronal reflex action." In other words, the crack neurosurgeon from Montreal was saying that the mind is not in the brain.

"It is all very much like programming a private computer," he wrote of the mind/brain connection. "The program comes to an electrical computer from without. The same is true of each biological computer. Purpose comes to it from outside its own mechanism. This suggests that the mind must have a supply of energy available to it for independent action." In another passage he again revealed himself as a card-carrying neo-Cartesian dualist: "As Hippocrates expressed it so long ago, the brain is 'messenger' to consciousness. Or, as one might express it now, the brain's highest mechanism [which Penfield tentatively located in the higher brain stem] is 'messenger' between the mind and the other mechanisms of the brain." The "highest brain mechanism," then, plays a role rather like Descartes's pineal gland, and the mind itself hovers somewhere outside the machinery like a guardian angel.

Apart from the general problems of mind/body dualism, there are several fallacies in Penfield's argument. The fact that the patient's "real" stream of consciousness (the one that is aware of being on an operating table) isn't being activated by electrodes does not mean that it doesn't depend on neuronal activity. Presumably, since the patient is alive and conscious, neurons are firing in many parts of his brain. Indeed, both streams probably depend on neuronal activity. How does the patient separate the real impressions from the ersatz? How does he know he's in the hospital having flashbacks of South Africa and not in South Africa having hospital flashbacks? That can be explained without invoking an aloof, observing mind. The patient's ongoing perceptions of the surgery, the doctor's conversations, and so on flow in a continuous, uninterrupted sequence in which every moment is connected with the immediate past. The vision of South Africa, on the other hand, is a sharp detour in the conscious stream. From these sorts of clues, the patient is able to label one experience real and the other a flashback.

But if the phenomenon of dual consciousness is not hard-and-fast proof of a disembodied mind, it is nonetheless extremely interesting. How many different selves can inhabit a brain? After all, we've seen that there is more than one knowledge/memory system in us and that a mysterious somebody can operate the controls when nobody's home (as in automatism). The real puzzle, perhaps, is not that pathological/extraordinary consciousness should on occasion resemble one of those chimera—the sphinx, the manticore, the centaur—that combine the torso of one species with the head or hindquarters of another but that "ordinary" consciousness should be unitary at all.

The Silicon Garden Slug

On a mild may day, the campus of the California Institute of Technology (CalTech) seems deserted except for the ubiquitous gardeners clipping hedges. The carefully groomed lawns, uncluttered by benches, falafel stands, or loitering undergraduates, suggest the little patches of green in an architectural model of a city. (Perhaps students are imported from a nearby community college when it is necessary to have a photo depicting "Student Life" for the college catalog, or perhaps no one cares.) But we didn't come here for Sigma Chi toga parties; we had an appointment with biophysicist John Hopfield's model brain, one of the few computer programs that is shedding light on the puzzle of human memory.

"Okay," he tells us, as green numbers flash across his computer screen. "The system has one hundred 'neurons,' each of which at any time has a value of zero or one. One means on, firing; zero means it's not firing. Some of the neurons are making inhibitory connections to the off neurons to keep them off. Some make excitatory connections to the firing neurons to keep them firing. The memories are in the pattern of the connections."

The "neurons" of which Hopfield speaks aren't real neurons but mathematical equivalents of neurons. With a set of equations he has endowed a computer with the ability to set up simple neural nets, to remember and forget, to free-associate, to create false memories, and generally to operate much as a flesh-and-blood brain does. Despite the fact that its reminiscences are expressed as strings of ones and zeros, this system's memory is altogether different from ordinary computer memory.

"A typical computer," explains Hopfield, "keeps memories in a way that can be likened to a very tall, very skinny library—with a hundred thousand floors and one book stored per floor. If we write the information we want to keep connected together in one book and store the book on one particular floor, all we have to know to get that information out is the floor it's stored on." That sort of memory is known as "addressable" memory, and it is not the way brains work. Unlike a Cray computer, you don't store your memories at particular addresses and you can use fragments of a memory to retrieve the whole. *(Let's see, her name started with a D, I think . . . She was engaged to that guy, you know, who kept the gerbils—Bernie Somebody from Sioux Falls or Sault Sainte Marie or something . . . She was always talking about the military industrial complex—Daphne . . . Daphne Quackenbush!)* You can lose a certain percentage of brain cells between the ages of twelve and fifty, and still be smarter at fifty than you were at twelve; yet, says Hopfield, "If one percent of the transistors in a computer go bad, it won't do anything at all." Those are just some of the differences between machine intelligence and the biological kind. Another key difference is that every brain cell makes thousands of connections, whereas a typical computer chip has only two or three connections per gate.

So when Hopfield got interested in creating a mathematical simulacrum of associative (biological) memory, he built in three hundred connections for each of the one hundred "neurons."

"Every memory is embedded in many connections, and each connection is involved in several memories," he tells us. The result is a system that can use incomplete or ambiguous information to find a memory. "Okay, I'm going to turn off a bunch of ones and then take a bunch of zeros and turn them on and make a bunch of garbage information." Hopfield deliberately falsifies the input, but after just four turns, the computer produces memory 22. "If I throw more garbage at it, though, it will start to give me some of the other memories some of the time. The memories are the stable states of the system. Imagine raindrops flowing downhill. Water droplets landing somewhere nearby will follow a path to the lowest point on the valley floor. You can think of the precise information as that particular location in the valley."

If that sounds a trifle abstract, you should know that Hopfield's computer can be trained to act like *Limax*, the garden slug with the conditioned aversion to potatoes. The scientist types some numbers on the keyboard and the display terminal says: TASTING A NEW FOOD. "I'm trying to make a simple neural network behave like *Limax*," he says. "In this case the food memories are the stable states. When a new food comes in—I have the system always learning—it will learn the food. Then if something else happens to it, a 'punishment,' it will associate it with the food."

How does the computer model compare to a real slug?

"I've learned some interesting things about networks by modeling a real biological system. In the classical conditioning paradigm, *time order matters*. In the conditioned eye-blink reflex, the bell has to come *before* the puff of air for the animal to learn. Same with *Limax*. If you give it potatoes and then give it quinidine—it's a bitter-tasting chemical that slugs don't like—*Limax* learns to hate potatoes. If you give it quinidine *before* potatoes, it doesn't learn anything."

"Is that because the animal is internalizing a crude notion of causality?" we ask. "Potatoes cause the bitter taste; the bell causes the puff of air?"

"Yes. Time is so important for a biological system because it must learn to predict the future better. It must ask, 'What's likely to happen next?' So you get *Limax* to learn a food. No problem. It eats food one, then food two, then food three. Then you give it quinidine, the punishment. It's supposed to know that food three is to blame. But how does it know which memory is most recent, which food it had last?"

"The system I showed you before had these stable memory states, but it had no idea of the sequence of states. The learning algorithm was completely symmetrical. If *A* came before *B*, or *B* before *A*, it learned just as well. Well, it turns out that with a minor change in the hardware you can make the system understand time order."

"What sort of change?"

"It's a question of the rules you put in for changing the strength of the synaptic connections. You know there was a rule described by Hebb for neural nets: The strength of a memory is proportional to the strength of the synaptic connections. It's a fine rule, but it has no sense of time order. But you can change the rules and modify the net so that locally—at the level of the synapse—you understand the direction the information is flowing. Then it's capable of knowing that A comes after B and behaving differently if the time order is reversed. The synapse really does have direction.

"If you do that, if you convert a standard Hebbian synapse into one with a time lag between the two sides, the thing can learn causality or what passes for causality. *Post hoc ergo propter hoc.*"

"So a sense of time," we ask, "is really built into the brain?"

"It really is," he says. "If I ask you, 'What's the letter after x?' you'll say y without hesitation. But if I ask, 'What's the letter before x?' You have to think. You learned the alphabet in time, and you can't go backwards so easily."

Hopfield's brainlike system also spews out bogus memories on occasion. "In a machine you can't get anything out that you didn't put in. But with our system we do. We get these spurious things—maybe they're errors, maybe brilliant new insights—which are produced by the correlations between memories. It just starts doing it." It also free-associates like an analysand on a couch. "If we built 'habituation' or 'fatigue' into the neurons—so they turn themselves off if they've been on for a while and turn on if they've been off—the memories are no longer absolutely stable. The system starts going from one memory to another. It will just naturally free-associate."

The secret to this is what Hopfield calls *collective properties*. "When you make the leap from one cell to a hundred cells or to a billion cells, you see new phenomena you wouldn't have dreamed of," he says. "Many physical systems are like that. If you put two molecules in a large box, every once in a while they'll collide and you can study the collisions. You can put a thousand molecules in the box and get more frequent collisions, but the collisions will look the same as they did when there were only two molecules. However, if we put a billion molecules in the box, there's a new phenomenon—sound waves. There was nothing in the behavior of two molecules—or ten or a thousand molecules—that would suggest to you that a billion molecules would make sound waves. Sound waves are a collective phenomenon."

Many neuroscientists labor like Hercules cleaning out the Augean stables under the reductionist assumption that billions of separate single-cell recordings pieced together will yield a circuit diagram of thought. But studying cell membranes won't tell you about collective properties, according to Hopfield. He sees individual neurons as a little like Rosencrantz and Guildenstern in *Hamlet*, minor characters who unknowingly play a role in some grand scheme of memory, intelligence, or consciousnesss. Or, to put it in physical terms, they're like the atoms in a magnet. "Individual atoms have electron spins that point up or down—which is what magnetizes the metal. But each guy just interacts with the other spins and has no idea that because of these interactions the whole bar is going to be magnetized in one direction. All the behaviors you see on a large scale are the consequence of a bunch of atoms, or what have you, simply interacting, without any idea of the global panoply of events."

It isn't necessary, therefore, to invoke a cosmic Programmer to explain how random accretions of cells could evolve to produce "Call me Ishmael." The magic arises spontaneously out of the collective properties as long as there's a little chaos, a little noise, in the system. "Computer people usually try to avoid noise," says Hopfield. "But I've tried to mimic noise—randomness—in my system. The brain, of course, is an open system. There's always this stuff coming in, this whimsical noise from the outside. That's why the chances of predicting what thought will be in your head a minute from now are about zero.

"How did cells get together," he continues, "and create more and more complicated life-forms without some guiding force saying 'Now do this'? I think all the mysteries of the brain come from the fact that there are new laws when you have many things around. That manyness is the central thing."

8

The Many-Chambered Self

> She went on and on, a long way, but, wherever
> the road divided, there were sure to be two finger-
> posts pointing the same way, one marked
> 'To
> TWEEDLEDUM'S HOUSE,'
> and the other
> 'TO THE
> HOUSE OF TWEEDLEDEE.'
> "I do believe," said Alice at last, "that they live
> in the *same* house! I wonder I never thought of
> that before.
> —LEWIS CARROLL,
> *Through the Looking Glass*

> I find that I am at two with nature.
> —WOODY ALLEN

WAKING UP after brain surgery, the patient said he felt fine except for a "splitting headache," and, though still woozy from the anaesthetic, he could repeat the tongue twister "Peter Piper picked a peck of pickled peppers." To prevent his grand mal seizures from ricocheting back and forth between the two cerebral hemispheres, doctors had severed the big cable of 250 million connecting fibers called the corpus callosum. It was the third in a series of historic "split-brain" operations that would eventually earn a Nobel Prize (in 1981) for Roger Sperry of CalTech, but back in 1961 nobody was entirely sure what a person lacking a bridge between his hemispheres would be like. Remember that each cerebral hemisphere controls the opposite, or *contralateral*, side of the body and links the brain to half a sensory world. Given the facts, you might think that a person without a corpus callosum would be a flailing, unstrung puppet, unable to integrate information coming in through his senses, incapable of walking down the street or dressing himself. You might think splitting the brain in half would leave a mind without a center, a self fractured and misshapen like a portrait by Willem de Kooning. The first marvel was that it did no such thing.

Sperry had already tested the waters with split-brain monkeys at the University of Chicago (otherwise, the operations would not have been done on human beings). But he and neurosurgeon Joseph E. Bogen, of the University of Southern California, were nonetheless relieved to see their patients speaking, joking (asked "How do you feel today?" one man quipped, "Which half of me?"), scoring normally on intelligence tests, and betraying no obvious signs of brain damage. Occasionally the two hemispheres would be at odds, and a patient would find her left hand unbuttoning her blouse as quickly as the right hand could button it, but in general, says UCLA's Eran Zaidel: "If you met such a person you wouldn't be able to tell him from your next-door neighbor. It takes extremely subtle tests to find anything wrong." But extremely subtle tests *did* reveal a surreal situation.

For starters, a split-brain patient would categorically deny the existence of an object placed in his left hand. With special *tachistoscopic* (from the Greek for "quickest view") equipment, Sperry launched a series of now-legendary experiments. Asking the patient to fix his gaze on a dot in the center of a translucent screen, he'd flash a picture to either the right or left side for a fraction of a second—too fast for a person to shift his gaze and pick up both visual fields. If a picture of a spoon appeared in his right visual field (which communicates with the *left* hemisphere), the patient would name it readily. But when it was presented to the right hemisphere—via the left visual field—the patient drew a blank or made wild guesses. "Pencil? Cigarette lighter? I don't know." Why? In the bisected brain the speech centers in the left hemisphere (in a right-handed person) are cut off from the experience of the other side of the brain. The patient's right hemisphere knows about the cup in the left hand, but can't talk, and the left hemisphere can talk but doesn't get the sensory message. The left hand *could* sometimes point out the cup among a pile of objects or even draw a picture of a cup, proving that the voiceless right brain was not a complete cretin.

In this first group of split brains, operated on in California between the years 1961 and 1969, science found a remarkable experimental laboratory, for Sperry's tests soon revealed two separate domains of awareness. Neither hemisphere seemed to know what the other was doing; they might have been in two different heads. When the word *heart* was flashed across the whole screen, with the *he* portion to the left of center and the *art* to the right, patients would report having seen the word *art*. But when asked to point with the left hand to one of two cards, *art* or *he*, they pointed to *he*. (The right hemisphere could sometimes recognize words.) In one memorable experiment, Sperry presented a nude pin-up photo to a patient's right hemisphere. The patient, a young woman, blushed and giggled nervously. Asked why, she replied, "Oh, Dr. Sperry . . . that funny machine."

It was a puzzle: Had an "emotional tone" somehow leaked across the border—perhaps through still-intact subcortical structures—which the spokesman left brain felt compelled to explain, even though it didn't know exactly what the right side had seen?

In hundreds of such tests Sperry could document a strange *doubling* of the stream of consciousness. "The surgically separated hemispheres of animals and man," he concluded, "have been shown to perceive, learn, and remember independently, each hemisphere evidently cut off from the conscious experiences of the other." The scientists who studied these patients fell into the habit of speaking of the two halves of the brain as if they were two distinct personalities—as in "The left hemisphere did X" or "I flashed a picture to the right hemisphere and it did Y."

Two Minds in One? THE BISECTED BRAIN began to suggest a wondrous monstrosity, like a two-headed man in the circus. If each hemisphere has an inner life, do two hemispheres mean *two* minds or even, horror of theological horrors, two souls? If so, why does a single, imperious "I" take credit for all our thoughts, beliefs, and actions? The great Charles Sherrington had written, "The self is a unity . . . it regards itself as one, others treat it as one. It is addressed as one, by a name to which it answers. The Law and the State schedule it as one." Is the unitary self a fiction?

Even before the split-brain operations there were hints that each hemisphere had a mind of its own. One garish example was the 1908 case of a woman whose left hand would travel up to her neck and try to strangle her unless she forcibly pulled it away and sat on it. Her neurologist, Kurt Goldstein, reasoned that damage to the corpus callosum had uncoupled her two hemispheres. The neurology texts also tell of weird "neglect" syndromes. A patient with a large right-hemisphere lesion may comb his hair only on the right side and put on his jacket with only the right arm in the sleeve, as if the left side of his body did not belong to him. In his book *The Nervous System* Dr. Peter Nathan, a London neurologist, recalls:

During the last war I saw a patient with a severe injury of the right parietal lobe. When I held up his left arm in front of his eyes, he would take no notice of it; and when I asked him whose limb it was, he answered, "Oh that! That's the arm Sister puts the penicillin injections into." In such cases, the patient may think that the arm on the opposite side to the brain lesion is someone else in his bed, and he may give it a name. Another of these patients . . . used to say that the limbs were his brother. He strongly objected to their presence in bed with him and would try to hurl them out of bed.

After the surgical removal of an entire hemisphere (hemispherectomy) many a patient is still demonstrably "himself," proving, in Bogen's opinion, that "one hemisphere is sufficient to sustain a personality or mind." If so, then two hemispheres would constitute two selves and the "I" would be an ontological bystander—unless, of course, the minor (right) hemisphere is *not* self-aware. Well, Sperry had shown that a patient's right hemisphere could recognize a picture of the patient and generate "appropriate emotional responses," but the issue of right-brain self-consciousness is far from settled. To say nothing of the larger puzzle: What is consciousness, anyway? An all-or-none phenomenon, or a continuum? Not to mention a smorgasbord of subproblems: Where is the boundary between the mental processes we call "conscious" and those that are "preconscious"? Can you have thought (consciousness, self-consciousness) without language? To what extent are higher human faculties localized in one hemisphere or another— language on the left and drawing on the right, for instance—or in even smaller compartments? "Is recognition of animate objects a faculty separable from recognition of the inanimate . . . ?" Bogen mused in a 1969 essay, "Is love of children a function to be localized in some particular part of the brain as Gall once maintained?" The split-brain pioneers themselves were not unmindful of the metaphysical oddness of the frontier they'd opened. "As knowledge of brain function and the mind/brain relation advances," Sperry wrote, "one would anticipate that terms like 'mind' and 'person' would have to be redefined, or at least more precisely defined."

To the conundrum "How many minds in a brain?" there seemed to be four possible answers.

1. Despite the subjective voice in your head that says, "I am a person named Randy Black, with a social security number and a valid driver's license to prove it," you are really a dual being. At least, that's what Bogen thinks: "Pending further evidence, I believe," he wrote, "that each of us has two minds in one person."

2. Though "divided in the bisected brain," consciousness is "unitary in the normal brain," according to Sperry. "Since each side of the surgically divided brain is able to sustain its own conscious volitional system . . . ," he said in a 1983 *Omni* interview, "the question arises, Why, in the normal state, don't we perceive ourselves as a pair of separate left and right persons instead of the single, apparently unified mind and self we all feel we are?" He decided that the everyday miracle of "I" was an emergent property. "The normal bilateral consciousness can be viewed as a higher emergent entity that is more than just the

sum of its right and left awareness and supersedes this as a directive force in our thoughts and actions."

3. Only the dominant, vocal hemisphere is truly conscious. As John Eccles ("Brain and Free Will") sees it, the Cyrano de Bergerac of the left brain is "uniquely concerned with giving conscious experiences to the subject and in mediating his willed actions." A lesser consciousness dwells in the mute right brain, to be sure, but "the absence of linguistic or symbolic communication at an adequate level prevents this from being discovered. It is not therefore 'self-conscious.' " How could it be self-conscious, he argues, since a split-brain patient, divorced from all the happenings in his minor hemisphere, is nevertheless "recognizably . . . the same person that existed before the brain-splitting operation and retains [his former] unity of self-consciousness"?

4. Selfhood is multiple, not double. The mind is not only divided between two hemispheres but splintered into many neural subsystems. Neurologist Michael Gazzaniga, a 1966 graduate of the Sperry lab who now works with his own "stable" of split-brain patients at Cornell University Medical College, writes in *The Integrated Mind*: "The mind is not a psychological entity but a sociological entity, being composed of many submental systems."

The Right Brain: Imbecile or Sleeping Prodigy?

ONE OF THE FIRST QUESTIONS confronting split-brain researchers was (as Gazzaniga would phrase it in a 1967 *Scientific American* article): "Did this [linguistic] impotence of the right hemisphere mean that its surgical separation from the left had reduced its mental powers to an imbecilic level?" The answer, it seemed, was no. When shown a picture of a cigarette, the silent right brain could select an ashtray from a group of objects— although even with the ashtray clutched in his left hand, the patient could not name it or the corresponding picture. It demonstrated rudimentary language comprehension (reading the word *pencil*, for instance, and understanding spoken instructions) and responded with thumbs-up or thumbs-down signals to photos of familiar faces, including Winston Churchill (up), Joseph Stalin (down), and Richard Nixon (a horizontal thumb). The search was on for tasks the minor hemisphere could do better, and by 1968 Sperry and his star graduate student Jerre Levy—who, in the 1970s, launched a whole hemispheric dominance factory at the University of Chicago—were reporting that "the mute, minor hemisphere is specialized for Gestalt perception, being primarily a synthesist in dealing with information input. The speaking, major hemisphere, in contrast, seems to operate in a more logical, analytical, computerlike fashion.''

The two hemispheres weren't just a verbal/nonverbal combo but two radically different mental landscapes, two "cognitive styles." Levy used photographs of two vertical halves of a face and other nonverbal tricks to reach the languageless right hemisphere. She showed that if the left brain broke things down into component parts and excelled at logic, the right brain perceived things "wholistically," as "gestalts." The right hemisphere was good at visuospatial tasks; it could draw well; it was better at recognizing faces; it had musical skills. As early as 1745, doctors had pondered the case of a man with severe aphasia (the only word he could say was "yes") caused by a left-hemisphere stroke. Nonetheless, they observed, "He can sing certain hymns which he had learned before he became ill, as clearly and distinctly as any healthy person."

There are suggestions that the right hemisphere is more "emotional" than the left. Patients with right-hemisphere damage are often strangely nonchalant about their condition, even when one side of the body is completely paralyzed. In 1982, noticing that victims of right-hemisphere strokes typically speak in flat monotones even about the most emotionally charged matters, a University of Texas researcher, Elliott Ross, coined the term *aprosodia* (from the word *prosody*, referring to pitch, melody, rhythm, and intonation) to describe a sort of right-hemisphere version of aphasia. The damage, he says, is to "emotional centers" in the right hemisphere that are mirror images of the left-brain speech centers. There is one center on the right for the *perception* of feelings, corresponding to Wernicke's area in the left hemisphere, he hypothesizes, and another for emotional *expression*, corresponding to Broca's area.

Thus the perennial tug-of-war between emotion and reason, "heart" and "mind," Freud's "primary process" (primitive, mythic thought, as in dreams) and "secondary process" (rational analysis), seemed to have a real embodiment in the twin hemispheres. Joseph Bogen was among the first to hail the dual brain as a fundamental human dichotomy. (He baptized the left brain "propositional" and the right "appositional," noting "this term [appositional] implies a capacity of apposing or comparing of perceptions, schemas, engrams, et cetera.") A widespread cult of the right brain ensued, and the duplex house that Sperry built grew into the K-Mart of brain science. Today our hairdresser lectures us about the Two Hemispheres of the Brain and mail-order pop-psych tapes urge us to awaken the latent creativity of our neglected right hemisphere. We even met a psychologist who runs workshops for people who are sloppy or neat because of right- or left-hemisphere dominance and who are unhappily mated to a person with the opposite tendency. Is any of this true?

Well, some of it. But in this chapter we'll tell you that: (1) Your mental life isn't neatly zoned along right or left lines. (2) The right hemisphere isn't as gifted as the human-potential gurus think. (3) If your husband leaves the cap off the toothpaste it probably has nothing to do with cerebral dominance.

What Do You Mean, Right?

"IMAGINE waking up one morning and—to paraphrase Kafka—instead of finding yourself a cockroach, you find yourself a split-brain patient," says Eran Zaidel. "What would you do? Well, at first you'd be scared because you wouldn't have normal control over your body maybe. Things would happen to the left hand that you don't really understand. . . . But the remarkable thing is that these patients behave like normal human beings in most everyday situations. In fact, they deny there's anything unusual going on."

From a drawer he extracts a set of four pictures drawn in the plain, didactic style of elementary-school textbooks: a fingernail, a nail, a hammer, and a mailbox. "Say I show the right hemisphere these four pictures, and I ask it to point to two pictures whose names sound alike but which mean different things. It's a fairly linguistic task—you wouldn't expect the right hemisphere to be able to do it. But it can. It points to *nail* and *nail*. I say, 'Right.'

"The patient says, 'What do you mean, *right*? How could I do it? How can I tell you those two pictures have the same names when I don't know what the name is?' The one who is talking is the left hemisphere, and it's getting upset because I'm praising the right hemisphere, and it doesn't know what the hell is going on. It *never, never* comes to terms with its inability to know what the other hemisphere is experiencing."

An engineer and mathematical linguist by training, Zaidel spent his graduate years at CalTech trying to teach computers to understand English. But the human side of the man/computer communication problem began to obsess him instead, and by 1970 he was part of Sperry's charmed circle, doing neuroscience. Eventually he focused on half a brain: the right. We meet him in his narrow office at UCLA on an April day when brisk Pacific breezes blow acacia blossoms, purple jacaranda flowers, and eucalyptus leaves across a hard, blue sky. From Zaidel's window the landscaped greens and subtropical flora of the Bel Aire Country Club on a distant hilltop are supernaturally clear in the uncustomary smogless air.

"My focus is language, especially in the right hemisphere," he tells us.

"How much language is there in a normal right hemisphere, and if there is some, as we believe there is, when is it used and how?

"There are patients called *deep dyslexics* who are very interesting. Because of large left-hemisphere lesions they have problems with language and reading. When they read words aloud, they'll read *chair* as *sofa*, *hat* as *tie*, *orchestra* as *band*. That shows they got to the general meaning somehow but not to the exact meaning address. They also read concrete nouns better than abstract function words like prepositions and conjunctions. If you give them the word *in*, they can't read it, but add another *n* and they can. They also can't read nonsense words aloud, sound out words phonetically, or do rhyming tasks.

"These are the very same symptoms we see in a split right hemisphere. So the question is, Are deep dyslexics using the right hemisphere for reading? The answer is sometimes. The patients made more errors when we flashed words to the right hemisphere. This suggests that when the left hemisphere can't do it, they shift to the right hemisphere, which supplies the general meaning. Then they go back to the left hemisphere for the name, and it gives one but not the precise one. Sometimes it says 'orchestra' instead of 'band.' "

A wispy undergraduate enters to report a problem with the testing equipment on the next floor. "Umm, the key monitor isn't working," she says. A numbing litany of technical problems follows. *Key monitor . . . start stimuli . . . light . . . goes off . . . press button . . . sometimes it doesn't stop the clock . . . sequence is screwed up. . . . I have a test tomorrow so I can't stay . . . subjects tomorrow.*

"What does the right side contribute to language in the normal brain?" we ask Zaidel after the student leaves.

"We don't know exactly. There's evidence that right-brain damage results in some loss in the appreciation of humor, metaphor, and connected theme—what the point of the story is. Our research suggests that the meaning structures in the right hemisphere are very rich, full of nuances. Maybe it's important for creating a rich semantic structure when you're reading. The left hemisphere is very literal."

Id and Ego

IT IS TEMPTING to picture the logical, rational left hemisphere as a sort of "ego" and the right hemisphere as an "id." In some circles the right brain is treated as a Rousseauian noble savage, bursting with raw creative energy. On the other side of the coin, there are those Kafkaesque case histories of evil, idlike right hemispheres, as in the case of the woman with the rogue, self-strangling left hand. Is the left brain, with its gift of gab, the brain's ego, and does the id live in the right?

"I don't think the ego is the left hemisphere," says Zaidel. "There has been a push to assign unconscious, primitive, idlike creature behavior to the right brain and egolike behavior to the left. But I worked with a girl who had her whole left hemisphere removed at age ten because of a tumor. She was severely aphasic, but she was kind and pleasant. There was nothing dark in her personality. So where is that dark, negative right hemisphere?"

"I saw a movie," he continues, "of a patient with a natural callosal lesion who was performing a block-design test. The *left* hand [controlled by the right brain] builds the design, and it does a good job. Then the *right* hand starts taking it apart. Finally, the man gets so frustrated he sits on his right hand and completes the design with the left. The French have a name for this syndrome: *la main étrangère,* 'the strange hand.' "

Furthermore, when Zaidel gave a personality test to the left and right hemispheres, the right came out more "superegolike." "It behaves like a goody-goody, always does the right thing, doesn't interrupt in class, follows the teacher's instructions. The left hemisphere tends toward more idiosyncratic responses." But he takes the results with a grain of salt, since they were based on a test designed for preliterate children.

Do those of us with normal brains and intact corpora callosi have two parallel streams of consciousness in our heads?

"Yes," says Zaidel. "But they're talking to each other. But how often and through which channels? We know nothing about this. How do two systems, each of which carries on complex analyses of the environment, interact? Are there situations when you're better off *inhibiting* callosal traffic because the conflict would make it impossible to behave? I think so, and I think there are ways for a human being to stop callosal traffic at will. We now have evidence that anxiety may do this a bit."

Unlike Bogen and others, Zaidel doesn't see a metaphysical dilemma in the split brain. "So you get conflicting responses from the two sides of the brain," he says. "Is that really so unusual? We all sometimes have conflicting feelings about the same thing. Each of us has two or more different perspectives depending on our mood, the time of day, and other circumstances. Why should that be fatal to a unified theory of consciousness?

"To me, the mind is the brain," he continues. "Consciousness is a particular pattern of cerebral activation. To say that someone has consciousness is to say he has a complex enough cognitive system to produce what we consider signs of consciousness: namely, a concept of self, a sense of the past, a sense of the future, maybe a fear of death, some kind of internal representation of the self as part of the environment. I don't think of consciousness as an absolute; it is a continuum. Some people, some creatures, are *more conscious* than others."

Why Two Hemispheres?

ACCORDING TO JERRE LEVY, the grande dame of hemispheric-lateralization research: "Cerebral dominance evolved because it's an efficient use of space, particularly when you've got an animal whose biological fitness . . . became more dependent upon intelligence. Two hemispheres absolutely identical in function would be sheer redundancy. We can hardly afford that feature if we live by our wits." Ergo, evolution built two separate neural programs, side by side. The brain's left half is tuned to time (sequential logic, counting, and so on are organized temporally), the right half to space. Since the 1970s Levy's lab at the University of Chicago has been churning out landmark studies on the neurological basis of sex differences, handedness, even neuroaesthetics (the human brain, it seems, favors pictures in which the eye-catching features are on the right side). She tested for subtle differences in cerebral lateralization in left-handers (particularly the interesting 30 to 40 percent who have language centers on both sides of the brain), dyslexics, mathematical prodigies, autistic children. To Levy's chagrin, this labor often turned to cliché in Sunday-supplement features, and in the public consciousness women were indelibly branded as "verbal" and "left-hemisphere dominant" and men as "right-brain dominant" and whizzes at spatial relations—as if a female architect or a male novelist were a biological impossibility. "People seem to have an irresistible tendency to simplify data," she said in a 1985 interview in *Omni*. "The fact is that for each sex each hemisphere may specialize in a different skill. It has been endlessly verified that males excel in three-dimensional, spatial visualization. But if you look at studies that measure lateralization in the understanding of emotion . . . the female right hemisphere is more specialized than that of the male, in this instance. It may be less specialized for spatial relationships and very specialized for understanding the meaning of facial expression. . . ."

Some psychologists became convinced that the two sides of the brain ought to be educated differently. If Johnny can't read, it may be because he is a right-hemisphere–dominant child stuck in a left-brain–oriented world (few would deny that the school is designed around the left hemisphere). Along came special remedial classrooms where Johnny does his spelling lessons to the tune of taped Vivaldi strings and where visualization exercises are used to coax out the peculiar genie of the right hemisphere.

Indeed, there is new evidence that learning disorders like dyslexia and discalculia (trouble with numbers) result from defects in the prenatal "hard-wiring." Slicing up deceased dyslexic brains, neurologists at Children's Hospital in Boston saw little clumps of nerve cells, particularly on the brain's left side, that were askew, as if hooked up incorrectly. Norman Geschwind of Harvard pointed to the following statistics: (1) Boys far outnumber girls among the learning disabled; (2) left-handed children are ten times more likely than right-handers to be learning disabled; (3) left-handers have a high rate of immune disorders, such as allergies; and (4) the left side of the brain develops more slowly than the right (to judge from rat experiments). The link between these seemingly disparate factors, Geschwind speculated, is the male hormone testosterone. When the fetus produces excess testosterone, it stunts the growth of the left hemisphere—causing left-handedness, learning disorders, and immune diseases (testosterone is known to weaken parts of the immune system).

"It is common to hear that our Western educational system discriminates against the right brain," writes Eran Zaidel (1978). "The left is constructive, algorithmic, stepwise, and logical. It benefits from narrow examples and from trial and error; it can learn by rule. The right hemisphere, on the other hand, does not seem to learn by exposure to rules and examples. It needs exposure to rich and associative patterns, which it tends to grasp as wholes. Programmed instruction is certainly not for the right hemisphere, but I am not sure what is the proper method of instruction for our silent half. It is part of the elusiveness of the right hemisphere that we find it easier to say what it is not than what it is." Nonetheless, some seers do not hesitate to hail it as a pipeline to the oversoul, a sleeping prophet, an exotic Eastern antidote to our sterile Western logic. In a way, the mystical right hemisphere has become a substitute for the soul that scientific rationalism has banished.

The Emperor's New Clothes

THIS WHOLE right brain/left brain thing has gotten out of hand," says Alan Gevins, in fine debunker form. "The underlying model is basically a dual-processor computer system, a left computer and a right computer connected by two hundred fifty million fibers. And the left computer is specialized for language and sequential processing, and the right for holistic, spatial function. It made a good metaphor for the early seventies when the Now Generation, or the Me Generation—or whatever that generation was called—was trying to emphasize the necessity for nonlinear, nonlogical thought. But it's grossly oversimplified.

"We did EEG recordings of people doing reading, writing, arithmetic, mental block rotation [a spatial task], and so on. At first the data looked great. With eight EEG channels I could tell whether a person was reading or writing or doing arithmetic just by looking at his brain waves. The problem was, though, I couldn't tell the difference between writing English and scribbling. I was just measuring motor control. So then we did a second experiment where everything was very controlled—the position of the hands, the difficulty of the task, et cetera—and there wasn't an iota of difference in the EEG. The amount of energy coming from those eight channels was the same whether the person was doing arithmetic or writing or block rotation!"

When Gevins and his colleagues at the EEG Systems Laboratory published these results in *Science* in 1979, they did not endear themselves to most scientists in the hemispheric-lateralization business. "I wasn't real popular," he says. "But I figured somebody had to do it—you know, it was like the Emperor's New Clothes. I stood my ground. I can say to this day I know of no study that has recorded the ongoing, continuous EEG and found a difference in pattern that could be attributed to a spatial versus a verbal kind of intellect. The studies that reported that sort of thing were just not controlled."

The real story, like most brain stories, proved to be more convoluted. The EEG Systems Lab found that even the most austere, scaled-down mental task generated a complex weather map of wave fronts, spreading rapidly over the entire scalp. "When you're reading or writing, it isn't as if the left half of your brain is turned on—if you're right-handed—and the right is turned off," he explains. "True, there are these critical areas for language on the left side, Wernicke's area and Broca's area, that have very specific functions. It looks as if Wernicke's area is a phonemic decoder for understanding language. Broca's area assembles strings of words into a syntactical framework. I think they are more like input/output areas than anything; it isn't like the *thinking* is there.

"There are many areas on both sides of the brain involved in the process of comprehending and expressing language. The same is true of spatial tasks. When you construct a map of the world in your mind, or you find your way through a dark room based on a memory of what that room is like, the left brain isn't *shut off*."

The War Between the Selves

WHITE COLONIAL CHURCH SPIRES point heavenward in the sleepy, tree-shaded New Hampshire town where Joe (known in the journals as case "J. W.") lives. A good-looking, dark-haired man of thirty-one, Joe underwent split-brain surgery for epilepsy in 1982 at Dartmouth Medical College and now lives an unexceptional life, working in the local egg-packing plant—except that once a month a large, air-conditioned recreational vehicle crammed with tachistoscopic equipment, cameras, computers, and Cornell University scientists pulls up to his house.

The word *pear* appears on the right side of the translucent screen (projected, of course, to Joe's left hemisphere).

"Pear," says Joe.

The word *bike* is flashed on the left.

"I don't see it. I saw a flash but I didn't see the word."

Dr. Michael Gazzaniga, the chief of the Cornell team, asks him to draw a picture with his left hand. Joe sketches a bicycle, complete with spokes and handlebars. Asked why he drew a bicycle, he shifts in his seat and mumbles awkwardly like a teenaged boy at a dance.

Banana and *red* flash on the screen, *banana* on the left, *red* on the right. Paul's nonverbal right hemisphere sees *banana*, and the verbal left sees *red*.

Picking up a red pen, his left hand carefully draws a naturalistic banana. Asked why, he gives a convoluted explanation about how a banana seemed a natural thing to draw with his hand in the position it was in.

Paul, a/k/a case "P. S.," sits facing a screen with a red dot in the center. A slide projector behind the screen flashes two pictures, a snow scene and a chicken claw, to the left and right sides of the "fixation point," respectively. (See Figure 8.) The snow picture is perceived by Paul's right hemisphere; the chicken claw by the left. As the impassive eye of a mounted video camera records the scene, Paul selects pictures of a shovel and a chicken from a group of four.

"Good," says Dr. Gazzaniga gently. "What did you see?"

"I saw a claw and I picked the chicken," he says, explaining: "You have to clean out the chicken shed with a shovel."

Vicki, or "V. P." is a divorced mother in her mid-thirties from Ohio whose corpus callosum was surgically severed in 1979. The operation curbed the recurrent seizures that had plagued Vicki since the age of nine, but for a time it made getting dressed in the morning a surreal Marx Brothers routine. The left hand chose clothes "she" didn't want; it snatched things like a perverse child; sometimes Vicki found herself putting on two pairs of shorts, one on top of the other. And tests at Cornell continue to reveal the presence of two Vickis.

A picture of an Indian headdress is projected on the left, a submarine

FIGURE 8   In classic experiments Dr. Michael Gazzaniga demonstrated that the left hemisphere in a split-brain patient will give false "explanations" for the perceptions of the right brain. Here, Paul's right hemisphere sees the snow scene, while the left side of his brain is shown a chicken claw. His right hand (controlled by the left brain) points to the chicken while the left hand (controlled by the right brain) picks out the shovel. Asked to explain, Paul—or rather, his left hemisphere—said, "I saw a claw and I picked the chicken, and you have to clean out the chicken shed with a shovel." (After Gazzaniga)

on the right. Asked to choose the correct drawings from a set of four, Vicki's right hand points to a picture of water; her left to a picture of a feather. Gazzaniga asks her why.

"I pointed to the water because it was a boat . . . uh, Indians. And the boat goes in the water. That's what I've seen."

"What did you see that time?"

"I saw a boat. A boat would float in the water and on the boat there could be Indians and they would have feathers. I guess that's all."

With their talking right hemispheres, Joe, Paul, and Vicki are the three stars among the hundred-odd split-brain patients in the "East Coast series" (patients who live in the states from Minnesota eastward fall into Gazzaniga's research stable). When Paul's right hemisphere began to express itself twenty-six months after surgery, Gazzaniga thought at first that the left hemisphere was doing the talking, that sensory information was leaking from Paul's right brain to his left through remaining interhemispheric connections. But tests showed that the two sides of his brain were still incommunicado. Then nine months after Vicki's operation, her right hemisphere began to write and then talk. Joe's right hemisphere can't speak, but it has the artistic skill to convey its thoughts in drawings.

"We focus on these patients because a right hemisphere without language is very boring to study," Gazzaniga tells us. "It can't respond to any verbal stimuli or follow instructions. It can't even do some of the so-called right-hemisphere tasks. . . . What we don't know yet is whether the engrams for language are over there, but there is no 'executor.' To use a loose computer metaphor, the executor is the thing that accesses and manipulates data. It may be that the amount of right-hemisphere language in the disconnected right brain depends on the extent to which the executors are present."

The ninth-floor offices where Gazzaniga and his team work are an interior decorator's meditation on variations of brown and beige: institutional-beige linoleum corridors, beige walls, mud-puddle-brown carpeting. The buzzing fluorescent lights and schoolroom-style clocks evoke the torpid eternity of a Friday afternoon in grade school, but there are invisible radiations of fervid intensity. For one thing, our visit coincides with grant-proposal season, when this country's neuroscientists must petition the funding bodies of the NIMH much as Renaissance artists had to curry favor with their Medici patrons. Besides, split-brain research seems to inspire a high intellectual passion in its devotees, for good reason.

A *talking* right hemisphere becomes an "assertive agent," in Gazzaniga's words, no longer the tongue-tied servant of the left. In the divided brain with two voices the Cornell researchers found the ideal test tube for experimentally induced states of conflict. Flash the message *smile* on one side of the screen and *frown* on the other, and "you can see the person fighting to get out both responses; parts of the mouth try to smile, while other parts frown." No doubt about it: There are two people in there, and they may not even be compatible. "Here's Paul," he says, pulling out a multiple-choice test. "We made up a five-point scale of the things we knew he was interested in. He had to rate them from 'like very much' to 'dislike very much,' and we had each hemisphere do the evaluation. One day he was absolutely polar. If one side liked something, the other side didn't. And he was *impossible* that day—abusive, bad tempered. . . . A month later we had him do it again, and each side rated things the same. That day he was calm, pleasant, engaging.

"Now, what happens when you and I experience states of anxiety? We're sitting here with two parallel mental systems evaluating the same stimuli differently. The biological system tries to resolve the conflict, and that may be what gives rise to our anxiety."

What Gazzaniga wondered was this: How does the dominant left brain cope with behaviors and statements initiated by the newly vocal right side? What manner of French farce would occur when "conscious" and "unconscious" processes collide? One answer surfaced in experiments like the three described above. Apparently the language centers in the left hemisphere will turn mental cartwheels to rationalize the puzzling behaviors emanating from the right. Thus the left brain will solemnly explain that it drew a banana because a banana could be drawn with several downward-sweeping strokes of the pen or that it picked a picture of a shovel because the concept of chicken suggested the idea of cleaning out a chicken shed. In short, it is the nature of the dominant linguistic hemisphere to *construct theories* about the world, including the unseen or unknown part.

Dumber Than a Chimpanzee

THERE IS a war on in the academic journals these days between Eran Zaidel, who thinks the average right hemisphere stores crucial language skills, and Gazzaniga, who believes a talking right hemisphere is a very rare bird. "Zaidel and I disagree about this. In Sperry's lab in the sixties, two of our first three patients had right-hemisphere language, and so we thought it was common. We were living in a statistical illusion. I think the percentage is really quite small. In our series of a hundred patients we have only three cases."

The average disconnected right hemisphere without language is a pretty dim bulb, in Gazzaniga's opinion; its abilities may be "vastly inferior to the cognitive skills of a chimpanzee." It may not even be self-aware. "A chimp can be conditioned to respond to a picture of itself with thumbs down or thumbs up. I don't know if that means it knows itself or not."

Before it could speak, Paul's right brain answered the question "Who are you?" by spelling out *Paul* in building blocks, a feat that was interpreted as self-awareness at the time. "Yet," says Gazzaniga, "that same 'smart' right hemisphere can't take the words *pin* and *finger* and point to the most appropriate answer, *bleed*, when it's told to set these things in a causal relationship. We worked through it with pictures and demonstrations to see if this right hemisphere could make inferences, and it couldn't. It's stupid."

What is the right brain good for then? "It does a lot of things. First of all, it's controlling half the body. It might also be a sort of fast processor for things that don't require verbal analysis: Get in or get out; match the sample; make quick perceptual judgments. It doesn't need to go through this analytical naming and classifying that the left side does. Bogen views it as a sort of mismatch detector, which is probably correct."

We visit a cluttered testing room, where a translucent screen with a red + in the middle sits on a scuffed metal desk next to an Apple IIe computer and a slide projector. Labeled 35-millimeter slide boxes ("Horizontal and Vertical Dots") line the shelves. White lab coats hang like discarded ghosts from a wooden coat tree. If a mute right hemisphere is below chimpanzee level, a talking one may still lag behind the Premacks' "Sarah," the ape who has theoretically mastered elementary logic and inferential reasoning. That, anyway, is the drift of Gazzaniga's recent experiments. "Vicki's right hemisphere is something else," he tells us. "It can talk, but it still can't compute. It can't subtract, multiply, or divide. And it has a rotten time generating mental images. If it is shown a capital *Y* and told to make a mental image of the lowercase version and say whether any part of the letter goes below the line, it can't do it.

"The right hemisphere has a hard time making inferences about events that go beyond simple association. If you flash *dog*, it points to *cat*. That's a simple associative response. But if you flash *dog* and *leash*, and it has to go to *walk*, it can't do it. It's too abstract."

"It sounds," we say, "like you agree with Eccles's idea that the right side of the brain has only a rudimentary consciousness."

"Well, there's more to that than we originally wanted to give him credit for," he says with a grin. "My sense of these patients is that they live in the left hemisphere, even the ones who talk out of both sides."

The first split-brain cases seemed to offer a rare opportunity to study thought without language. But, ironically, the Cornell group may have discovered just the opposite. "The assumption has always been that language is the basis of cognition," says Gazzaniga. "But this experiment of Mother Nature's has allowed us to see something very interesting. Here you have a right hemisphere with clear language skills but no real cognition. Now, the question is, what does that mean about language in the normal left hemisphere?

"It may mean that language is merely the press agent for these other variables of cognition. There are many parallel, co-conscious systems in the brain, not just two. There is no 'general' in charge. To make sense of all the different behaviors, there has to be a system that interprets and formulates theories. Language is closely related to it, but it isn't the thing itself."

"What is the thing itself?"

"That's what we're trying to get at. I can't say anything more. That's *my* book. It's called the *Social Brain*—that's a hint."

"The idea we're pushing around here," he continues, "is that the brain has a modular, parallel organization—well, it's silly to argue whether the brain is serial or parallel because it's obvious the system has to be serial in some ways and parallel in others. Think about a small home computer. If one bit is down, the whole thing's down. But I can take you across the street"—he points to the grave, gray towers of New York Hospital rising in the mauve November dusk like a massive stone effigy—"and show you people with pounds of brain gone who are sitting there reading the *Times*. If the brain were organized as a general serial system, a lesion in any region would be devastating."

The Self as Public Relations Agent

The center that he sought was a state of mind,
Nothing more, like weather after it has cleared.
—WALLACE STEVENS,
"Artificial Populations"

MENTAL UNITY, according to Gazzaniga, is as fraudulent as a Cecil B. DeMille movie set of ancient Rome. The sense of "I" is a slick public relations job. "The emerging picture," he notes, "is that our cognitive system is not a unified network with a single purpose and train of thought. A more accurate metaphor is that our sense of subjective awareness arises out of our dominant left hemisphere's unrelenting need to explain actions taken from any one of a multitude of mental systems that dwell within us."

This picture of the mind as an uneasy coalition of *multiple* subminds—of many parallel "subroutines," in computerspeak—is much in vogue. The late Dr. Norman Geschwind regarded our thought organ as a "loose federation" of neural systems. "The extent of the disunity varies from person to person," he told author Jonathan Miller in *States of Mind*. "In any case, there does not seem to be a central prime mover overseeing all behavior." Rather, our various behaviors are ruled by countless controllers in the brain, some of which behave like warring Balkan states. For example, a spontaneous smile and a consciously produced smile (as when the photographer tells you to say "cheese") are under the control of separate brain systems, according to Geschwind:

[There is] a region in the depths of the brain which contains the innate program for smiling. If we ask a patient who has suffered paralysis of one half of the face after a stroke to smile, he cannot produce even a poor smile on one side since the face area of the cortex has been destroyed on the opposite side of the brain. Yet when something amuses the patient, the region in the depths is still intact and produces a smile.

Consider: In earlier chapters we described two separate memory systems, one of which seems to operate semiautomatically, even "unconsciously." We met florid examples of epileptic automatism, of human beings running on "automatic pilot," seemingly without benefit of conscious awareness. We met people with "blindsight," who see without knowing they are seeing. Even in nonpathological brains conscious and unconscious mental processes are often at odds. Paul MacLean's three-in-one brain gives us a mind trisected into semiautonomous reptilian, paleomammalian, and neomammalian centers of consciousness. It's safe to say that the drama of the dueling hemispheres is only one instance of a "split brain."

If the brain is a menagerie of subselves, how do we experience ourselves as one? To Gazzaniga, the unitary self is a "sociological" creation, a tale concocted by a mental system that is kin to but not identical with the left-hemisphere language centers. Bogen thinks the self is double-headed like Janus; Sperry sees it as a higher emergent property bridging the mirror worlds of the two hemispheres; Eccles views it as an incorporeal entity that whispers to the left hemisphere. Computer aficionados speak confidently of a "self symbol," an internal "self-representation" inside the biocomputer.

In a perplexing syndrome known as borderline personality disorder, psychiatrist Arnold Mandell (1980) sees a parade of actor-selves upon an empty stage:

The stability of self called *character* is disturbed so that over the years such people have periods when they may behave like distinctly different people: an unconscionable psychopath, a guilty obsessional, a hysteric with a paralyzed limb, hypersexual, frigid, a born-again religious convert, a depressive with hypochondriasis, a bizarre psychotic, and for months or years even, an apparently normal individual with little of the previous manifestations. Whereas most of us have a limited number of what [William] James called *tendencies*, a narrow range of stable states . . . these "as if" people can be anything, but *not for very long*. Deeper looks at them . . . have revealed (between clinical "periods") feelings of insubstantiality, a continuing feeling of nervousness, "pan anxiety," along with feelings of emptiness, lack of identity, and an absence of meaning. Some use social roles to pretend a continuity of self they do not feel.

But that is solidity compared with the strange affliction of multiple personality disorder.

Multiple Perspectives

I am thirty-five years old and I was a multiple for thirty-two years, because I was three when it started. I was molested a lot by my stepfather, and when I was six I was raped. My core personality went out then, at age six, and my host personality, Mary, took over.

Only one person in my family knows. That's the case with most multiple personalities. You just don't see it if you're not looking for it. My first husband, poor dear, never knew what hit him.

See, part of my personality went to sleep for a year and woke up married to Eddie—that's my ex-husband—and I could not tolerate him. Monica was the one who married him. What happened was that Mary's fiancé had drowned and when he drowned she konked out for a year. When she woke up married to Eddie she couldn't stand him. She also resented being thrown into this situation because she didn't know she was a multiple at the time. She didn't know that Monica existed.

In 1983 we wrote a short magazine article about multiple personality disorder (MPD), the bizarre psychiatric syndrome known in the vernacular as "split personality." You may know it as *The Three Faces of Eve* syndrome, after the 1957 best-seller. (The real Eve actually developed twenty-two different personalities before she was healed in 1974; the eponymous "Sybil," a midwestern woman, had sixteen.) Several weeks after the article appeared, we received a well-written and thoughtful letter from "M. M. George," a self-described "multiple." We wrote back, eventually establishing contact with Marion, the thirty-five-year-old western Massachusetts woman behind the pseudonym (M. M. George is an amalgam of her three major personalities, Mary, Monica, and George). Marion is not her real name, either; proper names and certain personal details in these passages have been changed to protect her identity.

Marion's story is painfully real. Like most multiples, she has been through more trials than Job, including misdiagnosis as a schizophrenic, commitment to a Bedlamesque state mental hospital, repeated suicide attempts, inappropriate drug treatment, even a would-be exorcism. Yet, as she wrote us in one letter, "I am all in favor of educating the public and letting them know that we multiples are really ordinary people with a bit of an odd illness . . . but we live and survive. That's what it's all about, a unique and wonderful defense mechanism that not everyone can have.''

Until recently, multiple personality disorder was usually dismissed as a rare and rococo psychiatric hoax. If a many-faced Eve or Sybil appeared on the couch, mainstream psychiatry labeled her (for most multiples are female) a schizophrenic, a manic-depressive, or a clever, manipulative fake. Psychiatrist Frank Putnam discovered his first multiple languishing in a ward for depressives at NIMH—glum, suicidal, totally unresponsive to treatment. "She had been presented at grand rounds as a classic example of various neurological diseases—brain tumor, epilepsy, you name it," he tells us. "In my therapy group she went through a series of startling changes that she did not acknowledge. Usually she was withdrawn, rigid, hostile, and quiet, and then she'd suddenly shift and become funny and witty, laughing and making puns."

That was 1979, and over the next few years, Putnam went on to assemble some 150 "Eves" and rigorously analyze their brains as well as their psyches. "When I got into multiple personality disorder, I got so involved in it I essentially gave up everything else," he says. He and his co-workers at the NIMH and St. Elizabeths Hospital in Washington can now report that the alternate selves inside a multiple are more real and more autonomous than anyone suspected. If Eve has three faces, she also has three voices, three separate memory circuits, indeed (in a neurophysiological sense) three different brains. This fact could force some revision of our old notions of selfhood.

The Several Brains of Eve   First, Putnam and EEG veteran Monte Buchsbaum (then at NIMH) analyzed the brain waves of ten multiples, mapping the patterns of event-related potentials (ERPs) in response to light flashes. "In each multiple we studied at least three different personalities that were capable of cooperating—usually, the core personality, a child personality, and an obsessive-compulsive personality," he explains. "And we tested each personality at least five times. For controls we used normal actors, who merely imagined being different people." His results elevated "split personality" from late-late-show melodrama to hard neuroscience: While the actors' EEG patterns didn't change much from one feigned personality to another, the Sybils, Joes, Harriets, and Marys inhabiting each multiple patient looked like different people, neuroelectrically speaking. MPD—which California psychiatrist Ralph Allison likens to a cancer of the personality, because selves multiply wantonly like malignant cells—proved to have a basis in biology.

Putnam did not rest on his laurels. With Daniel Weinberger, he did cerebral blood-flow studies (in which inhaled radioactive xenon is used to illumine active brain regions) and reported "striking differences" between different personalities. Since it's common to find both left-handed and right-handed characters inside a multiple, Putnam did a series of physiological tests and found corresponding shifts in hemispheric dominance.

"We now know of a thousand cases," says Putnam. "So while it's a rare disorder, it may not be as rare as we thought." Women comprise 85 percent of the victims. "But," says Putnam, "I suspect that there are many unrecognized male multiples in the criminal justice system, because they usually have one personality that's violent." In 1978 William Milligan of Columbus, Ohio, became the first person in the United States to be acquitted of a major crime (four counts of rape) by reason of multiple identity. His ten personalities included an intellectual named Arthur who spoke in a clipped, British manner; several child personalities; two lesbians; "Ragan," a feisty male with a Slavic accent who threatened to fire his lawyers; and an escape artist named Tommy, who once slithered, Houdini-like, out of a straitjacket in ten seconds flat. Although each personality knew the difference between right and wrong, all of them together did not compose a whole person, according to the seven psychiatrists and psychologists who testified at the trial—ergo, Milligan could not be held responsible for his crimes.

Many multiples, however, shuffle through their pack of selves inconspicuously, working as corporate lawyers, secretaries, PTA presidents, or dentists—incognito even to themselves. The first hint may be odd gaps in the temporal stream, disquieting memory lapses, perhaps the "Twilight Zone" experience of waking up in a strange motel room with a perfect stranger (if not married to one).

One day in 1979, I woke up—or rather, Mary, woke up—in a motel room with somebody Monica was involved with. I called my psychiatrist at four a.m., and said, "All right, what's going on here?" He said, "Okay, it's time we talked."

That's when we discovered Monica. And shortly afterwards, we discovered George, and we have that on tape. Since I have it on tape I can listen to all three personality voices—Mary, Monica, and George—and they're all different. George had kind of a deeper voice. People would kind of look when he came out. Monica's voice was very light and lilting. Daphne's was sort of low and sexy.

Lurking somewhere behind all the personae is the "original," the core personality, which may take years to unearth. In the meantime the "host," the facade that the patient uses to simulate unity, presides like a long-term guest host on the "Tonight Show." Usually no one perceives the change.

Virtually all multiples have a child-self, an opposite-sex self, an obsessive-compulsive self, and a self that is depressive, suicidal, or violent. There may also be several incomplete "personality fragments." Typically some of the personalities are more charismatic, more flamboyant, than the rather drab original. But despite their myriad identities, most multiples are not psychotic, according to Putnam, and may function quite well, often delegating different tasks to different personalities.

Mary was a marvelous artist, a good writer, a moderate singer. Monica was the real singer in the bunch; she had a beautiful voice. In my high-school chorus I was listed in three different categories—second soprano, which was Mary; alto, which was Monica; and George was first tenor. It didn't happen very often but whenever my singing teacher needed an extra voice he'd put me in wherever, because I had a three-octave range. Mostly I was in the alto range, which was Monica's range . . . I don't consider myself as good now. My husband thinks I have a chance to be as good as Monica was if I just practiced.

Therapists who treat multiples often find themselves in dialogue with different voices—some male, some female, some childlike—eerie as the alien voices emanating from a medium at a séance. In 1983 neurologist Christie Ludlow of the National Institute of Neurological and Communicative Disorders and Stroke (NINCDS) tested this phenomenon by making high-tech "voiceprints" of some of Putnam's patients. Using a computerized technique called spectral analysis, which essentially sorts out the different frequencies composing a single sound, Ludlow confirmed that the subvoices were indeed very distinct.

One multiple has three menstrual periods every month, one for each of her identities. Others require different prescription glasses for their alter egos. A multiple can harbor one identity that knows how to drive and another that doesn't; one that speaks a foreign language fluently and another with a tin ear. Chicago psychiatrist and MPD authority Bennett Braun studied a man who was allergic to citrus drinks in all personalities but one. Putnam has met multiples who are actually married to two different people. "I wouldn't be surprised," he adds, "if a certain percentage of people who lead double lives—spies, double agents, bigamists—are actually multiples. Some mediums and victims of 'demonic possession' probably are, too." The repertoire of a multiple includes dramatic shifts in facial expression, accent, vocabulary, body language, clothing and hair styles, handwriting, phobias, and—above all—memories.

For twenty-eight years of my life I was amnesic. When I was younger I didn't notice it; I just thought everyone had these moments. Later, as things got more traumatic there was more and more time I would miss. I just thought I was crazy.

Mary, the "host," the one who was "me" the majority of the time, didn't know about the other personalities. Monica knew about Mary but not about about George. She was amnesic when George came out. George knew everything. He is the one they call the link or the bridge, the one who has all the memories.

So there were all these things that happened, but to an observer it just looked like I was acting strange some of the time. My mother never believed that I tried to commit suicide because she said I called for help, that I was just doing it to get attention. The point is, Mary would try to commit suicide and Monica would wait till she started to fall asleep and then she'd get up and call for help. But an outsider would just see that this person took a bunch of pills and then called for help.

Sometimes Eve fails to keep Lucille's appointments or (more ominously) mild Bruce does not recall the crimes committed by Harry. Multiple amnesia made for high courtroom drama at the trial of Kenneth Bianchi, the Los Angeles "Hillside Strangler," when Bianchi convinced several psychiatrists that he was unaware of the activities of a murderous doppelgänger named "Steve." The jury didn't buy Bianchi's multiple routine, but what of the selective amnesias of genuine MPD patients? With a battery of sophisticated tests, Putnam and NIMH psychologist Herbert Weingartner determined that multiples' memory circuits are well and truly compartmentalized. Personality X may remember nothing that happens to Y, while Z is consistently aware of Y but not of X, and so on. Braun believes that MPD may be an extreme case of state-dependent learning, which is the psychological law that information encoded during a given psychophysiological state is best retrieved in the same state. (In other words, if you misplaced the car keys while drunk, a couple of piña coladas may be the best route to finding them.)

What causes a personality to split apart in the first place? The clear and chilling answer is child abuse: 85 to 90 percent of MPD patients were beaten, cut, burned, half-drowned in bathtubs, locked in closets, hung out of windows, and/or sexually assaulted as children (generally before the age of ten), and their early histories are sagas of criticism, betrayal, abandonment, and inconsistency. "It is a coping mechanism," says Putnam. "The child compartmentalizes his or her pain so as not to have to deal with it all the time. A form of self-hypnosis is probably involved. The child goes into trances, and that trance-state consciousness grows more and more autonomous and differentiated."

When I was six, the "Topper" series was on TV and I was madly in love with George Kirby, the ghost who always helped to get Topper either into or out of trouble, who mostly helped him against the bad guys. I used to think, "Gee, I wish I had a George who could protect me against my stepfather." And then the night I was raped, bingo, there was George, and I (Marion) was gone. I went out with a scream, that's what I heard. George was there to save me. He pulled me away from my stepfather. Then Mary was born a few instants after. She was like the temporary host of the body. I never actually knew her because I went to sleep and when I woke up she became part of me.

Monica, who was born when I was three, also went to sleep when I was six and stayed gone until I was fourteen. She came back then to help out. Monica was the domestic one, the cheerful, the happy one. She was the one everyone liked best.

Unfortunately it isn't very easy to put Humpty-Dumpty together again. MPD is not cured in a day. "I don't believe there are any medications that work," says Putnam. Integration, as the healing process is called, can take years. Therapy takes the form of an intrapsychic encounter group, in which the various buried identities are coaxed into the open, sometimes via hypnosis. "The first step in treatment," Putnam explains, "is to get the personalities to meet each other."

The Reintegration of Marion

Fourmillante cité, cité plein de rêves,
Où le spectre en plein jour raccroche le passant.
—CHARLES BAUDELAIRE

As for Marion, six different personalities took their turns upon the stage of her life for thirty years. Despite her potpourri of nicknames (three of her personality-monikers appear under her picture in the high-school yearbook), her three-part harmony in the chorus, her often baffling behavior, her own family didn't notice her psychic multiplicity. Like many multiples, she was (and is) intelligent and talented, an accomplished singer, artist, and writer. But depressions, mental breakdowns, suicide attempts, and confusion inevitably aborted all her career plans.

Not until 1979, after her sobering morning-after in the motel room with "Monica's" date, did she learn she was a multiple personality. With a therapist, she began the slow, painful process of reconnecting her scattered selves, establishing lines of communication between them. Mary, the acting "host," learned of George and Monica; Monica began to leave notes for Mary ("Oh, by the way, I made an appointment for you . . ."); the personalities heard one another's voices and traded memories. On Halloween 1982 integration occurred, and all her "personal spirits" coalesced into a whole person. With her self-taught psychologist husband (who "fell in love with all of us" and married them/her in 1982) acting as hypnotist and guide, the real Marion returned after her long, Rip Van Winkle-like sleep. She now assists with the reintegration of other multiples and is working toward a career as a therapist for abused children. This is her story.

There were six personalities in all, Mary, Monica, George, Daphne, Ginny, and me. There was also a fractional personality, Nancy, but she never really developed into anything. She was a reaction to a car accident and then she was integrated, so we don't really count her.

Each personality was born from a crisis; it's an elaborate defense mechanism. You're in a situation you can't handle and you hypnotize yourself into being someone else who can. When I was raped at the age of six, George *came in and he saved me; he was the one who pulled me away from my stepfather.* Mary *was also born then. She was the host-personality after the real self,* Marion, *went to sleep. She was not a happy person. As she got older she got severely depressed and negative. She gained weight as a defense against men. At one point she allowed the body to reach a peak of 310 pounds.*

Monica *was the one I call "our little homemaker"; she was cheerful and bouncy, the one everyone liked best. She was created when I was three, when my stepfather started molesting me. But then she went to sleep when I was six and came back at age fourteen. At that point things got really bad at home and Mary couldn't handle it, so Monica came back to help out. But Monica could get depressed, too. Usually it was Mary who tried to commit suicide, but Monica tried to kill herself once. She was the one who fell in love with Eddie, my ex-husband, and married him. Later she had a brief affair with a guy who reminded her a lot of Eddie and she went home and tried to kill herself.*

Daphne *came out in 'eighty-one. She was sexual revenge, feminine anger. Men had treated me very badly and then when I lost weight and men started paying attention to me, Daphne was there to get even. She was this seductive eighteen-year-old siren. She was the one my [present] husband first fell in love with.*

A major trauma happened in late 'eighty-one that caused me to feel very abandoned, and Ginny *was born. She was six years old and an orphan. She actually started out as an infant and my George personality adopted her and raised her to the age of six.*

Once I was in a car accident and had severe internal injuries, and a fractional personality, Nancy, *was born from that. All she'd do is just lay there in internal pain. The problem was, though, she wanted to die. My doctor thought it wouldn't be a good idea to integrate her with all that pain, so she healed Nancy and then integrated her. So if you have a personality that is really negative you would probably work to change that personality before integrating it.*

I'm unlike a lot of multiples in that I don't have a whole slew of people. I knew a girl who had nineteen personalities and I sat down with a piece of paper and worked out all their attributes. . . . When I got married, there were three other multiples there who were all patients of my doctor. So we had a picture taken and we called it the Multiple Exposure. Between all of us, we figured out, there were forty-two people in that picture.

One psychiatrist told me that anyone who believed in multiples was deranged. Many of us have had people try to exorcise us. My mother tried to bring in a priest once. . . . She still won't believe it.

Before I was recognized as a multiple I was classified as a schizophrenic and, another time, as a manic-depressive. They tried lithium on me and it did absolutely nothing. You see, what they were seeing was first Monica, then Mary, then George—so, you know, elation, depression, then anger, in rapid succession. In 'seventy-seven I had a major breakdown. I was in the hospital almost more than I was out of it, first as a voluntary patient and then I was committed. Being committed to a state institution is a sheer hellhole. I didn't know what was going on; I didn't find out till two years later.

In 'seventy-nine I woke up. I was sitting there in this office with this doctor, who looked familiar to me. I thought some little kid had come in, because that's what it sounded like, a kid whispering. It was Monica whispering to me. I just started slowly and finally got to the point where I could easily carry on conversations with her. We discovered George not long afterwards.

My husband and I started working together in September [1982]. I couldn't afford a therapist and he said he was willing to be my lay therapist. We used all the material I already had, all the experiences I'd gained from my therapists. We had charts of all the major incidents in my life, all the major memories that had to be dealt with.

On Halloween I integrated. We took the personalities in reverse order, integrating Ginny first and working back to Monica. We did it with hypnosis because we figured it would be easiest. Some people integrate in their sleep. I know of one girl who went to sleep and woke up the next morning integrated. There's no tried-and-true way. We taped it, but I don't remember much of it. I embraced each of them, and when I embraced them they became one with me.

When I got to George, I just broke down and cried. He'd saved my life.

He'd been there for me so many times. But I realized later I didn't give him up. He's still a part of me.

One night, my girlfriend Lynn and I were in the car. It was shortly after integration. I hadn't seen any sign of the others [personalities] yet, but when you first integrate you aren't sure whether it's really happened. You won't know till there's a real crisis. So I was in the car with Lynn singing to a song on the radio. She said something, and I got angry with her. All of a sudden, she heard my voice drop and she looked over. George always wore his glasses down on the end of his nose. And she looked over and there were the glasses hanging down on the end of the nose. So at first she thought it was George yelling at her. But then she saw it was me; she could tell I hadn't left.

Lynn always knew when George was in the room. She wouldn't even have to look up; she could sense it. She'd just say, "Hi, George." See, Lynn was George's lover, and that's something that does happen quite often with multiples. George defined himself as a man; therefore he had an interest in women. And that bothered me. Other people would have seen us as lesbians, I suppose, if they had known. But George was very discreet; no one knew. But that's why they were so close. Lynn had a really hard time giving up George.

Anyway, after that incident in the car, I looked at her and said, "That was me*. I got angry." I had never gotten angry before. When I got angry I'd let go and George would take over. That wasn't my role.*

George was about anger. And destruction, protection, firmness. He had many sides to him. He grew up to have quite a temper. Once he grew up to age fourteen, he stayed fourteen for a number of years. It's a volatile age. It's more acceptable for a fourteen-year-old to have temper tantrums and throw things. So he stayed fourteen till he was discovered and my therapist aged him hypnotically.

There is a humorous side to being a multiple. My Daphne personality liked to go out partying and dancing with Lynn. One night Daphne started drinking and dancing, forgetting that I had just taken some pretty potent medication. Halfway through the wine, it hit her hard and Lynn had to drive her home. Daphne happened to comment that Ginny—my little one—was drunk, on the inside. (At this point I was close to fusing and there was a great deal of cooperation between personalities.) Lynn couldn't resist and asked to see the six-year-old in such a condition. Ginny came out, glassy-eyed and feeling silly. She was curled up in the stuffed chair staring around in a way that suggested the room was moving around her. She focused on the shelf where she kept her four stuffed animals. She looked amazed and said, "I got three Teddy Bears, and three Katrina Kitty Kats, and three

Tommy Tommy Tom Cats and three Pokey Turtles . . . I got more animals than I thought I got."

Since I am integrated now, I have all the memories. I am still affected by some of them; I can still go into withdrawal over some of them. My husband and I had to go over them several times to neutralize them. He would give me what we call a volume control on the pain and I could observe the scene with no commitment at all, and then turn up the volume and get a little closer, and a little closer, until I could accept the whole thing.

I think my stepfather may have been a multiple himself. He has a lot of different names. He was severely abused as a child. And there were times when his personality would just switch. He'd be beating me and then, boom, he'd just stop and walk away as if nothing had happened. There was one incident when I, as George, got angry and sideswiped him across the head with a bowl, and he just walked away.

He also had this strict religious side, and I've never known a multiple without a religious, almost fanatical side to them. My Mary personality was obsessed with certain things; she was obsessed with religion for a while. Another thing is migraines. I don't know a single multiple who doesn't have them. Mary had migraines all the time.

This summer I may try to see my stepfather, whom I haven't seen in years. I am thinking of going back to visit the house where I grew up, where all this happened. See, logically, I know that that house is a nice little house on a nice little street in a normal city. But in my mind it's the Amityville horror. I've got to go back to put it in perspective. . . .

It's hard being integrated. There are so many situations when you wish some of them were around to take care of it. You're totally responsible for all your actions now.

A doctor I once worked with said that in a sense we are all multiples. To his seven-year-old he's "Daddy"; to someone else, he's "Doctor"; he plays different roles. It's just that with a multiple the roles are a little more for keeps.

A few months after this conversation, we got another letter from Marion, which read, in part:

To be perfectly honest, I have re-split but we don't think it is a serious situation. There were stressful circumstances involved with the possibility of seeing my stepfather again. That on top of an overloaded work schedule and doing volunteer work, too. . . . I just blew a fuse. We feel (my doctor and I) that as soon as I can calm down, put my stepfather out of my mind, and rest from the overload, I should be able to reintegrate George and the new young personality named Anna (aged 15). They seldom come out, and when they do, it startles my husband. After all, I had been integrated for 16 months. But I think I can reintegrate soon. . . .

It's time that people understood that this illness is a *reality*, not just a figment of someone's imagination.

Some Embarrassing Questions

LIKE THE "SPLIT BRAIN," MPD raises some awkward, even embarrassing, questions. Will the Real Self please stand up! Who is in charge? How does it feel to share a body with a host of other minds? Is a person morally responsible for the actions of alternate selves he/she doesn't know about?

Given the often-astonishing gifts of their satellite personae—like the ability to converse in fluent Russian or to perform Houdini-like escape feats—multiple personalities make a strange showcase for the untapped potentials inside every brain. Rather than freaks, multiple personalities are like you and me—only more so, or so some psychiatrists maintain.

Maybe you, too, harbor closet "selves" in various degrees of evolution: an intellectual, a Don Juan, a bon vivant, an ascetic, a hero, a melancholiac, a housewife, a revolutionary, a hysteric, a lonely child, a Machiavellian power broker, an artist. Perhaps mental unity is a matter of *repressing* the alternate selves struggling to be born. And consider the dream self, your nocturnal alter ego: Is *that* you? What about your pack of previous selves: four-year-old, bed-wetting Stevie, teenage Steve with the ducktail haircut, and so on? You are amnesic for your own infancy; "you" disappear in anesthesia, deep sleep, coma, and certain twilight states. Where's the self?

So far no electroencephalogram, no PET scan, has pinpointed the neuron, or network of neurons, that encodes the "I." Obviously, the self is a global property of the brain—if, that is, it is "in" our gray matter at all. Even in this age of neurotechnological miracles, selfhood remains a deep, dark mystery.

ALTERED
STATES

9

The Hanged Man:
Altered States of Consciousness

> The Hanged Man is suspended from a gallows, a
> T-cross of living wood. His arms, folded behind
> his back, together with his head form a triangle
> with the point downward; his legs form a cross.
> . . . There is a deep nimbus about his head, and
> his face expresses deep entrancement rather than
> suffering.
>
> —EDEN GRAY, *The Tarot Revealed*

THE ORTHODOX VIEW is that the mind is a biological computer, totally self-contained and limited by physical laws," Charles Tart tells us in his house in the Berkeley hills, as the late-afternoon sun illumines a row of sedate Buddhas on the window curtains and a dreaming house cat stirs on the carpet. "If you have an experience of leaving your body, becoming one with the universe, or meeting a spiritual being, Western science tells you it's an illusion. Just as if you programmed your Apple computer to say 'I have just attained oneness with the Ultimate Chip.'

"However, it seems quite possible that things like precognition and remote viewing, which violate our assumptions about physical laws, do happen. There are certain altered states in which, moreover, such phenomena seem neither illogical nor unnatural."

Beneath the thin patina of ordinary mental life lies a glittering emporium of "altered states of consciousness" (ASCs). They range from the exotic (the peyote trips of South American *curanderos*) to the routine (sleep and dreams); from the sordid (angel dust nightmares) to the sublime (Saint Theresa's ecstasies). Tart is the man who put them on the map, scientifically speaking. Back in 1970 the University of California at Davis psychologist edited a fat, sky-blue volume, *Altered States of Consciousness*, which was touted in the *Last Whole Earth Catalogue* as a must-read "if you're doing anything with meditation, dope, hypnosis, dreams, subjective exploration of any kind." Today, after all the Indian-print bedspreads have faded, the book is still the ASC connoisseur's bible, and Tart is still scrutinizing the human mind's outback.

Not haphazardly, and not by zoning out into a chemical never-never land. Rather, Tart proposed scientific methods for cataloguing out-of-the-ordinary states, for testing them, for mapping their varied terrain. He even fathered a new science, *state-specific science*. Remember the drug experiments of the 1960s, in which aloof, white-coated technicians observed college students stoned on marijuana or LSD in sterile, windowless labs? "Eyes bloodshot, thinking impaired, subject confused and disoriented," the scientists would note down. Altered states, Tart believes, can't be mapped that way. To an "objective," note-taking observer, someone on LSD (or a yogi in deep *samadhi*) may appear catatonic, but inside the subject's head the Hallelujah chorus may be playing. That's where state-specific science comes in.

The basic idea is to get *inside* the subjective world. For instance, Tart asked pot smokers if they could identify the moment of transition from "straight" to "stoned" (they couldn't) and codified their experiences in a landmark marijuana study. He discovered that LSD users typically transit a whole series of unstable, rapidly metamorphosing states of consciousness. Early on he pointed out that drug dosage X did not automatically produce psychological state X, for so much depended on setting, mood, the helper/guides, and the user's own psychic structure.

If Tart had his way, a new breed of state-specific scientists would be

The Hanged Man of the Tarot deck: His inverted position symbolizes the complete reversal of ordinary thought patterns that occurs in altered states. (*The Bettmann Archive*)

trained to enter various ASCs and report the landscape in scrupulous detail. Is time oddly dilated? Space foreshortened? Are the colors vivid, pulsating? What happens to memory, identity, thought processes? "Then," he adds, "once a researcher has identified a certain state, he can go back and do more minute mapping. For example, most reports of the near-death experience include traveling through a tunnel. One could ask people to describe the tunnel in detail. What are the sides made of? How many people touch the sides? What is the means of locomotion? These are questions we never thought to ask before."

But why bother? Who cares if acid heads see luminous, Day-Glo colors, or if some turbaned ladies squinting into the Absolute have funny brain waves? What's this ouga-bouga stuff doing in a book about the brain?

Our subject here is consciousness, which can't be ground up and analyzed in a petri dish. We can't stick electrodes into it, see it in a radioimmunoassay, or control it with inescapable foot shock. So just as neurologists have studied brain tumors and bullet wounds to map the topography of the cortex (if region X is down, the big toe won't work), researchers can use altered states to illumine little-known regions of the mind. Hallucinations and dreams can tell us about the brain's perceptual machinery as well as about the psyche's back streets. "Much of the brain's information is stored as images," says UCLA's Ronald Siegel, the Leif Erikson of the hallucinatory world, whom we'll meet in Chapter 10. "By studying hallucination we are learning about the brain's storage and retrieval processes."

A great deal of information is stored in ASCs in fact. We have mentioned the well-known psychological law of state-bound knowledge, which says, in essence, that information learned in a given state is best retrieved there, too. Since information isn't easily transferred from one state to another, one wonders what uncharted human abilities and what valuable state-bound knowledge lurks in ASCs. The chemist Kekulé solved the structure of the benzene ring in a dream after all. "Most religious teachings are actually state-bound knowledge," Tart notes. "They make excellent sense in certain altered states, but in other states they turn into empty creeds that people are forced to believe in."

If the first part of this book described the "machine," this section is about the "ghosts." The division is a bit meretricious, of course, for we've already encountered a whole funhouse of altered states: schizophrenic hallucinations, the strangely truncated mental life of multiple personalities, the "auras" of temporal-lobe epilepsy, various distortions of memory. It goes to show just how difficult it is to set up any apartheid between what is "altered" and what is "normal" in human consciousness.

Among the ASCs known to humankind are dreams, daydreams, drug and alcohol intoxication, whirling dervish rites, the ecstatic ! kia dance of the ! Kung bushmen of Africa, fire-walking ceremonies, ESP visions, mystical reveries, a medium's trance, the "auras" preceding a migraine attack, the near-death experience. Fasting, meditation, prolonged sleeplessness, the monotony of an arctic winter or a total body cast, hypoglycemia, a high fever, chanting, hypnosis, brain-wave biofeedback, and isolation tanks are all possible routes to our inner gardens.

The quintessential ASC includes these features: distorted time perception or a sense of timelessness; "depersonalization," or loss of self; lowered inhibitions; ineffability; and heightened empathy, even a sense of merging with other people or objects. Whether he or she has just swallowed five micrograms of LSD, meditated on a blue vase (as in a classic experiment by psychiatrist Arthur Deikman), or is merely dreaming, a person in an altered state typically links thoughts associatively and metaphorically rather than logically, dwells on paradoxes, prefers the concrete to the abstract, and may enjoy "synesthesia," an overlapping of the senses in which words evoke colors or a Strauss waltz tastes like lime sherbet.

Because of strong "family resemblance" among disparate ASCs, some scientists believe they all spring from a similar brain state. The common denominator often seems to be either sensory isolation (e.g., monastic life, an isolation tank, meditation, dreams) or sensory overload (e.g., repetitive chanting, Holy Roller revival meetings). But can science explain the exact electrical/chemical/physical mechanisms that cause auditory hallucinations, *satori*, or a medium's trance? Can it find God (or the experience of God) in the brain?

That's the great hope, and at first it looked easy. The first ASC to be quantified in the laboratory was sleep, Everyman's route to nonordinary reality. When researchers in the early 1950s discovered that distinctive EEG patterns and rapid eye movements (REM) characterized dreaming, some hopeful investigators foresaw an exact science of altered states. Maybe clairvoyance or the hypnotic state would be accompanied by a certain sawtooth-shaped brain wave. Maybe Zen meditation would make a bio-feedback machine's needle move. In the early 1960s, biofeedback pioneers Elmer and Alyce Green, of the Menninger Foundation in Topeka, Kansas, traveled to India, wired up some yogis, and brought their neuro-transcendent secrets back to the lab. At Langley Porter Psychiatric Institute, in San Francisco, Joe Kamiya compared the brain-wave, breathing, and heart-rate patterns of Zen monks, Tibetan Buddhists, and ordinary daydreamers. A group of sleep researchers at Maimonides Hospital in New York worked on experimentally induced psi. By the early 1970s, when Maharishi Mahesh

Yogi's Transcendental Meditation (TM) started producing a standardized, Middle-American type of meditator that made a perfect experimental animal, mantras entered the lab.

The results? A few flashy EEGs here and there in the yogis, many ho-hum statistics about heart rate, galvanic skin responses, and lack of "stress" in the meditators. But, by and large, altered states did not make for hard science. Only in sleep and dreams do EEGs precisely mirror states of consciousness, and they still can't tell what you're dreaming *about*. Scientists can explain how LSD tampers with brain chemistry but not whether a given tripper will merge with the universe, jump off a ledge, or merely groove on the wallpaper pattern. The two-hundred-year-old science of hypnosis so eludes scientists' probes that some doubt it's an ASC at all. As for meditation: Research at Yale University's Center for Behavioral Medicine turned up the surprising fact that regular "reading therapy"—that is, reading a book for half an hour a day—is neurophysiologically equivalent to the practice of TM. (Whether this means the Maharishi's mantras are comparable to *Heidi* or merely reflects the crudeness of our measuring devices, we'll let you decide.)

Nonetheless, there *are* a few places where hard science and altered reality meet, and we'll take you to them in the next chapters, in which we'll meet:

· A no-nonsense behavioral psychologist at UCLA who is compiling the world's first hallucination "dictionary."
· A pair of Harvard sleep researchers who, after years of probing dreams with microelectrodes, propose a drastic revision of Freudian dream theory.
· A Stanford researcher who has made "lucid dreaming" scientifically kosher and who is training a corps of "oneironauts," or dream travelers, to consciously direct their dream life.
· A hard-nosed Atlanta M.D. who launched an empirical study of the near-death experience (NDE) in order to disprove the phenomenon and wound up a believer. And some psychologists who concur.
· A heterodox group of neuroscientists with startling opinions on "God in the Brain." What modern neurochemistry and mysticism, the opiate receptor and William Blake, have in common.

We have tried to stick to good, hard neuroscience: studies of neuroreceptors, EEG recordings, models of brain circuitry, and the like. Unfortunately "state-specific science" is still a science in search of a lab. "No one has ever systematically applied the idea," says Tart. We would count Ron Siegel's anatomy of hallucination (Chapter 10) and Stephen LaBerge's lucid-dreaming studies (Chapter 11) as the closest approximations. But the following section could be viewed as an outline of possible methodologies, the scattered pieces of a future science of the subjective universe. If some of the scientists interviewed here are renegades, if their theories clash with the worldviews of *Science* and *The Archives of General Psychiatry,* that's because mainstream brain science has mostly neglected altered realities.

When someone has visions, orthodox science says, "Oh, schizophrenia. This is what happens when the brain is diseased." (And, more often than not, the diagnosis is correct.) If a biblical figure had a tête-à-tête with God on the road to Damascus, well, okay, that's in the Bible, but if the conversion occurs today on the highway to Peoria, cerebrospinal-fluid samples are ordered. If several million Americans tell pollsters that they had a classic near-death experience (NDE), scientists say, "Severe depersonalization." Altered states are, for the most part, considered pathologies.

Out-of-the-ordinary realities aren't just difficult to quantify and control in the lab. They also challenge conventional ideas of the brain/mind. People who are revived from near-death, for example, typically report afterlife-type visions, which the scientific orthodoxy views as lunatic-fringe stuff (Chapter 12). If the near-death experience is genuine, it would come close to proving Plato's doctrine that the nonphysical mind can exist apart from the bodily hardware. How would neuroscience handle that? The world's mystics, as well as many drug messiahs, also speak of a reality quite contrary to our sacred scientific paradigms. After tasting transcendent realities, John Lilly discarded his former scientific beliefs and decided that the mind can float away from its physical container. (Ron Siegel, in contrast, is convinced by his altered-states research that mind and brain are one and the same.)

So-called normal consciousness, as Tart sees it, is merely "consensus reality," that safe, tidy plot of mind that our culture calls home. Thus the generic term *altered state* has been banned from his vocabulary and replaced by "discrete state of consciousness" and "discrete altered state of consciousness" and other phrases that don't exactly roll off the tongue. "Western science implicitly assumes that there is a normal state of consciousness and that all others are degenerate forms of it," he says. "But that's not true. What one person experiences as an altered state may fall into the sphere of ordinary consciousness for another. We don't all start from the same baseline consciousness, and we vary widely in our ability to transit between different states." In his everyday consciousness, for instance, the inventor Nikola Tesla could design a machine in his head, specifying the parts to one ten-thousandth of an inch.

Besides, ASCs are as all-American as apple pie and the Superbowl. As Amazonian Indians have their tribal ceremonies, we have ours: cocktail parties, discotheques with strobe lights, Superbowl fever, the febrile cadences of Billy Graham. In fact, 90 percent of the world's cultures have some sort of institutionalized mind-altering ritual, according to Ohio State University anthropologist Erica Bourguignon. "The fact that they are nearly universal," she tells us, "must mean that such states are very important to human beings."

Why? No one really knows. As Chapter 11 will tell, science has yet to explain why nature gave us sleep and dreams, our nocturnal theater of the absurd. But there are theories. In Chapter 10, we'll hear why Ron Siegel believes higher mammals need periodic vacations (via altered states, chemical or otherwise) from quotidian, workaday reality, and we'll meet Dr. John Lilly, the former *enfant terrible* of the NIMH, who has taken a permanent, mind-altered vacation. Perhaps without ASCs we'd all go insane.

Every night, regular ninety-minute cycles of REM and non-REM (deep, dreamless) sleep alternate in the human brain. And during the waking hours—according to studies at the University of California at San Diego—human beings fall into spontaneous daydreams every ninety minutes if left to their own devices. Maybe these natural cycles of reverie are as necessary to the organism as REM sleep is. (Deprived of REM, animals and people are known to go quite bonkers.) Yet modern, nine-to-five life is obviously not designed around them. "My hypothesis," muses Patricia Carrington, a psychologist and meditation authority who teaches at Princeton, "is that we are starved for the natural rhythms, the biological alternation of rest and relaxation we see in animals. Only in man is there such a thing as seventeen hours of constant wakefulness." Deprived of our own mini-ASCs, we have the three-martini lunch, angel dust, and Disneyland.

ASCs may serve other purposes, too. "Altered states remind us that we're more than we think we are," says Tart. "There is tremendous human suffering because we've banished them. We live so immersed in our own ongoing psychological processes that we're in a kind of waking trance. And it's 'normal'—everyone is in it. All science has to tell us about ourselves is that we're locked inside our skulls, that we're automata totally shaped by our environment, and that, whatever happens, we'll just die, anyway, so what does anything matter?"

10

Anatomy of Hallucination: Prophets of the Void

> If we tested Socrates or Joan of Arc, I think we'd
> be able to classify their experiences comfortably
> with our code.
> —RONALD SIEGEL

> The miracle is that the universe created a part of
> itself to study the rest of it, and that this part, in
> studying itself, finds the rest of the universe in its
> own natural inner realities.
> —JOHN C. LILLY, M.D.,
> *The Center of the Cyclone*

W E CAN NOW TELL YOU that pigeons see a lot of red dots and circles when they hallucinate and that monkeys see food-related objects," Ronald Siegel, of UCLA, tells us. "The technique has its limits, of course."

The forty-one-year-old Siegel is probably *the* world expert on scientifically engineered hallucination, which sounds like an oxymoron and possibly is. We're sitting in the muted modern interior of the Westwood apartment that houses his office. Vivid tropical fish swim languidly in the artificial paradise of a large glass tank, a row of South American peyote cactuses creates a little desert metaphysic on the windowsill, and a phone in the next room rings every twenty minutes or so with mysterious, possibly glamorous, emergencies.

The animal hallucinations he's describing occurred in a psychology lab at Canada's Dalhousie University in the early 1960s, long before Siegel became a drug savant. He was a psychology graduate student experimenting with such austere things as pigeon memory and Skinnerian conditioning. One day a Dalhousie student was arrested for marijuana possession, and the student's lawyer phoned Siegel to ask what he knew about the drug. He didn't know very much, so he had some grass sent over to the lab and made a potent extract, which he fed to one of the lab's pigeons. Then he opened the window (for this was a *homing* pigeon) and watched the weird flight patterns of a stoned bird.

Ronald K. Siegel, psychopharmacologist, cartographer of inner space, and encyclopedist of hallucination. (*Courtesy of Ronald K. Siegel; reprinted with permission*)

"He did this kamikaze nosedive to the ground," Siegel recalls. "I thought, 'Fascinating.' Since there was a little of the extract left, I took it and *I* did a kamikaze nosedive to the ground, where I was laid up for about eight or nine hours, surrounded by these wondrous images."

How do you study hallucinations in a Skinner box? No problem. Siegel had already trained pigeons to match a flashing light on a screen by pecking a button of the same color. So he simply adapted this standard animal-learning paradigm to the internal world. He'd give LSD to a test pigeon and show it a blank screen: If the bird pecked a blue light, say, or a circle, Siegel would know what it *thought* it saw while under the influence. Because, make no mistake, animals *do* hallucinate.

"You know, animals are religious, too," he confides, a faint smile at the corners of his thin, chiseled lips. "At Dalhousie we trained a pigeon named Noah to have religious experiences. It was kind of cute; he would genuflect superstitiously in front of a cross. . . . Now Noah's preaching to all the pigeons in the parks." It tells you something about Siegel's opinion of religion.

As it happens, there's no shortage of messiahs in Los Angeles the spring we visit Siegel. There were reports of at least five different ones in a single week. But this is a land where hallucination is cheap. Shopping malls look like Spanish missions; French châteaus couple with Moorish arches; and the painted billboards look more real than the orange-toned sky. If you drive up to the Griffith Observatory at night, you tend to look for constellations in the vast, glittering electronic grid of the city below.

We figure that Siegel, as a sometime psychopharmacologist to the stars, might have a handle on some of the local alternate realities. Savvy and relentlessly articulate, he's a medium-cool character, the sort of person you'd imagine would have a high freak-out threshold. He also happens to be the only U.S. scientist who continued to do LSD research in the post-psychedelic era. (For scientific purposes the LSD age ended in 1966, the year the compound became a "controlled substance," surrounded by more red tape than an official tour of the Soviet provinces.) But without breaking a single law, Siegel has served up LSD, mescaline, marijuana, amphetamines, cocaine, psilocybin ("magic mushroom"), angel dust, barbiturates, and other psychoactive drugs to hundreds of volunteers at the UCLA Neuropsychiatric Institute. And no one, he says, has ever had a bad trip in his lab.

Tunnels at nine o'clock . . . moving toward me in a pulsating, explosive way . . . with 560 and 780 millimicrons . . .

The story of the first scientific dictionary of inner space is marked by some interesting psychopharmacological karma. For instance, Ron Siegel was born in the same year (1943) that Albert Hofmann, a chemist working at Sandoz Laboratories in Switzerland, accidently ingested an obscure lysergic acid compound and took the world's first acid trip. History doubled back on itself a quarter century later, when Ron Siegel was doing chemistry-of-memory experiments at Dalhousie and weighing out the fine white powder that was pure Sandoz LSD–25—the *Ding-an-sich*, the Pouilly-Fuissé of acid. Some of it must have stuck to his fingers and entered his bloodstream, because the researcher soon found himself in a decidedly altered state. "There is no way pigeons are going to tell us about this!" he told himself when he came down.

Rather than disappearing into the Om, Siegel looked for a way to apply his habitual behaviorist sangfroid to the subjective world. It wasn't long before a new science of "experimental introspection" (another Siegel oxymoron) hit the scene.

"In the early years of psychedelic research," Siegel remembers, "the drug experience was considered too complicated to describe. About the most articulate statement you could get from a user was 'Wow!' "

"Wow" being too soft for Siegel, he went to work on a standardized hallucination code. Through ads in underground newspapers in 1971, he recruited a pioneering group of inner-space explorers to his lab at UCLA. Before giving them a single drug, he used colored slides to teach them a new visual vocabulary. "They wouldn't just say, 'That's sort of a sick green, or a pea-soup green,' " Siegel explains. "They'd say, 'That's 540 millimicrons [the precise wavelength],' and they'd be accurate within a couple of millimicrons." The other landmarks of the mindscape were geometric forms and patterns of motion. If a picture was flashed at Siegel's trainees for eight milliseconds ($\frac{1}{125}$ of a second) they could classify its color, form, and movement dimensions as precisely as zoologists label genera and species.

Later, with a certain dose of a certain psychoactive drug circulating in their bloodstreams (the drug and the dosage varied each week), the "psychonauts" entered the lab's darkened, soundproof chambers. (We're not allowed near the hallucination zone, for Siegel is smart enough to avoid the publicity that tainted Timothy Leary's Harvard experiments in the early 1960s.) There, they'd communicate their visions, in the prearranged code, over an intercom about twenty times a minute. "We took these reports from all our subjects and did a statistical analysis to get the mean prototypical image," Siegel recounts. "Then we'd get a graphic artist to draw it. The images were played back to the subjects, who then picked the ones that best matched their hallucinations."

After several years of painstaking mapping of these psychic never-never lands, Siegel discovered an extraordinary thing: The mind of man contains only so many visions.

When the psychonauts closed their eyes and looked inward *without* drugs, they saw black, white, and violet hues. Under the influence of psychedelics the predominant colors were reds, oranges, and yellows, while THC (tetrahydrocannabinol), the active ingredient of marijuana, brought out cool blues. On placebos, depressants, and amphetamine, the volunteers saw mainly boring black and white forms moving randomly; on LSD and mescaline, they hallucinated geometric shapes that became increasingly intricate as the trip progressed. As the experience got more intense, these forms rotated, pulsated, and exploded—and then gave way to personal, idiosyncratic images (more about that later).

But what most interested Siegel was this: No matter what hallucinogen they were on, the psychonauts kept hallucinating four basic, recurrent geometric forms—the same four shapes, or "geometric constants," interestingly enough, that a University of Chicago scientist, Heinrich Klüver, had deciphered in mescaline hallucinations back in the 1920s. It was Klüver who named them: the spiral, the tunnel or funnel, the cobweb, and the lattice (or grating or honeycomb).

Being a collector of drug-influenced art, Siegel can show us lattices and

This yarn painting, made by one of the Huichol Indians of Mexico, is part of Siegel's collection of drug-influenced art. The Indian at the left, carrying a basket of freshly harvested peyote, is witnessing visions of pulsating and exploding colors and shapes. The peyote cactus is depicted on the right. (*Copyright 1977, Ronald K. Siegel; reprinted with permission*)

tunnels from other lands too. A trio of Huichol yarn paintings faces us from a wall of his office, like a race of gaudy alien gods. The psychologist not only visited the artists in the rugged Sierra Madre *cordillera* of Mexico, he can tell you the blood level of peyote that produced each painting. "Structurally," he explains, "they are very similar to what our subjects would see on mescaline—latticelike tunnels with bright lights at the center. The revolving deer heads are cultural, of course. *You* might see revolving magazines or something." The lesson is that a human brain, whether it belongs to a UCLA sophomore or to a Huichol shaman, is built the same way and hallucinates along similar lines. All possible visions are predetermined by our electrochemical wiring.

On the weekend Los Angeles's Venice Boardwalk is one large, rather surreal yard sale. Dozens of vendors sit cross-legged facing the Pacific, each presiding over a semicircle of objects that appear entirely random. A rusted hot plate, a pair of mirrored sunglasses, a faded Indian-print bedspread, a 1965 issue of *Time*, a wrinkled paisley blouse, a souvenir ashtray from Yosemite, a New Riders of the Purple Sage album. Hundreds of people pause to examine these little displays, as if they were artifacts

The lattice pattern in this Huichol embroidery is one of four "geometric constants" found over and over again in hallucinatory imagery. According to Siegel, schizophrenic art shows a similar preoccupation with repetitive geometric designs.

In Siegel's studies, phenobarbitol and amphetamine induced "black-and-white random forms moving about aimlessly." The visual hallucinations fueled by psilocybin, LSD, mescaline, and tetrahydrocannabinol (THC), the active ingredient of marijuana, became less random, more organized and geometric, more colorful and pulsating, as the experience progressed. (*Copyright 1977, Ronald K. Siegel; reprinted with permission*)

from Pompeii. What is the attraction of such prosaic relics? Perhaps each is a mundane haiku, a momentary configuration of the personal.

Hallucinations have a similar property, if you believe Ron Siegel. Our brains store information in the form of images, and these old images are discharged whenever we turn our senses inward. Siegel has his own favorite metaphor, derived from the landmark 1931 theory of the late British neurologist Hughlings Jackson:

"Imagine a man sitting in his study," says Siegel, "looking out his window at the trees swaying, at passing cars, and so on. . . . As night falls, he can't see out the window anymore, but he has a fire burning brightly in the fireplace behind him. Now when he looks out the window, what does he see? His own reflection, and the images of the 'furniture' inside his brain.

"When it's 'dark' outside, when your senses don't give you access to the real world—as in sensory deprivation, cardiac arrest, or sleep, for example—you see the furniture of your own mind, its stored images. The other way to hallucinate is to stoke up the 'fire,' overstimulate the brain with a lot of LSD or something, and see your internal images superimposed on the outside world."

To be precise, there are two stages of hallucination. Phase one is the geometric one we've heard about. Phase two is more complex and its imagery is idiosyncratic, personal: white rabbits, little green men, three-headed serpents, angels, demons, "Lucy in the Sky with Diamonds," out-of-body travel, the face of your dead grandmother. What had been a simile in the first phase ("I feel like I'm flying") becomes literal reality in phase two ("I *am* flying!"). Phase two obviously does not lend itself as readily to a scientific classification system—yet. But, says Siegel, there are still certain rules of motion hidden in all the weirdness (things tend to pulsate and then revolve, for example). There are laws that govern how images metamorphose—birds commonly turn into bats, bats into brooms, and then into witches. Details tend to cluster in the peripheral visual field, and bright lights at the center. And these rules are really *neural* rules, says Siegel.

"Look," he says, pointing to his Huichol paintings. "There's something that happens here that we call multiplication or duplication. It's a common hallucination phenomenon. You see one little toy soldier and then up pops an army of toy soldiers going across the visual field. The Huichol Indians will see one maize plant, then a whole field of maize plants marching across the sky.

"The form suggests that a column of cortical cells, which store certain memories in image form, is being excited, and that triggers a row of images. A colleague of mine, Jack Cowan at the University of Chicago, has worked out a neurophysiological model, which he can stimulate to produce all the patterns that my subjects produce. You should talk to him." (We did, and we'll tell you about it later.)

The master of hallucination has also applied his cartography to a whole funhouse of nondrug altered states. Hyperventilation, hypoglycemia, marathon running, and the dementia of neurosyphilis, to name a few. Extreme fear states, dreaming, daydreaming, and the surreal "auras" that precede migraine attacks; glue sniffing, crystal gazing, sensory bombardment, sensory deprivation, rhythmic dancing, and strobe lights. Not to mention shipwrecked sailors and spelunkers trapped in caves, who sometimes have visions resembling those of saints.

"I think," he says, "there is a continuum of mental phenomena ranging from thoughts to fantasies to dreams to hallucinations. How far you travel along this continuum depends on the degree of cortical arousal."

QUESTION: Why altered states?
POSSIBLE ANSWER: Because they're there.

One reason, of course, is simple curiosity, also known (especially in lower mammals) as "exploratory drive." In a classic psychology experiment, monkeys housed in a sensory-deprivation box would repeatedly press a lever that opened a window. Siegel tried a takeoff on this. "We wondered what would happen," he says, "if the monkey's only window to the world was a chemical window. After about eight days of darkness, of sensory deprivation, two out of three monkeys started taking DMT." DMT is a potent, fast-acting hallucinogen often called the businessman's-lunch-hour-high, which nonhuman primates usually eschew.

The moral: "All primates, and especially the human organism, seek to adjust their levels of arousal," says Siegel. Which brings him to the theme of new and improved chemical utopias—safe, custom-tailored recreational drugs. "I know this sounds like an advertisement for the Bionic Man, but we can make them better, stronger, faster, safer—and I'm talking about drugs." One of his pharmacologic daydreams is a real-life equivalent of Aldous Huxley's fictional *moksha*, a "truth-and-beauty pill." It would be something like psilocybin (the drug that the psychonauts preferred over all others) but would be completely nontoxic and capable of having its effects turned on or off at will.

"If we don't develop these drugs, our underground chemists will," Siegel points out. "We need to recognize that people are already selecting chemicals to alter their consciousness. They're not happy with one two-week vacation a year."

The quest, however, is not without its casualties, and Siegel points to the toll cocaine has taken among our folk heroes and other inhabitants of America's high circles. And recently Siegel has spotted signs of a psychedelic renaissance, at least on the Coast. "I don't think there's a cocaine *consciousness* in the sense that there's a psychedelic consciousness," he says. "Coke moves you in the direction of arousal, narrows down the gates of perception. It's speedy, focused. Negative hallucinations—not seeing things that are there—are very common in cocaine psychosis.

"Psychedelics, on the other hand, are very plastic. The experience is very much shaped by the setting and the user's programming. LSD is an asocial drug, by the way; animals on LSD isolate themselves. Nonhuman mammals usually won't self-administer psychedelics. They avoid them."

Normal spider web

Hashish-inspired web

Mescaline-inspired web

Do different drugs produce qualitatively different altered states? How do LSD visions differ from mescaline visions, for example? According to the *Psychedelics Encyclopedia* by Peter Stafford, connoisseurs tend to rate mescaline and peyote as "earthy" and LSD as more "cerebral," but people are notoriously inarticulate about such things. Spiders, it seems, are quite eloquent. These photos show the results of a curious experiment in which spiders wove their webs under the influence of various mind-altering drugs. Note the perfect symmetry of the LSD web, compared with the helter-skelter caffeine web. (*Peter Witt, Berlin 1956*)

Don't mistake Ron Siegel for a drug guru. As a frequent expert witness at drug trials he's seen the chemical hell realms at close hand (Leslie Van Houten of the Manson family, the case of Elvis Presley's doctor, the chemical circumstances surrounding the Howard Hughes will). At our second

LSD-inspired web

Web after a high caffeine dose

meeting he surprises us by jumping up to pull a stack of police snapshots from his files. Then he tells us a true story about LSD in Chicago, about a man full of lysergic acid and alcohol, his lover, and her twelve-year-old son. Siegel produces Polaroids in sequence, as if dealing out a hand of seven-card stud or an especially black series of Tarot cards. The first twenty shots are prosaic interiors: a dinette set with kitchen objects, a living room with all the appliances unplugged. Finally Siegel quietly sets down his ace, a photo of what appears to be a sleeping boy in pajamas. Except that he is not asleep and there is a huge jagged red crack where his head should meet his neck. Siegel notes that after the suspect decapitated the little boy, he also repeatedly raped the mother.

"So you see," says Siegel, "LSD experiences are not necessarily transcendent."

On the coffee table the face of John Belushi stares out at eternity from the glossy cover of *People* magazine. Our host recounts a dream:

I went into the future—it was after the War, of course, when everything was destroyed and rebuilt. My guide was taking me around, showing me the architecture and stuff, and then he said, "Would you like to see a movie?"

I entered the theater and sat down. I remember the lights going off and there was a white light on the screen that started to glow and glow and glow. It got bigger and bigger, and the audience was saying "Oooooh, Aaahhhh!" Then the lights came back on, and I said, "That was a marvelous experience, almost a sexual experience."

I asked my guide how they did that, and he said, "That was an experiential projector." Then I went to the local drugstore, and on a rack of books I found one called *Build Your Own Experiential Projector*. I went to the corner to buy the book, but I didn't have the coin of the future. . . . I woke up.

The next night I went back into the dream of the future, back into the drugstore, and I pulled the book off the shelf and read it right there.

When he woke up, Siegel wrote down the dream instructions and found he had a schematic design for a device he now calls FOCUS, a pair of goggles that can simulate a psychedelic experience. The lab psychonauts get hallucinogenlike images when they wear them. "FOCUS does something to visual perception that is like what stereo headphones do to the audio modality," he explains. "With stereo phones, you know, the sound isn't really in your left or right ear; it's someplace between. With FOCUS, the image is projected directly on your retina. You have the sense of images being inside your head and out there at the same time."

There are other futuristic fantasies in Siegel's head. He wishes he had a "little camera" he could stick into his pet cat's brain and watch the world through its eyes. He sees interspecies communication as a possible application of his cartography. He also thinks his inner-space research might help man deal with outer-space realities: "On one *Apollo* mission, I remember, one of the astronauts got very excited and compared the experience of orbiting the moon to what he imagined having a baby would be like," he tells us. "We need a more refined vocabulary to describe those experiences—of weightlessness, of being on another planet. . . . When we contact extraterrestrial worlds, populated or not, we're going to be overwhelmed by a lot of alien sensory input, and understanding an alien environment of our own can prepare us."

Among our everyday alien worlds are dreams, daydreams, and reverie states. These altered states contain a lot of untapped information, to which Siegel's methodology could give us access. Imagine, for example, a more exact science of dream interpretation. Or a new visual language for communicating with schizophrenics in midhallucination—which is something Ron Siegel has already done.

One of his patients, a schizophrenic artist, had a private hallucinatory land called Nid, where her job was to draw murals on the castle walls. In real life she painted dreamy Nid landscapes, full of ethereal winged wolves and dragons, one of which hangs in Siegel's collection. "She was suicidal," he recalls. "Her therapists were always pulling on one hand, telling her,

'Come back. Nid isn't real,' while a dragon was pulling on the other. I asked her to give me a mind tour of Nid. She did, and she introduced me to all the characters, who started talking to me. Because of my own hallucination experiences, I was able to teach her techniques for controlling and describing her images."

> Oh, Mama, can this really be the end,
> To be stuck inside of Mobile
> With the Memphis blues again?
> —BOB DYLAN

Paradox City. Here's a no-nonsense behaviorist who studies the most mercurial mindstuff. Who speaks casually of contacts with aliens but does not believe in a soul beyond the complex wiring of the human brain. Though he uses passages from *The Tibetan Book of the Dead* as a training manual for his psychonauts, Siegel takes a jaundiced view of the mystical and enjoys telling anecdotes about one psychonaut who "became one with an ashtray." Whenever anything transcendent creeps into his hallucination chambers, he brings his subjects back to earth and wavelengths in millimicrons as rapidly as possible.

"It's safe to say," he tells us, "that the similar characteristics of the so-called mystical states—tranquility, bliss, et cetera—don't reflect a common objective reality but simply an *internal* landscape that is common to all Homo sapiens. If we tested Socrates or Joan of Arc, I think we could classify their experiences comfortably with our code."

There is an old story about the drunk who hunted for his lost keys under a street lamp because the light was better there. Siegel sticks to the form, color, and movement dimensions of visual hallucination because the light is better there. Yet isn't phase two of visual hallucination, which falls outside Siegel's categories, the more interesting part? And what about auditory "visions" (the voices that spoke to St. Paul on the road to Damascus and to Joan of Arc) and queer happenings in other senses? Can eight-miles-high *emotions* ever be described in millimicrons?

This is not to denigrate Siegel's considerable accomplishments. He doesn't claim to map the entire visionary scene, for an experimentalist must measure the measurable. And if he hasn't cracked the whole hallucination code, he has at least isolated some of the mind's basic grammatical units. We need such a refined language of introspection—and not merely measurements of twitching rabbit ears or the squeals of foot-shocked rodents—to tackle the mind/brain problem.

A week after our meeting with Siegel, we phone Jack Cowan in Chicago and ask him about the mechanics of a hallucinating brain. Cowan is a biophysicist-mathematician who designs mathematical models of the brain. "With a student I worked out what actually goes on in the individual brain when a person sees hallucinations," he tells us. "This tells you a lot about what the circuits are like in the cortex."

Lo and behold, funnels, cobwebs, spirals, and lattice/honeycombs— Klüver's four geometric constants—materialized in the abstract realm of Cowan's computer simulations, just as they had in Siegel's visionary chambers. Cowan's equations demonstrated that whenever electrical excitation exceeds a critical threshold, the cortex will generate the familiar hallucinatory forms. That these geometries resemble other patterns in nature, notably the rising-and-falling convection currents in heated fluids, is no accident, according to Cowan, for the same mathematical laws apply to brains and to turbulent fluids.

"If you heat liquid in a saucepan, you'll see honeycombs in it," he explains. "The patterns are the same as the patterns that turn up in hallucinations. The mathematics of this is known as symmetry breaking. Whenever you have a physical system with symmetries—such as the resting state of a fluid where all the molecules are moving randomly and are more or less evenly distributed—and you disturb the system, the symmetries get broken. Then patterns form." In the brain the equivalent of the heat under the saucepan might be LSD, a petit mal seizure, a psychotic state, or anything that overstimulates the cortex.

If you were to actually look *inside* a hallucinating brain you would see stripes. "If you know the map from the eye to the brain you can work out the patterns in the cortex," Cowan explains. "They are very simple— stripes, basically. The stripes are really standing wavefronts of firing neurons, separated by columns of inactivated neurons." Cowan has even calculated the wavelengths of the stripes and says they correspond to the "hypercolumns" that Hubel and Wiesel mapped out in the visual cortex. The optical pathway translates the stripe patterns into the spirals, lattices, and tunnels the hallucinator sees.

"What one learns is that the brain is intrinsically unstable," says Cowan. "Any excitation that destroys the normal balance can produce hallucinations or epilepsy."

The control switches are the chemicals norepinephrine and serotonin. "When you increase norepinephrine or shut down serotonin," he explains, "you stimulate the cortex and destabilize the brain." LSD does this; so do our other favorite mind-benders; and so do, Cowan suspects, near-death crises, migraine attacks, and other visionary states.

"And phase two?" we ask him. "How about white rabbits and little green men?"

Cowan doesn't have that worked out yet, but he can tell us that as hallucination progresses, the "stripes" move forward from the visual cortex, in the back of the head, toward the more symbolic forebrain. "When a column of cells gets activated here, each of those cells codes not just a simple geometric property but something very, very complicated," he says. "We just don't know how to read that yet.

"But we can account for some things. A hallucinating person tends to see a whole row of faces instead of a single face. And there's also megalopsy and micropsy, when objects grow very huge or very tiny, like Alice in Wonderland. We know the mechanisms for this aren't in the primary visual cortex but farther forward, in the inferior temporal cortex. So the excitation is already moving forward, and we can probably get our hands on some of these phenomena."

> I pushed back through, I would estimate, two thousand generations and suddenly the face of a hairy anthropoid appeared on my face. My humor came to the fore at this point, and I said, "Oh, you can project anything, including the Darwinian theory of the origin of Man." I started to laugh, enjoying the spectacle. Suddenly the face of a saber-toothed tiger appeared in the place of mine, with six-inch fangs coming out of his mouth.
> —JOHN C. LILLY, M.D.,
> *The Center of the Cyclone*

If Siegel and Cowan are right, if the central switchboard of reality is in the cortex, then you are a very complicated dream machine. Think about it. Columns of neurons fire and produce images—real, remembered, or hallucinated—and those images are the only world you'll ever know. Can you ever get out of the machine and experience reality directly? Of course not, says Siegel (and most of his peers), because you *are* the machine.

John Lilly, on the other hand, has spent the better part of his adult life as a brain-machine escape artist.

You may know him as the Dolphin Man (George C. Scott played a sanitized, Disney-fatherly Lilly in *The Day of the Dolphin*). Or maybe you saw the Paddy Chayevsky/Ken Russell film *Altered States*, whose isolation-tank–crazed hero is modeled on Lilly or someone very much like him. (Unlike the mad scientist of the film, however, Lilly never exactly regressed into a prehominid and trashed the lab. It was his friend and fellow-tripper, the late Dr. Craig Enright, who "became" a prehominid—and that was only in his head. But that's another story.) What you may not know, unless you've read his autobiographies, is that John Lilly, M.D., was a straight neurophysiologist before he fell in love with the Void.

As a whiz kid at NIMH in the 1950s—he was fluent in neuroanatomy, neurophysiology, electronics, biophysics, and computer theory—Lilly helped illumine the brain's pain and pleasure circuits. It was his technical genius that gave science the first electrical recordings from the cortexes of unanesthetized animals. In 1954 he turned to a classic neuro-puzzle: What would happen to the brain if it were deprived of all sensory input? Most scientists assumed it would go unconscious in the absence of stimulation, but no one had ever tested it out. So Lilly built the world's first isolation tank—a pitch-dark, soundproof, ultrasaline void, the first version of which required wearing a skindiver's mask—and immersed himself in it.

Instead of going to sleep in this tranquil, man-made sea, Lilly's brain surprised him by experiencing dream, reverie, and trance states, mystical illuminations, and out-of-body travels. "There you are suspended in an embryonic silence one hundred miles out in deep space," he would report in *The Deep Self*, his tanking memoirs, "and suddenly the Logos, the Universal Vibration, begins to pervade the fabric of awareness, coming at one from inside and all directions." These aren't the sort of data that science journals print, and Lilly's previous "belief system," the basic NIMH doctrine that the brain *contains* the mind, gave way to what he would come to call his "leaky-mind hypothesis."

"A human being is a biorobot with a biocomputer in it—the brain," he tells us. "But we are not that brain, and we are not the body. A soul essence inhabits us, and under acid, under anesthesia, in a coma, you'll find that the essence isn't tied to brain activity at all. Brain activity can be virtually flat and you can be conscious—off somewhere in another realm."

It is August, the season when the Malibu hills have a supernatural look. In our rented Ford Escort we drive through a landscape of steep canyons, sagebrush, yucca, and twisted oaks, thinking of fires, Santa Ana winds, and other wild forces.

It hadn't been easy to track the Dolphin Man here. We'd asked his various acquaintances where Lilly lived and had received answers like, "You mean, what dimension?" Someone said he worked at Redwood City's Marine World, with the performing dolphins, but the receptionists who answered our phone calls had never heard of the illustrious Dr. Lilly. When, at last, we got a Malibu phone number, Lilly himself answered and agreed to see us on the condition that we arrive within the next hour. His driving directions turned out to be accurate to the tenth of a mile.

A grave, life-size wooden Indian guards Lilly's doorway. We knock,

John C. Lilly, M.D., and friends. The king of altered states invented the isolation tank in order to experience a dolphin's world. (*Courtesy of Human/Dolphin Foundation*)

and the high priest of human/dolphin communication appears in a navy-blue zippered jumpsuit. The sixty-eight-year-old Lilly is lean, tan, and athletic-looking, a landlocked Lloyd Bridges with haunted, extraterrestrial eyes. "Hi," he says, in a flat voice, and ushers us silently into a spacious living room, where trapeze-artist iron rings hang from the ceiling and the picture windows frame a Wild West movie set of arid mountains, scrub oaks, sagebrush, and a deep, shadowed gorge.

"We have one rule in this house," says our saturnine host. "No one can take any drugs—even aspirin—and drive back down that mountain."

Since his latest near-death experience occurred on the hairpin turns of Malibu Canyon Road, Lilly knows whereof he speaks. With forty-two milligrams of angel dust dancing in his head he rode his bicycle down the mountain. The brakes failed, and he ended up in a five-day coma. While his pain-wracked body lay in the hospital, Lilly's mind visited alternate universes, where guides took him on a tour of a bleak future. It was the year 2500, and the "solid-state entities" (which inhabit computers and other silicon-based forms) had wiped out most of water-based, biological life, including man. Later Lilly would disown the SSEs as a temporary paranoia—"I was just getting in touch with my bones and teeth"—but other parts of his experience were eerily real.

"I can't make up my mind whether that was an experience of genuine realities or just a projection of the damage to my body," he tells us. Anyway, he begged the guides to let him go back to his wife, Toni, on Earth, and they told him, "You can stay here, in which case your body dies, or you can go back." He chose to go back, as evidenced by the fact he is here being interviewed by us, but we get the feeling he'd sometimes rather be elsewhere.

Assuring him we won't take any drugs, we take out a tape recorder. Lilly counters by producing his own matchbook-size Japanese tape recorder and carefully adjusts the microphone. He watches us through his blue-gray gimlet eyes, his face a mask, and answers our first questions in cryptic monosyllables. The interview isn't going well.

"Do you want some acid, some K, some pot?" he asks suddenly. (Or did we hallucinate that?) It could be a test, a challenge, or a strange koan. There's a chill of paranoia in the air. "No, thanks," we say, remembering the hairpin turns and feeling like tourists with cameras and Hawaiian shirts blundering up the steps of a sacred temple.

Lilly's early isolation-tank trips were drug free. He was not to get his first taste of LSD until 1964, which was when his leaky-mind experiments really took off. While floating around in the Epsom-salted waters at the NIMH, though, his thoughts turned to dolphins: "I thought, 'Gee, I wonder what it would be like to be bouyant twenty-four hours a day.' A friend of mine said, 'Well, try the dolphins.' " He did and eventually resigned from the NIMH and went to sea to talk to the large-brained mammals that, he was sure, were not only smarter than man but had ancient "vocal histories" as well. In 1961 he set up the Communications Research Institute in the U.S. Virgin Islands and Miami and became acquainted with cetaceans (whales, dolphins, and porpoises) as no other human ever has.

"Because they have voluntary respiration," he explains, "dolphins are interdependent in ways we aren't. They have a group mind. If a dolphin passes out for any reason, his friends must wake him up. Otherwise, he'll drown. So every dolphin is aware of where every other dolphin is, just in case he's needed. 'Do unto others as you would have them do unto you' is one of their rules, and unlike us, they follow it twenty-four hours a day. They're also more spiritual, since they have more time to meditate. Try the isolation tank and you'll see what it's like." (We will.)

Whenever Lilly talks about a dolphin, he uses the pronoun *he*, never *it*. His fine, chiseled-granite features turn gentler, and he seems to come down from the remote, glacial realms behind his eyes. Why, we ask him, if the Cetacea are the most intelligent beings on earth, do we humans assume we're God's chosen creatures?

"Because we can't talk to anyone else. The highest intelligence on the planet probably exists in a sperm whale, who has a ten-thousand-gram brain, six times larger than ours. The problem is that that big brain is in a body that can be killed by man. Maybe he wants to get out of that body."

Because Lilly would like to get out of his—or out of the cramped human *weltanschauung* anyway—he spends a good deal of time at Marine World these days, trying to see the world through a dolphin's eyes. His current attempt at an interspecies dialogue uses a computer system called JANUS (the name stands for the two-faced Roman god and for Joint Analog Numerical Understanding System) to exchange messages with the dolphins. Unlike the baby-talking Hollywood dolphins that called George C. Scott "Faaa," real dolphins communicate in "acoustic pictures."

"We're trying to develop a sonic code as the basis of a dolphin computer language," he says. "Our computer system transmits sounds underwater, via a transducer. If a group of dolphins can work with a computer that feeds back to them what they just said—names of objects and so forth—and if we can be the intercessors between them and the computer, I think we can eventually communicate. I think in about five years we'll have a human-dolphin dictionary."

If tanking led to dolphins, it also led to LSD. And the two parallel romances of Lilly's life, interspecies communication and altered states, proceed from the same break-on-through-to-the-other-side longing.

"There were a lot of 'LSD pushers'—all legal of course—at the NIMH when I was there in the fifties," he reminisces. "But I didn't take it then. After about ten years in the tank I decided there was something new to be learned. So I came out here to California, in 1964, where a lady I knew who had access to Sandoz LSD–25 gave me the LSD for my first two trips.

"On my first trip I went through all the usual stuff: seeing my face change in the mirror, tripping out to music. During the first two movements of Beethoven's Ninth I was kneeling in heaven, worshipping God and His angels, just as I had in church when I was seven years old. On that trip I did everything I'd read in the psychedelic literature so as to save time and get out of the literature the next time."

The phone rings and Lilly answers it. "Who are you?" he demands. His end of the conversation is curt, and he hangs up without saying good-bye. Small talk is not his long suit. "That was just someone asking about the solid-state entities," he says.

The LSD initiation was the beginning of an unparalleled hallucinogenic high-wire act. With the single-mindedness of a God-crazed medieval monk, Lilly spent the next two decades stalking the brain's truth with LSD, PCP, and—above all—"Vitamin K," the superpotent hallucinogen he prefers not to identify. In the Virgin Islands, in 1964, he mixed tanking with LSD for the first time and got even higher highs, like the following (from *The Center of the Cyclone*):

I traveled through my brain, watching the neurons and their activities. . . . I moved into smaller and smaller dimensions, down to the quantum levels, and watched the play of the atoms in their own vast universes, their wide empty spaces, and the fantastic forces involved in each of the distant nuclei with their orbital clouds of force field electrons. . . . It was really frightening to see the tunneling effects and the other phenomena of the quantal level taking place.

He floated through Pascalian infinities great and small, from interstellar space to the minutiae of his own cells, and met otherworldly beings who "reminded me of some of the drawings I had seen of Tibetan gods and goddesses, of ancient Greek . . . gods and of some of the bug-eyed monsters of science fiction. . . ." Some became his "guides."

By now Lilly was no longer writing up his research for scientific journals or even reading other people's physiology papers. Instead he started authoring popular books to record his state changes, from Roman Catholicism to CalTech electronic wizardry to medical science and psychoanalysis; from NIMH neuroscience to tanking, dolphins, and LSD, and finally to Esalen–New Age mysticism. When the vibes started to go sour around 1965–66 (his second wife filed for divorce, LSD became a controlled drug, and some of the dolphins at the institute reacted to captivity by committing suicide), he set the dolphins free and came out to California to join the human-potential Gold Rush.

But the LSD and tank excursions of 1964–65 were, in their way, as methodical as Ron Siegel's research. If Lilly used his own nervous system as an experimental laboratory, he did so in the tradition of the great J. B. S. Haldane, who, when he wanted to measure the brain's temperature, had thermocouples inserted through his jugular vein into his own brain. Lilly wanted to map successive slices of inner space, and he did it systematically, using ascending doses of LSD and tank immersion. In fact, he found that one hundred micrograms corresponded to x level of internal reality, two hundred micrograms to y level, and so on, up to "infinite distances—dimensions that are inhuman."

A certain reentry shock was to be expected.

"If you get into these spaces at all," he tells us, "you must *forget* about them when you come back. You must forget you're omnipotent and omniscient and take the game seriously, so you'll have sex, beget children, and the whole human scenario. When you come back from a deep LSD trip—or coma or psychosis—there's always this extraterrestrial feeling. You have to read the directions in the glove compartment so you can run the human vehicle.

"After I first took acid in the tank and traveled to distant dimensions, I cried when I came back and found myself trapped in a body. I didn't even know whose body it was at the time. I felt squashed."

The leaky-mind/escaping-self hypothesis had turned into a living-on-the-edge life-style. "Acid and K," he explains, "set up the chemical configuration of your brain so as to loosen the connection between the brain/body and the soul essence. Then the essence can move into alternate realities. That's the the leaky-mind or escaping-self hypothesis. . . . There are lots of ideas about the soul's location in the body. In Spanish, when you're scared out your wits, you say your soul is in your mouth—you have *el alma en la boca.*

"But the junction between the biocomputer and the essence is not localized in the brain; it's throughout your body. If you get out of your body, you can assume a fake body, an astral body, which can walk through walls. Your essence is represented in every cell of your body."

We were used to scientists who discussed the mind in terms of dopamine metabolites, refined bioassays, and tighter parameters, and so we ask Lilly if he thinks the human mind can be mapped in that way. He doesn't. "Neurochemistry is interesting, but not specific enough yet. I suspect we'll find there are a million different compounds operating in the nervous system.

"You know," he adds, "[mathematician Kurt] Gödel's theorem, translated, says that a computer of a given size can model only a smaller computer. It cannot model itself. If it modeled a computer of its own size and complexity, it would fill it entirely and it couldn't do anything."

"So the brain can never understand the brain?" we ask.

"That's right. We are biological computers. And Gödel said that you cannot conceive in full a computer the size of your own, for it would take up all the space you live in. But a sperm whale, with a brain six times the size of ours, could model a human brain and do a pretty good job of it. Since the model would take up only one-sixth of his software, he could use the remaining five-sixths to manipulate the model, predict its actions, and so on."

Is Lilly a Whitehead or an Ouspensky? His so-
lipsistic, hallucinogen-facilitated head burrowing
into brain and space has the appearance of a rational search. I know of that sound, its disguises,
its path near suicide. I too have looked to the
brain's cortical mantle, the moonless sky, and the
empty space inside that comes from hours of the
mantra. . . .
—ARNOLD MANDELL, M.D.,
Coming of Middle Age

If there were an Association for Scientists Ten Tokes Over the Line, many
of Lilly's former colleagues would elect him president. Some say he's brilliant but strange. Some think that too much acid and K or his many standoffs
with death have damaged his nervous system. To Ron Siegel, who knows
him pretty well, Lilly is "one of the bravest explorers of the inner world,"
a Jacques Cousteau of the psychic undersea.

"The trouble with Lilly is that he's in love with death," one psychiatrist
friend of his tells us, and mentions *Thanatos*, the Freudian death wish.
That Lilly has flirted flagrantly with death on at least three occasions is a
matter of record. During his early acid phase, he once gave himself an
antibiotic injection with a hypodermic that contained foam residue and it
sent him into a coma. A few years later, during a period of daredevil
"Vitamin K" use, he almost drowned. And then, in 1974, there was the
bicycle accident.

"Were these accidents or quasi-suicides?" we ask Lilly.

"The whole issue of suicide is very complex," he answers. "I think the
brain contains lethal programs, self-destruct programs, below the level of
awareness, which LSD or K can release or strengthen. My accidents were
near-death learning experiences. There's nothing like them for training you
fast.

"We have a saying in our workshops: 'If you pass the cosmic speed
limit, the cosmic cops will bust you.' I got busted in 1974. I'd spent most
of the year in *satori*, a state of grace, mostly living in alternate realities. I
had a ball. But I'd been out there too long and hadn't paid enough attention
to my planetside trip. So the ECCO guys called me back by throwing a
bike accident at me."

"The echo guys?" we ask, picturing an infinite inner echo chamber.

"The Earth Coincidence Control Office—ECCO. They're the guys who
run Earth and who program us, though we're not aware of it. I asked
them, 'What's your major program?' They answered, 'To make you guys
evolve to the next levels, to teach you, to kick you in the pants when

necessary.' I appreciate what they did. They're not cruel; they're in a state of high indifference."

Lilly leads us outside and around a semicircle of manicured lawn to his rustic workshop/office. He turns on his computer, and the table of contents of his book-in-progress, *From Here to Alternity: A Manual on Ways of Amusing God*, appears on the terminal. TIME, BITS, BYTES AND TOASTED HONEY, we read. BEGIN GOD. THE DUSTBOWL GOD. It has the feel of a cosmic programming language.

"I can run this thing on very high doses of K," he says. "In spite of everything vibrating."

Alternity is about Lilly's journeys on K, his favorite chemical nirvana. He once spent a hundred sleepless, dreamless days and nights on K, tuning his "internal eyes" to the dim borders between alternate realities, rotating universes, yin and yang, hyperspace from within. We ask him about contacting God.

"In many cases," he says, "I didn't know whether I was taken on a trip by God or by one of His business officers in the outer galaxy. Guides at each level above ours pretend to be God as long as you believe them. But when you finally get to know the guide, he says, 'Well, God is really the next level up.' God keeps retreating into infinity."

If there is a bureaucratic feel to these infinite spaces, if Lilly's heaven sometimes resembles a vast civil-servant hierarchy, it may not be accidental. You can find such multitiered hierarchies in the brain, as Lilly well knows from his former lifetime in the neuroanatomy lab. You can find them in computers, along with infinite loops and iterations like a God retreating into infinity. (Lilly is a computer master, too, and in the merciless confessionals of his books he often bemoans the "stainless-steel computer" side of his being.) What this says about the mind/brain relationship we're not entirely sure.

We ask what or who the Dustbowl God is.

"Oh," he says, "in my book I have a theory about the Dustbowl God. God got bored with this universe and the distribution of intelligence in it. So He made a dust bowl out beyond the galaxies. In this dust cloud every particle is intelligent; on the atomic level each particle is as intelligent as a human being. The dust particles made themselves into stars and planets and animals and humans, and everything was totally aware of everything around it. . . . Now, the problem is: If every particle is equally intelligent, what are the traffic rules for relations between, say, humans and elephants?

"It would be nice to see such universe, wouldn't it?" he says. "The Dustbowl Universe."

Later, submerged in the wet, dark, womblike void of Lilly's Samadhi tank, we try to get a handle on these things. The water temperature is 94 degrees, close enough to body temperature so the junction between inside and outside, body and water (if not body and mind), is blurred, but slightly lower to allow some heat loss so the tanker doesn't die of hyperthermia. We float weightless, a crouton in a primordial soup, with no sights, no sounds, no time—in the same tank where Jerry Rubin, Charles Tart, est mogul Werner Erhard, Nobel laureate physicist Richard Feynman, anthropologist Gregory Bateson, and other luminaries have floated and had visions.

Ours are pretty rudimentary. Lilly's "metaprogrammings," "belief-system interlocks," and "Earth Coincidence Control Offices" echo in the head like mantras. We seem to see him in various disguises: a reincarnated Old Testament prophet waiting out the locust years; Cybernetic Man, with a brain full of codes; a wounded sorcerer; a shipwrecked hero befriended by dolphins. It occurs to us that the mind/brain problem may not be solvable in this universe.

When we emerge the low sun casts elongated shadows over the canyons. We locate Lilly back in his living room, but he seems indifferent to our presence, like someone who is just about to board a plane and is already mentally in a different time zone. From another room the canned laughter of what sounds like an "I Love Lucy" rerun drifts out to us. Then Toni Lilly walks in, smiling, carrying a bag of groceries. By all accounts, Lilly's third wife is the life force that keeps him around the planet these days, and he comes noticeably alive in her presence. He jumps up to help her unload firewood from the car. We call good-bye to his receding back and try to thank him for the interview.

"Well, we'll see how it comes out," he says and disappears into some zero-g universe beyond us.

11

Chuang-tzu and the Butterfly:
Dreams and Reality

> Anyone who when he was awake behaved in the
> sort of way that [he does] in dreams would be
> considered insane.
> —SIGMUND FREUD,
> *The Interpretation of Dreams*

> What if you slept? And what if in your sleep, you
> dreamed? And what if in your dream you went
> to heaven and there plucked a strange and beau-
> tiful flower? And what if when you awoke, you
> had the flower in your hand? Ah! What then?
> —SAMUEL TAYLOR COLERIDGE

WHEN she's ready to dream, Beverly Kedzierski checks into what looks to be a small, California–ranch-style motel behind the ultrasuburban Stanford Shopping Center. The technician who pastes electrodes to her head, chin, and the skin just below her eyes will stay up all night in the room next door, watching seven parallel streams of squiggles course over polygraph paper. That doesn't cramp Kedzierski's style. She's the Stanford sleep lab's star lucid dreamer. By now the task of controlling the protean substance of dreams boils down to a pragmatic ritual: Plug wires into headboard. Rehearse the eyeball-movement code that she'll use in her lucid dreams. Rehearse that night's specific task. Go to sleep.

Lucid dreaming is nothing new. You can find references to it in Aristotle, in various mystical texts, and in rapturous Victorian memoirs full of séance tricks like astral projection and precognition. Perhaps you have a friend who does it spontaneously; or perhaps you have at one time or other "awakened" in middream to discover you could rewrite the plot and shuffle the characters like an imperious Hollywood director on location.

Kedzierski started lucid dreaming when she was a five-year-old child with a recurrent nightmare about witches. "Every night they chased me around and around the yard," she remembers. "I'd say, 'Listen, you can have me in tomorrow night's dream, but just let me go free now.' They'd let me go, but sure enough, the next night they'd be chasing me again. So one night I just said, 'Okay, enough is enough. What do you want?' They didn't answer, but they never came back after that."

It took a young Stanford sleep researcher named Stephen LaBerge to make lucid dreaming a science. No reputable scientist before him had ever considered breaking the communication barrier between dreams and waking life—for what could be more private than a dream, that twilit cloister guarded by the ever-vigilant "censor"? The best one could do was to reconstruct one's dream the morning after (when its "soul" was already cold) and fumble around in its gnomic gibberish for symbols planted by the subconscious. But LaBerge's solution was surprisingly unmystical.

If dreams were soft science, sleep research was hard. Since 1953 dreaming sleep was known to be accompanied by characteristic rapid eye movements (or REM), which are easily detected by a sensor under the sleeper's eyes. If it really was possible to be conscious in a dream, LaBerge mused, why couldn't the dreamer "speak" to the outside world; and why not use his eye movements as the lexicon? For several nights running, in 1978, he hooked himself to a polysonograph, a lie-detector-like device that auto-

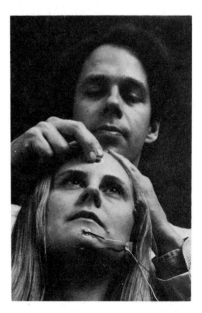

Lucid-dreaming researcher Stephen LaBerge prepares oneironaut Beverly Kedzierski for a night's sleep in the Stanford sleep lab. The electrodes will monitor her brain waves, eye movements, and facial muscles throughout the night. (*Christopher Springmann*)

matically monitors eye muscles and other physiological signals; each time he dreamed a lucid dream he moved his eyes in a prearranged sequence: left-right-left-right. When he scanned the record later, there, embedded among the slow EEGs and familiar eye flickerings of REM, was his coded message—four giant, sweeping zigzags on the eye-muscle channel. Lucid dreaming was no hallucination, and it *did* occur during sleep.

LaBerge graduated to fancier feats. He began using a complex series of eye and body movements to send out Morse code signals, once spelling out his initials from within a lucid dream. For several years he meticulously recorded a total of 389 dreams, and still there were scoffers. "People were saying 'Oh, this lucid dreaming is just a dissertation effect: LaBerge is the only one who does it.' " Finally he stopped sleeping with electrodes himself and trained an elite corps of *oneironauts*, or "dream navigators"—including Kedzierski, the first and most gifted—to communicate from the vaporous land of dreams to the high-noon world of technicians, EEG machines, and science journals.

We meet him in his office, an unprepossessing cubicle off the labyrinthian cinder-gray corridors of the Stanford Medical Center's R wing. From floor to ceiling the bookshelves are crammed with large cardboard boxes of graph paper covered with serpentine tracks of red ink. The place might pass for a cheerless medical technician's annex and the thirty-five-year-old LaBerge for any boyish jean-clad student but for his aura of quiet authority and a certain laserlike intensity in his eyes.

"Let me show you one of our experiments," he says, opening one of the boxes. Each box contains the psychophysiological record of one night's sleep, and this is one of Kedzierski's. Over his shoulder we peer down at the special calligraphy of sleep: Taut little bunches of alpha brain waves (the subject is awake); the slower, "sawtooth" dreaming waves; the flat-lands on the chin-muscle line that distinguish dreaming from dreamless sleep. "The top two channels are EEGs," LaBerge explains. "The next two are eye movements—see, up and down means left and right. This line is chin-muscle tone. The bottom two are skin potential, or galvanic skin response, a measure of excitement.

"Now we'll see when she's having a lucid dream." He shuffles through the perforated pages. "Right here, see, she's dreaming—those are the so-called sawtooth waves of REM sleep, and here are the eye movements. The muscle tone is depressed, as it always is in REM sleep. She's definitely asleep. But now there's the eye-movement signal—left-right-left-right! She's telling us she knows she's dreaming." There's no way to miss it: The lucid dreamer's call to the waking world jumps off the page like a famous face in an old group photograph.

The ink tracings don't reveal anything about how it *feels* to wake up inside a dream, though, and it's hard for the oneironauts themselves to describe the peculiar, surreal *frisson* they experience. "When I notice something doesn't fit or someone doesn't belong there," Kedzierski tells us, "I say, 'Hey, wait a minute, this might be a dream. If I test it out and realize that it *is* a dream, it's very thrilling, very emotional. It's like being at the Grand Canyon for the first time, and I think, 'Wow! I've never seen it look like this before; I want to remember everything, every detail.' "

Back around 1967 lucid dreams were the farthest thing from Stephen LaBerge's mind. He was just a nineteen-year-old Stanford prodigy working on a doctorate in physical chemistry. Then the Acid Age came along and attracted him to the nascent "chemistry of mind." He began taking more and more extended leaves of absence and even found himself a job synthesizing hallucinogens at the University of San Francisco. "I wanted to test a series of LSD analogues," he recalls, "to see if I could find any interesting improvements." After a while, the grants dematerialized like the visions they fueled, but by then LaBerge had hit a familiar psychedelic cul-de-sac, anyway. "I'd take LSD, and I'd feel that I *almost knew*—that state of incipient knowledge. I think the drug turns on a 'significance' signal in the limbic system, but without any particular content. So you come back empty-handed the next day."

Eastern metaphysics turned out to be a better route to the study of consciousness; and LaBerge was drawn to the notion that normal, waking consciousness is a kind of collective dream. One day in 1970 he attended a lecture at Esalen, where a Tibetan master spoke of maintaining waking consciousness in the dream state. That night LaBerge did something he hadn't done since he was a small boy in Florida swimming underwater for hours in his dreams: He had a lucid dream.

"I was climbing K–2, the second highest mountain in the world. There I was going through these snowdrifts and I noticed I was wearing a T-shirt. I instantly recognized that I was dreaming and flew off the mountain. . . . Today, of course, I wouldn't fly off the mountain; I'd climb to the top to see what was there."

It took a few more years and much dissertation *angst*, but by the late 1970s, LaBerge had found a place for his unorthodox specialty within the sleep-research mainstream. By that time, too, he'd gained remarkable mastery over his own dream life and had a few tricks to pass on.

One was a technique called MILD (mnemonic induction of lucid dreams) that can help the novice convert ordinary dreams into lucid ones. While using MILD, LaBerge had an average of 21.5 lucid dreams a month. He found it most effective in the early morning hours, when dreams are frequent, and right after waking from a dream. Here is how it works:

Step one: Train yourself to wake up early in the morning right after a dream.

Step two: Recall your dream, fixing all its details in your mind; then spend ten to fifteen minutes doing something (like reading) that requires full alertness.

Step three: Before you go back to sleep, tell yourself, "Next time I'm dreaming I'll recognize I'm dreaming."

Step four: Visualize yourself asleep in bed. At the same time imagine that you are inside the dream you just recalled—and that you're aware that you are dreaming.

Now repeat steps three and four until your intention is firmly lodged in your mind. With a little practice, you may train yourself to wake up at a Transylvanian masked ball and alter the script as you see fit. (Recurrent dreams are particularly fertile soil for lucidity.)

Can anyone do it? Theoretically, yes, but LaBerge estimates that only one person in ten is a natural lucid dreamer. At the University of Northern Iowa, a psychologist named Jayne Gackenbach has done a survey that concludes lucid dreamers are less neurotic, less depressed, and have higher self-esteem than nonlucid people. They also tend to have excellent emotional balance (if you don't keep your cool when a dream turns lucid, it quickly evaporates), and their *physical balance*, as measured by walking on a balance beam, is equally superior—a fact that might explain dream-flying ability.

The plain criterion of lucidity is to be aware that you're dreaming. Or as LaBerge puts it to his oneironauts, "You have to remember you're in a sleep lab doing an experiment; you have to remember there's an outside world." Beyond that, there are infinite shades and variations. "Full lucidity," says the dream maestro, "is knowing, 'Every part of this dream is in my own mind and I take full responsibility for it.' If you don't fly because you don't think you can, then you're not fully lucid."

Beverly Kedzierski tells us, "To test whether I'm lucid I'll float up into the air. If I can fly I know it's a dream." Then she recounts how she has fine-tuned her aerodynamics over the years. "In the beginning I was flapping my arms as a little bird would do. When I woke up, I thought, 'Well, if I can fly, it shouldn't take any effort; it's all a dream anyway.' So in my next dream I tried just gliding through the air like Superman. It worked fine, but I was still avoiding rooftops and telephone poles.

"Later, I thought, 'Why do I have to do this? I should be able to fly right through rooftops.' Now when I'm flying in a dream, I can fly right through things—as long as I believe I can do it. When I *don't* believe it, I crash into the rooftops and fall down."

Toppling Freudian Towers

He understood that modeling the incoherent and vertiginous matter of which dreams are composed was the most difficult task that a man could undertake, even though he should penetrate all enigmas of a superior and inferior order; much more difficult than weaving a rope out of sand or coining the faceless wind.

—JORGE LUIS BORGES,
"The Circular Ruins"

THE FOURTH FLOOR of the medical center overlooks a disjointed geometry of red-tile roofs, domes, towers, treetops, and white–gold meadows. We try to imagine how this campus would look from the aerial view of a lucid dream. Would the dreamer set his or her compass by Hoover Tower—that unabashedly tumescent monument always known in these parts as "Hoover's Last Erection"? Would the gnarled live oaks, mournful eucalyptus, and neurotic, attenuated palms seem to possess souls?

To Freud, flying in dreams usually meant sex. To LaBerge and his protégés, flying is psychic freedom. When lucid dreamers choose to dream about sex, they do so frankly, like the female oneironaut who made love to a giant department-store Easter bunny. This is only one of the differences between the old school and the new psychology of dreaming.

Freud's dreamworld was a musty, semidarkened, red-brocaded Victorian parlor cluttered with phallic symbols, distortions, inversions, wish-fulfillment fantasies, condensations, and bizarre associations. Although repressed yearnings from the unconscious could leak into dreams when the rational cortex went to sleep, there was, between the conscious mind and the unconscious, an ineradicable wall of frosted glass. Everything was filtered, sifted, censored, coded. And dream analysis was a Hermetic science accessible only to initiates.

Consider for a moment this quote from *The Interpretation of Dreams* (1900): "We shall take the unconscious system as the starting-point of all dream formation. Like all other thought-structures, this dream-instigator will make an effort to advance into the preconscious and from there to obtain access to consciousness."

This rigid trinity of conscious-preconscious-unconscious is the very cornerstone of psychoanalysis. What does LaBerge's new science do to that? Instead of furtive, sybilline mutterings between the "conscious" and the "unconscious," there is frank discourse in lucid dreams; the ego *directly* intervenes in the dreaming self's operations. Could the blockade that Freud posited between different compartments of the mind be a phony one?

An accomplished lucid dreamer doesn't just lie there like a supine analysand and have nightmares and anxiety dreams. He/she takes control and changes things, as Beverly Kedzierski did with her witches at the tender age of five. And the dreamer can lucidly search for solutions to real-world problems. Recently, faced with writing a proposal for her computer-science dissertation, Kedzierski had a bad bout of writer's block. "I told myself I'd dream about it," she said. "So when I had a lucid dream I remembered to try sitting down at my computer terminal. Well, as soon as I tried to sit there, there was all this turbulence that just sort of swished me away. When I woke up, I realized my problem wasn't that I didn't have enough ideas or that I wasn't capable of writing. The problem was that I wasn't sitting down at my desk." The solution? Back in waking life, she just sat down in front of her terminal and pretty soon she'd done the proposal.

A peculiar Instant Karma operates in dreamland, too, according to LaBerge. "In a dream," he explains, "there's a perfect reciprocity between 'you' and 'them.' As soon as you change your attitude toward them, they change. Loving your enemies in your dreams works instantly, because who are they to have swords when you love them? They don't have any being independent of you. . . ."

As we talk, a dragon-shaped cloud scuttles across the hard cobalt sky outside the window. In the parking lot below a coagulated rainbow hides in an oil slick, and several new, shiny Audis and Volvos maneuver around a life-size gameboard of coded A, B, and E spaces. Is the world a different order of dream, as the mystics say? If so, lucid dreams may guide us to higher states of consciousness, offering us a glimpse of what it would be like to awaken from the common slumber.

"In the dream state the person I'm seeing is my construction, just an image in my mind," LaBerge comments. "Now, in waking life the 'you' I'm seeing is an image in my mind, but there is somebody out there, too, and it's an autonomous being.

"Right now we're agreeing on consensual reality. We're observing certain social rules about an interview—what's appropriate, what's not. But most people just accept the situation as a given and don't recognize that they help construct it. If you experience lucid dreaming, though, you take *full* responsibility for your experience. And that carries over into waking life. You try out different approaches to real situations; you develop psychological flexibility."

Anyone who when he was awake behaved in the sort of way that he does in dreams would be considered insane. Maybe, maybe not.

But how does the brain generate a lucid dream—if it *is* the brain that does it? "Here's stage-two sleep, dreamless sleep," LaBerge says, pointing to some telltale EEG "spindles" on the polysonograph record. "Now, here she enters REM sleep—look at the sawtooth waves and the rapid eye movement. And after just thirty seconds, there's the lucid dream signal!

"What happens," he continues, "is that in the transition from non-REM to REM, the cortex is turned on by the reticular activating system down in the brain stem. We've measured cerebral blood flow and found a large increase in the transition from non-REM to REM sleep, and the eye movements are also a sign of cerebral activation.

"It's very interesting: Lucid dreams often occur right at the beginning of a REM period, as you saw here in this chart. It's like a control system: As the nervous system goes from a lower to a higher level of activation, I think you sometimes get an overshoot—you can demonstrate mathematically that this often happens when you go from one state to another—and that can result in a lucid dream."

"Is lucid dreaming a state-specific science, in the Charles Tart sense?" we ask LaBerge.

"Well," he pauses, scanning his internal data bank for the most precise answer. "State-specific science is based on the idea that you can't carry some kinds of knowledge from one state to another, and I think that's mistaken. You can learn to remember your dreams, and you can learn to be awake in your dreams, too. What we're doing is trying to relate lucid-dream reality to waking reality."

He and Kedzierski have just been comparing dream time to real time, as a matter of fact. And, at least in these rather austere experiments, ten seconds in a dream takes just as long as ten seconds in reality. When Kedzierski estimated the passage of ten seconds during a lucid dream—signaling with her eyes before and after to mark off the interval—she was off by two seconds, just as she had been when awake. Dream counting and dream singing mimic wide-awake counting and singing. That's not to say that all oneiro-chronology—like flying from the Grand Canyon to your grandmother's house in Omaha in a flash—obeys real-world laws. But it does prove a neat "psychophysical correspondence," in LaBerge's lingo, between the two realms.

"When you're dreaming about doing something," says LaBerge, "your brain is going through the same patterns it would if you were awake. And, indeed, if you believe the mind is in the brain, that would seem obvious. But if you believe that when you go to sleep your mind somehow leaves your body . . . well, it's clear where the 'astral silver chord' is."

Since he speaks like a mind-is-brain believer, we ask him about it. Here is his answer:

"The brain is the most wondrous piece of organized matter—in the local universe at least. We don't know what's in other galaxies," he says. "And it's capable of what look like miraculous things, so miraculous that we're tempted to say it's divine, that it's not 'natural.' But I don't think there's any mystery about where different levels of mind come from. I see them as the result of various complex interactions in the brain."

Stephen LaBerge is not one of those flat-footed reductionists who only believe in things that move a dial, however. Lately he's been thinking that if the mind can heal the body, it might do it best in the comparative sensory vacuum of the dream state. As a first experiment, he plans to make tiny scratches in oneironauts' arms (both arms, in each case) and then instruct them to heal only *one* arm during a lucid dream. (He doesn't rule out psi, either, though he'd prefer to keep his dream science out of the paranormal hinterlands.)

As for Beverly Kedzierski, the splendor of her dreams has not distracted her from artificial intelligence. In a way she's found a link between the silicon world and lucid dreaming. "We're working with automatic programming of a knowledge-based system," she tells us. "Our system is self-referential; it knows about itself. And that circular knowledge about itself is sort of like a consciousness.

"Knowing in a dream that this is a conscious body and that there is another body in bed that is dreaming, I think, is similar to the architecture of these computer systems."

Why Do We Dream?

THERE'S THE RUB. *Nobody knows* exactly why nature invented REM sleep, with its accompanying little theater of mirages. The fact that all animals and birds do it, though, argues that dreaming sleep must have some evolutionary purpose beyond providing cerebral jigsaw puzzles for analysts. Fetuses engage in REM sleep in the womb (what they might dream about, we don't know); newborns dream about half of every day; and adult human beings rack up a total of about an hour and a half of REM a night. And if they don't, they're in deep trouble.

Much of the basic science of REM, or "paradoxical sleep," as it used to be called—the paradox is that the dreaming cortex is cut off from normal sensory input yet remains active—comes from the landmark research of the French physiologist Michel Jouvet. In his lab in Lyons, in the 1950s, Jouvet proved that REM sleep was controlled by a part of the brain stem's reticular activating system (RAS) called the pons, or "bridge," and that another part of the RAS gives us dreamless, non-REM sleep. One day the father of modern sleep physiology turned his laboratory into an archipelago of small islands surrounded by water and placed cats precariously on the islands. The cats were fine as long as they were awake or in deep, slow-wave sleep, but whenever they went into the characteristic muscular relaxation of REM, they lost their grip, automatically slid into the man-made sea, and woke up. After a few weeks of REM deprivation the animals became extremely weird—some even died—proving starkly that the mammalian brain needs dreams.

Why?

Theory number 1: Dreams are the mind's safety valve, a way of sneaking dangerous, taboo, emotionally charged or contradictory messages past the prim, Oxford-donnish superego. This was Freud's idea, in a nutshell. Memory traces or residues of daytime happenings commingle in an intracranial forest primeval with "regressive" material from our deep dark past. The dreamscape reenacts not only our own personal infancy but the whole phylogenetic childhood of the race. "We may expect," wrote Freud, in *The Interpretation of Dreams*, "that the analysis of dreams will lead us to a knowledge of man's archaic heritage, of what is psychically innate in him. Dreams and neuroses seem to have preserved more mental antiquities than we could have imagined possible."

No doubt there is a lot of truth to the psychoanalytic theory of dreams, but it doesn't explain why your dog has REM sleep. And how repressed can a week-old infant be?

Theory number 2: We need dreams for psychological equilibrium. "If you've received an insult to your self-esteem during the day," notes Stephen LaBerge, who has one foot in the psychological-balance camp, "you'll try to compensate in your dream with an ego-enchancing dream." Theory number 2 can be seen as a variation on number 1, except that instead of Freud's dual (or maybe triune) self, we must picture the mind as a sort of Hindu heaven with multiple gods. Or, to use the more fashionable parlance, as a multilevel information-processing system.

"We have many different goals, ranging all the way from higher goals like 'Be a better person' to lower-level ones like 'Buy a magazine,' " says LaBerge. "How to arrange all the goals in an effective order—how to get everything one wants—can be a mathematical problem. One thing dreams probably do is work out possible solutions."

Theory number 3: Dreams serve another kind of information-processing function, namely memory consolidation. This would account for the famous Midterm Effect (it's better to sleep a few hours after memorizing the reigns of the English monarchs than to cram all night) as well as the popularity of mail-order sleep tapes ("Learn Yoga/Serbo-Croatian/Double-Entry

Bookkeeping in Your Sleep"). It may also explain why reptiles and fish don't dream and why newborn humans dream so much.

The idea is this: The mammalian brain, born without all of its neuronal connections ready-made, relies on experience to weave meaningful patterns. What dreams do is to replay experiences and reinforce the crucial synaptic connections. Think of a child's connect-the-dot drawing. Add a three-dimensional structure of multiple superimposed images so that each dot is intersected thousands of times to take part in thousands of different drawings. A young brain that is still laying down synapses, says the we-dream-in-order-to-remember school, needs a lot of REM sleep to hook up all this wiring. Conversely, reptiles, which are relatively hard-wired at birth, have no special need of dreams.

Theory number 4: This is a brand-new one, and it's the reverse of number 3: *We dream in order to forget.* We'll need a little space to explain why Francis Crick, the eclectic co-discoverer of the double helix, and Cambridge researcher Graeme Mitchison think that you should forget your dreams. But hang on to the connect-the-dot image, for it comes in here, too.

The Overwrought Computer

ISN'T IT INTERESTING, mused Crick and Mitchison, that the only creatures endowed with REM sleep are those that have a neocortex—or in the case of birds, an analogous structure called a wulst? A single mammal lacks REM, and it is more of a pseudomammal: the primitive, small-brained, egg-laying spiny anteater. Do dreams fulfill a special neocortical need, the scientists wondered, and if so, what?

Consider again the human cortex with its 50 billion interconnected neurons and 500 billion glial cells all packed into two fistfuls of thick custard. Somewhere in the dense web of local cell connections that brain scientists call a neural net is stored the face of your first-grade teacher, the definition of *amanuensis*, the knowledge that a turnip is an edible vegetable and not a volcanic rock. Or at least that's the reigning hypothesis. As we saw in Chapter 7, the great Canadian psychologist Donald O. Hebb postulated that the stronger the synaptic connections are in a specific neural net, the stronger the engram it encodes. But isn't there an upper limit to information storage? Wouldn't it sometimes make sense to "erase" your first-grade teacher's image or the ancient Greek pluperfect subjunctive to make space for other, more useful patterns?

To test this idea, Crick and Mitchison used a computer program to simulate a neocortical neural net and endowed it with the Hebbian law of information storage (the information stored is proportional to the strength of the synapses). Such artificial-intelligence models can nowadays be trained to "recognize" a certain stimulus when the computer equivalent of "synaptic strength" is set at a certain level—which is to say they can mimic brains in a primitive way. With a neat computer-graphics attachment they can even turn an incomplete or blurred glimpse of a face into a realistic portrait, just as your neocortex does every day of your life. But what Crick and Mitchison wanted to know was this: What would happen if a neural net got overloaded, if it were force-fed too many superimposed, overlapping patterns?

The result was a computer gone berserk. Their model neocortical net displayed "parasitic modes of activity," wherein it printed out bizarre associations, fantastic silicon ravings. Sometimes it became "obsessed" and gave multiple versions of the same memory or else it printed out only a bare handful of memories in response to any stimulus. At other times it "hallucinated," generating a completely inappropriate picture out of input that should have been ignored. If all this evokes the locked wards at Bellevue, it's because flesh-and-blood neural nets are also vulnerable to information overload. Or so Crick and Mitchison speculate.

Although the human neocortex possesses many more "bits" (and therefore more storage capacity) than the Crick/Mitchison model net, the bulk of its synapses are excitatory; and self-excitation can lead to electrical instability—and epilespy, psychosis, and other pathological states, according to the scientists. Fortunately most of us aren't mentally ill or epileptic. Crick and Mitchison believe that's because REM sleep *erases* unwanted synaptic connections, all those associations and memory traces that, if filed permanently, would overwhelm us. Nocturnal "unlearning" or "reverse learning," then, is evolution's solution to the mathematical dilemma posed by the gargantuan mammalian neocortex. (Unbeknownst to Crick and Mitchison, John Hopfield of CalTech had independently conceived the idea of reverse learning, though he hadn't connected it with dreaming. In Hopfield's simulations "unlearning" did indeed improve the behavior of a neural network.)

Instead of knitting up raveled sleeves of care or anything else, Crick and Mitchison propose, dreams are the fleeting shades of neural nets *unraveling*. Thus, in their 1983 article in *Nature*, they counsel us to ignore them: "In this model," they write, "attempting to remember one's dreams should perhaps not be encouraged, because such remembering may help to retain patterns of thought which are better forgotten. These are the very patterns the organism was attempting to damp down."

The Deinterpretation of Dreams

I was lying in bed and a gentleman who was known to me entered the room; I tried to turn on the light but was unable to; I tried over and over again, but in vain. Thereupon my wife got out of bed to help me, but she could not manage it either. But as she felt awkward in front of the gentleman owing to being "en negligée," she finally gave it up and went back to bed. All of this was so funny that I couldn't help roaring with laughter at it. My wife said, "Why are you laughing? Why are you laughing?" but I only went on laughing until I woke up.

—FREUD: a patient's dream from *The Interpretation of Dreams*

POOR FREUD. Everybody's dismantling his theoretical castles these days, and now a pair of eminent sleep physiologists, armed with microelectrodes, EEG machines, and pseudoneurotransmitters, are demystifying the dream.

One might nitpick about the correct decoding of certain dream specimens in *The Interpretation*, of course, or about Freud's knee-jerk responses to towers and caves, but never, never about the central sacrament, the dream's meaning. Until now. To Harvard's J. Allan Hobson and Robert W. McCarley, two high priests of modern sleep research, dreams are just a glitzy sideshow, not the main act.

Hobson, who studied with Michel Jouvet in France, and his colleague McCarley co-direct the Neurophysiology Laboratory at the Massachusetts Mental Health Center. The dreams they "analyze," in a basement laboratory in Boston's Back Bay, are the dreams of cats. It is a long way from the Viennese boudoirs of Freud's rambling neurasthenics. From a microelectrode in a sleeping cat's brain, the firings of a single neuron can be heard crackling over an audio-amplifier like a bad car radio. Hobson and McCarley inject microscopic drops of chemicals and change the neuron's firing rate. They have their fingers, in short, on the on/off switch for dreams.

The REM on-switch, or "dream state generator," is the concerted activity of a collection of cells in the pons (bridge) of the brain stem. Unlike the parochial neurons of the cortex, these pontine neurons are gangly giants with long-distance fibers reaching all the way from the top of the spinal column to the neocortex. By secreting a neurotransmitter called acetylcholine, they "wake up" the sleeping cortex and produce dreams. As for the off-switch, that's controlled by a part of the brain stem called the locus coeruleus. The locus coeruleus cells make the chemical norepinephrine and automatically inhibit REM. Together, these two reciprocal systems generate cycles of REM sleep in the human brain every ninety minutes of the night. (In the cat, the cycle takes thirty minutes; in the rat, twelve.) Like genies out of the *The Arabian Nights*, Hobson and McCarley have managed to conjure dreams (or at least the right electrical correlates in a cat brain) with a drug that mimics acetylcholine. And they turn them off again, plunging the animal into dreamless, non-REM sleep, with a drug that acts like norepinephrine.

But, Professor, how can these feline brain waves tell us anything about the interpretation of dreams?

In late 1977 Hobson and McCarley took on this psychoanalytic sacred cow in an article in the *American Journal of Psychiatry*. After all, wasn't Freudian dream theory based on the outmoded, turn-of-the-century neurophysiological model? Although they stop short of saying that dreams are meaningless, Hobson and McCarley push psychic motives to the back burner:

Freud believed that the dreaming sleep state (D) and dreaming were initiated and powered by the combination of the day residue (certain memories of the day) with the energy contained in a repressed unconscious wish. . . . It can now be categorically stated that there is *no* experimental support for Freud's theory . . .

Freud could not have known . . . that neurons are elements of a signaling network, that neurons have their own metabolic sources of energy and influence one another by the transmission of *small* amounts of energy. Freud . . . believed that all neural energy was entirely derived from outside the brain, chiefly from . . . instincts. Neurons acted as passive conduits and storage vessels for this energy.

In short, Freud was wrong, say Hobson and McCarley. Dreams are powered by the spontaneous firing of neurons, not by repressed libido energy. Even dream *content* sometimes has less to do with veiled Oedipal wishes or castration panic than with purely neural events. Take the common nightmare of being chased. That can be explained by the physiological paradox that motor commands are given during REM sleep, but the immobilized dreamer is powerless to obey them. If you should feel paralyzed or dream of running in slow motion through a field of thick oatmeal after a train that keeps receding, you now know why. (When the motor-inhibiting parts of the pons are removed, cats actually *act out* their dreams. They run, chase dream mice, and arch their backs in a facsimile of attack.)

Why are dreams so distorted, fragmented, and fantastic? Freud said that in our dreams we revisit a psychic Jurassic Age, prehistoric, irrational, garbled, full of fabulous monsters. "Condensation," "displacement," and symbol formation, according to Freud, are the dream's way of disguising the forbidden wishes of the dreamer. Hobson and McCarley have a simpler explanation: The brain, like a fairytale princess lost in a haunted Schwarzwald, is faced with the task of weaving together a lot of contradictory and nonsensical information. Some of our senses, like vision and sound, are very active in REM, while others—pain, taste, and smell—hardly function at all. Our limbs don't move when the brain tells them to. The sudden, uncoordinated eye movements of REM may make the dreamworld move in odd ways, so that we dream of floating on a magic carpet over an undulating landscape.

In analyzing hundreds of dream reports compiled by Cincinnati dream researcher Milton Kramer, McCarley pursued correspondences between dream content and neurophysiology. One thing he observed was the curious tendency of dreams to truncate, dissolve, or shift suddenly in midstream. Freud explained this as the dreamer's attempt to elude the unpleasant and the taboo, but McCarley thinks the normal cycles of neuronal activation are responsible. One group of cells simply runs its course—and voilà!—a brand-new dreamscape.

While McCarley and Hobson allow that dreams still make nice "physiological Rorschach tests," they think you shouldn't *overinterpret* them. As Freud himself once said, "Sometimes a cigar is just a cigar." And sometimes a flying-carpet ride over Machu Picchu is just an ephemeral shadow show scripted by the neurons in the pons. "Even in dreams," Hobson concludes, "the mind and the brain are one."

It is an impressive picture: the slumbering cat in a little glass box, the waves and troughs on the sea-green oscilloscope, the electric cackle of the brain's tiniest components. But it cannot strike anyone as a complete theory of dreams. What about the rich sepia interiors of "Irma," "Herr M.," and the other turn-of-the-century analysands? Do we find the dream's "soul" in a cat's intracerebral chatter any more than we can relate Proustian memory to the conditioned reflexes of *Aplysia californica*?

Gordon Globus, of the University of California at Irvine, would say no. But then he left the technological miracles of sleep physiology about ten years ago for the pure domain of "existential psychiatry," which he practices at Capistrano-by-the-Sea Hospital, a place that looks a lot like its name.

To get there (from Los Angeles) you don't so much drive as get swept south by the straight, seventy-mile-an-hour current of the San Diego Freeway. Past the sprawling industrial badlands between Long Beach and the interior, past a dozen or more luminous green exit signs for overnight condo havens—always called Something-Vista or Something-Mar; though usually there's neither a "mar" nor a "vista" in sight. Finally, just as Irvine vanishes behind you, an exit in the middle of nowhere announces "Pacific

Coast Highway" and fifteen minutes later, you're there. The sudden apparition of palms and ocean, a new marina with its perfect crescent of Spanish Mission-style stores and seafood restaurants feels curiously like a dream, a movie set, or maybe a mural in a mall. Nearby, atop a little windswept, eucalyptus-fragrant hill overlooking the whole shimmering Pacific Ocean is Dr. Globus's hangout.

"I was a psychophysiologist for many years," he tells us with the bemused detachment of someone recalling a previous incarnation. He is mid-fortyish, intense, reserved, with an academic's manner of pronouncing his ideas slowly and as if in perfect paragraphs, so that the listener can end up with legible class notes. "I was interested in dreams, sleep-cycle physiology, biological rhythms. But my talents aren't suited to the lab. I'm not very compulsive. I was spending all my time at the computer center programming statistics, when what I was really interested in was consciousness. So as soon as I got tenure I gave up my laboratory."

Isn't neurophysiology a route to consciousness? we ask him.

"Most bench scientists, who are studying at the neurochemical level, the cellular level, the single-unit level, don't care about consciousness," he says. "That level of investigation is so molecular that consciousness doesn't make a difference. It's only at higher levels of the nervous system that consciousness matters.

"What brain science has done in my career is amazing. That's where the Nobel prizes lie, not in molecular biology any more. However, all you're really finding out is *correlates*. We know that certain conscious processes co-vary with the amplitude and latency of the P300 wave of the evoked potential, for instance. This principle of *psychoneural covariance*"—we imagine the invisible student underlining the italicized phrase— "is a good place to begin in trying to solve the mind/brain problem. By itself, though, it doesn't prove any particular theory. It's compatible with identity theory, with crass materialism, with dualism, with parallelism, with anything. . . ."

The mind/brain problem is to Gordon Globus what the pole star is to a sailor: the fixed point of his cerebral navigational system. Over the years, as he approached it first from one angle and then from another, the solution has sometimes hovered just above the horizon—only to recede, or, by a curious philosophical parallax, to shift with the position of the observer. But Globus is a patient man. He is, he tells us, prepared to devote his lifetime to solving it.

The Infinite Library

NOT LONG AGO he had a dream. On the surface it wasn't particularly remarkable— or at least it had none of the phantasmagoric, topsy-turvy, now-you-see-it, now-you-don't quality of many dreams—but it became the centerpiece of an abstruse paper called "The Causal Theory of Perception: A Critique and Revision through Reflection on Dreams." Here is the simple, crystalline dream fragment that concealed a radical metaphysics:

I am swimming out of the ocean into a rocky grotto. I gaze up, and against the dark vaulted ceiling I perceive a starry display of luxuriant, green, luminous growth, which I experience with some feeling of pleasurable awe.

For Freud dreams were composed of second-hand stuff, memory traces and "day residues," all decomposed and rearranged. The new composite might *seem* original, but each of its elements harked back inevitably to some real-world impression, however obscure and fleeting. Vivisecting one of his own dreams in *The Interpretation of Dreams*, Freud theorized:

What I did was to adopt the procedure . . . of family portraits: namely by projecting two images on to a single plate, so that certain features common to both are emphasized, while those which fail to fit in with one another cancel one another out and are indistinct in the picture. In my dream about my uncle the fair beard emerged prominently from a face which belonged to two people and which was consequently blurred.

Globus doesn't think dream perception works that way at all. True, he could track a few of *his* dream's details to daytime impressions. The day before he'd been "gazing ruefully" at his swimming pool, envisioning a Plexiglas half-dome that would cover half of it, and that memory might account for the bare outlines of the grotto's shape. For the vegetation on the dream-grotto's ceiling he could summon up a more remote memory: "I once unexpectedly came upon a place where water very slowly seeped into a small niche in the face of a rocky cliff. It was filled with a fantastic and beautiful luminous display of green slimy growth of all kinds." However, these "family resemblances," failed to explain his dream. "Freud's conception," he observes, "is that the dream object concatenates properties of previously experienced objects and averages across them. But the grotto of my dream is not a patchwork assemblage or collage of the dome and seep or a blurry average. . . ." Globus hadn't even seen the Plexiglas dome, for that matter, only *imagined* it: It was an abstraction, immaculate of sensory input. Furthermore, he'd never gone swimming in a grotto in his life. Yet the world of the dream was totally convincing, compelling, and real—at least to the dreamer, Globus thinks: "Not only does the dream self feel like my usual self, but the dreamworld also seems entirely authentic. The rocky dream grotto appears just as real as if I were 'actually' swimming in such a grotto. Even if I were to fly like a bird, it would still seem like 'my' world I was seeing (from a bird's-eye view). . . . Thus, my dream experience is both authentic and novel."

The dreamworld à la Globus is not a pale, lunar reflection of waking life; nor are dream objects poor, flimsy, hand-me-down versions of past sensory messages. Although day residues may influence dream images, the dream is a totally original creation.

And here's the radical corollary: Waking perception is not fundamentally different. Once you suspend the question of whether anything exists or not (in philosophical lingo, that's called bracketing existence), you find that the dreamworld and "real world" have the same ontological status. Globus writes:

It must be remembered that there are strong *biological* grounds for supposing that perception utilizes comparable mechanisms across waking and dreaming. It is biologically absurd to hold that evolution would abruptly bifurcate into two distinct forms with distinct mechanisms at its very pinnacle—human consciousness. . . . (As Freud . . . indicates, dreaming is but a special form of waking thinking, taking place under the peculiar conditions of sleep.)

Basically Globus argues against the commonsense notion that sensory input is a message from external reality—that the tree in your head is a copy (maybe an imperfect or transmuted copy, but a copy nonetheless) of the tree outside it. For Descartes, the simple tree message was carried to the pineal gland and then to consciousness. Though we now know that perception is far more complex, that the brain subjects each message to elaborate analysis and computation, most scientists still believe that when a sensory message finally reaches consciousness its basic order is preserved. (Hubel and Wiesel's model of visual perception is a case in point.)

Globus's perception of perception is an extreme departure: "There is no message received from the external reality," he asserts. "Instead a model of reality is created *de novo*." To explain what he's getting at (it's a long way from the glass beakers and micropipettes we're used to), here's a partial record of our conversation:

WE: You've said that you're an "identity theorist." Do you mean that the mind's operations boil down to workings of the physical brain?

GLOBUS: Yes. Otherwise you're stuck with dualism—two different substances, which would be impossible. But it has taken me ten years to understand identity theory. It's much more radical than people think. Naive realism, you know, is the doctrine that what you see now is a reality that you directly perceive. It's the traditional, commonsense view: As much as your brain might transform, analyze, or compare the sensory input, the original message is retained. Perceptual order conserves input order.

But any neuroscientist knows that couldn't be true. The world you see is a *representation*. If you follow that to its logical conclusion, you have the existential dilemma of Carlos Castaneda's *Journey to Ixtlan*, where Don Juan tells Carlos that we're all enclosed in a "bubble of perception." That's what's really radical about identity theory. Although it seems you and I share this world here now, strict identity theory says we are totally isolated, that each of us individually constructs this world. . . .

WE: So we're all locked inside our separate skulls, experiencing the world only indirectly through the filter of our senses—or, worse, perceiving total chimera?

GLOBUS: That's the loneliness of the journey to Ixtlan. Don Genaro discovers that the people he had always seen as warm, flesh-and-blood humans are but apparitions. The other person is an apparition, a construction.

WE: Is there any way I can tell that you are not an apparition?

GLOBUS: No, there is no *empirical* way to know. Reality is a distant thing, which we know only by inference. What you're doing, what your brain is doing, is telling a good, comprehensive story.

WE: Is that what a neuroscientist does—construct a "good story" about the brain?

GLOBUS: Yes, that's why the phenomenologists, like [Maurice] Merleau-Ponty and Husserl, rejected science—because they rejected the commonsense view. The scientist was just reading a meter or something. Husserl was after transcendental, absolutely certain knowledge, not empirical knowledge. But he was working with an impoverished conception of the brain.

WE: You're not in favor of ignoring the physical apparatus?

GLOBUS: No. If you're going to solve the mind/brain problem—and I think it's a solvable problem—you have to think about the brain the way a brain scientist does in order to make any headway. But if you're going to translate between brain and consciousness, you also need a model of consciousness, and neuroscience has a very impoverished one. Some of the best definitions of consciousness come from the phenomenologists.

WE: How do you think about consciousness?

GLOBUS: Well, Walter Weimer [a mind/body theorist from Pennsylvania State University] says, "The organism is a theory of its environment." That's a koan, it's beautiful. In my terms the organism is an abstract classification system. By that I mean it has a program, a set of rules for taking input and generating the life-world, the objects we see.

WE: How do we know there is anything out there at all?

GLOBUS: Brain scientists tend to be realists—antimetaphysical. Is there a world out there? Well, that's just an assumption. It would be intolerable if it weren't, though. I'm interested in nice theories—that's a California term, as in "Have a nice day"—and a nice theory postulates existence. My theory says that all the worlds we might perceive exist *a priori* in the brain. The world we see now is selected from this infinite *a priori* store. How do you get a particular "book" out of this infinite library? Well, there's input from the senses. The input is classified by the brain and it provides a selection signal, a rule of explication; it picks a particular book out of the infinite library. But all the books are already there. They're built in genetically. From moment to moment we generate the world. When we fall asleep it goes away.

WE: That brings us to dreams. How does your theory of perception account for dream phenomena?

GLOBUS: Well, it explains why the dreaming world is infinitely creative. The dreaming mechanism selects out of that infinite library worlds we've never seen before, whole new created worlds.

WE: Say I took a spaceship to the planet Remulak, twenty-four light-years away, where the scenery resembles nothing whatever on Earth. Does your theory predict that I would be able to perceive this entirely foreign reality by selecting certain pictures out of the infinite store in my brain?

GLOBUS: Yes, and that's what you do in your dreams. It's an extremely mystical notion. If it's all there *a priori*—or at least the mechanisms for constituting it are—that means that from moment to moment we uphold the world we see.

Alice Meets Bishop Berkeley

AS NEUROPHYSIOLOGY, Globus's theory is a bit threadbare—or at least science has yet to invent the instrument that could detect his abstract perceptual "mechanisms." (One suspects he's not that interested in down-and-dirty neuroscience, anyway.) His metaphysics, on the other hand, take us right to the nerve center of an age-old philosophical conundrum.

> "He's dreaming now," said Tweedledee. "And what do you think he's dreaming about?"
> Alice said, "Nobody can guess that."

"Why, about *you!*" Tweedledee exclaimed, clapping his hands triumphantly. "And if he left off dreaming about you, where do you suppose you'd be?"

"Where I am now, of course," said Alice.

"Not you!" Tweedledee retorted contemptuously. "You'd be nowhere. Why you're only a sort of thing in his dream!"

"If that there King was to wake," added Tweedledum, "you'd go out—bang!—just like a candle!"

"I shouldn't!" Alice exclaimed indignantly. "Besides, if *I'm* only a sort of thing in his dream, what are *you*, I should like to know?"

"Ditto," said Tweedledum. . . .

"I *am* real!" said Alice, and began to cry.

—LEWIS CARROLL,
Through the Looking Glass

The Red King's dream is a metaphysical hall of mirrors. Alice, being a seven-and-a-half-year-old pragmatist, adopts the commonsense, "naive-realist" position: "I *am* real!" She accepts everything she perceives, including the snoring Red King, as solid objects in a solid world. She "knows" herself to be a real, sentient being named Alice—just as Descartes knew himself as a thinking "I." Tweedledee and Tweedledum, on the other hand, are disciples of Bishop Berkeley, to whom all material phenomena were only "sorts of things" in the mind of God, the Big Dreamer Upstairs.

Alice's plight is that nothing she can do, not even her "real," salty tears, can get her out of her painful existential position. She is, she's informed, a figment in the Red King's dream, and no one can prove otherwise. Furthermore, the entire looking-glass universe—the King, Tweedledee and Tweedledum, and the dream-character Alice included—exists in a dream of Alice's. (Hence her retort: "If *I'm* only a sort of thing . . . what are *you*, I'd like to know?") In the looking-glass tale, the question of who-dreamed-whom reverberates forever.

"A sort of infinite regress is involved here in the parallel dreams of Alice and the Red King," the philosopher/mathematician Martin Gardiner writes in his annotated *Alice in Wonderland.* "Alice dreams of the King, who is dreaming of Alice, who is dreaming of the King and so on, like two mirrors facing each other, or that preposterous cartoon of Saul Steinberg's in which a fat lady paints a picture of a thin lady who is painting a picture of the fat lady who is painting a picture of the thin lady, and so on deeper into the two canvases."

Oh, come on, you say (for you're a commonsense realist), this is a game for world-weary philosophers. I know I exist, and there's a world out there that *we all agree* exists, and everybody—except perhaps poor Aunt Sadie who went off her rocker twenty years ago and has been getting valentines from Henry VIII ever since—knows the difference between dreams and reality. If I crash into a real door I get a bump on my head, but a dream door may be so insubstantial I can slip through it like a ghost. Besides, my dream is my own private cosmos, whereas you and I and the gardener all see that the lawn needs weeding.

Yes, as Stephen LaBerge's oneironauts attest, there are clear and palpable differences between a dream (wherein you can fly and tamper with time and space) and "reality," with its crude, ineluctable physical laws. But consider the dilemma of Chuang-tzu, the Chinese philosopher (a contemporary of Plato) who dreamed of being a butterfly, and then awoke and asked himself, "Am I a man dreaming I'm a butterfly, or a butterfly dreaming I'm a man?" Chuang-tzu, like Alice, was faced with the possibility that ordinary, waking life, not the dream, might be the unreal interlude. This happens to be a doctrine that the Senoi people of Malaysia, who put more stock in dreams than "real life," take as an article of faith. Many cultures view dreams as a separate reality, parallel to our normal waking world, in which one may commune with gods, spirits, and departed ancestors.

Okay, you reply, but what about the fact we all perceive the same world while awake? Actually, we don't necessarily experience *exactly* the same world (your "blue" and my "blue" may be quite different), but we do agree about enough of its physical features to construct a consistent "story." So far, so good. But we're still left with the unsettling possibility that this whole physical universe, from the strange celestial objects called black holes down to the equally bizarre quarks, is a grand, collective "dream."

Maybe we perceive it as we do only because the brain of Homo sapiens is built that way. Recall how Ron Siegel attributed the similarity of all near-death visions to the neural wiring common to humans: By the same token, couldn't we also dismiss "reality" as a mass hallucination? Maybe a God-brain, or a differently evolved extraterrestrial brain, would "construct" a different universe. If Dr. Lilly's dolphins can ever tell us how their world works, would it or would it not resemble our own?

12

Border Stations:
The Near-Death Experience

I remember reaching the hospital entrance and
them dragging me out of the car. That's when I
started going out. . . . I remember them saying,
'He's had a heart attack.' During this stage, my
whole life flashed in front of my face . . . like
when we got married . . . flashed and it was gone.
. . . That's when I went into a tunnel. . . . At the
end of the tunnel was a glowing light. It looked
like an orange—uh, you seen the sunset in the
afternoon?

> —Cardiac arrest victim, interviewed by
> MICHAEL SABOM, M.D., in *Recollec-*
> *tions of Death*.

In 1976, when he was in his first year of cardiology at the University of
Florida in Gainesville, Dr. Michael Sabom was conversant enough with
death. No gaunt, apocalyptic horsemen, of course; death and near-death
visited routinely, if dramatically, in the form of "Code Blues," or "Code
99s," hospital-intercom distress calls for a patient in extremis. Doctors,
nurses, and technicians would rush through the halls with defibrillators,
oxygen, injections of lidocaine, and the other paraphernalia of modern
medical resurrection, and quite often the patient was snatched from clinical
death, or something very close to it. Being so invested in high-tech life-
saving, it did not occur to Dr. Sabom to wonder about the fate of those
who did not return.

During that year a friend introduced Sabom to the book *Life After Life*
by Dr. Raymond Moody, the first popular account of the near-death experience (NDE), published in 1975. Dr. Moody had talked to people who
had been at death's door and who returned with rapturous tales of the
"afterlife." They told him of dark tunnels and ethereal golden lights, technicolor life flashbacks, and visions of their own lifeless bodies being worked
over by doctors. There were also rendezvous with departed relatives, heavenly landscapes complete with biblical characters in robes, and an eventual
re-descent into the body—all of which was much too "far-out" for the

skeptical cardiologist to swallow. "I thought Moody's claims were ridiculous," Sabom recalls. But since resuscitation-from-near-death was part of his business, he decided to query patients informally about any peculiar experiences they might have had on the life-death border. He certainly didn't expect to hear anything Moodyesque.

The third patient he approached was a middle-aged Tampa housewife who'd passed through several near-death crises and was in the hospital for routine tests. The cardiologist slipped in a question about her experiences while unconscious. "As soon as she was convinced that I was not an underground psychiatrist posing as a cardiologist," he recalls, "she began describing the first near-death experience I had heard in my medical career. To my utter amazement, the details matched the descriptions in *Life After Life*. I was even more impressed by her sincerity and the deep personal significance her experience had had for her." He decided to do some NDE research in earnest. Five years and 116 interviews later, he published his own startling findings in a book, *Recollections of Death: A Medical Investigation*.

Before we tell you the details, you should know what a life-after-death chapter is doing in a book about the brain. So let's go back to our original question: Is the mind (consciousness) in the brain? To the average neuroscientific bench-worker that's like asking whether the earth is round. To conceive of mental activity outside a working brain is to regress to the level of medieval spirits, pallid ghosts in the machine, everything science has worked so hard to exorcise from the rational universe. But what if the psyche *could* detach itself from its physical container—even for a moment— and continue to see, hear, reason, and remember? If that were so, we would have to conclude that brains are unnecessary, a notion that violates every axiom of brain science. No wonder neuroscientists queried about NDEs tend to mention the *National Enquirer*.

You've seen the headlines: NEW PROOF OF LIFE AFTER DEATH, right next to AMAZING ARTHRITIS CURE and I WAS HELD HOSTAGE ON A UFO. At the time Sabom tackled it, the NDE was hardly respectable. Medical textbooks mention the phenomenon, when they mention it at all, in chapters on "Psychiatric Complications." The rare NDE descriptions that Sabom came across were lodged among paragraphs on "severe personality decompensation," "acute brain syndrome," and "other psychiatric reactions." In 1961 a parapsychologist named Karlis Osis published a collection of deathbed visions, most of which came from doctors' and nurses' retrospective reports, and no one paid much attention. In the early 1970s Dr. Elisabeth Kübler-Ross, of death-and-dying fame, lectured passionately on the subject, claiming to have interviewed hundreds of NDE veterans, but her statistics remained vague. The scientific establishment was not impressed by Moody's best-sellers, either, though the physician gets credit for coining the term *near-death experience* and for cataloging the common pattern of experiences: the feeling of overwhelming serenity, floating out of one's body, moving through a darkness (often a tunnel), perceiving a warm light, encountering a "being of light" or some supernatural presence, entering a beautiful supramundane "world," meeting dead relatives, and so on.

Later, more systematic studies corroborated the classic Moody NDE and brought a bit of scientific rigor to a field that was, at best, anecdotal and fraught with strong religious overtones. Psychologist Kenneth Ring, of the University of Connecticut, for example, collected and analyzed hundreds of NDEs over a six-year period using standardized statistical methods. Among other accomplishments, Ring codified the "core" features of the NDE—tunnel, brilliant light, out-of-body travel, panoramic life flashbacks—that were first observed by Moody. Other scientists, such as UCLA's Ronald Siegel and even Sloan Kettering's Dr. Lewis Thomas, added weight to the field by offering physical explanations for the NDE.

But it was Dr. Sabom who attacked the NDE head-on. Moody's statistical vagaries and lack of objectivity had disturbed Sabom. How many of Moody's subjects had the full NDE with all the prototypical features, he wondered? And how typical were these people anyway? Were they just plain folks, or weirdos? Had they really been clinically dead? Were their recollections real or fabricated?

Sabom's methods were more scrupulous. He approached a random sample of patients who had survived a brush with death (three-quarters had been in cardiac arrest) without tipping them off to the purpose of his inquiries. He tracked down the medical records and culled only those NDEs that occurred during a true near-death crisis ("any bodily state that caused physical unconsciousness and that could reasonably be expected to result in irreversible biological death" without medical intervention). He collected data on the patients' socioeconomic, educational, and religious backgrounds to determine whether any of these factors had a bearing on the NDE.

To his surprise fully 40 percent of his patients remembered their "deaths" in lucid and often wondrous detail. A third of them recalled floating above the operating table, hospital bed, or scene of the accident where the temporarily discarded body lay. Half reported close encounters with beautiful lights, unearthly landscapes, and other transcendent phenomena. Many had both the *autoscopic*, or "self-visualizing," experience and the *transcendent* part. Even more remarkably, dyed-in-the-wool atheists were just as likely to have NDEs as born-again Christians—although the pious more often communed with a biblical God, the nonbelievers with a "warm presence" or a holy light.

Autoscopic Realism

BUT SABOM'S REAL COUP was to focus on the one element of the NDE that, unlike life flashbacks and scenes in heaven, might actually be tested empirically: the autoscopic experience.

He began his investigation with the "Code Blues," those modern-day Lazaruses revived from cardiac arrest in the ordered, antiseptic world of the hospital—where detailed medical records were filed. "I anxiously awaited the moment when a patient would claim that he had 'seen' what had happened in his room during his own resuscitation," Sabom recalls. "I intended to pit my experience as a trained cardiologist against the professed visual recollections of laypersons. I was convinced that obvious inconsistencies would appear that would reduce these purported visual observations to no more than an 'educated guess.' " He was wrong.

"Mr. P" was a fifty-two-year-old security guard who went into cardiac arrest in a Florida hospital. He blacked out for a moment, he told Sabom, and when he came to, there was his body below him, curled up like a fetus on the black-and-white tile of the emergency room floor. With an odd sense of detachment, he went on observing the scene from ceiling level, as several people placed his body on a gurney and wheeled it down the hall to another room, where it was hooked up to a strange machine and "thumped." Here is a portion of the interview, recorded in *Recollections of Death*:

MR. P: I thought they had given my body too much voltage. Man, my body jumped about two feet off the table. . . .

SABOM: From where you were, could you see the monitor?

MR. P: It was like an oscilloscope. Just a faint white line, running with a little fuzz dropping down to the bottom. . . .

SABOM: Where did they put those paddles on your chest?

MR. P: Well, they weren't paddles, Doctor. They were round disks with a handle on them. No paddles. They put one up here, I think it was larger than the other one, and they put one down here.

SABOM: Did they do anything to your chest before they put those things on your chest?

MR. P: They put a needle in me. I thought at the time it looked like one of these Aztec rituals where they take the virgin's heart out. They took it two-handed—I thought that was very unusual—and shoved it into my chest like that. He took the heel of his hand and his thumb and shot it home. I thought that was very unusual.

SABOM: Did they do anything else to your chest before they shocked you?

MR. P: Not then, but the other doctor, when they first threw me up on the table, struck me. And I mean he really whacked the hell out of me. He came back with his fist from way behind his head and he hit me right in the center of my chest. And then they were pushing on my chest like artificial respiration, not exactly like that but kinda like artificial respiration. They shoved a plastic tube like you put in an oil can, they shoved that in my mouth. . . .

This account of the minutiae of cardiopulmonary resuscitation was remarkably accurate in all its details, Sabom noted, including "the proper sequence in which this technique is performed—that is, chest thump, external cardiac massage, air-way insertion, administration of medications and defibrillation." (The defibrillator is the machine that "thumped" the patient's body with electricity, jolting it two feet off the table.) And this was a man, Sabom discovered, who'd never even seen a CPR scene on television. It was his first heart attack, so he was no veteran of the cardiac wards. "At no time did I find any indication that he possessed more than a layman's knowledge of medicine," reports the cardiologist, who thoroughly examined his subjects on this score. "I was particularly struck by his reaction to my inadvertent use of the word *paddle* to describe the instrument that is held on a patient's chest during electrical defibrillation . . . ," he comments. "The man demonstrated his unfamiliarity with the term and with the resuscitation technique by his response: 'They weren't paddles, Doctor. They were round discs with a handle on them.'" Of course, the patient would not have known the medical nomenclature for the strange round discs he saw.

Mr. P. was one of thirty-two patients who claimed to have witnessed their own resuscitation from above and whose reports squared with doctors' accounts—down to the color of an oxygen mask, the number of shocks administered to the chest, and the serious or trivial conversations of doctors and nurses. But could some chronic cardiac patients simply have fantasized realistic autoscopic "recollections" on the basis of prior knowledge of resuscitation techniques? To find out, Sabom asked twenty-three long-term cardiac patients to give a detailed account of the resuscitation procedure. Twenty of them made major errors.

Patients who traveled out of their bodies during surgery described such gritty details as the placement of clamps and sponges, the appearance of their exposed organs, and the doctors' remarks: "It seems Dr. C. did most everything from the left side," reported a fifty-two-year-old man of his open-heart surgery. "He cut pieces of my heart off. . . . They even looked at some of the arteries and veins and there was a big discussion on whether they should do the bypass up here. . . . All but one doctor had scuffs tied around his shoes, and this joker had on white shoes which had blood all over them." A forty-two-year-old woman who suffered cardiac arrest during back surgery recalled the scene thus: " 'Arresting,' I think he said, 'arresting.' He said, 'Close' and all of sudden they started pulling out clamps real fast out of my back and closing up my skin. I was still down close to the operation and they started sewing up from the bottom. They were sewing up so fast that when they got up to the top there was a gaping piece of skin on my back. I was really annoyed. . . . I was thinking: I could have done better than that."

Out-of-Body Perception?

OKAY, but maybe these "dying" patients were really semiconscious, and maybe everything they supposedly saw autoscopically was no more than ordinary sense perception: fragments of overheard conversations or scenes glimpsed through half-closed eyes. That's one of the standard theories, and for obvious reasons, it remains more palatable to the medical mind than the disturbingly paranormal alternative of a patient ejecting from his body, in full possession of his faculties, like James Bond bailing out of one of his sportscars. But consider the case of Mr. S, a retired air force pilot who during a cardiac arrest in 1973 coolly observed every step of his resuscitation, including the intricate movements of the defibrillator's gauges.

In the operating room, Mr. S. was lying on his back, the oxygen mask obstructing his vision. Even so, he remembered the hospital personnel pulling over the cart with the defibrillator and the shape and details of its meter. ("It was square and had two needles on there, one fixed and one which moved.") Mr. S. also described how the fixed needle "moved each time they punched the thing and somebody was messing with it."

Mr. S. is Sabom's star witness. As far as the cardiologist could determine, even if Mr. S. had been partially conscious, he could not have seen the defibrillator—still less, the needles on its meter—from the position his physical body was in at the time. An oxygen mask covered his face and the defibrillator machine was located out of his visual range, yet his reportage was rigorously correct. "I was particularly fascinated by his description of a 'fixed' needle and a 'moving' needle on the face of the defibrillator as it was being charged with electricity," Sabom notes. "This charging procedure is only performed immediately prior to defibrillation, since once charged, this machine poses a serious electrical hazard. . . . Moreover, meters of [this] type . . . are not found on more recent defibrillator models, but were in common use in 1973, at the time of his cardiac arrest."

The man said he had never seen a working defibrillator before, and Sabom had no cause to doubt him. Despite his materialist-reductionist training, the cardiologist was forced to conclude that Mr. S. must have witnessed his temporary death from an out-of-body vantage point. "I couldn't pinpoint the position where I had been," said S., "but it was almost like I was in an amphitheater, and I was observing. I was at the foot of the bed to either side. . . . I could have walked around or whatever. I was free to do whatever I wanted, move around, watch what was going on. . . ."

The Big Secret

MR. S.'S SUPREME INDIFFERENCE to the grave physical facts was typical of the autoscopic scene, during which patients felt like disinterested bystanders watching a remote movie or a scene in a play. As one patient put it, it was "like being up in a balcony looking down and watching all this and feeling very detached as though I was watching someone else." In this incorporeal state there was no pain: "That's when Dr. A. began to do the pounding on the chest," a patient reported, "and it didn't hurt even though it cracked a rib. . . ." Nor was there any death anxiety: "I knew I was going to be perfectly safe, whether my body died or not."

But indifference to physical realities was rarely accompanied by philosophical or emotional indifference. Most near-death survivors, Sabom reports, were deeply moved by their walk on the weird side:

That was the most beautiful instant in the whole world when I came out of that body! . . . I can't imagine anything in the world or out of the world that could anywhere compare. Even the most beautiful moments of life would not compare to what I was experiencing. —Fifty-five-year-old heart attack patient at the Atlanta V.A. Medical Center

I feel it was God, and it was a very religious experience for me. —Thirty-seven-year-old woman relating the NDE she had at age fourteen

I think once you've penetrated the big secret just a bit like I did, it's enough to convince you, enough to convince me that I'm going to have no fear. . . . I don't think God wanted me to die. . . . He wanted me to get a peek into this big secret and shoved me right back again. —Heart-attack victim

Not all of Sabom's subjects met a Sunday-school Jesus or became overtly religious during an NDE, but virtually all of them returned with an unshakable belief in postmortem survival. ("Before I had this experience I figured when you're dead, you're dead. That's all. I believe now that your spirit does leave your body.") And this foretaste of the hereafter, if that is what it was, had definite aftereffects. "For the NDE survivor, life in the here-and-now became more precious, more meaningful," Sabom tells us. "Some people even took on jobs where they could help others struggling with the fact of death. And these profound psychological changes can last for years. We interviewed some people who had an NDE thirty or forty years ago and still professed no fear of death."

"Dying," he adds, "may not be the universal 'horror and agony' many of us were brought up to believe. All the people I interviewed recalled the overall experience as pleasant, though some were temporarily afraid or bewildered during the moving-through-the-void phase, and some felt remorse at the thought of the loved ones they were leaving." Sometimes the nagging memory of unfinished business, children left behind, et cetera, played a part in the person's "decision" to return. "At that time," said one typical patient, "I thought about my family and all and I said, 'Maisie, I better go back.' It was just as if I went back and got into my body."

Condos in Paradise

THE "TRANSCENDENT" NDEs in Sabom's sample included a broad spectrum of otherworldy environments, ranging from a children's illustrated New Testament–style heaven and "the Sea of Galilee" to realms of "cottony clouds," radiant pastures, and landscapes full of people "of all different nationalities . . . all working on their arts and crafts." None of these small eternities resembled a damnation scene out of Hieronymus Bosch or even a garden-variety Baptist hell, which must have come as a great relief to some. Here is what two of Sabom's subjects saw in the Beyond:

I went out the window. I guess you've flown an airplane into the clouds when the sun shone on it? All it was was a bright light that got brighter and brighter but it didn't hurt your eyes.

Just as clear and plain the Lord came and stood and held his hands out for me. . . . He was tall with his hands out and he had all white on, like he had a white robe on. . . . It [the face] was more beautiful than anything you've ever seen. His face was beautiful, really and truly beautiful.

"It's very interesting," Ronald Siegel, the hallucination master of UCLA, tells us with a knowing smile. "In the afterlife the loved ones are always fully clothed, looking just the way we remember them from the family album. . . .

"I hardly believe they're going to be fully clothed on the Other Side, if there is an Other Side, or that they're not going to show any physical changes. You know, we've had descriptions of golf courses, even condominiums, in the afterlife." He pauses to savor the joke. "What we're looking at," he continues, "is the projection of your own internal images onto the outside. It's your own projector, your mind, which is generating these images. I don't think we have to postulate a lot of untestable constructs like the hereafter. We can explain it all by the well-known dissociative properties of hallucination."

With his silver-tongued skepticism and his impeccable credentials as a connoisseur of altered states, Siegel has emerged lately as a high prophet among NDE nonbelievers. Not that he is a lone debunker. His view that the so-called near-death experience is an unholy marriage of wish fulfillment, superstition, and hallucination is still the basic scientific doctrine. Freud declared that the belief in immortality is a pathetic attempt to deny the terrible reality of physical annihilation, and Siegel wouldn't disagree. "The most logical guess," he wrote in a paper, "The Psychology of Life After Death," published in *American Psychologist* in late 1980, "is that consciousness shares the same fate as that of the corpse. Surprisingly this commonsense view is not the prevalent one, and a majority of humankind rejects [it]."

Indeed, it does, to judge by George Gallup, Jr.'s recent poll of 1,500 people, 70 percent of whom said they believed in life after death. (The survey also revealed the extraordinary statistic that some eight million American adults have probably experienced a textbook NDE with all the mind-boggling trimmings.) But to Siegel, the 70 percent are no less deluded for being a majority, and the happy hereafter is a psychological talisman, a teddy bear for grown-ups afraid of the existential darkness. And Homo sapiens isn't the only superstitious animal. Even elephants, he tells us, bury their dead comrades with fruit, flowers, and other little *memento mori*, as if they too believed in life everlasting. He also likes to point out that the people interviewed by Moody, Sabom, and other NDE researchers weren't really dead. "No one has died and come back to give an interview on the 'Johnny Carson Show,' " he says.

Here Siegel is attacking a straw man. Except for Kübler-Ross, who did not endear herself to serious scientists by saying she knew "beyond a shadow of a doubt" that there was life after death, the NDE fraternity carefully avoids this claim. "My research does not prove life after death," Michael Sabom tells us. "The people I studied were *near* death, not dead and resurrected. My study suggests that the physical brain and the non-physical 'mind' are distinct and that they may split apart somehow in the process of dying. Otherwise how can we explain accurate out-of-the-body perceptions? Whether this immaterial 'mind' persists beyond ultimate biological death, however, is purely speculative."

So leaving the immortality of the soul out of the picture, let's focus on the rest of Siegel's argument. His best case against the NDE's validity is its family resemblance to the hallucinatory states he has cataloged so exhaustively. Tunnels, bright lights, the sensation of floating out of one's body, luminous extraterrestrial landscapes, celestial guides, ineffable peace, and all the other NDE phenomena, he points out, are also commonplace landmarks of drug trips. For example, listen to two Moody subjects describing the passing-through-the-tunnel experience:

I found myself in a tunnel—a tunnel of concentric circles . . . [a] spiraling tunnel.

I felt like I was riding on a roller-coaster train at an amusement park, going through this tunnel at a tremendous speed.

And here are two of Siegel's subjects narrating their psychedelic journeys, as reported in his 1980 article "The Psychology of Life After Death":

I'm moving through some kind of train tube. There are all sorts of lights and colors.

It's sort of like a tube, like, I sort of feel . . . that I'm at the bottom of the tube looking up.

If the NDE people saw wondrous lights, so did the UCLA hallucinators:

And it seems like I'm getting closer and closer to the sun, it's very white . . . and there's like a geometric network or lattice in the distance.

Panoramic life reviews? Supernatural beings? Heavenly scenes? Siegel can find those in the annals of drug intoxication, too. And if you want a sensational out-of-body trip, try this one, which Siegel culled from the drug aficionado magazine *High Times*:

My mind left my body and apparently went to what some describe as the 'second state.' I felt I was in a huge, well-lit room in front of a massive throne draped in lush red velvet. I saw nothing else but felt the presence of higher intelligence tapping my mind of every experience and impression I had gathered. I begged to be released, to return to my body. It was terrifying. Finally I blacked out and slowly came to in the recovery room. That's my ketamine experience.

Ketamine, a superpotent hallucinogen related to angel dust, simulates the classic near-death experience extremely well, Siegel claims. "This thing of floating above one's body and looking down is a very common dissociative phenomenon," he tells us. Not just drugs like ketamine, but sensory deprivation, extreme fear, and other mind-altering states can also dislodge the "mind" from the body, NDE-fashion. As you might have guessed, Siegel reads in the core features of the NDE no more than the old universal grammar of human hallucination.

"We've studied a group of hostages and also a group of people who claim to have been abducted by a UFO," he tells us. "The phenomenology of their experiences—the visions of the inside of the craft, of floating out of their bodies down a corridor or tunnel into a well-lit room where they are examined—is structurally identical to the so-called NDE."

One of the key arguments for the NDE's reality is its uniformity. Grade-school dropouts and college graduates, red-clay walk-with-me-Jesus Christian fundamentalists, Orthodox Jews and free-thinkers, men, women, small children, people of every demographic shape and size float disembodied among tunnels and beautiful lights, and so on. To this Siegel retorts, "NDE believers are naive about hallucination. They think hallucinations are quirky, variable, individual, but hallucinations are *not* variable."

Remember the perceptual-release theory of hallucination, the image of the man looking out his window at nightfall with the fire stoked up in the background? Applying it to life-after-death experiences, picture the daylight of sensory input fading at the moment of death, while the "interior illumination" (central-nervous-system arousal) keeps shining. In this state, says Siegel, "images originating within the rooms of the brain" are perceived as if they came from outside. "Like a mirage that shows a magnificent city on a desolate expanse of ocean or desert," he notes in a burst of lyricism, "the images of hallucinations are actually reflected images of objects located elsewhere."

What exactly causes the brain of a dying (or almost-dying) person to hallucinate? Here are Siegel's hypotheses: "Phosphenes, visual sensations arising from the discharge of neurons in the structure of the eyes," could create such phantasmagoria. So might the shutdown of physical sensory systems at the hour of death, which would certainly qualify as an extreme sensory-deprivation state. Other factors like oxygen deprivation (hypoxia), neural overexcitation, medications like morphine, or the progressive death of organs could also turn the patient's consciousness inward toward mirages of heaven. Then, of course, there's the psychological phenomenon of depersonalization, which is the ego's way of distancing itself from a really bad scene. But whatever the exact neural mechanism, Siegel is convinced that the so-called NDE is hallucination pure and simple and "just isn't an experience of the afterlife.

"When the Book of John tells us," he concludes, " 'In my Father's house there are many mansions,' or when the Apache tells us, 'There are many tents in the camps of the dead,' there are probably no more mansions and tents than there are images of those structures in our own brains."

But Seriously, Folks . . . A Review of the Standard Medical "Explanations"

· *Psychodynamic explanations*: The NDE is a psychological defense used by the freaked-out ego to deny death. According to this school of thought, the "illusion" of viewing the death scene dispassionately from outside the body is an extreme case of *dissociation*, or *depersonalization*. "Depersonalization is a frequent reaction to life-threatening danger," says Russell Noyes, a psychiatrist at the University of Iowa: "It alerts the organism to its threatening environment while hiding potentially disorganizing emotions in check. As a psychological mechanism it defends the endangered personality against the threat of death. . . ."

To this Michael Sabom replies that the death anxiety/depersonalization theory would require the patient to perceive the threat of death. Therefore, it fails to explain why patients who suffered Stokes-Adams attacks—in which the heart stops without warning, producing a sudden loss of consciousness—had full-fledged NDEs.

There is also a logical flaw here. Death anxiety, denial, wish fulfillment, and other psychodynamic bogeymen may well hover around the near-deathbed, but none of these explanations tells us anything about the reality or unreality of the NDE. "There are compelling psychodynamic explanations for a person's belief in God," says Menninger Clinic psychiatrist Glenn Gabbard, who has studied the NDE in depth. "These, however, say nothing about whether or not God exists." Having surveyed a hefty 339 out-of-body experiences, Gabbard and coworker Stuart Twemlow can report that people who leave their bodies have no greater death anxiety than those who don't.

· *Semiconsciousness*: The NDE voyagers were never really unconscious and certainly never left their bodies. They merely constructed an accurate mental picture of the death-and-resuscitation scene out of conversations they heard while in a semiconscious state.

That's what Sabom's colleagues said when they heard about the NDE, but the cardiologist asserts that this explanation won't wash. The semiconscious perception theory doesn't fit with the characteristic lucidity and visual richness of the autoscopic reports. According to Sabom, research has shown that when semiconscious patients overhear conversations, they remember them only aurally, without any accompanying visions. Moreover, patients who undergo a painful procedure like defibrillation while in a drug-induced twilight state commonly describe it as "like having everything torn out of your insides." NDE memories, in contrast, are blissfully painless.

· *Hallucinations*: Ron Siegel is only one avatar of the hallucination theory. Many NDE skeptics have pointed to hospital medications, hypoxia, hypercarbia (a buildup of carbon dioxide in the brain), temporal-lobe seizures, or some combination of the above, as probable triggers. Physician/author Lewis Thomas, among others, has speculated that endorphins, the body's natural opiates, might have a lot to do with the near-death high.

But if the euphoric, painless state of the NDE was caused by a massive release of endorphins, Sabom retorts, it would last longer than the several seconds to several minutes typical of the experience. The instant these patients "return" to their bodies, they're right back in a pain-wracked world. Besides, opiates, natural or otherwise, aren't known for producing states of hyperalertness like the autoscopic NDE. Temporal-lobe seizures? Not likely, says Sabom: NDE patients don't experience the feelings of fear, sadness, loneliness, and the perceptual distortions that the neurosurgeon Wilder Penfield recorded among the common effects of temporal-lobe epilepsy. Hypoxia? Hypercarbia? Morphine visions? Read on.

"Ron Siegel is totally invested in a reductionist paradigm, and he never supports his theory that the near-death experience comes from the same 'neural status' as hallucinations," Menninger's Glenn Gabbard tells us. "NDEs have occurred in thoroughly oxygenated patients and in patients with unclouded minds. As a matter of fact, *undrugged* patients are more likely to have them." Other NDE investigators we queried agreed.

No Bad Trips
the NDE Way

CAN A HALLUCINATION THEORY really account for the legions of ordinary people—35 to 40 percent of those who reach death's door, according to all the surveys—who not only have been to the "other side" but will swear up and down that it was no dream? Could so many people be so deluded?

Well, let's go back to the ketamine trip quoted by Siegel. "I begged to be released, to return to my body," this patient recalled. "It was terrifying. Finally I blacked out and slowly came to in the recovery room." This terror resembles nothing we've heard about NDEs, which are almost invariably tranquil if not downright ecstatic, according to every single researcher who has inventoried them. For all the touted resemblances, then, there seem to be some interesting differences between drug hallucinations and NDEs.

"I can honestly say we've never run across a negative experience, even in people who attempted suicide," says University of Connecticut psychologist Kenneth Ring, who has systematically collected and analyzed hundreds of NDEs. Drug hallucinations, in contrast, can often be hellish, grotesque, or just so-so.

Siegel may speak of chemical netherworlds so vivid they appear as real as browsing through Macy's housewares section, but Ring has his doubts. "I think if Siegel had talked to more people who'd had NDEs he'd reach different conclusions," he tells us. "Again and again, these people say, 'I *know* it was real; it really happened.' When somebody hallucinates, on the other hand, he usually recognizes he's hallucinating—at least afterwards." Some of Ring's NDE veterans had had previous experience with drug hallucinations, and they "just laughed" at the idea that the two phenomena were the same. So did those of Sabom's patients who had also known morphine visions.

Another point: "Most hallucinations," Ring tells us, "don't have the profound psychological aftereffects that the NDE does." After their little death-and-rebirth, Ring's subjects (like Sabom's and Moody's) underwent quasi-conversions, typically becoming "kinder, more compassionate, more tolerant, more spiritual, though not necessarily more religious."

But if the NDE is not hallucination, fabrication, or fantasy, what *is* it? Sabom theorizes that during a near-death crisis the mind and brain fly asunder, and the mind goes on doing its thing outside the physical organ. Toward the end of his book he invokes Wilder Penfield's mind/brain theory (mind as a disembodied pilot, brain as computer) and wonders: "Could the 'separate self' in the NDE represent the detached 'mind,' which according to Penfield is capable of experiencing contentment, happiness, love, compassion, and awareness, while the unconscious physical body represents the remains of the 'computer'—a lifeless automaton?"

Platonic Dualism Revisited

SOUND FAMILIAR? It should. Two millennia before Sabom began accumulating evidence of minds casting aside their physical vehicles on operating tables and in intensive-care units, Plato enunciated the doctrine that man's soul was imprisoned in his body in life and delivered from it at death. As a matter of fact, death should be the philosopher's finest hour: "For then, and not till then, the soul will be parted from the body and exist in herself alone. . . . And thus having got rid of the foolishness of the body we shall be pure and hold converse with the pure, and know of ourselves the clear light everywhere, which is no other than the light of truth."

Like Plato, the NDE traveler is oblivious to the lowly physical self. "I said to myself, 'Oh, that girl is going to have a tracheotomy,'" one of Ring's subjects recalled. "It was 'that girl.' It wasn't 'me.'"

"It is at this moment [during the NDE]," Ring observes, "that we may come to a realization of who and what we truly are. Death punctures a hole in the tight fabric of the ego, which allows us to slip through in a moment outside of time to experience ourself as infinite perfection." When this happens, he adds, "we realize in the depths of our own being the truth of Meister Eckhart's dictum that 'God is at the center of man.'"

Natural scientists are not very high on Plato, however, and for good reason. If all sense impressions are flickering shadows on the walls of a cave, and if the "truth" lies in the chaste soul domain, then anything one can observe through electron microscopes, PET scans, the giant radio dishes at Arecibo, Puerto Rico, or any other mechanical extension of our senses, is illusory. But scientific truths are derived from empirical observations of the physical universe, of course. To the scientific mind, Plato's world of ideas, wherein abstractions such as Beauty float about devoid of substance, is rank nonsense. "Because science deals with concrete entities only, because it acknowledges only properties of such entities rather than properties in themselves," Mario Bunge of McGill University writes in *The Mind/Body Problem*, "it has no use for properties . . . [that are not properties] of some concrete entity or other, be it atom or neuron, brain or galaxy."

And Plato's dualism poses special problems. If mind and body are separate, how are they so coordinated that a brain event (such as a stroke) is paired with a simultaneous mental event (such as aphasia)? If the mind is immaterial and autonomous, it should be immune to blows to head, chemicals, surgery, electrical brain stimulation, disease, and so on. But, of course, it's not. "The only way the dualist can evade this conclusion," avers Bunge, "is either by ignoring the huge heap of experimental evidence or by claiming that the brain is governed by an otherworldly spirit."

Leibniz's Clocks

"WE KNOW that when people are knocked over the head, they go unconscious," says Daniel Robinson, a philosophical neuropsychologist from Georgetown University, who is one of the last of the pure dualists. "So how do we account for the remarkable correlation between the mental and the physical? Well, [the seventeenth-century philosopher Gottfried von] Leibniz said we must assume that mental life follows its own natural history and so does the physical body. The two run their respective courses in parallel; there's no interaction between the two but the correlation will be perfect. It's as though two watches had been synchronously wound. An observer would say, 'How remarkable! When one watch moves, the other watch moves, too,' and such an observer would be inclined to see a causal relationship between the two. Leibniz's solution, of course, was the Great Clockmaker in the Sky—a 'pre-established harmony.' You-Know-Who set the clocks in motion, and the mere destruction of one clock has no bearing on the other."

As you might imagine, *psychophysical parallelism*, or *preestablished harmony*, as Leibniz's theory is known, is not popular in this age of neuroscientific wonders, when the magenta, pink, and emerald-green patches on PET-scan or EEG maps are taken for states of mind—schizophrenia, dementia, aphasia. Robinson invokes it only as a last resort, after finding flaws in all the other solutions to the mind/body problem. "When it comes to the affairs of the universe," he tells us, "I only work here. I don't know the answer. I only know that the answer I find most compelling is preposterous on its face." There's no question that psychophysical parallelism is unscientific. The cornerstone of the scientific method is causality, but the doctrine that brain and mind glide along their parallel paths, never directly interacting with each other yet never falling out of step, is based on an acausal principle: synchronicity.

Synchronicity and the Mind

SYNCHRONICITY found an articulate twentieth-century partisan in Carl Jung, the psychiatrist. In his essay "The Interpretation of Nature and the Psyche," he expressly applies it to the mind/body problem:

We must ask ourselves whether the relation of soul and body can be considered from this angle, that is to say, whether the coordination of psychic and physical processes in a living organism can be understood as a synchronistic phenomenon rather than as a causal relation. Leibniz . . . regarded the coordination of the psychic and the physical as an act of God, or some principle standing outside empirical nature.

Guess what Jung's prime example is? It seems that one of his patients told him about a remarkable experience she had during childbirth. Her labor was difficult, complications set in, she lapsed into a coma, and presto:

The next thing she was aware of was that, without feeling her body and its position, she was *looking down* from a point in the ceiling and could see . . . herself lying in the bed, deadly pale, with closed eyes. Beside her stood the nurse. The doctor paced up and down in the room excitedly, and it seemed to her he had lost his head and didn't know what to do. . . . Her mother and her husband came in and looked at her with frightened faces. . . . [Behind her, she saw] "a glorious park-like landscape shining in the brightest colors, and in particular an emerald green meadow with short grass, which sloped gently upwards beyond a wrought-iron gate leading into the park and [she knew that] if I turned round to gaze at the picture more directly, I should feel tempted to go in the gate and thus step out of life. . . ."

Had this woman simply been in a "psychogenic twilight state in which a split-off part of consciousness continued to function?" Jung wondered. No, by all indications, she had completely blacked out. Yet "she could observe actual events in concrete detail with closed eyes. . . ." How? If conscious mental faculties (perceiving, thinking, willing, desiring, and so on) really operate outside the physical brain and its sensory apparatus, we're stuck with two equally absurd propositions. Either we must suppose, against all neuroscientific evidence, that extremely primitive parts of the nervous system are more conscious than we think. Or we're stuck with the heresy of dualism.

As for the first possibility: Although "the cortex or cerebrum which is conjectured to be the seat of conscious phenomena" is out cold in a comatose patient, Jung muses, "the sympathetic system is not paralyzed . . . and could be the possible carrier of psychic functions." Consider bees, he says. Their nervous system is very rudimentary, but they perform complex dances to communicate information about food sources—an activity that we would call "conscious" if it were carried out by human beings. Maybe, he speculates, there is a "kind of intelligence in lower centers of the brain and nervous systems" after all. Maybe so, but it seems unlikely that the vivid perceptions and thoughts of the NDE are the work of the sympathetic nervous system.

The only other possible explanation, in Jung's view, is that "the processes that go on during loss of consciousness are synchronistic phenomena, i.e., events which have no causal connection with organic processes." In other words, there is no biological substrate for this peculiar consciousness.

We are accustomed, of course, to operating in a physical universe dominated by three despotic rulers—space, time, and causality—so acausal connections strike us as supernatural or weird. But consider our inner universe. As Jung points out, "most psychic contents are non-spatial, and time and causality are psychically relative," and he's right. Thoughts and memories occupy no space and wander crazily through time, backward as well as forward. And the whole notion of cause and effect presupposes a mind to perceive the connection. Jung suggests that the "fact of a causeless order, or rather, of meaningful orderedness" may be as valid for mental life as the stodgy trio of space, time, and causality. "Synchronicity is a phenomenon," he notes, "that seems to be primarily connected with psychic conditions, that is to say, with processes in the unconscious."

Maybe the events we interpret as amazing coincidences, extrasensory perception, or the clairvoyant hunches of Madame Zodiac, are manifestations of a fourth law of the universe, synchronicity. These, of course, are phenomena that scientists dismiss as ougabouga stuff, because they can't explain them in causal terms. But ours is not the only way of viewing the universe. As Westerners worship the god of causality, the Chinese mind, for instance, kneels at the altar of chance and coincidence. In his famous foreword to the *I Ching*, the ancient Chinese "Book of Changes," Jung finds synchronistic order in this game, in which a toss of coins or yarrow stalks is interpreted in the light of sixty-four wise hexagrams.

Just as causality describes the sequence of events, so synchronicity to the Chinese mind deals with the coincidence of events. The causal point of view tells us a dramatic story about how *D* came into existence: it took its origin from *C*, which existed before *D*, and *C* in its turn had a father, *B*, etc. The synchronistic view on the other hand tries to produce an equally meaningful picture of coincidence. How does it happen that *A'*, *B'*, *C'*, *D'*, etc., appear all in the same moment and in the same place? . . . In the *I Ching* the only criterion for the validity of synchronicity is the observer's opinion that the test of the hexagram amounts to a true rendering of his psychic condition.

The flavor of the moment necessarily includes the observer (a particular mind) as well as the thing observed, just as in quantum physics the experimenter's consciousness is an inextricable part of his experiment. "It is only the ingrained belief in the sovereign power of causality that creates intellectual difficulties," says Jung.

Accidental Satori?   By now you may have noticed that many NDEs sound a lot like the states of grace described by mystics from St. Theresa of Avila to Ramakrishna. Both conditions are characterized by a sense of timelessness, ineffable beauty and serenity, divine lights, and a conviction that earthbound things are mere phantoms (or *maya*) and that the "real self" is not the physical one.

Like mystics, NDE returnees commonly undergo profound personality transformations, "conversions" of a sort. Is the near-death experience a case of accidental *satori*?

That's how Kenneth Ring sees it. "I think what happens," he says, "is that the person is thrust inadvertently, for a brief period of clock time, into a transcendental state of consciousness. It's like involuntary yoga. Your breathing is interrupted, your sensory systems are shut down. . . . But the difference is that the NDE is accessible to everyone. You don't need special training. You don't need to meditate for twenty years. It's like the spiritual principle being democratized."

He tells us about the ancient Egyptian mystery schools, in which seekers were put into deep hypnotic trances to learn the supreme secret of immortality. "If we can believe the accounts, these schools were mystical training programs in which initiates were taught the great secret: that there is no death. The trainees then were just a handful of people who went on to become the priests or hierophants for the masses. Well, today millions of people are involuntarily going through the same mystery rites and coming back to say, 'There is no death. It's all perfect.' They're the initiates. The hierophants are the doctors who resuscitate them, and the initiation, of course, is the NDE.

"Any explanation of the NDE," he adds, "is going to have to account for transcendental experience in general."

The Clear Light in Atlanta

Thine own consciousness, shining, void, and inseparable from the Great Body of Radiance, hath no birth, nor death, and is the Immutable Light, Buddha Amitabha.
—*The Tibetan Book of the Dead*

AS TRANSCENDENTAL NDEs GO, the *Bardo Thodol*, which Westerners call *The Tibetan Book of the Dead*, is probably the crème de la crème. Basically a traveler's guide to the after-death realm, or *bardo*, this text (committed to writing in the eighth century A.D.) was intended to be read into the ear of the dying person—and then to the corpse—for forty-nine days to help him sort out the phantasmagoria on the road between death and the next incarnation. (For Tibetan Buddhists, of course, there is not one death, but innumerable deaths and rebirths.) It begins, very courteously, thus:

O nobly-born [so and so], the time hath not come for thee to seek the Path. Thy breathing is about to cease. Thy guru hath set thee face to face before with Clear

Light; and now thou art about to experience it in its reality in the Bardo state, wherein all things are like the void and cloudless sky, and the naked, spotless intellect is like unto a transparent vacuum without circumference or center. At this moment, know thyself, and abide in that state.

"It is highly sensible of the *Bardo Thodol*," writes Jung in a commentary, "to make clear to the dead man the primacy of the soul, for that is one thing which life does not make clear to us. We are so hemmed in by things which jostle and oppress that we never get a chance, in the midst of all these given things, to wonder by whom they are given." Note that the first thing the departed man encounters in the *bardo* plane is the clear, colorless light of the soul, the same light, perhaps, that was glimpsed by the patients who "died" and were revived in the cardiac wards of the Atlanta V. A. Hospital. This is the ultimate reality, the Godhead itself, which to the Buddhist takes the form of a Void, and not an anemic-looking person wearing a halo and sandals.

The reason we invoke *The Tibetan Book of the Dead* at this point is that, in the manner of many an Oriental paradox, it supports both Ron Siegel's theory *and* the claims of NDE believers. How is that possible? Remember the condos in heaven about which Siegel quite rightly scoffs. How seriously can we take after-life golf courses, Jesus in hippie sandals and robe, or dear old Aunt Maude still wearing her gingham apron? Siegel maintains that such images are mental projections, and the *Bardo Thodol* couldn't agree more. After the Clear Light (which is the only reality in the universe according to this cosmology), the rest of the text is a manual of hallucination. All the other phenomena the dead wayfarer runs into, it plainly states, are apparitions "issuing from the [eastern quarter] of thine own brain." Before it finds a new womb in which to be reborn, the soul drifts though a series of well-defined *bardos* populated by serene Buddhas, shades of dead relatives, hungry ghosts, hideous demons, and other phantasmagoria. These realms degenerate progressively until, at last, the grotesque Lord of Death himself appears, gnashing his teeth. But the guide counsels the dead man, over and over again, to pay no attention: "Apart from one's own hallucinations," it insists, "in reality, there are no such things existing outside oneself as Lord of Death, or god, or demon, or the Bull-headed Spirit of Death. Act so as to recognize this."

Carl Jung notes, very astutely, that the *Bardo Thodol* can be read backward as a handbook for spiritual/psychological progress. Traveled in reverse, its various *bardos* describe stages of increasing perfection, culminating with the Clear Light of spiritual illumination. Perhaps this is its supreme message.

In any case, the lesson of *Bardo Thodol* is that the NDE is part reality, part dream. The soul's survival is real, as is the radiant light. But just as Tibetans might hallucinate the "dull red light of the Preta [hungry ghost] world" or the "Greenish-Black Elephant-Headed Big-Nosed Goddess holding in the hand a big corpse and drinking blood from a skull," you and I might wander through Middle-American *bardos* full of kindly Jesuses, billowy cumulus clouds or, yes, even divine golf greens.

No Answer

"MAYBE we make a mistake in thinking that death has to be just one thing. You might go to Christian Heaven One-B. I might be reincarnated as a shoehorn," Arizona State University death-and-dying researcher Robert Kastenbaum tells us. Kastenbaum is basically an agnostic on the NDE issue. He thinks endorphins might explain the experience or that it might be a matter of switching from the rational, analytical left hemisphere to the visionary, magical right. But he admits he's not sure about anything.

The NDE, if it is genuine, raises questions to which there are no answers. How could one ever *prove* (or for that matter, disprove) life after death? Kastenbaum brings up the notion of using electrodes to track the brain waves of dying animals into the Beyond, but he's speaking half tongue-in-cheek. And what would EEGs tell us about out-of-body perceptions anyway, if such mental states are *not* tied to brain states? If the mind can be uncoupled from the physical apparatus, then the brain is not the organ of consciousness, and all our neuroscientific know-how tells us it is. Otherwise why spend years mapping opiate receptors, designing better mind drugs, or hunting for the biological cause of schizophrenia?

Sorry, but we have to leave this chapter without an answer. Perhaps, as the legendary Maine curmudgeon said to the tourist, "You can't get there from here."

"We must consider, at least," Sabom tells us, "that there may be more to the human experience than what the nerve cells and chemicals of our bodies and brains can account for."

And from Kastenbaum, the man who claims to be sure of nothing, one prediction. "I will say," he says, "that somewhere down the pike—and Mike Sabom's work is bringing us closer—there's going to be a wonderful crisis in the minds of scientists."

13

God in the Brain:
Cleansing the Doors of Perception

> I have always found that Angels have the vanity
> to speak of themselves as the only wise. This they
> do with a confident insolence sprouting from sys-
> tematic reasoning. —WILLIAM BLAKE

I T WAS NOT your basic Fillmore West, paisley-poster acid trip. At
eleven o'clock one brilliant May morning in 1953, in the Hollywood
hills, Aldous Huxley, the writer/philosopher, swallowed a small white
pill. Half an hour later he became aware of "a slow dance of golden lights"
and of "sumptuous red surfaces" swelling, expanding, and vibrating. After
another hour, he was lost in contemplation of a small glass vase containing
a pink Belle of Portugal rose, a large magenta-and-cream carnation, and
a pale purple iris. At breakfast the same arrangement had seemed garish
but now it was a living icon. "I was not looking now at an unusual flower
arrangement. I was seeing what Adam had seen on the morning of his
creation—the miracle, moment by moment, of creation."

This transubstantiation had a lot to do with the chemical structure of
mescaline sulfate, as Huxley was well aware. Though he didn't know that
his incantatory pill was a chemical cousin of the neurotransmitter serotonin,
he certainly knew that alterations in various "enzymes" in his brain (and
a drop in brain glucose) caused the room to resemble a still life "by Braque
or Juan Gris" and Huxley to perceive "the Dharma Body of the Buddha
in the hedge at the bottom of the garden." He also noticed that his artificial
paradise strongly resembled the mystical epiphanies of Meister Eckart, the
Zen masters, and the enlightened seers of the *Bhagavad-Gita*. Perhaps the
Sat Chit Ananda, the Godhead, the Beatific Vision, was available to Everyman in his double-mortgaged duplex with the metal awnings and the im-
itation fieldstone veneer.

It wasn't an entirely new idea. In *The Varieties of Religious Experience*
(1929), the psychologist William James catalogued similarities between
saintly rhapsodies and the nitrous-oxide visions of a Boston dentist, for
example, and noted that the religious experience did not necessarily have

to occur in a Gothic-style building with a stained-glass window. If Huxley's mescaline-transfigured flowers assumed a celestial glow, James would have methodically filed them alongside Blake's "world in a grain of sand" and St. Francis's conversations with birds. Mystics of all cultures (as well as acid poets merging with the wallpaper) tend to read cosmic truths in the meanest particulars.

"If the doors of perception were cleansed," William Blake wrote, "the world would appear to man as it is—infinite." Borrowing Blake's phrase, Huxley wrote a classic essay, "The Doors of Perception," about his mescaline experiment. In it he suggested that the main function of the human nervous system is to *filter out* infinity.

Each person is at each moment capable of remembering all that has happened to him and of perceiving everything that is happening everywhere in the universe. The function of the brain and nervous system is to protect us from being overwhelmed and confused by this mass of largely useless and irrelevant knowledge, by shutting out most [of it]. According to such a theory, each of us is potentially Mind at Large.

Surely all the information in the universe would overload our circuits. Our brain's sensory equipment is tuned to rather narrow bandwidths, such as visual wavelengths between about 375 and 750 nanometers. Other waves of electromagnetic energy swirl around us all the time, but we don't see them. If our senses were more acute, we might hear random movements of molecules (perhaps this is the Zen "sound of one hand clapping"?) or see ghostly coronas of UHF waves around TV-transmission towers. We might find ourselves in the unendurably bright, cacophanous, and portentous world of Norma MacDonald, a Canadian nurse who described her psychotic break in *The Journal of the Canadian Medical Association* in 1960. On the streets of Toronto she experienced an "exaggerated awareness" such that every passerby seemed to bear messages from either God or Satan. "To feel that the stranger passing on the street knows your innermost soul is disconcerting . . . ," she wrote. "The real or imagined poverty and real or imagined unhappiness of hundreds of people I would never meet burdened my soul, and I felt martyred." In Huxley-like fashion, she imagined that a protective "filter" in her brain had broken down.

"To make biological survival possible," Huxley concluded in *The Doors of Perception,* "Mind at Large has to be filtered through the reducing valve of the brain and nervous system. What comes out at the other end is a measly trickle of the kind of consciousness that will help us stay alive on the surface of this particular planet."

If a person manages to *bypass* the reducing valve, on the other hand, "all sorts of biologically useless things" can happen, according to Huxley, such as extrasensory perceptions, spiritual illuminations, a glimpse of "naked existence" in all its glory, even perhaps an encounter with the Creator on the road to Damascus (or Mecca, or Benares, or Peoria).

It was a metaphor when Huxley invoked it. But perhaps there is a real, biological "reducing valve" in the brain, the circumvention of which could open the mind to nonordinary realities. In this chapter we'll explore some possibilities.

The Real Reducing Valve

THE NOTION that "normal" consciousness is a wan illusion, a paltry slice of life, is a mystical commonplace. According to the mystics, most of us view the world "through a glass darkly" (St. Paul), "through a narrow chink" (Blake) and, like Plato's cave dwellers, mistake flickering shadows for real things. "The Atman [the soul] is the light; the light is covered by darkness," says the *Bhagavad-Gita,* the gospel of Hinduism. "This darkness is delusion; that is why we dream." Reality, with a capital *R*, lies beyond the world-of-appearances that Eastern texts call *maya* (illusion) and we call "real life."

"Our brain defines how much reality is let in," says Candace Pert. "Reality is like a rainbow or like the electromagnetic spectrum. Each creature is a finely evolved machine built to detect the electromagnetic energy most useful for its survival. Humans can see the part of the spectrum between infrared and ultraviolet, while bees can see up through several shades of ultraviolet."

But it isn't just the receptors in our skin and nostrils, the rods and cones in our retina, the minute cilia in our ears, that restrict Mind at Large to a utilitarian trickle. What matters more is how we *interpret* and edit the incoming messages. Human gray matter, after all, is 90 percent interpretation equipment, 90 percent storyteller. "The cortex," says Francis Crick, the master of the double helix, who now practices neuroscience at the Salk Institute in La Jolla, California, "is a machine looking for correlations. It spends most of its time talking to itself."

When our brain cells talk to one another, they use a chemical code, which can turn to gibberish if even one chemical messenger is missing or overabundant. When brain cells are starved of acetylcholine, a person develops Alzheimer's dementia and forgets his wife's name. A brain bombarded with dopamine may hallucinate. To say that neurochemicals color reality is an understatement. But for the moment let's focus on the endorphins, our internal opiates.

"We're developing the concept that the opiate system filters input from every sense—sight, sound, smell, taste, and touch—and places it in an emotional context," says Pert. "Through our natural opiate system we screen signals from the environment. The brain's criteria for selecting what to pay attention to and what to ignore are not ones that you and I made up last week. They're standards our ancestors worked out about a million years ago. They have to do with survival, and with pleasure or pain."

In Pert's opinion, the internal opiate system is a dead ringer for Huxley's hypothetical reducing valve. "If Huxley were alive today, his mind would be blown," she muses. "He'd probably be a pharmacologist." If it is true, as T. S. Eliot remarked, that "humankind cannot bear very much reality," endorphins may reduce reality to bearable levels. They are our natural defense against physical pain, for one thing. Even before the discovery of endorphins and their receptors, scientists spoke of "opiate gates" regulating the flow of pain impulses through the nervous system. But what of emotional pain, esthetic or spiritual pain, the soulsickness of Eliot's Wasteland, the mechanical amours of the typist and the "young man carbuncular"? In Chapter 3 we saw that endorphins soothed freaked-out baby animals after they were separated from their mothers. And there's an ancient human tradition of escaping from a too-grim world into a narcotic fog, into heroin, morphine, or opium. A series of experiments at the NIMH suggests that endorphins do, in fact, buffer some people against too much reality.

Some schizophrenics are extremely insensitive to pain—you could use their hands as pincushions and never evoke a wince—and unreactive to other sensory stimuli, as well. Several years ago psychiatrist Monte Buchsbaum, then at the NIMH, measured such patients' brain-wave responses to electrical shocks and auditory signals and found these EEGs to be abnormally flat, especially at higher levels of intensity. He concluded that a subgroup of schizophrenics were "reducers" (as opposed to "augmenters"), that their brains naturally reduced, or dampened, sensory stimuli. When he gave the "reducers" naltrexone, an opiate-blocking drug, their EEGs became almost normal. The implication was that endorphins were filtering environmental messages on the way to consciousness. Then Buchsbaum noticed something else: Schizophrenics who were "reducers" were more likely to get well than those who weren't. "If schizophrenics are able to 'turn off' with internal opiates," he tells us, "perhaps it's an adaptive response to their illness." Perhaps endorphins dull emotional as well as physical pain.

What does this tell us about the nature of reality? Do we glimpse only the narrow spectrum of Mind at Large that our chemicals select as important and miss everything else? As Pert puts it, "We don't even know if there is a world out there. The first pages of Hume say it all. If a tree falls in a forest and nobody's there. . . ."

But the opiate system is not the only candidate for the real reducing valve.

The Pharmacological Bridge to God

Daiju visited the master Baso in China.
Baso asked: "What do you seek?"
   "Enlightenment," replied Daiju.
   "You have your own treasure house.
Why do you seek outside?"
               —*Zen Flesh, Zen Bones*

NEARLY FIFTY YEARS AGO, a Swiss chemist tinkering with derivatives of an ergot grain fungus synthesized something called lysergic acid diethylamide, or LSD–25. It had no apparent effect on laboratory animals and didn't interest him much. But five years later, in 1943, Albert Hofmann returned to his creation and accidentally absorbed a little of the powder, whereupon he fell into an unusually vivid daydream among his beakers and pipettes. Several days later he took what he thought was a tiny experimental dose, .25 milligram, and when the funhouse images in his head made work impossible, he bicycled home. As he watched the staid streets of Basel metamorphose into the phantasmagoric shapes of a Grimms' fairy tale, Hofmann marveled, as scientists still marvel, that a quarter of a milligram of anything could so transform reality.

Years later the peculiar djinn of LSD was traced to its chemical resemblance to serotonin, which plays a largely inhibitory role in the brain. By plugging up the serotonin receptors and thereby removing inhibition from many brain structures, hallucinogens such as LSD and mescaline unlock the mind's secret gardens, for better or worse. Or so the prevailing theory goes. "Hallucinogens alter what seems important or trivial," says Stanford psychiatrist Philip Berger. "LSD does exactly that. It opens up the part of the brain that confers significance on things."

Sometimes the significance is such as to constitute a religious experience, as the father of LSD himself discovered. "To see the flowers in my own garden is to see all the mystical wonder of creation," said Hofmann. "You don't have to go to India to see it." Alan Watts, the philosopher, took LSD–25 at San Francisco's Langley Porter Clinic in 1959. "In the course of two experiments," he recounted in *Does It Matter?: Essays on Man's Relation to Materiality*, "I was amazed and somewhat embarrassed to find myself going through states of consciousness which corresponded precisely with every description of major mystical experiences I had ever read." What LSD told Watts was that "you yourself are the eternal energy of the universe playing hide-and-go-seek (on and off) with itself. At root, you are the Godhead, for God is all there is."

This might sound like blasphemy to the average "Phil Donahue Show" audience. Indeed, in early times, many people were roasted alive for less. Our Judeo-Christian heritage has no good translation of *samadhi* or *satori*, Watts noted, "because our own Jewish and Christian theologies will not accept the idea that man's inmost self can be identical with the Godhead, even though Christians may insist this was true in the unique instance of Jesus Christ." The Judeo-Christian God is monarchical, a "King of Kings" up in his remote Delft-blue dome, encircled by adoring choirs of cherubim, seraphim, powers, dominions, principalities, angels, and archangels. At times He has been more approachable, making deals with prophets and sending His only son to Earth, but mostly He (and He is a *He*) is far above us.

Not so the God of Buddhism, Hinduism, Taoism, Sufism, and the esoteric Christian and Jewish traditions. Divinity may assume the shape of many-armed gods and goddesses; it may answer to the name of Allah, Jehovah, Krishna, Brahman, Buddha, or I-am-that-I-am; but, in the words of the *Katha Upanishad*: "The Supreme Person, of the size of the thumb, dwells forever in the heart of all beings." Eastern religions consider every human being a God-in-embryo, a potential Christ or Buddha, which is the meaning behind one of the fundamental credos of Hinduism, *Tat Tvam Asi,* or "That art thou."

While the God-within has not always been popular with ecclesiastical councils, it is the true mystical God. *The Way of the Pilgrim* says: "Everywhere, wherever you may find yourself, you can set up an altar to God in your mind by means of prayer." Meister Eckhart declared: "My soul is my kingdom . . . and this kingdom is greater than any kingdom on earth." St. Paul preached, "Not I, but Christ in me." And, finally, Jesus himself is quoted as saying, "The kingdom of heaven is within."

Is the kingdom of heaven within the *brain*? So says Arnold Mandell, the iconoclastic neuro-philosopher of the University of California at San Diego: "William James, the great turn-of-the-century psychologist, found that the transcendental experience was the same wherever he examined it," he notes, "and its most commonly invoked source, God, was actually in the brain." But where? In an unorthodox paper called "God in the Brain: Toward a Psychobiology of Transcendence," Mandell proposed an answer that owes something to LSD, which Hofmann called his "problem child," and something to a disease called temporal-lobe epilepsy.

Temporal-lobe seizures are known to trigger déjà-vu and jamais-vu, dreamy "fugue states," ineffable cosmic insights, strange islands in the memory stream. There are even cases of "clinical mysticism," according to Karl Pribram. "A lesion in the temporal lobe near the amygdala can produce something akin to mysticism," he tells us. "There is a disruption in self-awareness. There is a kind of consciousness-without-content, like the oceanic consciousness of the mystical state. The distinction between the self and the other disappears."

> As a man in the embrace of his loving wife knows
> nothing that is without, nothing that is within, so
> man in union with the Self knows nothing that is
> without, nothing that is within.
> —*Bridhadaranyaka Upanishad*

Between seizures some temporal-lobe epileptics experience long-lasting beatific states, permanent personality changes, even religious conversions, according to Mandell. St. Paul's conversion may have been a case in point. Another temporal-lobe saint, Mandell thinks, was Fyodor Dostoevski, a known epileptic, who ascribed to his characters states of grace that resemble classic temporal-lobe epilepsy. When a flash of light goes off in his mind, the epileptic Prince Myshkin of *The Idiot,* for example, savors an immortal second, "the very second which was not long enough for the water to be spilt out of Mahomet's pitcher, though the prophet had time to gaze at all the habitations of Allah." This sort of timelessness, in which the history of the universe contracts into the blink of an eye or a second dilates into eternity, is typical of the mystical state. Are all mystics undiagnosed temporal-lobe epileptics then?

No, but Mandell thinks mystical revelations spring from a similar brain state.

Epilepsy is the result of a process called "kindling," in which nerve signals are amplified exponentially, causing a raging electrical storm in part of the brain. In temporal-lobe epilepsy the storm spreads over the temporal lobe and underlying limbic structures, particularly the hippocampus. Ordinarily, says Mandell, the hippocampal cells are inhibited by serotonin. But if the brain is deprived of serotonin, they fire in an overexcited, kindlinglike fashion.

So one route to God in the brain might be to repress brain serotonin, which, of course, is precisely what hallucinogens do. No wonder that these drugs have been dubbed a "pharmacological bridge to transcendence"; that mescaline awakens a "benign empathy" with "inanimate and living things, especially small things," according to California pharmacologist Alexander Shulgin, an independent drug designer; that Albert Hofmann, and many latter-day acid prophets, found God in less than a milligram.

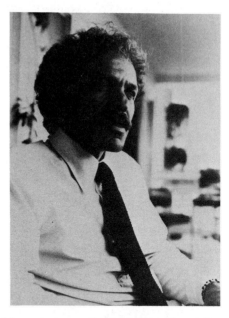

Arnold J. Mandell, M.D.: After a "nightmare season," a mid-life crisis, and a psychic metamorphosis, he has a different outlook on the brain. (*Courtesy of University of California, San Diego*)

But how exactly does tampering with brain serotonin levels produce transcendental consciousness?

Mandell's hypothesis is this: The hippocampus is a meeting place between two different circuits, one from the external world via the senses and the other from inside the organism. One job of this sea-horse-shaped structure is to adjust moods and emotions to incoming information from the environment. When "lightning" strikes the hippocampus, however, this reality check is gone. Internal reality and external reality fly out of sync, and the inner experience predominates. "The *Bhagavad-Gita* suggests that transcendent consciousness is associated with 'detachment' from the objects of desire," Mandell notes, and synchronous, epilepticlike brain waves in the hippocampus of monkeys have been associated with a decline in social bonding and sexual interest. Is this the "neurological substrate" of holy detachment?

Of course, Lao-tzu, St. Theresa, and the Buddha weren't smoking funny herbs. There are other ways to dampen serotonin activity, including marathon running and meditation, according to Mandell. Perhaps the world's great mystics have done it with prayer, fasting, repetitive chanting, the sensory deprivation of monastic life, or by some completely unknown means.

The consequence, in Mandell's words: "William James called it a 'mystical experience'; St. Paul called it 'the peace that passeth understanding'; Thomas Merton, the 'transcendental unconscious'; . . . Lao-tzu, 'the absolute Tao'; Zen Buddhism, 'satori'; Yogis, 'samadhi'; St. John of the Cross, 'living flame.'" And so on through Blake and Brother Lawrence to Plotinus, Gopi Krishna, and *The Tibetan Book of the Dead*.

Anatomy of a Conversion

THAT'S what Mandell used to think anyway. Today, in the wake of his own conversion—or series of conversions—he sees the formula for God in terms less pharmacologic. When we visit him at the U. C. San Diego campus, he reflects, "Hallucinogens did contribute to a religious revival. They let thirty or forty million Americans into a place that only fourteen Arabs in the desert ever knew about. There is a close physiological relationship between the primary religious experience and hallucinogens. But the context changes it. Fifty thousand of you got lost in the hills. You have twenty thousand kids in Santa Cruz who can't find the bathroom. Topology [the mathematical science of forms] tells you why the context is more important than the content."

These days Mandell jogs on the beach in a T-shirt ensloganed: BOUNDED CHAOTIC MIXING PRODUCES STRANGE STABILITY. The motto—which must mystify the surfers at Del Mar and Laguna—comes from chaotic dynamics, a far-out branch of mathematical physics that is Mandell's current obsession. What it means, he says, is that "you have more stability if you surrender to God." Mandell himself surrendered to God in the early 1980s, at a local charismatic Christian church. But that came after an epic midlife crisis, which "on another level was a religious conversion, though I didn't recognize it at the time."

Before his conversion, Mandell was founding chairman of UCSD's psychiatry department, a post he attained as a workaholic *wunderkind* of thirty-five. He lived in a fancy apartment on the La Jolla coast, the Southern California Riviera, drove a Lincoln Continental, and by his own accounts lived out a competitive, grant-grubbing scientific success story. Then came legal troubles, a divorce, a heart attack, a nervous breakdown, and a desert of the soul. One of the events that shattered his old life was a scandal involving the San Diego Chargers football team. In 1975 the Chargers' head coach had hired Mandell to investigate the psychological factors behind the team's erratic ups and downs. The psychiatrist stumbled on what he called "The Sunday Syndrome"—massive amphetamine abuse. To keep them away from dirty street drugs, Mandell (as he later testified) wrote amphetamine prescriptions for some veteran users, an action that would come to haunt him. He wrote a book, *The Nightmare Season,* alleging widespread amphetamine abuse in the National Football League, and when it came out in 1976, all hell broke loose. A year later an administrative judge found Mandell guilty of "clearly excessive prescribing of a dangerous drug" and placed him on five years' probation. Though he later won on appeal, the psychiatrist lost his chairmanship.

Waking up in a plastic-tent-covered bed in the coronary unit to the muted hum of the heart monitors and the steady drip-drip of IV bottles, the former boy wonder confronted the psychic badlands beyond "Darwin's climactic hill of fighting and fucking." He had thoughts that put him in the psychiatric unit for a while. At one point Arnold Mandell, M.D., metamorphosed into an alter ego called Dr. Sam Shambhala, a self-described shaman, whose emergence is chronicled in a remarkable 1978 autobiography, *Coming of Middle Age.* The Shambhala persona spoke out of his Dionysian right brain—"Out of a blackened middle brain to the blue-white of the upper one. High and Free"—and turned away from the smooth parabolic dose-response curves of the laboratory. He turned away from mechanistic wiring diagrams and Freud's phallocentric universe. He turned away, above all, from his father's legacy.

Mandell's father was "a virulent Jewish intellectual," a rigid taskmaster who forced his son to practice the piano for hours every day and berated him constantly. One day, after one of his father's tirades, the young Arnold Mandell found a phrenology chart in a book, which prompted the reassuring revelation that "there were biological forces beyond good and evil that caused good and evil—maybe it was my forehead." The brain became his religion from then on. He would run rats, figure dose-response curves, and investigate Oedipal complexes to extract its secrets. "It was probably a vicarious religious quest," he reflects.

But the neuroscience he was taught was "very molecular, deterministic." The brain was "a big piece of machinery," whose parts certainly did not answer the most important questions on his mind. One of these questions was: "How does a person change into an entirely different person in an hour? And change forever. You know, some nasty drunk who beats his wife turns into an elder of the church. The religious conversion phenomenon is well documented in the turn-of-the-century psychological literature. It happened to about thirty percent of the population. William James wrote about it. This is something our modern deterministic biology can't account for."

So Mandell strayed from biological determinism. In the late 1970s, he took up long-distance running and a mantra. The brain, to which he had devoted his whole life, began to appear in a different guise, more like a living cathedral than a box of wires. He dreamed of a new psychophar-macology in which marathon running, psalms, and mantras were the drugs: "Cold, heat, music, overwhelming beauty, simplicity and repetitious daily routine, hypnosis, muscle-relaxation training, and short periods of swamp-ing psychological overload are all powerful mutators of the color pool." He even pioneered an unusual chemoliterary criticism, as in this passage from his book.

Amphetamine brings red and sometimes pink, if that brain's high white comes from winning. The quick, flashing prose of Tom Wolfe and the sacking of a quar-terback are in the bag of red. Kerouac was on amphetamine when writing the red, restless prose of *On the Road;* on pot to make the cool blue sounds of *The Sub-terraneans.*

Today Mandell does not call himself Dr. Sam Shambhala, but he did not revert to his old ways either. In 1982 he followed his sons into what some might call Jesus freakhood, a movement Mandell himself used to consider "lunatic fringe, filled with righteous persecutors of liberal causes." He doesn't sound like your average Jesus freak, though. He certainly doesn't talk like the rapt young man with the broken guitar who had talked Scripture at us the day before on the beach at Venice, a long, rambling speech about fornication, the whore of Babylon, and the Book of Daniel. Mandell is more likely to talk about mathematical models of enzyme rates. But in the local talking-in-tongues Christian community he evidently found an antidote to sterile scientific rationalism.

We ask him if he still believes God is in the brain.

"He's always been there and he always will be," he answers. "God is the essence of the state of bounded mixing. A personality is an interplay of stable and unstable forces. How do you keep your brain from getting so organized you're rigid or obsessive, and not so flexible you're bizarre or hysterical? I think the key is the surrender of the self. The charismatic Christians say, 'Jesus died for you.' It's an exercise in bounded madness.

"In psychoanalysis, you talk about the same event over and over again. It doesn't get rid of the ego; it glorifies it. I've been there; I know. As an organizing force I think charismatic Christianity is better. I see sick people coping that way. In some ways they look rigid, but inside they're freaky. They speak in tongues, hear God's voice, and talk to it.

"I read the New Testament every day—and the Old Testament too. I haven't left Judaism, but Judaism doesn't have a charismatic movement. I want God to get up and walk around with me, right here and now. Let me see him."

Heaven and Hell in the Brain

> I can hardly clap as some did, Phil, about the fact you're going to hell.
>
> —BOB JONES III, president of Bob Jones University, on the "Phil Donahue Show," January 20, 1982

PERHAPS in some corner of our universe there are sulfurous hells stoked by horned devils with cloven hooves, where bad people go. Perhaps there are heavens full of saints in pastel robes and angels playing harps. But it seems more likely that these are realms of the mind (or brain).

Long before PET scans and EEG machines were heard of, poets and philosophers described our inner universe quite well. We could explore parallels between Dante's tripartite afterlife—*inferno, purgatorio,* and *paradiso*—and our three-layered brain. We could view mental illnesses as underworlds, and vice-versa. Seen through Dante's eyes, the schizophrenia ward might resemble the Fifth Circle, where: "There are souls beneath that water. Fixed in slime/they speak their piece, end it, and start again." The depressives, futilely circling a piece of their past, again and again, might bring to mind the wan, dolorous shades of the *Aeneid*. Angels and demons; muses, sirens, furies, and gods; hells, limbos, purgatories, and paradises; the Garden of Eden and the archetypal Babylon: Don't they live inside the brain?

Recall the varied demons and angels uncovered by electrical brain stimulation. If we wanted vivid illustrations of the Oriental concept of *maya*, the world of appearances, we'd need look no farther than to Olds's famous "self-stimulating" rats, swimming across moats, navigating complex labyrinths, even going without food and water for the pleasure of a few milliamps of current to the brain. Not to mention the electrode-implanted cats hissing at invisible enemies or running in terror from mice; monkeys "displaying" to shadows; human beings threatening murder under the influence of minute electrical currents. We recognize that the emotions elicited by electrodes are mere simulacra, shadows flitting across the walls of the brain cave. But are our "real" emotions any less illusory?

The chemical brain, as Pert and others depict it, is a Manichean battlefield of opposites. Valium and anti-Valium, endorphins and Substance P, hunger and satiety, heat and cold, love and rage. Our neurochemicals sort all possible experiences into two piles, "Like" and "No Like." Their code is relentlessly binary. As Paul MacLean told us, emotions are either pleasurable or painful, never neutral. The nervous system could be likened to a paranoid person who translates all his inputs into a fixed delusional system: "You can't trust people from New York," or "Communists are trying to put fluoride in our water supply."

Eastern mystical texts preach that the "sweet and bitter fruits of the tree" are alike *maya*; they are like the laughter and tears in a movie, compelling only so long as we're inside the darkened theater. God lies outside the "world of opposites," heaven and hell, I and thou, subject and object, and the eternally spinning hamster wheel of pleasure and pain. To enter this realm beyond duality, one must free oneself from the "addictions of the senses," in the words of the *Bhagavad-Gita*.

The Chinks of Perception

IF THERE IS one semimystical message of the Brain Age it is that the universe we see, taste, feel, smell, and hear *is not the real universe*. As the British neuropsychologist Richard Gregory puts it, "Brain states represent the world rather as a letter on a page represents fiction or truth."

Around the turn of the century, William James, using the bare tools of introspection, observed in *The Principles of Psychology*:

There is no reason whatever to think that the gap in Nature between the highest sound-waves and the lowest heat-waves is an abrupt break like that of our sensations; or that the difference between violet and ultraviolet rays has anything like the objective importance subjectively represented by that between light and darkness. Out of what is in itself an undistinguishable, swarming *continuum*, devoid of direction or emphasis, our senses make for us, by attending to this motion and ignoring that, a world full of contrasts, of strong accents, of abrupt changes, of picturesque light and shade.

Too bad James could not have witnessed the brilliant, Nobel Prize–winning experiments of David Hubel and Torsten Wiesel. "In the visual system," Hubel reported in *Scientific American* in 1979, after two decades of painstaking single-cell mapping expeditions, ". . . it is contrasts and movements that are important, and most of the first two or three steps [of visual processing] is devoted to enhancing the effect of contrast and movement."

Your brain has certain *idées fixes* about this world. In the late 1950s MIT scientists discovered neurons in the frog brain that fired whenever a convex object moved across the visual field. The object had to be moving and it had to be the right shape or the cells wouldn't respond. If a dead fly was dangled in front of a frog's nose, the animal would ignore it, even when ravenous, but if the string was jiggled slightly, it would stick out its tongue and eat the fly. Such was the discovery of the "bug detectors" with which nature has equipped the frog brain.

Then Hubel and Wiesel came along to prove that we, too, come prewired with something like "bug detectors." (Well, strictly speaking, their experiments were conducted on macaque monkeys, but given the similarity of the primate visual system, we can safely extrapolate to man.) Boring a tiny hole through the skull with a high-speed dental drill, the scientists would drive a minute electrode, less than a thousandth of an inch in diameter, into the monkey's *striate cortex*. The striate (or "striped") cortex, on the underside of the occipital lobe, is the primary visual cortex, where our visual universe is first interpreted. As images were projected to the animal's visual field, the electrode would pick up the firing of a single cell. Then Hubel and Wiesel would spear another neuron, and another, listening to the popping and crackling over a loudspeaker, until they had charted the whole striate cortex.

What they discovered were *feature detectors,* highly specialized cells that "recognize" lines or bars with horizontal, vertical, or oblique orientations. Rotate the line 10 degrees, and the cell quieted down. Rotate it 30 degrees, and it stopped firing altogether. When all the single recordings were pieced together, the six layers of the striate cortex formed an "intricate edifice of orderly columns," as Hubel put it. If you pushed an electrode down through the area you'd find a neat ledger-book column of neurons that respond to lines or edges of a particular orientation.

"The brain takes input from the eye and puts it in a preengineered machine," says Francis Crick, who on a chilly November evening in Baltimore is giving a guided tour of the cortex at a "Mind/Brain" symposium at Johns Hopkins Medical Center. As he lectures, he waves a pointer at what looks to be a serried geological cross section of the earth but is, in fact, a cross section of monkey striate cortex. "See, there are clear architectonic differences between the different cortical areas. There are stripes, discontinuities, edges.

"The system is not a general-purpose computer. The brain has been engineered to do a specific job. Mammals have been looking at the same sort of visual world for a long time, a world that consists of solids with surfaces. So through natural selection we have evolved some special gadgetry for that."

That single neurons have preferences and that these mirror the geometric features of nature would have gratified Immanuel Kant. Kant said that certain "pure concepts," or "categories," exist in our brains *a priori,* before we perceive anything outside us. Space, time, causality, quantity, and certain other concepts are features not of the external world, but of the human mind. The ethologist Konrad Lorenz, who was a disciple of Kant, thought that these hereditary notions were comparable to the inborn instincts of animals. According to Kant, our innate laws of thought forever prevent human beings from perceiving true reality—the "thing-in-itself," or *Ding-an-sich*.

"Perhaps Immanuel Kant was right," muses Bela Julesz, a prominent psychophysicist at Bell Laboratories in New Jersey, who has uncovered what may be the psychological counterpart of Hubel and Wiesel's feature detectors. Julesz set out to unravel the earliest stage of the visual recognition process. "We're like astrophysicists," he jokes in a Central European accent in which *R*s and *W*s are interchangeable. "We asked, What happens in the first seven seconds?" What he turned up were the "quarks of perception," the elemental building blocks of vision. Human beings, he determined, are capable of a kind of preconscious, or "preattentive," seeing, processing an entire visual field in a flash, without scrutiny or conscious attention. The reason, Julesz's experiments determined, is that the human brain is hard-wired to perceive three basic forms, or "textons": (1) "elongated blobs" (rectangles, ellipses, or line segments of particular colors, orientations, lengths and depths); (2) "terminations" (ends of lines or blobs); and (3) "crossings of elongated blobs."

"How to find a needle in a haystack?" he says. "Well, if the needle is of a different texton from the hay, we can find it very easily."

The brain, in short, perceives the world in terms of stereotypes, "categories" not so different in principle from those that dictate that "for the frog a dark, moving convexity must be a fly," as Daniel Robinson observes. We may look down on the lowly frog in his lily pond, for whom the entire phenomenal universe is an array of buglike forms, but what would a differently wired alien make of us? "Our experiments show conclusively that Earthlings are incapable of perceiving uqqwzzzs. When a moving uqqwzzz is dangled in their visual field, they mistake it for a flying saucer." Our doors of perception are tailored to a particular planet with a particular gravitational field, at a particular distance from a particular star. (Unless this world is the *effect*, not the cause, of our particular brain. Perhaps consciousness created the universe, instead of the other way around.)

"Perception is not direct," says Karl Pribram. "It is a *construction*." In order to see the broken yellow line down the center of the highway or hear the Veteran's Day marching band, your brain performs complex mathematical operations on the frequencies coming into it. "When I move my eyes even slightly there's always a little jiggle in the image on the retina," Pribram adds. "Yet I perceive the environment as still. Obviously the brain is doing very complicated computations to subtract out the motion and keep the world still. It's like what the NASA computers do in the Venus flyby."

DEVIL'S TUNING FORK

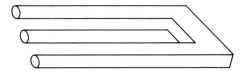

FIGURE 9

The image in your head is not a straightforward copy of anything. Palm trees and Ella Fitzgerald's high notes are represented in your brain by abstract codes. There are no colors, no sounds, no smells in your neural tissue. As Vernon Mountcastle puts it, "Sensation is an abstraction, not a replication of the real world." Your neurons tell a story—usually a good, plausible story—about the world outside. You can witness this yourself with a simple experiment:

Study for a minute or two the "devil's tuning fork" in Figure 9. Now look away and draw it.

Not so easy, was it? This tuning fork could not exist in our universe. It is a two-dimensional image containing paradoxical depth clues, like M. C. Escher's blatantly impossible staircases. Your brain, however, automatically interprets it as a three-dimensional object and tries to match the marks on the page with an internal model of a fork.

Now consider the Necker cube (Figure 10).

Why does the cube flip back and forth from a hollow square to a solid block? Because, according to the distinguished professor of illusion Richard Gregory, the information on the retina isn't sufficient to allow the brain to frame a single "model." So it must entertain two rival hypotheses simultaneously. Such illusions speak to Gregory of the brain's magical capacity to construct rich worlds out of bare sticks and lines.

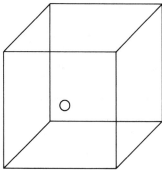

FIGURE 10   NECKER CUBE

Relativity by M. C. Escher. This lithograph employs reversible perspectives like that of the Necker cube. Unable to make sense of the paradoxical perspective clues, the brain is forced to juggle alternative interpretations of this impossible building. Such pictures remind us that seeing is not a passive process but "a dynamic searching for the best interpretation of the available data," in the words of neuropsychologist Richard L. Gregory. We are constantly matching what we see to our internal theories of staircases, buildings, faces, and so on. (*Photograph by courtesy of the National Gallery of Art, Washington, D.C. 20565*)

The eminent Cambridge University visual physiologist Kenneth Craik proposed that the brain builds "small-scale models of external reality" and tests them out. At U. C. Berkeley, physiologist Walter Freeman has discovered an olfactory "search image" in the rabbit brain that supports this idea. No doubt you have an internal space-time map of the route between your home and your office. A rabbit has a model of the smell environment in its brain—specifically, in its "palatial, beautifully organized" olfactory bulb. With advanced multiple-electrode recordings, Freeman managed to decipher the three-dimensional electrical pattern corresponding to a rabbit's "theory" of its world. "The animal has a template in its brain to which it matches any incoming odor input," he explains. "This template, or search image, is constantly being refined and updated. Smell is actually a process of hypothesis testing." With every breath it draws, the rabbit revises its theory of the environment.

Freeman props his heavy work boots on the desk and leans back in his chair, puffing on a cigar. With his grizzled beard, jeans and lumberjack shirt, and his off-the-cuff manner he suggests a mountain man teleported inexplicably to a university campus. His office, on the ground floor of the Life Sciences Building, has the run-down, cluttered look of a storage room in a natural history museum. Next to his desk a prehistoric-looking lizard, a dinosaur in miniature, gazes unblinking from a glass terrarium, in stony reptilian freeze time. A staring contest with a reptile gives you an inkling of where the image of the Medusa came from. Needless to say, Walter Freeman is anything but the eccentric, out-to-pasture naturalist one might at first mistake him for. "He's light-years ahead of everybody else; he's probably the smartest man in the neurosciences," one EEG expert tells us. "His work is so advanced that no one else knows how to do it." In a field where most scientists count spikes from single cells or chart the voltages emanating from two electrodes, we gather that Freeman's analysis of the complex electromagnetic patterns of 64 channels is like a passage from *Finnegan's Wake* inserted into a seventh-grade class discussion on *Great Expectations*.

"The brain has this incredible capacity to make images," he reflects. "It can take random numbers or words and make poems. We're wired up to make patterns. The essential nature of brain function is to make sense of the mass of raw stuff coming in. The operation I described in the rabbit brain is a metaphor for how scientists work. When you do an experiment you've got to have a search image, a reason for doing it in the first place. We're constantly selecting images and looking for them on the outside— in the data. If there's no discrepancy, we don't learn anything."

Beyond the Senses

Turn therefore from your outward senses and do not work with them neither within nor outside yourself. All those who undertake to be spiritual workers . . . and believe that they should hear, smell or see, taste or feel spiritual things . . . surely are deceived and are working wrongly against the course of nature.

—*The Cloud of Unknowing*

SCHOPENHAUER saw that Kant's *a priori* categories were equivalent to the Hindu/Buddhist *maya*, the veils of illusion obscuring pure reality. To the Western mind the *a priori* forms seem God-given and immutable. Eastern philosophy, however, insists that one can *suspend* the Kantian categories of three-dimensional space, time, and causality—all of which is just a projection, anyway. If the senses deceive, the truth seeker would do well to circumvent them.

"One can look at some religious aphorisms as a form of *psychophysical noise reduction,*" says Charles ("Chuck") Honorton, who directs the Princeton Psychophysical Research Laboratories in New Jersey. "Purity, poverty, contemplation, and so on aren't just for the sake of piety. These are methods of removing sensory distractions and increasing mental concentration. A good example is Patanjali's *Yogasutras*, composed in the second century B.C. in India. All the practices can be seen as systematic noise reduction, which eventually culminates in *samadhi*, a transcendental state in which the normal boundaries between the self and others disappears. It may not be dissimilar to what people experience on marijuana when they find themselves staring at the wallpaper for twenty minutes."

Sensory deprivation is a common religious practice. One thinks of the monotony of monastery life; of hairshirts, beds of nails, strict dietary laws, and other saintly mortifications; of the solitary mountain caves of holy men. "The tortoise can draw in his legs," says the *Bhagavad-Gita*. "The seer can draw in his senses. I call him illumined." To withdraw his senses from the world, the anchorite St. Anthony (ca. 250–355 A.D.) went to live in the desert, where (if we believe Brueghel the Younger and Gustave Flaubert) he experienced a carnival of grotesque and beatific hallucinations on the path to God. St. John of the Cross wrote his mystical "Spiritual Canticle" in a solitary prison cell. The Buddha's enlightenment followed a long arid spell of disenchantment and renunciation.

When John Lilly tested his prototype isolation tank in the 1950s, the elders of the NIMH preached that a brain cut off from all sensory stimuli would simply "turn off," like an unplugged appliance. Today this notion of a mechanistic brain powered by external inputs seems astounding, for we now know that brain cells are spontaneously active, as, for example, during REM sleep, when spontaneous electrical activity in the brain stem generates the opulent magic of dreams.

It was, in fact, in a dream lab at Brooklyn's Maimonides Hospital in the 1960s that Honorton got his basic training. Reasoning that the "sixth sense," if it existed, would be more accessible when the ordinary senses were turned off, Honorton and his fellow researchers tried transmitting telepathic messages to their dreaming subjects in mid-REM. When a distant "sender" gazed at a photo of the Firpo-Dempsey fight, one subject reportedly dreamed of Madison Square Garden, according to Honorton. After the dream lab dissolved, Honorton went on to preside over the computers, psychic video games, brain-wave biofeedback machines, and random-number generators of his high-tech parapsychology palace in Princeton.

"John Eccles argues that the mind is more than the brain, that there's a nonphysical aspect of mind," he tells us. "Every time you carry out a volitional act you are literally invoking psychokinesis, mind over matter. From that perspective what we call parapsychological phenomena are the channels through which mind and brain connect. PK [psychokinesis] is the way the mind acts through the body.

"If Eccles is right, then an act of normal will, such as raising your hand to your forehead, should have a psychokinetic correlate that can be measured."

Indeed, Honorton believes this theory is testable. To detect PK, he uses a psychic geiger counter called a random-number generator (RNG), a box containing a small sample of radioactive material, such as strontium 90. At random intervals some of the strontium decays, setting off the geiger counter, which, in turn, signals a computer to display either a one or a zero, depending on the time interval between counts. Radioactive decay being one of nature's truly random processes, if a subject can *will* the counter to stop at a certain number, this is considered evidence of PK. Anyway, Honorton rigged subjects up to an EEG biofeedback machine as well, and preliminary tests showed that RNG hits were most likely to occur when a person was "successfully controlling his own brain circuitry."

"We do have some evidence that is consistent with Eccles, though it's not conclusive. . . . I don't think," he adds, "that we're in a position yet to say with authority what is or is not unlikely in the mental domain."

We are not especially interested in psychic research, which seems a tedious business of combing a jungle of variables for "statistically significant" results, with all the glamour of an H & R Block workbook. We are more interested in Honorton's Ganzfeld chamber. The German scientist who invented this sensory-isolation technique (*Ganzfeld* means "homogenized field") immersed his subjects in a uniform, foglike atmosphere. Figuring that the messages bombarding our eyes, ears, nose, skin, and taste buds might be drowning out the faint small voice of psi, Honorton puts his test psychics in a Ganzfeld chamber to do their thing. We are given a guest pass.

A technician tapes the split halves of a Ping-Pong ball over our eyes, and as bug-eyed extraterrestrials we enter a small, soundproof cubicle. Through our translucent orbs we stare into a rose-colored light. Our ears are encased in headphones, through which a calm taped voice tells us to relax all our muscles in sequence. We count backward, as directed. Then as swooshing noises—a jetty rocked by the incoming tide? ancient winds trapped in a conch shell?—serenade us, we fall into a vague daydream.

Time dilates. Old memories surface like gaily colored tropical fish. We do a random-number test. We become excruciatingly aware of our breath. New York *Post* headlines flood our mind like ancient curses: DEATH BID BY MAN WITH NO FRIENDS ON NEW YEAR'S EVE: HEARTLESS CROWD YELLS "JUMP." We do not hear any celestial voices in this artificial desert, nor do we achieve any of the yogic powers itemized in Patanjali's *sutras*, such as, "By making *samyama* on the relation between the body and the ether, or by acquiring through meditation the lightness of cotton fiber, the yogi can fly through the air." Later, we learn that our psychic ability tests at "significantly below chance," a score that is sometimes considered evidence of "negative psi." Obviously we are not latent Jeane Dixons.

The Joan of Arc Personality

"THERE'S a democratic assumption that we're all at the same level of consciousness, and that's wrong," says Theodore X. Barber (the *X* stands for Xenophon), an eminent hypnosis authority and altered-states connoisseur who works at Cushing Hospital in Framingham, Massachusetts. "Just recently, we found a group of people who live in a different place *all the time,* and this has important implications for consciousness." Barber calls these natural visionaries "fantasy-prone personalities" (FPPs). The altered states that others use drugs, hypnosis, or long years of yoga or meditation to attain are home base to them. FPPs comprise about 4 percent of the population, the majority of them are female, and, according to Barber's controlled study, they are no better or worse adjusted than the average nonvisionary. They are simply the Mozarts of introspection, blessed with a remarkable talent.

Seventy-five percent of the fantasy-prone people Barber and colleague Sheryl Wilson studied could reach sexual climax by pure fantasy. All of them could weave imaginary scenes "as real as real" in all five senses, mentally touring the Hanging Gardens of Babylon even while carrying on cocktail-party small talk in Fort Lee, New Jersey. As children, they had a menagerie of imaginary playmates, fairies, elves, and guardian angels and regarded their dolls and toy animals as real, sentient beings with distinctive personalities. Typically they grew up without TV sets and were avid readers. They are extremely hypnotizable, vivid dreamers, whizzes at guided imagery, and so easily overwhelmed by LSD and marijuana that they give drugs a wide berth.

"You see, it's all the same state," says Barber. "They're hypnotized and they go into deep hypnosis. They go to sleep and they have lucid dreams. They take drugs, and their hallucinations become much too vivid. It's the same fantasy state behind it all the time."

The life of a typical fantasy-prone person is also full of clairvoyant dreams, precognitions, past-life regressions, psychic healings, out-of-body experiences, and other paranormal adventures, according to Barber. He thinks that the world's great visionaries—the likes of Joseph Smith, Madame Blavatsky the Theosophist, St. Bernadette, Joan of Arc—were fantasy-prone personalities. St. Joan's divine voices were compelling enough, of course, to convince the king of France to let her, a mere female child, command his armies. "Does this mean these things are just fantasy?" Barber muses. "Maybe. Or maybe these people really are perceiving other realities."

If so, where are these nonordinary realities that a handful of mystics, saints, clairvoyants, and table-tappers glimpse and the rest of us don't? Karl Pribram of Stanford has a hypothesis.

The Brain as Hologram

> I confess I do not believe in time. I like to fold my magic carpet, after use, in such a way as to superimpose one part of the pattern upon another. Let visitors trip. And the highest enjoyment of timelessness—in a landscape selected at random—is when I stand among rare butterflies and their foot plants. This is ecstasy, and behind the ecstasy is something else, which is hard to explain.
>
> —VLADIMIR NABOKOV, *Speak Memory*

A HOLOGRAM is a three-dimensional photograph made from light beams. You may have seen one hanging lifelike in midair at a science museum, or in the cinematic heavens of *Star Wars* or *Superman,* in which case you probably were not reminded of brains. But you are not Dr. Karl Pribram.

We arrive to find the father of the holographic brain hunched over a computer terminal in Stanford's psychology building, a modern building that rather resembles a napkin dispenser from afar. A small-boned, compact man in a pea-green T-shirt, forest-green slacks, and beads, he has the lush, gray beard and wizardly eyes of a Druid sorcerer. His magic evidently lies somewhere in the data, in the pale numbers glowing on the phosphorescent ocean of the screen. Even at a glance, one senses how a problem could obsess Karl Pribram like a sphinx's riddle. When he finds the answer, he jumps up and ushers us into his office, where a nearly life-size stuffed orangutan—"my newest graduate student"—slouches in an armchair and other simian memorabilia decorate the walls and desk.

Pribram's life has been full of monkeys, apes, and chimpanzees. He has meticulously taken apart thousands of simian brains and chronicled untold hours of monkey learning, sex life, social relations, and colony politics. In 1980 he lost a finger to a chimpanzee, and no ordinary one at that. He was visiting Washoe the "talking chimp" at the University of Oklahoma's Primate Research Institute. "Washoe and I were getting along just fine," he recalls, "until I reached over to feed her from a sack that Roger Fouts, her trainer, was holding. Washoe must have interpreted my gesture as an attack on Fouts." Reverting to a lower level of communication, the chimp reached through the feeding hole of her cage, bit Pribram's right hand, and then raked it against the sharp extruded metal. The scientist looked down to see his middle finger hanging from a string of flesh. While he was frantically flushing the wound with water, Washoe reportedly signed, "Sorry, sorry, sorry."

The finger was reattached by microsurgery at Oklahoma City's Presbyterian Hospital in a five-hour operation. The next day Dr. Pribram climbed out of his hospital bed and rode the elevator downstairs to the hospital's new clinical neuropsychology department, where, clad in his hospital gown and with an IV needle still in his arm, he delivered his scheduled dedication address. "The talk was very well received," he says. He later lost the tip of his finger above the first joint to gangrene, but that did not keep Pribram from performing delicate neurosurgery on animals. When his swollen, bandaged finger could not be stuffed into a standard surgical glove, he put a condom over the injured finger and then donned a regular glove with the middle digit cut out. "You can imagine the jokes when it came to sterilizing the condom along with all the other stuff required for surgery," he remarks.

The story tells you something about Karl Pribram. A man who would give a public address in his hospital gown and perform neurosurgery with a prophylactic finger is the sort of man who would also boldly propose—in the face of widespread peer skepticism—that the brain works like a hologram.

Holography is a form of lensless photography invented by Dennis Gabor in 1947. Unlike an ordinary two-dimensional photograph, a hologram is an eerily lifelike three–dimensional image. Its code, stored on the film, bears no resemblance to the object photographed, but is a record of the light waves scattered by the object. Suppose you drop two pebbles into a still pond and then immediately freeze the rippled surface. In the overlapping wavefronts is stored a complete record of the pebbles' passage through a moment of time. So it is with a hologram.

A beam of light energy—a laser, in most cases—is split in half. One part, called the reference beam, travels directly to the holographic film; the other is bounced off the object to be photographed before continuing on to the film. The two beams collide on the film, forming an interference pattern like that of the pebbles' intersecting wavefronts. It looks like a meaningless tangle of swirls. As Gabor himself said, "It looks like noise." But when the film is illuminated with a "reconstruction beam," a laser beam identical to the original reference beam, the object is magically reborn. It's as if the wavefront had been frozen in time in the holographic plate and then released to continue its path to your eye. And behold, there's Uncle Sid in his Naugahyde armchair, in vivid 3-D, so lifelike you reach out to touch his can of Budweiser—but only slice through thin air.

Archimedes had his Eureka experience in the bathtub; Pribram's hol-

Dr. Karl Pribram demonstrates a Multiplex hologram, composed of holographic strips, each of which represents a frame of a movie. Pribram believes that the neurons in the visual cortex function much like this type of hologram. (*Courtesy of News and Publication Service, Stanford University, Stanford, California*)

ographic brain theory was born of a chance reading of a 1966 issue of *Scientific American.* Perusing an article on holography, he was struck by several interesting properties: A hologram can store nearly infinite amounts of information in almost no space at all. Any part of the hologram contains information about the whole. Should you drop and shatter the plate, you can salvage a fragment of the wave pattern and reconstruct the entire image. The "message" in a hologram is located paradoxically everywhere and nowhere.

Pribram thought of the dead-end quest for the engram, in which he had briefly participated, hunting memory traces in the chimpanzee brain under Karl Lashley's tutelage in the 1950s. If the brain used a scattered, holographiclike code for information storage, it would explain why rats with massive brain damage can still remember mazes and why human stroke victims don't lose discrete parts of their memory store—the years from 1966–1974, say, or all words beginning with *h*. It would also account for the fact that an organ the size of a cantaloupe can hold a lifetime of memories. Just as many different holograms can be superimposed, Pribram speculated, so can infinite images be stacked in our brains. When we recall something, we may be using a certain "reconstruction beam" to zoom in on a particular encoded memory.

At first it was a metaphor. But by the early 1970s, the holographic brain had become something more. "Of course, there are no laser beams or reference beams in the brain," Pribram tells us. "I'm simply saying that our brains use a holographiclike code. The brain performs certain operations, which can be described by the mathematics of holography, to code, decode, and recode sensory input. There is no other technique known to man that allows for the storage of so much information."

Holography is based on a mathematical operation called *Fourier transforms.* Roughly speaking, this is a method of breaking down any complex pattern into sets of simpler waves. The outline of a face, for example, can be represented as a series of sine and cosine waves, ultimately as a set of numbers, a Fourier series. Satellites use Fourier transforms to filter out irrelevant shapes and zero in on the forms that mean submarines on the move. CAT scans and other imaging techniques use them to construct three-dimensional pictures of the body. Scientists use them in their computers to cull statistical wheat from chaff.

When you see something, your retina works pretty much like a camera. But then, Pribram believes, a "scatter effect" takes place. "You see, your brain is operating in two modes simultaneously. You have the spatial representation which maps the retinal image onto the cortex. And then, in the membranes of the cells, the image is transformed back into the frequency mode—the scatter that you'd see if you saw without a lens. The neuron's code for storing information resembles the interference patterns on the holographic plate." Thus, according to Pribram, your brain does not store a literal reproduction of your grandmother's face, but something like a Fourier transform of her face. If you could look inside the brain, you'd "see" an abstract code of wave-phase relationships no more like the perceived world than the overlapping patterns of light and shade on the holographic plate are like Uncle Sid in his armchair.

Why doesn't the brain simply print an image, like a photograph? Hubel and Wiesel discovered neurons that are tuned to the physical dimensions of the external world: Why not suppose that the brain starts with bars, lines, and edges and builds up to complex images such as faces and buildings? The ultimate extension of this idea is the "grandmother cell," a hypothetical neuron that lights up when your grandmother walks in the room. But think about it: How could the same cell detect Grandma five hundred yards away in profile, as well as across the breakfast table? How, moreover, could the brain contain cells that are prewired to see toasters, calico cats, apple trees, ten-speed bicycles, and discotheques?

"In the midsixties," Pribram recounts, "everyone believed that feature detectors were the basis of perception. That's the idea that each neuron responds to a particular feature of the sensory input—such as redness, greenness, or verticality—and that these features are later combined into a whole image. But how is it that when I view your face from different distances or different angles, I still perceive the same face? There can't be a single brain cell that says 'Bzzz—Judy's face' or 'Bzzz—Judy's nose.' Perception must be a very flexible thing, not a pattern that's wired in. Brain cells do selectively respond to features but not uniquely so. Each cell is something like a person with many traits. So when you abstract blueness, you must address all the cells in the network that detect blue. . . .

"A holographic code automatically takes care of imaging from different distances and angles. The problem of grain is solved; you can have very fine-grained textures. But perhaps the most important reason is the same reason Fourier transforms are used in computers: In the Fourier domain, correlations can be performed almost instantaneously. That's exactly what our brains do when we instantaneously process the table's color, texture, dimensions, luminosity, distance, and relation to all other tables we've seen."

What does all this have to do with God in the brain? As Pribram was quick to perceive, the kingdom-of-heaven-within may be the holographic realm. At least, it is as good a place as any to look for the counterpart of the City of God, the Realm of Light, the Beatific Vision, the Clear Light of Tibetan Buddhism.

Consider: A cross section of the airwaves at any moment would resemble a hologram. It takes a radio or TV receiver to transform this "noise" into auditory and visual images, into "Love Boat" or the classical hour on KFEX. In the same way, your senses take frequencies and make objects out of them. They translate William James's "undistinguishable swarming continuum" into the forms, colors, sounds, and shapes of our ordinary, three-dimensional world. But is this the "real world" or just a movie?

"If we got rid of our 'lenses,' " Pribram proposes, "we'd experience the interference patterns themselves. We would be in the pure frequency domain. What would that domain look like? Ask the mystics. Though they have trouble describing it, too. . . . Space and time would be collapsed, or, as I prefer to say, enfolded. Think of an EEG recording. On the vertical axis you have amplitude; on the horizontal axis, frequency. There's no space and no time.

"Our brains can apparently perform the transforms back and forth between space-time reality and the frequency reality, the light domain. Or maybe they keep track of both sides of the equation. A computer using Fourier transforms does this in performing rapid correlations."

Outside Pribram's window Stanford undergraduates cycle through a flawless green-and-gold afternoon. Most of them look as if they had spent the morning mountain climbing and then got together to film a soft-drink commercial. Does the mind, we ask, dwell in the physical brain like a ghostly hologram, everywhere and nowhere simultaneously?

"Yes, mind isn't located in a place," says Pribram. "What we have is holographiclike machinery that turns out images, which we perceive as existing somewhere outside the machine that produces them. We know our eyes are involved, but I don't image you on the surface of my retina. Even though the codes are in my brain somewhere, I perceive you over there on the chair.

"I've always felt," he continues, "that dualism is okay in the ordinary image-object domain—the domain where the eye constructs images and the brain operates on the sensory images to make objects. Dualism's okay for the Newtonian domain. But it doesn't apply to the holographic, enfolded order. There is no space and time, no causality, no matter and no mind. Everything is enfolded. There are no boundaries; so you can have neither mind nor brain."

The Universal Hologram

Even so large as the universe outside is the universe within the lotus of the heart. Within it are heaven and earth, the sun and the moon, the lightning and all the stars. Whatever is in the macrocosm is in the microcosm also.

—*Chandogya Upanishad*

THE HOLOGRAPHIC THEORY finds some experimental support in the work of U. C. Berkeley scientists Russell and Karen DeValois, who have identified cells in the visual system that respond to spatial frequencies instead of lines, edges, and other features of three-dimensional space. And there is good reason to think that distributed nerve networks, not single "wise neurons" (in Francis Crick's phrase) are the important units in the brain's information-processing code. As Crick puts it, "We don't think a neuron by itself can do very much." Most scientists we met, however, had not embraced the holographic-brain faith. "It's absurd," said one. "There are no Fourier transforms in the brain." Others said that it was a useful metaphor, as long as it was understood as a metaphor.

Even if it is only a metaphor, though, the hologram is a compelling one for the brain's magic show. It suggests how a finite lump of matter, the brain, could contain an infinite mindscape. It may be a better model in many ways than the oft-evoked computer. "The computer's mind is a creature of the linear, Euclidian world of its origin," notes Paul Pietsch, an anatomist at Indiana University, who has written a book on the holographic brain called *Shufflebrain*. "Its memory reduces to discrete bits. A bit is a binary choice—a clean, crisp, clear, yes-no, on-off, efficient choice. . . . The hologramic continuum is not linear; it is not either-or; it is not efficient."

Holography may also explain why time and space in the brain do not resemble physical space-time. "People have dreamed ten-year scenes within the span of a ten-minute dream," notes Pietsch. "The reverse also can happen. . . . A character in a recent Neil Simon play tells how during a bout of depression he couldn't cross the street because the other side was too far away." Said Albert Einstein: "When a man sits with a pretty girl for an hour, it seems like a minute. But let him sit on a hot stove for a minute—and it's longer than an hour. That's relativity." Psychological time is relative, and holography is built on relativistic principles. Instead of quantities, its code is based on relationships between waves, phase relationships. Compressed into a hologram is the entire history of the waves, just as your entire past is contained in your memory. Time is collapsed in a hologram as it is in the mystical state.

Perhaps it was a case of Jungian synchronicity that while Pribram was dreaming up the holographic brain, a renowned quantum physicist six thousand miles away in London was coming to the conclusion that the whole universe was a hologram. The two scientists did not know of each other at the time; only later did they compare notes and start appearing on the same lecture circuits. Physicist David Bohm, who is a disciple of the Indian philosopher Krishnamurti, relates the image-object domain (the "unfolded order") and the frequency domain (the "enfolded order") to the Hindu Manifest and Unmanifest. According to Hindu philosophy, all of creation is latent, "enfolded" in the Unmanifest, rather as a potential human being is "enfolded" in DNA. Out of the formless Unmanifest is born the Manifest, the world of myriad objects, creatures, and forms. The enfolded order to which quantum theory has led Bohm is "a reality immensely beyond what we call matter. Matter is like a small ripple on a tremendous ocean of energy. And the ocean is not primarily in space and time at all. . . . Space and time are constructed for us for our convenience."

There are other deep spiritual principles embodied in holography. "In a hologram every part is distributed in the whole, and the whole is enfolded in every part," Pribram tells us. This recalls the Hermetic doctrine: "As above, so below," the microcosm that recapitulates the macrocosm. A hologram is like the "network of pearls in the heaven of Indra" of Buddhist legend, so arranged that "if you look at one you see all others reflected in it." Just as each creature is a compressed record of the Godhead, so is the individual hologram part of the universal hologram, according to Bohm. "Each individual manifests the consciousness of mankind," he observes.

Sick Souls and Mad Saints

SINCE LANGUAGE is embedded in dualism (subject and object), the mystical state is said to be "ineffable." In Lao-tzu's phrase, "The Tao that can be told is not the eternal Tao." The fourteenth-century mystical handbook *The Cloud of Unknowing* instructs the seeker that the way to know God is through "unknowing." Paranormal realities tend to come clothed in obscure paradoxes, oxymorons (St. Theresa's "pain of God"), riddles, and koans ("What is the sound of one hand clapping?") expressly designed to short-circuit the rational mind. To rational ears, mystical pronouncements sometimes sound like the babbling of madmen.

Indeed, many famous saints were, in William James's words, "sick souls." St. Paul showed symptoms of epilepsy. St. Theresa has been called the "patron saint of hysterics." George Fox, the founding father of Quakerism, was a "hereditary degenerate," according to James. The unsavory visions of St. Anthony in the desert do not suggest a healthy, well-rounded mind. Many saints have practiced what we would regard as excesses of self-mortification: Both St. Catherine of Siena and St. Catherine of Genoa, for instance, subsisted for weeks on nothing more than consecrated Communion wafers. Obsessions, compulsions, rituals, "religious melancholia," brooding dark nights of the soul, and manic highs are at least as common among religious geniuses as they are among artistic ones.

To Freud mysticism represented an infantile "regression" to the oral stage, even to the primal unity of the intrauterine life. Modern psychiatry, for the most part, takes an equally dim view of the phenomenon. In 1960 the Group for the Advancement of Psychiatry (GAP) issued a report on mysticism, stating: "The psychiatrist will find mystical persons of interest because they can demonstrate forms of behavior intermediate between normality and frank psychosis." A surefire way to be diagnosed as schizophrenic at the state hospital is to punctuate your conversation with references to God, Satan, sin, or miracles.

But one culture's lunatic may be another culture's shaman, *curandero*, or holy man. Perhaps some of the shopping-bag ladies mumbling to themselves in Greyhound bus terminals are latter-day sybils attuned to the equivalent of Delphic oracles. What the American Psychiatric Association calls *depersonalization* or *poor ego boundaries* may fit the criteria for *samadhi* in parts of the Himalayas. In a 1971 article, "Eastern and Western Models of Man," in the *Journal of Transpersonal Psychology,* Ram Dass (formerly Harvard Professor Richard Alpert) observed:

There are some beings that we call psychotic who in India would be called "God Intoxicants." They are people who have experienced compassion outwardly and then their entire energy turns inward to inner states that they are experiencing. We see them as catatonic. Because we are not getting an elicited response out of them, we project onto them a certain kind of psychological state. Now in India they project another kind of interpretation . . . so that a God-Intoxicant is treated with great reverence and respect. Ramakrishna, a very famous mystic in India, was often God-intoxicant.

"For aught we know to the contrary," mused James in *The Varieties of Religious Experience,* "103 or 104 Fahrenheit might be a much more favorable temperament for truths to germinate and sprout in, than the more ordinary blood-heat of 97 or 98 degrees." This was his reply to the learned doctors who dismissed mystical insights as the by-products of "hereditary neurasthenia," a "gastro-duodenal catarrh," a bad liver, tuberculosis, or some other organic ailment. Against the medical materialism of his day James argued, "To plead the organic causation of a religious state of mind . . . is quite illogical and arbitrary. . . ." If you explain away our spiritual insights as mere by-products of a disturbed biochemistry, James pointed out, then "none of our thoughts and feelings, not even our scientific doctrines . . . could retain any value . . . for every one of them without exception flows from the state of its possessor's body at the time."

James's argument seems timely. If the belief in God is no more than a series of neurochemical reactions, then why not also ascribe atheism— or the doctrine that thoughts are merely chemical reactions—to chemical reactions in the nonbeliever's head?

It is interesting that the path to God seems to be a negative path, a path of "unknowing." All the methods of tapping into heaven-within-the-brain involve *getting rid* of something. A protective filter, a reducing valve, a lens, a set of hard-wired perceptual "categories," serotonin, endorphins, or some other neurochemical keep us earthbound. The face of God is veiled by the *maya* of the nervous system.

If our brain were a different size and shape, what would our religions be like? If we had a single cyclopean eye in the center of our forehead, if instead of two hemispheres we had three, if we navigated by echolocation like bats, would our philosophies, our geometries, our mythologies, our notions of causality, space, time, and number be radically different?

Perhaps we'd perceive an "effect" before the "cause." Perhaps, instead of experiencing temporal continuity, we'd feel ourselves at each moment to be altogether different beings (as, in *Ulysses,* Stephen Daedalus joked that since all the molecules composing him were different, he was no longer bound to repay the money he'd borrowed seven years earlier). Maybe we'd live several parallel lives simultaneously (as some multiple personalities may). Or perhaps space would flow by us at a uniform pace, like our clock time, while time could be traveled in any direction.

Some people's brains are wired up so as to experience synesthesia, a "cross-wiring" of the senses in which one sense evokes another. The most common form of synesthesia is *audition colorée,* or colored hearing, immortalized by the poet Arthur Rimbaud in his famous poem "Les Voyelles" about the hues of vowels. When Maryland neurologist Richard Cytowic studied the brains of synesthetes in mid-*audition-colorée,* he found that the blood flow decreased in the neocortex and increased in the limbic system. "The brain's higher information processing turns off during colored hearing," he told *Brain/Mind Bulletin.* "An older, more fundamental way of viewing the world—more mammalian than language-related—takes over."

Even more exotic realities occur in certain neurological syndromes. "I shall never forget a group of patients with deep lesions of the right hemisphere . . . ," writes the Russian neurologist A. R. Luria in *The Working*

Brain. "They firmly believed they were in Moscow and also in another town. They suggested they had left Moscow and gone to the other town, but having done so, they were still in Moscow, where an operation had been performed on their brains."

In certain brain states time flows more slowly or stops completely, arrested, like Pompeii, at the scene of some primal tragedy. In others, like the postencephalitic states described by neurologist Oliver Sacks in *Awakenings*, "cinematic vision" occurs. One such patient, "Hester," was seeing the world at about "three or four frames a second" when she received a visit from her brother. As she watched him light his pipe, some of the "frames" appeared out of sequence, and she saw the pipe being lit *before* she saw her brother's hand, holding the lit match, approach the pipe. Notes Sacks, "Thus—incredibly—Hester saw the pipe actually being lit several frames too soon; she saw 'the future,' so to speak, somewhat before she was due to see it."

Should we dismiss this kind of thing as a quaint pathology? Or can we regard people like Hester as neurological Marco Polos who have been to remote and otherworldly climes of mind? After all, our stolid reality, with its familiar "categories" of space, time, and so on, is simply one state of brain that we happen to call normal.

THE
BRAIN / MIND
CONNECTION

14

Chaos, Strange Attractors, and the Stream of Consciousness

> A great disorder is an order. Now, A
> And B are not like statuary, posed
> For a visit in the Louvre. They are things chalked
> On the sidewalk so that the pensive man may see.
> —WALLACE STEVENS,
> "Connoisseur of Chaos"

FOR five days in a row, a Stanford psychiatrist has been watching the "shopping-bag ladies" in a public park. By his calculations each of the women has a stereotyped routine of postures, gestures, and monologues that is repeated over and over again like a musician's set. Later he jots down some equations for dopamine synthesis in the schizophrenic brain.

Fiddling with his parameters just a little, a scientist in Pennsylvania makes a high-speed computer "epileptic." A Chicago biophysicist studies the "hallucinations" he conjured with digital representations of neurons. In Santa Cruz, California, a mathematician adds stress variables to ROVER, a computer simulation of a dog's adrenal cortical system. "When we add ACTH," he says, "it responds just like a dog."

In La Jolla, rats on LSD, amphetamine, cocaine, antidepressants, lithium, and caffeine wander at random in cages. Each time their tails pass through a photobeam, an electrical blip is transmitted to a computer, which calculates the "frequency" and "amplitude" of their journeys. Studying the patterns, a neuroscientist reflects, "The stream of consciousness is a random walk, but an order emerges over time."

These scientists are "connoisseurs of chaos," practitioners of a science so new it doesn't have an official name, only a nickname—chaos. (Officially it is known as nonlinear dynamics, or sometimes as chaotic dynamics.) The Christopher Columbus of chaos was an MIT meteorologist named Edward Lorenz. While working on the problem of long-range weather forecasting in 1963, he proved mathematically that the weather was impossible to predict. This may be big news for Willard C. Scott—and for you when you're worried about rain on your parade—but what does it have to do with the brain?

Well, years after Lorenz's quiet discovery (known for a decade only to readers of an obscure meteorology journal), it became apparent that the laws he discovered also governed water flowing through a pipe, hurricanes, airplanes in flight, chemical reactions, the waxing and waning of wildlife populations, economic cycles, the ebb and flow of hormones in the body—and the 10^{11} interconnected nerve cells of the brain.

"The mind does not easily grasp nonlinear interactions between billions of cells," says Stephen Grossberg, a mathematician and interdisciplinary scientist at Boston University's Center for Adaptive Systems. "That is why we need mathematical models." Says Arnold Mandell, "The machinery of the brain is just too complicated. Two hundred neurotransmitters, each with seventy thousand receptors! How can we ever understand all the plumbing? We have to get away from the plumbing to see the brain's deep messages." Of course, many researchers have made brilliant careers out of digging up the "plumbing." Out of Eric Kandel's microscopic scrutiny of cell membranes came the elementary building blocks of memory; from Hubel and Wiesel's single-cell recordings, a map of the visual cortex. But can this explain how you *think*?

Mandell, Grossberg, and the other scientists you'll meet in this chapter don't think so. If you want to know how New York City functions, would you interview three passersby in depth? Or would you take a helicopter ride over the city and look down on the different boroughs and the major traffic routes, the clusters of skyscrapers that mark the financial centers, the densities of flashing red lights that might mean dangerous neighborhoods? If you are looking for the brain's basic organizing principles, its "deep messages," mathematics can lift you above the gritty details. The lingo of chaos is esoteric, and many of its pioneers labor in rarefied and otherworldly realms of theoretical physics. But the interesting thing about it is that chemists, mathematicians, biologists, physiologists, meteorologists, and neuroscientists are all tuning in to the same "deep messages." There are some who think chaos is a universal language of nature.

The Dripping Faucet as Microcosm

"ONLY ONCE OR TWICE in a millennium," says mathematician Ralph Abraham, of the University of California at Santa Cruz, "is there a true scientific revolution, a paradigm shift. Newtonian mechanics and the invention of calculus in the seventeenth century brought about the last one. The current scientific revolution will synthesize the whole intellectual discourse of the species." While Abraham makes this prophecy, in a Szechwan restaurant in downtown Santa Cruz, ragged armies of sixties' casualties drift by the window, hollow-eyed, laden with knapsacks, like refugees from an Antonioni film. If there is a dark side to the third millennium, these are the people who will gather on mountaintops to witness the end of the world. Abraham and his fellow chaos theorists expect to witness quite the opposite.

Up the hill, the University of California at Santa Cruz (UCSC) is a land of sun-bleached, windblown meadows and cool redwood groves. Something of the zeitgeist of the sixties lingers in the air; the students do not look like accounting majors, and it is possible here to obtain a Ph.D. in the History of Consciousness. Perhaps it was the right objective correlative (as T. S. Eliot might have called it) for the Chaos Cabal.

In 1977 physicist Rob Shaw was just winding up his Ph.D. dissertation on superconductivity when a professor asked him to take a look at some puzzling differential equations. He programmed them into an analog computer he'd salvaged from the basement of a defunct engineering department and got the shock of his life. By having the computer perform iterations—essentially repeating the same equations over and over again—he fell into a looking-glass world where order spun off into chaos. Soon he lost all interest in superconductivity (the dissertation was never completed) and took to sleeping in his lab and staying up all night to ponder the enigmatic shapes on his screen. (They were "strange attractors," though Shaw did not know that yet.) When three friends, also physics students, dropped by to see what he was doing, they became possessed too. In late 1977 the Santa Cruz Dynamical Systems Collective—or, colloquially, the Chaos Cabal—was formed. (Abraham, who had heard the gospel of chaos a few years before, became a sort of chaos elder.)

To enter Shaw's office is to walk into the bowels of a dismantled appliance—a maze of meters, dials, plugboard, wires, terminals, plotters, and gauges. "I'm a technotwit," he confesses. He takes us next door to see a contraption that looks like a precocious child's project for the science fair. A plastic tub of water is mounted above a brass faucet. The drops from the faucet interrupt a laser beam, which precisely records the intervals between them and transmits them as pulses to the computer next door. This is Shaw's famous chaotic faucet. "The fascinating thing about a standard faucet," he tells us, "is that it's got this random element in it. The flow is constant, the spigot doesn't move, and nothing has perturbed the system, but you get this chaotic pattern in it that never repeats itself. It's a microcosm."

When the Chaos Cabal first presented results like these at scientific conferences, other scientists would shake their heads dubiously and ask,

"Are you sure this isn't just a numerical error?" But chaos is not the result of a numerical error. It is a fact of nature.

Physical theories since Archimedes, Galileo, and Newton have been built around a stable, linear world, an idealized cosmos of frictionless pendulums, efficient machines, and eternal trajectories. The serene assumption—articulated by the French mathematician Pierre Simon, Marquis de Laplace—was that you could predict the future in its entirety if you knew the position and velocity of every particle at one moment in time. Alas, this is untrue. Half a century ago, the founders of quantum mechanics said that the subatomic domain was haunted by randomness, and the best measuring devices on earth could not make it less uncertain. Albert Einstein could not accept this idea, objecting, "God does not play dice with the universe!" Well, God does play dice, and not just with quarks. Waterfalls, cloud patterns, heart arrhythmias, waves crashing against a sea wall during a winter storm, the fluctuations of a predator/prey population, the collective song of your neurons, and many other systems in nature also have pockets of randomness that make them unpredictable. We can write equations for the orbits of remote planets, but the trajectories of tumbling dice forever elude us. Why?

Back in 1977 Shaw observed that the realm of chaos was ruled by certain laws. One of these was "sensitive dependence on initial conditions," a phenomenon starkly illustrated at the casinos of Las Vegas. At the moment a roulette wheel is spun, the tiniest twitch of the finger controls the ball's trajectory. Similar infinitesimal influences determine how dice will land. In meteorology there is the so-called Butterfly Effect, the idea that the flapping of a butterfly's wings in the air over Peru in February could affect the weather in Los Angeles in March. Because of sensitive dependence on initial conditions, minuscule measuring errors are magnified into huge ones farther down the line, and prediction becomes impossible. So it is not necessarily your local weatherman's fault if he's wrong about the weather a week from Monday. We are condemned to live with chance.

One of the founding fathers of chaos, the German theoretical chemist Otto Rössler, once watched a mechanical taffy puller at work, pulling the taffy and folding it back on itself again and again. In his mind Rössler followed the diverging course of two imaginary raisins and jotted down equations for a new "strange attractor." Rössler was observing a second fundamental law of chaos, "rapid divergence of nearby trajectories." Variables that start out highly correlated—the mathematical equivalents of the raisins—drift apart and become uncorrelated. After lots of stretching and folding, which a computer does with "iterations," differences in the system widen and a deterministic system becomes indeterminate.

Shaw was to learn, of course, that the *terra incognita* he stumbled on was not entirely *incognita*. Edward Lorenz before him had discovered how "sensitive dependence" and "rapid divergence" produced lumps of chaos in the convection currents of the atmosphere. Then, in 1971, a study of fluid turbulence really put chaos on the map. Werner Heisenberg, the father of quantum uncertainty, once remarked that when he went on to the next world, he wanted God to explain two things. One was the mysteries of the quantum realm; the other was fluid turbulence. Generations of physicists had tried in vain to write equations for the hydrodynamics of waterfalls, cascading rivers, even water rushing out of a faucet, and concluded that these phenomena, for reasons no one could identify, were just too complicated to predict. But two European scientists, David Ruelle and Floris Takens, showed that a wild river had a form to it after all, albeit a strange one. In the dynamics of turbulent fluids they divined ghostly geometric forms similar to the one Lorenz had identified a decade before in the weather. They named them *strange attractors*.

So what is an attractor, and what makes one strange? Any physical system—a chemical reaction, the motion of a pendulum, a heartbeat, or the fluctuations in a population of gray foxes—can be plotted as a series of mathematical points representing successive temperature readings, velocity, amplitude, or whatever. In time the points describing the changes in the system are drawn toward the invisible geometry of an "attractor" like metal filings toward a magnet.

There are three types of attractors, two of which are old news. The *fixed point* attractor describes a system at rest, after all the motions have ceased. If you fill a pan with water and shake it up, the liquid will swirl around for a while and then stop. Mathematically speaking, it settles into a fixed point. After all the chemicals have stopped reacting, a chemical system would have a point attractor (equilibrium) structure.

The second type is the *periodic attractor,* or *limit cycle.* The periodic motion of a pendulum or metronome, the regular beating of a human heart, a smoothly oscillating EEG, or the mood swings of a manic-depressive might all be described by the limit cycle. The key thing about the fixed point and the limit cycle is that they are regular and predictable. If you know the initial state, you can plot all the future states.

Suppose you heat french-fry grease in a saucepan. At first the grease just sits there. As it heats, convection currents form, periodic wiggles that make a limit cycle. If you turn up the burner a little more, the patterns make doubly periodic wiggles (wiggles upon wiggles). At a certain critical value of heat, however, the grease abruptly "bifurcates," in the lingo, to a strange attractor motion.

Paradoxical Order　　　　WHAT does a strange attractor look like? Aiming a creaky school projector at the wall, Shaw shows us movies of the strange attractors captured on the local cathode-ray screens. "This is our local compulsion," he says, as the ten thousand mathematical points that represent ten thousand future states unfold in an instant, bringing these odd mathematical creatures to life. They are beautiful: baroque spirals, elaborate filigrees, intricate webs spun by non-Euclidian spiders, shapes like amusement-park rides as depicted by Marcel Duchamp.

There's a method to this madness, however. At first chaotic behavior seems to follow no rules, but in time it assumes a definite shape. Strange attractors may sprout extravagant thickets of randomness, but they never fly out of the "phase space," a determined mathematical envelope. And whether you're dealing with water in pipes or clouds or swirls of smoke or jet engines, certain rules and numerical constants always apply when nature "bifurcates" into disorder.

"By the very nature of our activities," says Shaw, "we try to avoid chaos. What do we try to do with our machines? Keep them stable and avoid oscillations, or if we have oscillations, try to keep those stable. But now we can see that chaos has a lot of order in it.

"The Old Guard—people like [information theorist] Norbert Wiener—used equations for *total* randomness as a model for nature," explains Doyne Farmer, a graduate of the Chaos Cabal who has carried the seeds of chaos to Los Alamos National Laboratories in New Mexico. "When you have complete chaos, you can perform probability studies. This is the case with the molecules in a gas, which get pretty evenly distributed. However, there are many situations in nature where orderly things happen in the midst of great chaos. Some systems have a 'clock' inside them that goes on keeping perfect time in the midst of very chaotic stuff. For those systems, deterministic chaos, with its strange-attractor structure, is the best model."

Paradoxically the study of chaos seems to lead into a higher realm of order. (Farmer's Ph.D. dissertation, "Order in Chaos," describes how order, information, and structure arise in these systems.) Under nature's polymorphous surface lies a finite set of hidden principles. "There are only a few movies, and everything we see around us is the working out of one of those movies," says Ralph Abraham. If you know how to look, the invisible blueprints of strange attractors determine the behavior of rivers and jet engines, chemical reactions and cloud formations, heartbeats, the Big Bang, EEGs, and economic cycles.

You can use nonlinear equations to model a two-nation arms race, as physicist Alan Saperstein, of Wayne State University in Detroit, has done.

"I think," he says, "the idea of a transition from laminar [smooth] to turbulent flow or, if you will, from predictable international relations to chaotic international relations is important." You can look at the economy this way, plotting the often-quirky "oscillations" of business cycles. You can analyze the heart as a dynamical system, as a pair of researchers at Montreal's McGill University did, and isolate the conditions under which a normal, periodic heartbeat will "bifurcate" into dangerous heart fibrillations. You can mix together certain chemicals and see the genesis of chaos. You can build a nonlinear model of the female endocrine system (the interlocking hormonal feedback loops of which act like coupled mechanical oscillators) to study the premenstrual syndrome. Ralph Abraham did, and he also fathered ROVER, the computer simulation of a dog's stress response.

"It is interesting, even comforting," muses W. Ross Adey, a neuroscientist who is conversant with chaos, "that the laws that determine atomic interactions in cosmic interstellar dust are the same laws that determine the interactions of molecules on the surface of brain cells."

Chaos and the Brain   THE WALLS of Don Walter's office, in the basement of UCLA's Life Sciences Building, are covered with graphs of different biological processes. Some, like the computer-graphics portrait of systolic and diastolic rhythms, resemble stylized mountain chains with Japanese-style clouds around their peaks. As we arrive, his computer terminal is displaying sawtooth waves of blue and violet. "Chaotic spikes," he explains.

By running equations for three linked neurons, Walter and Alan Garfinkel, of UCLA's Crump Institute for Medical Engineering, have conjured up a bit of chaos. *Orderly* chaos. "If you link together a bunch of neurons with cross-inhibitory coupling, they will fire erratically," says Garfinkel. "And yet there really is a pattern in that chaos that we can tease out with sophisticated methods." As a wallpaperlike pattern on the screen grows more intricate, Walter adds, "You can't predict the thing in detail, but it has *tendencies*."

If three coupled neurons make unpredictable patterns, imagine what 10^{11} billion interacting cells could do. A working brain is more like the weather or a turbulent stream than it is like a digital computer, according to the chaos connoisseurs. In the classic lock-and-key model, one molecule of a brain chemical fits into a specific receptor on a cell membrane. But neuroscientists now know that a population of receptors can fluctuate rapidly under the influence of many microscopic conditions inside and outside the cell. "Instead of receptors, it may be better to think in terms of *re-*

ceptivity," says Alan Garfinkel. The neuron itself isn't a hard, little marble or a microchip in a computer but a "complex chemical reaction in solution," a "bag of enzymes," prone to the same fluxes as other chemical reactions.

"There are some predictable things about the brain and some predictable things about people's behavior," says Walter. "You can predict when most people will get up tomorrow. You can predict that brains will get old and clanky and wear out and die. But for many brain processes you have to give up even the *ideal* of determinism. Chaotic dynamics tells us that many things that look deterministic can't be predicted in a practical sense for more than a short time."

Calculus describes a smoothly changing, predictable world, and its inventor, Gottfried von Leibniz, once declared, *"Natura non facit saltum"* ("Nature does not make jumps"). But nature *does* make jumps. When a parameter is increased beyond a critical value, metals snap, a smoothly flowing fluid becomes turbulent, chemical concentrations turn chaotic. These are some of nature's *nonlinearities*. A linear relationship is one in which if x equals y, $300x$ will equal $300y$, and so on, for all possible values of x and y. "But all of biology is nonlinear," says Garfinkel. "Double the dimensions of a bone and the result has eight times the weight but only four times the strength. That makes a thirty-foot-tall man impossible."

In the brain, twice the input may mean *four* times the output—or *half* the output. Perception, for example, is organized along log (decibel) lines. And whether you're measuring the behavior of an animal or a neuron, the effects of heat, chemicals, or electricity can have decidedly unpredictable effects. "The brain is funny," says Arnold Mandell. "If I gave you two milligrams of amphetamine you might feel very alert; at seven or eight milligrams you might feel sleepy; at twelve, you might be alert again; at twenty, full of rage; at fifty milligrams, totally out to lunch. So in the brain more is not necessarily more. Sometimes more is just different."

If there are universal patterns buried in the brain's "plumbing," if there is a grand theory—perhaps an $E=mc^2$—latent in all the data flowing out of electrodes and radiation counters, perhaps nonlinear dynamics can pry it out. "Now that people like Hubel and Wiesel and Mountcastle have made these marvelous discoveries about what single cells can do and a little about how columns [of neurons] are arranged," says Jack Cowan, the University of Chicago biophysicist whom we met in Chapter 10, "now comes the next problem. How is it all put together? What are the general organizing principles of the brain?"

Cowan has been working on a mathematical model of epilepsy and hallucination. These "bifurcations" occur in the brain, he thinks, when neuroelectric activity, cranked up past a certain threshold, forms "traveling and rotating waves." His abstract pictures of these crashing electrical wavefronts are identical to the scroll-like waves generated by the famous "cha-otic" Belousov–Zhabotinski chemical reaction. Meanwhile, Paul Rapp, of the Medical College of Pennsylvania, has also been tracking "seizures" in a computer. As electronic brains grow more complex, he reports, they begin to exhibit failures analogous to epileptic convulsions. Brains and high-speed computers both can be easily tipped into chaos.

The Secret Messages of Shopping-Bag Ladies

THE GRASS was still beaded with dew when Roy King arrived. Like a Margaret Mead of the park bench, King was keeping a meticulous record of several homeless "shopping-bag ladies" in a San Jose, California, public park. One of his subjects was sitting rigid on a bench, a petrified Pompeiian mummy with a masklike face. From time to time she'd lift her right arm in a stiff salute and rock back and forth for ten minutes, before going catatonic again. Another pushed a shopping cart full of yellowing newspapers and broken appliances around a fixed route, pausing at intervals to comb her hair with a dirty blue comb. A third woman obsessively circled a bench, head bowed, muttering the same malignant phrases over and over. The tape recorder in her brain seemed stuck in one place, condemned to repeat one terrible message forever, like the "black box" of a crashed airliner.

For five days in a row, King timed their behavior with a watch. Each of the women (who were evidently chronic schizoprenics) had a "stereotyped routine of movements, postures, and gestures," he noted. "Their activity had an erratically periodic course. The same routine was repeated in the same order roughly every twenty minutes."

Most psychiatrists-in-training don't hang out in public parks timing shopping-bag ladies, but King was chasing a theory. The outlines had come to him while he was still in medical school at Stanford in the late 1970s. He was working at an alternative psychiatric-treatment center in San Francisco, where he was able to observe the "natural evolution of psychosis" in unmedicated patients. Certain rhythms in their behavior struck him as curious. The acute schizophrenics were swaying like pendulums between agitated frenzy and catatonic withdrawal every twenty minutes. The mood and behavior swings of manic patients, in contrast, formed regular ninety-minute cycles, like the cycles of REM and non-REM sleep.

"What I saw was that people were fluctuating between opposite states," he tells us. "And a light bulb went off in my head. I saw that the key to psychotic behavior was not *too much* or *too little* of a specific neurotransmitter. It was unstable fluctuations in a chemical system."

Fortunately King had a Ph.D. in math from Cornell under his belt. He went to his computer, plugged in the variables for dopamine synthesis and release, and in 1981 "Catastrophe Theory of Dopaminergic Transmission: A Revised Dopamine Hypothesis of Schizophrenia" was published. (Catastrophe theory is not about earthquakes and towering infernos; it refers to the sudden jumps and phase transitions that nonlinear systems are prone to.) The gist of the theory is that the key to schizophrenia is chaotic fluctuations in dopamine production. As King explains it, he draws neat diagrams and graphs in our notebook: a synapse with DA (dopamine) hovering in the presynaptic terminal, a curve shaped like a *U*, a chain of jagged peaks and valleys (dopamine release plotted against time). When his equations spawned a telltale, U-shaped curve, King did a double take. That classic nonlinear curve said that the dopamine system was unstable, extremely sensitive to small inputs. A relatively minor influence could set off wild bursts of dopamine release. Plotting the time course, King got steep waves of dopamine release that spanned twenty minutes from peak to peak. This exactly matched the behavioral rhythms he'd observed in psychotic patients.

The model also said that a schizophrenic's dopamine neurons would start to fire in two different rhythms and rapidly become uncoupled. Could this be the organic basis of the psychological splitting Eugen Bleuler had in mind when he coined the word *schizophrenia*? "I think that in schizophrenia the brain fragments into active and inactive clusters of neurons and different parts of the brain become dissociated," says King. "You might get an asymmetry between the left and right side, say. Schizophrenics often feel that their minds and bodies are split apart. I had one patient who said her left hand was possessed by a foul, fuming substance and her right hand was pure light, ecstatic, blessed. Another patient said his father put a stake through the left side of his head when he was six years old and that the right side of his head was possessed by his mother, who wanted to have sex with him. When he was most psychotic, he said he felt like Humpty-Dumpty, all in pieces. Therapy helped him reconnect the different parts of himself."

The principle goes beyond schizophrenia. With equations for norepinephrine and its receptors, King has been studying the abstract geometry of panic disorder. "In panic attacks," he says, "you get these bursts of adrenergic [norepinephrine and epinephrine] activity that last five to eight minutes. You get symptoms like tachycardia, cold sweats, confusion, cold extremities, fear. I found that the system was very unstable, supersensitive.

"Why did nature design the brain this way, so that it is highly sensitive to small changes in input? If the brain were linear, you'd have the same sensitivity in every state. It would seem that an organism in the wild needs to be acutely aware of danger. The fight-or-flight reaction has to be very sensitive."

A Mathematics for Biology

IN KING'S MODEL the crucial difference between schizophrenia and sanity is not a quantity but a quality. Not x amount of dopamine or x amount of walking or talking, but the shape of the chemical curve, the *quality* of behavior. This is a key point.

"Topology, or qualitative dynamics [out of which chaotic dynamics grew] is the perfect mathematics for biology," says Alan Garfinkel. "In biology we see forms everywhere, but there is not the numerical precision found in much of physics. People all share the same form, but we differ in the details."

We meet Garfinkel one rainy evening in the bright, mirrored interior of a café-bar in Venice, California. When we leave, our cocktail napkins will be covered with ellipses, spirals, graphs, diagrams of the orbits of the sun, earth, and Jupiter. And the tape recording of our conversation will be laced with the tinkle of ice in glasses, juke-box songs, and shards of local conversations ("I'm getting into bioenergetics these days")—giving it a signal-to-noise ratio comparable to a bad Yoko Ono recording.

"Poincaré is really the father of this whole field," he tells us. "More than half a century ago, he realized that you can't get exact solutions to the equations describing many phenomena, and even if you could they wouldn't tell you what you want to know. If you're studying the motion of the earth around the sun, it's more important to know the shape of its path, its topological type, than the exact distances it travels. Is the orbit an ellipse, or a very long curved line that doesn't close—in which case the earth might eventually spin off into space? So Poincaré invented topology, the science of forms of motion."

At UCLA, where he teaches kinesiology, Garfinkel is applying Poincaré's mathematics to movement disorders, or dyskinesias. He tells us, "The hyperstability of Parkinsonism, the hyper*instability* of Huntington's chorea, and the oscillations seen in various tremors are each characterized by specific forms of movement, and by studying those forms you can infer the neurophysiological processes responsible." Just as coupled pendulums can be jolted into irregular oscillations, Garfinkel theorizes, so can the brain's interlocking chemical feedback loops. The result may be a dyskinesia, chaos in the motor system.

Chaos is not always a bad thing in biology, however, and Garfinkel briefly ticks off the virtues of chaos for us (including the "chaotic mixing" of the rum and coke molecules in our Cuba Libre). More to the point: "I think sensitive dependence on initial conditions in the embryo is what makes us individuals," he says. "As one undifferentiated cell develops into a zillion differentiated cells, there is a distinct sequence of changes. There are epochs of smooth, quantitative change, then—boom—qualitative change and differentiation."

The topological view may discern things in madness, for example, that spinal-fluid samples do not. What is the underlying "form of motion" of schizophrenia, for example? "In schizophrenia," says Garfinkel, "you see two distinct sets of symptoms that are exactly opposite. On the one hand, you have extremely labile [unstable] behavior. You wander quasi-randomly from one thought to another. That's extreme sensitivity to initial conditions. Then, on the other hand, you have very rigid behavior, fixed delusions and obsessions. Everything reminds you of x. Every little thing takes you back to the 'attractor.' Cindy Ehlers thinks chaos is the primary symptom in schizophrenia and the delusional symptoms are the brain's desperate attempt to regain order."

The Mysterious Geometry of Rats

WHEN WE VISIT the Salk Institute, in La Jolla, the Pacific is turning metallic under storm clouds that, depending sensitively on initial conditions, may or may not bring rain. In the room where Jacob Bronowski wrote *The Ascent of Man*, we meet Cindy Ehlers. "What is the difference between walking and dancing, and what does the brain have to do with that?" she says. "I don't think dopamine, a single transmitter out of hundreds, can explain the difference between a walk and dance. How do you measure the *quality* of activity?"

When Ehlers asked herself this question, she thought of what she knew best: EEG analysis. There are sophisticated mathematical operations, such as spectral analysis, for picking out salient patterns in brain waves. Could one analyze behavior as if it were an EEG?

"I took rats and put them in cages with photobeams to measure their locomotor activity. Every time a rat runs through the beam, you get a blip, and it's counted by the computer. Rats are nocturnal; so I recorded their activity at night for five-to-seven-hour periods. And I found there was a natural pattern of locomotor activity. It occurred in bursts every sixty to ninety minutes.

"Then, I thought, Why not use this model to study the effects of psychoactive drugs? The standard paradigm is to give the rat a very high dose of a drug and see whether it jumps up on a shelf or something. I wanted to see how drugs in *low dosages* would affect activity—the *quality* of activity. So I looked at the activity record as if it were an EEG. What were the frequency components? What is the amplitude? That is, if I draw a line through it and say this is the mean, what is the variance?"

The result? Sure enough, lithium, Valium, antidepressants, caffeine, amphetamine, and other mind drugs produced characteristic patterns in the rats' odysseys. Ehlers draws them for us on the blackboard: jagged spikes; little, bunched waves; lopsided waves; regular, languid waves. "On lithium the activity was much more randomized," she tells us. "It blocked the bursts. Antidepressants had the opposite effect: The spikes got bigger. On caffeine you got tight, little waves. It increased the mean activity, but the variance went down. That makes sense when you think of caffeine: People say they can be more focused. Amphetamine increased the mean and the variance."

Later she did EEG studies and found they corresponded strikingly to the behavior patterns. "Maybe what brings the whole system together from behavior to the EEG down to enzymes is this frequency organizer," she reflects. "Arnold Mandell says frequency is a basic language, a global property. . . . A description of consciousness may be a description of the variability of mental states and the organization of those states in time. In preliminary studies of TM meditators, for example, it looks like the variance of the EEGs is reduced. I'd like to find out, What does that state mean cognitively?"

When Farmer, Garfinkel, King, and other chaos cognoscenti checked out the waveforms Ehlers was getting out of her computer, "they started realizing the brain was emitting patterns similar to the patterns produced by equations for hydrodynamic flow."

Freud, Jung, and Strange Attractors

ARNOLD MANDELL sees a lesson for psychiatry in the nocturnal journeys of the Salk rats. If a computer followed *your* tail for many hours, many days, or many years, he thinks, your random odyssey would have a shape as distinctive as your signature. Human behavior has its underlying geometries, if you know how to look. "William James's 'preconscious stream' is a random walk," he says, "but an order emerges over time. How is it that your thoughts are in flux from moment to moment, yet you remain the same person with the same mind? The concept of deterministic chaos can resolve that paradox. It's like an almanac, which is better than a three-day weather forecast."

The first time he heard Doyne Farmer describe a strange attractor— "This thing just can't wait to roll itself up," he remembers Farmer saying of some hydrodynamic phenomenon—Mandell was hooked. To penetrate the cryptic geometries that, he felt, must be in neurons as surely as in convection currents and rising columns of cigarette smoke, he spent five or six years teaching himself difficult differential equations. "This is a bitch," he confides. "It's the hardest thing I've ever done." But he did it well enough, apparently, to win a MacArthur Foundation Prize in 1984.

"Whether you're talking about electricity or water or clouds or the brain or the behavior of crowds," he says, leaning forward in his chair and fixing us with his electric eyes, "there are only a few plays, a few dances.

"I think of Doyne's incredible image. You take a bunch of dots—those are the initial values in a computer system—and throw them on the attractor. Do they get together and make waves? Or do they spread out all over the attractor? The attractor is like a magnet. It looks random, but over the course of time it makes a shape. The brain is like that. A personality is like that.

"What Freud discovered was very profound. If you put a person in an office in Vienna in 1900, turned out the lights, and had him say whatever came into his mind, there were only a few basic patterns: the obsessive, the compulsive, the hysteric, the psychopath. Out of the infinite possibilities of free association, only a few 'myths,' like the Oedipal myth and the castration-anxiety myth, recurred again and again. The details of the personality might be different—one person might be a doctor, another might be a plumber—but at a deeper level there were only a few patterns of resistance against the stress of circumstances. In a sense when a psychiatrist looks at a person, he is taking infinite dimensions and making a 'low-dimensional attractor,' a simple myth that ties everything together. Oral desperation, or anal ambivalence; control, or pride, or sexual jealousy."

On his blackboard Mandell clears a "phase space" and draws a point attractor and a limit cycle. "If you get stuck anywhere," he says, "you might get a disease. This"—he indicates the point—"might be death. This"—his chalk goes round and round in the endless circle of a limit cycle—"might be manic-depressive disease." The limit cycle also reminds him of obsessions, fixed ideas, the circling "stereotypes" of rats on high-dose amphetamines, and the obsessive detail of speed art. "The obsessive style is too coherent, like a limit cycle," he says. "You go round and round in the same circle. 'People are bad.' 'Relationships are like that.' We all have a little of that.

"These were the only dynamical stabilities we knew about until a few years ago. Then this new one was found." He scrawls a spiky, bristling strange attractor. "This might be that Christian church I told you about. Those kids do a lot of far-out things. They speak in tongues, have visions, read the Bible, and say, 'I'll do it, Lord,' but they are stable because they've surrendered to God. I think that's the stability of the strange attractor. It is phaseless, but it's definitely a shape.

"I think," he adds, "we all oscillate between two brain states: the laminar [the smooth flow described by a fixed or periodic attractor] and the chaotic. You can see the dynamics of the two hemispheres that way. The left brain is laminar, orderly. It gets home by saying, 'Two blocks left, one block right, six blocks north.' The right brain just gets home by the geometry. It's a disorganized flow, a strange attractor. Freud saw the obsessive and the hysteric as the yin and yang of the personality continuum. I think these are the two basic brain styles, and every personality is some mixture of the two.

Hang out with chaos long enough and it will become a personal philosophy. The paradoxical "bounded madness" of the strange attractor is like a Zen koan, the mathematical equivalent of "What is the sound of one hand clapping?" Many of the chaos people we met spoke like poets and mystics—Ralph Abraham, who once spent seven months in India with a guru, is exploring the Vedic theory of vibrations in a computer simulation of neurons—and Mandell is no exception. The worldview he wears on his T-shirt (BOUNDED CHAOTIC MIXING PRODUCES STRANGE STABILITY) is not as succinct as $E = mc^2$. But it has cosmic resonances for Mandell.

It means: "You have greater stability if you surrender to God." It means Jung instead of Freud. "Freud's paradigm is ego determinism: 'I cause it.' Jung's is a different sort of causality—mythic, a word church. I think that's closer to the way the world works." It means "nonattachment, the mysterious theme of the *Bhagavad-Gita*."

He shows us a picture of a strange attractor spawned by a computer simulation of a pituitary cell's response to tropic hormones. "Otto Rössler, a German theoretical chemist, stood in front of his analog computer and saw one of the first ones like this and went psychotic," he tells us. "It was like a hallucinogen psychosis, I'm sure."

The Lewis Carroll landscape of chaos can do weird things to your head. If you make a cross section of a doughnut, you get a circle. If you make a cross section of a strange attractor, you get an infinite regress of folds-within-folds-within-folds like nesting Chinese boxes. Magnify an inch of one fold, and you'd see more folds inside, with the same rich detail repeated in miniature. It is like a map of the English coastline each curve of which, when enlarged, contains a smaller version of the coastline, and so on ad infinitum. Mandell thinks the brain is a little like that.

"Whatever way you slice it, the brain shows you infinity with the same face," Mandell says. "I've gotten the same patterns now from dopamine receptors, from the enzyme tyrosine hydroxylase that makes dopamine, from the serotonin receptors, from single-cell recordings, from EEGs, all the way up to behavior. Your style, whatever it is, is imprinted in every neuron. It appears in your EEGs and in your handwriting, in the way you brush your teeth and the way you keep your car. At every level, down to the atomic, I think you'd find you see the same dance, the same scenario. It's a signature. A year of your life, if we could describe it geometrically, would have the same 'coastline' as your day.

"If you give someone lithium, it changes all the dances, at all the levels. It randomizes things, creating an ionic mesh of 'noise' in the water. The waves are less bunched, less phased, less coherent. Tricyclic antidepressants [such as Elavil and Tofranil] do the reverse: They speed things up so you get to the next state faster.

"Cocaine and amphetamine produce kindling, the waves become phased. If you look at the character disorder that cocaine produces, it's as if random events become organized into one frequency. You're very positive about everything, arrogant, monotonic. I think Freud described a cocaine slice of the brain. He got very nasty, territorial, and defensive in his later papers.

"Hallucinogens, I think, are strange attractors. They scramble detail; they disorganize. When enough detail is scrambled, all you can hang on to is the underlying geometry. If you're used to the sequential, laminar mode, you can panic. But sometimes for the compulsive who has known only the laminar mode, they can add a new dimension."

Needless to say, the brain Mandell contemplates does not look anything like a wiring diagram. It is not a switchboard or a computer but something like a soup—uncertain, fluid, full of nonlinear eddies and currents.

"To study a neurotransmitter in a test tube," he explains, "you add the precursor enzymes and co-factor enzymes, then measure the rate at which the transmitter is produced. Most researchers add enzymes at concentrations a thousand times greater than those found in the brain. At such large concentrations, the biochemical reactions move toward equilibrium at an orderly rate. The graph is a smooth curve. But when we used low biochemical concentrations like those in the brain, the lines on our graphs started wiggling and dancing like crazy. I've flown all over the country with these graphs, and some of the finest brain scientists told me they were just noise, garbage, because they don't have a linear behavior. But I'm trying to *map* the wiggles.

"You get these wiggles in any nonlinear system. They're the vortices you see if you put a rock in the path of a fast-moving stream. They have an order of their own. We can map them, but they're not inches or milligrams; they're *dances*.

"I think we'll understand the global things about the brain—temper, impulsivity, obsession, hysteria—before we figure out how we see or how we drive a nail," he tells us. "There is deep order in there that we can get at with some of these mathematical tools. Now we're asking things like, When do you 'come down' from a hallucinogen? Maybe you never really do.

"The brain's gonna change," he assures us. "I should have been a buyer in a department store. I can call these things."

A Higher Form of Order

ONE OF THE KEY INSIGHTS of chaos is that, as Alan Garfinkel puts it, "Chaos is not disorder; it is a higher form of order." The loops of randomness in nature, the lumps, wiggles, whorls, eddies, and nonlinearities in a system, contain information. The "noise" self-organizes and creates complex patterns. When you heat a fluid past a critical value, for instance, millions of individual molecules, as if on cue, organize themselves into hexagonal cells. A similar process happens inside your brain.

"In the brain individual molecules may appear to be behaving randomly," W. Ross Adey tells us, over prefab chili dogs in the ultramodern cafeteria of Pettis Memorial Veterans Administration Hospital in Loma Linda, California. "And if you look at electrical processes, the noise at the synapse appears random. If you go from the atomic level all the way up to systems at the ganglia, you get randomness. But at each level some aspect of order emerges.

"When I say order," he explains, "I mean that a certain *graininess* appears that makes it nonrandom. It shapes itself into something."

One of the shapes is the EEG, the complex, shifting patterns of many neurons firing in unison. "There is an organizing principle in the EEG we don't really understand yet," as Cindy Ehlers puts it. "In the language of chaos, it may eventually be defined as an 'attractor.'"

On a warm April day we rent a car in Los Angeles and drive eastward to La Loma, a Seventh-Day Adventist town in the shadow of the San Bernardino mountains. They are stark, lavender, otherworldy mountains, the arid flanks of which make one think of John Wayne movies and the bleached bones of pioneers who never made it across the desert. Adey came here from UCLA's prestigious Space Biology Lab, which he directed during the 1960s and early 1970s. In a reductionist age, he became something of a lone ranger.

"Thirty-odd years ago, the British biologist J. Z. Young gave a series of lectures for the BBC," he tells us. "He said if he were to build a model of the brain he would liken it to a telephone exchange. Calls come in and the operators plug circuits in and out, directing calls to the proper recipients. But the operators would also be doing a lot of eavesdropping, and they would *whisper together* about the things they overheard. And Young saw this whispering as the fundamental function of brain tissue. Not the impulses going through the switchboard, but what the cells picked up from the traffic and whispered about among themselves."

In the traditional, connectivist model of the brain, all communication passes through the individual "switches" of the synapses, and the elementary unit of cognition, the essential information carrier, is the individual nerve impulse. Adey disagrees. "Every organism needs its sewage system," he says of the nerve impulse. He is part of the "globalist" camp, which sees the brain's real language as the synchronized "whispering together" of millions of neurons—the EEG.

"One of my earliest experiences in neurobiology," he says, "was studying the central nervous system of a giant, five-foot-long earthworm. It has a little brain with only two hundred neurons arranged in a pallisade. And yet the worm has a complex repertoire of behaviors. This would not be possible if everything depended on the impulse system. There aren't enough cells.

"The first thing that happens in the nervous system is the transmission of wavelike information between cells, and not impulses. There's this slow, wavelike process we call the EEG. God didn't put it there as something funny for humans to observe."

Unlike the discrete voltage spike of the nerve impulse, the EEG is a continuous wave that has sometimes been viewed as mere background noise, the "noise of the brain's motor." But to Adey the EEG has "signatures in it of great importance." At the Space Biology Lab he analyzed the EEGs of chimpanzees playing tic-tac-toe, of hallucinating schizophrenics, and of NASA pilots and astronaut candidates performing different mental tasks. Whether or not it could foretell how a mind would process celestial navigation data in a claustrophobic capsule on the far side of the moon, the EEG did contain signatures of "truthfulness," "correct decision making," "auditory vigilance," and "specific hallucinatory behaviors," according to Adey.

Furthermore, he insists, an individual brain cell "senses" the surrounding electromagnetic waves. If a weak electromagnetic field is applied to the head, neurons will synchronize their firing to the surrounding rhythm. When Adey's team put a monkey's head inside a radiomicrowave field that pulsed to the same frequency as the brain's alpha waves (a slow, seven-to-ten-hertz rhythm that accompanies relaxed states), the animal's EEG became locked in phase with the external field. Its brain started to produce more alpha. "In one case, the monkey had to press a lever every five seconds to get apple juice. When we applied a seven-hertz field, the animal's estimate of time sped up by one second. Maybe these fields alter our circadian rhythms."

If this is so, it's a bit ominous, for we're surrounded by weak electromagnetic currents. Can the waves flowing out of telephone lines, transmission towers, radar installations, video display terminals, and microwave appliances alter the mind like a psychoactive drug? Do they make us irritable or calm, sleepy, alert, forgetful, or depressed?

For years it has been rumored that the Russians have a mind-control machine. They do, and, as part of a Soviet-American scientific exchange program, they've loaned one to Adey. An odd-looking contraption made out of vacuum tubes and other components of World War II vintage, it is an electrical tranquilizer called the Lida. Adey and his colleagues tested it by putting a nervous cat in a metal box and the Lida next to it. When the machine began to hum and broadcast radio waves in the frequency of deep-sleep EEGs, the cat went into a trance. "Instead of taking a Valium to relax yourself," says Adey, "it looks as if a similar result could be achieved with a radio field." Soviet scientists claim they've used the Lida to treat insomnia, hypertension, anxiety, and "neurotic disturbances." (Of course, if a tranquilizing field is possible, so is an anxiety-producing field, and there are rumors of a more sophisticated version of the Lida that is capable of long-distance mind control.)

None of this is *supposed* to be possible, according to the switchboard doctrine, because these fields are far too weak to trigger a nerve impulse. But Adey showed that fields too weak to make a cell fire an impulse changed the way charged calcium ions bound to the membrane, setting off powerful chemical reactions within the cell.

"We have seen this terrible era in the last twenty years when engineers have proudly prated that the brain is like a computer," he tells us. "Well, it is and it isn't. The part that is *not* like a computer is the fundamental part of brain function. A computer is totally linear. We have evidence of tremendously nonlinear interactions in the brain. A linear equilibrium model cannot explain why a field at twenty hertz has much more powerful effects on brain chemistry than a field at sixty hertz."

Slime Mold and Society

Look at this egg: with it you can overthrow all the schools of theology and all the churches in this world. What is this egg? . . . How does this mass evolve into a new organization, into sensitivity, into life? . . . First there is a speck which moves about, a thread growing and taking color, flesh being formed, a beak, wing-tips, eyes, feet coming into view. . . . Now the wall is breached and the bird emerges, walks, flies, feels pain, runs away, comes back again, complains, suffers, loves, desires, enjoys. . . . And will you maintain, with Descartes, that it is an imitating machine pure and simple?

—DENIS DIDEROT,
d'Alembert's Dream

IF YOUR BRAIN had no "noise" in it, you would lack both free will and individuality. As Mandell puts it, "Your personality is the style of your noise." If every input triggered a determined, linear output, you would be a flesh-and-blood automaton, a "meat computer," incapable of hatching a new idea. "A linear system cannot generate new information," says CalTech's John Hopfield, the father of the forgetful computer. "If you are trying to build a system that can reconstruct a total memory from partial information, you need a nonlinear system."

"In a computer you have to round off at nine places," says Mandell. "There is noise at the boundaries, and if you let it, that noise can begin to shape itself into something. The not-quite-rightness gets bigger in time. It self-organizes. The brain has this spontaneous, self-organizing activity, like clouds, air, and water. It makes eddies and whorls. As you go from the level of neurons, to electromagnetic fields, to a person, to a family, to a society, you get emergent properties."

But how does noise shape itself into something? How does order arise out of disorder? How do cells floating in a sea of extracellular fluid give rise to ideas, the "causal potency" of which, in Roger Sperry's words, "[becomes] just as real as that of a molecule, a cell, or a nerve impulse?" Who or what is directing the traffic, giving the orders, drawing the blueprints?

Well, consider slime mold. Alan Garfinkel did, and was fascinated by the organism's ability to self-organize. "When I first saw it, I said, 'Alan, stop what you're doing; this is the most beautiful thing in the world.'" You and I might not see the attraction in the green slime that coats the surface of stagnant ponds, but to the connoisseurs of chaos it is a paragon of emergent order.

"The creature has two life phases," Garfinkel explains. "In the first,

The Belousov-Zhabotinski reaction, above, discovered in the early 1960s, is a classic example of self-organization in nature. Traditionally, chemical reactions were supposed to return to equilibrium, but as these particular inorganic chemicals react, a pattern of scroll-like waves unfolds in a shallow petri dish solution. If dyes are added, the solution can be seen oscillating from red to blue to red, as the constituent molecules spontaneously organize themselves into a "chemical clock." The equations describing the Belousov-Zhabotinski reaction can also be applied to the metamorphosis of slime mold, the internal dynamics of a hallucinating brain, and other phenomena in nature. (*Fritz Goro*)

it's a single-celled amoeba that crawls around, leading its own little life. But when it's deprived of food—bacteria—it undergoes a radical transformation, a phase transition. It starts pulsing a chemical messenger, cyclic AMP, which signals to all the other amoebas. They all start to cluster, in beautiful wavelike patterns, into colonies of thousands of cells. Then an amazing thing happens. The colonies, originally homogeneous, undergo an internal transformation and become *one differentiated animal*.

"The front part becomes a head; the back, a stalk. The body becomes spores covered with hard cases. They break away, the cases crack open, and out come individual amoebas, completing the life cycle. You get this incredible, structured, differentiated, organized piece of macroscopic order out of individual cells!"

Believe it or not, there are equations to describe this process, and the pattern the slime mold forms is the "solution." The equations have a self-organizing property that, in this case, transforms a loose collection of unicellular creatures into a single, many-celled animal. But the same property operates in many parts of nature, including the Belousov–Zhabotinski chemical reaction, and some scientists suspect it is the hidden factor in morphogenesis, turning a spherical, undifferentiated fertilized egg cell into a complex, structured, differentiated animal or human being. (Is this the answer to Diderot's question?)

Slime mold also offers a model for the emergence of human social order, Garfinkel thinks. How do societies, nations, global economic systems, trade unions, and so on arise out of the random, unpredictable behavior of individuals? How is it that we all agree to drive on the right side of the road, to observe a nine-to-five workday, and to file our income taxes on April 15? "The total state of the system will move to a certain attractor—say, cooperation—even if the individual doesn't consciously intend it," says Garfinkel.

The dramatic reorganization of slime mold occurs when the individual amoebas begin pulsing to the same rhythm, a phenomenon known as "phase locking" or "phase entrainment." Crickets and fireflies do this, too, chirping or flashing in concert, and there is a widely observed tendency for the menstrual cycles of women living together to become synchronized. Lovers sleeping together will naturally breathe in unison. And, Garfinkel tells us, a mechanical "breathing" teddy bear has been used to stabilize the breathing of infants with breathing arrhythmias, for the baby's respiration automatically becomes entrained to the bear's. Perhaps, he suggests, some of our social conventions, such as the nine-to-five workday, involve an analogous frequency entrainment. It is the nature of things to beat in unison—neurons not excepted (as we have just seen from Ross Adey's experiments).

> Kilgore Trout once wrote a short story which was a dialogue between two pieces of yeast. They were discussing the possible purposes of life as they ate sugar and suffocated in their own excrement. Because of their limited intelligence, they never came close to guessing that they were making champagne.
>
> —KURT VONNEGUT,
> *Breakfast of Champions*

Question: When you think, what thinks? Do your individual brain cells think? Does a neuron possess a quantum of consciousness? We think the answer is no—even though there is a school of thought that sees the neuron as an atom of cognition, as in Hubel and Wiesel's feature detector cells, which "recognize" lines or edges. It seems unlikely that a neuron can know, perceive, or feel sorry—even a little bit. A single neuron is mindless. How then does it produce a mind? No matter how many billions of mindless things you put together, they could never make a mind, could they? Well, the paradoxical laws of chaos suggest that they *could*.

There is no Hobbesian sovereign to hold the social contract of slime mold together; no king amoeba or supervisor amoeba to give orders: "Just move one centimeter to the right, next to Harry, there." And individual amoebas are no more aware of the grand scheme than the bits of yeast in Kilgore Trout's story. But nonlinear equations show that the behavior of a million amoebas, a million atoms, a million people, or a million neurons can be *totally different* from the behavior of one. Thus the slime-mold organism is emphatically more than the sum of its parts. No matter how conscientiously you probe a single amoeba, you won't uncover the dynamics of slime mold. Only when tens of thousands of amoebas are packed together does this startling self-organizing property operate.

A New Dialogue with Nature

THIS PICTURE of a self-organizing world constitutes a "new dialogue with nature," according to Ilya Prigogine, a Belgian theoretical chemist and 1977 Nobel laureate. "I think," he remarks, "we are beginning to perceive nature on earth in exactly the opposite way we viewed it in classical physics. We no longer conceive of nature as a passive object. . . . I see us as nearer to a Taoist view in which we are embedded in a universe that is not foreign to us."

The universe of classical physics is static and lifeless, according to Prigogine, because it is based on closed, equilibrium systems, which are artificial. "In order to produce equilibrium," he writes in *Order Out of Chaos*, "a system must be 'protected' from the fluxes that compose nature. It must be 'canned' so to speak, or put in a bottle like the homunculus in Goethe's *Faust*. . . . "

You might say we have been studying the brain in an airtight glass jar. When we refrigerate brain tissue and puree it in a blender, we freeze time. By studying artificial still lifes—dead tissue sections and static micrographs—we miss the brain's moment-to-moment transformations. A real, living brain is constantly reshaping itself, down to the level of synapses and receptors.

"The brain is self-organizing," says Berkeley's Walter Freeman, who uses nonlinear dynamics to discern the shape of an olfactory "search image" in the electrical din of sixty-four electrodes. "That's where free will comes in. This is only true of open systems, where there's traffic of matter and energy with the surrounding environment. As far as the brain is concerned, the body is just as much outside as the external environment."

Newton's universe was a rationalized machine wound by a clockmaker

God, and the mechanical Cartesian body harbored a ghost. Long after science tossed out the clockmaker and the ghost, the machine lives on. Our favorite contemporary model for the brain is the computer, which, of course, requires an external program to animate it. (The central faith of artifical intelligence, that the brain's "software" can be lifted from its organic "hardware" and duplicated by a processor of symbols, can be seen as a form of mind/body dualism.) In a world that is a cold, lifeless, perpetual-motion machine, man and nature, mind and matter, seem to be made of different stuff.

Now, however, we see that matter itself has a kind of soul. "Just heat it up and it will make itself into something," as Mandell puts it. Instead of winding down, as the second law of thermodynamics (entropy) predicts, the world progresses from disorder to order. The detritus of the Big Bang coalesced into stars and solar systems. Life-forms sprang out of the pre-biotic mush on earth and grew increasingly complicated as a result of chaos (copying errors) in the DNA code—eventually producing the exquisite information system of a human brain. (Doyne Farmer, for one, suspects that evolution wasn't *completely* random, like a million monkeys banging on the keys of a million typewriters until they accidentally produce all the plays of Shakespeare. Rather, he theorizes, the "DNA of higher organisms evolved to enhance certain errors 'on purpose' and to repress others.")

The quintessence of nature's self-organizing principle is consciousness. In an Oregon laboratory a well-known faith healer, Olga Worrell, recently tested her powers on the Belousov–Zhabotinski reaction. According to a report in *Brain/Mind Bulletin*, the chemical solution treated by Worrell produced organized waves twice as fast as a control solution. "We have demonstrated the ability of a healer to influence the self-organizing behavior of an experimental system," one of the researchers concluded. The idea was that "paranormal" healers might be enhancing the body's self-organizing processes, its ability to counteract entropy and decay.

But paranormal feats aside, consciousness arranges randomness into patterns every day. According to Hobson and McCarley's theory of dreams, the reticular activating system, for purely physiological reasons of its own, fires meaningless nerve signals, which the storyteller of the neocortex weaves into a dream tale. Human memory is a "story," not a faithful transcript. Out of Rorschach inkblots the mind makes faces, poplar trees, church spires; in the night sky it sees constellations, celestial bears, archers, and dippers. It orders biological forms into phyla, genera, and species; chemicals into the Periodic Table of the Elements; stones into cathedrals; letters of the alphabet into *Moby Dick* and *Don Quixote*. Confronted with a bunch of dots, the mind naturally plays connect-the-dots.

On Ghosts and Machines

WE ARE NEARING the end of our journey around the nation's brain labs, a journey we started with a handful of questions as ancient as Plato. Whence do our ideas, dreams, and emotions spring? Is the brain in the mind? Can a three-pound organ the texture of warm porridge account for consciousness?

We have talked to drug designers, computer jocks, dream technicians, pharmacologists, phenomenologists, hallucination engineers, Freudians, behaviorists, lucid dreamers, rat runners, mystical psychiatrists, mind controllers, and inner space explorers. We have looked inside the brain with PET scans and electrodes to find the source of dementia and madness. We have tracked the relation between chemical messengers and mental illness, between dreams and electrical activity in the reticular activating system, between memory and alterations at the synapse. We have met reptile superegos, surprise waves, pleasure centers, multiple personalities, "dream state generators," boss monkeys, talking apes, and talking right hemispheres.

Our initial questions began to fall by the wayside. Caught up in the marvels of opiate receptors and neural networks, we stopped asking about ghosts in the machine. The machine seemed remarkable enough, with or without ghosts. But have the ghosts been exorcised?

Several years ago we met a man who had built a ghost-catcher. It was an elaborate arrangement of random-number generators, polygraphs, amplifiers, and so on. A team of physicists had designed an electrically shielded box equipped with sensors, special metal gauges "extremely sensitive to vibrations." The gauges were connected to an amplifier, which multiplied any vibrations in the metal, and sent them to a polygraph machine for measurement. With this machine parapsychologist Karlis Osis was trying to "catch an apparition."

A pale, white-haired man of rather ghostly mien, Osis has investigated haunted houses, mediums, poltergeists, psychics, deathbed visions, and other paranormal phenomena for many years. One of his subjects was Alex, a Portland, Oregon, man who from time to time had out-of-body experiences (OBEs) in the lab of the American Society for Psychical Research in New York. While the physical Alex lay swathed in electrodes and electromyographic equipment in one room, his incorporeal self, which he calls "Alex Projection Two," would journey to the room next door. This was the "apparition" Osis wished to catch.

Alex was instructed to go into the room next door during his OBE and crawl inside the machine's little box ("Alex Two can change his size"), and "without telling him we were monitoring him," Osis and his colleagues

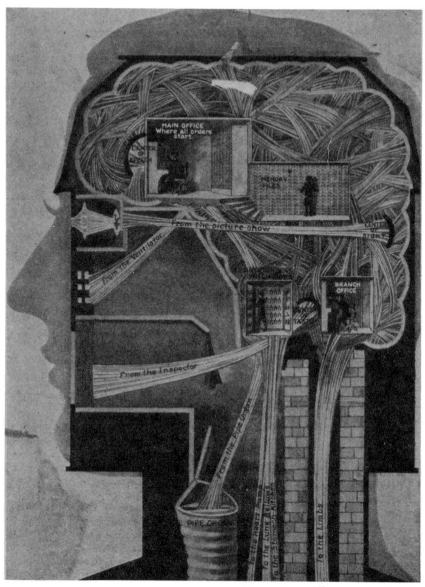

"Headquarters": One of many mechanistic representations of the organ of thought. Of course, memories are *not* neatly filed in one neural filing cabinet, nor is there a "main office, where all orders start." If the brain were structured as such a rigid hierarchy, the loss of a single neuron might suffice to turn us into vegetables. (*The Bettmann Archive*)

looked for any vibrations his etheric double would trigger in the metal. "So far," he told us, "we have very encouraging results."

Maybe so. But our encounter with Osis served to convince us that it is no easy matter to catch a ghost in a machine. "An apparition," as he put it, "is a very slippery fish." You may say you don't believe in ghosts, but in fact you are surrounded by them. Not wan beings of ectoplasm, perhaps, but things that are not easily caught in a material net. "Is what you thought yesterday still part of your mind?" Rudy Rucker asks, in *Infinity and the Mind*. "If you own and use an encyclopedia are the facts in that encyclopedia part of your mind? Does a dream which you never remember really exist? . . . Would the truths of mathematics exist if the universe disappeared? Did the Pythagorean theorem exist before Pythagoras? If three people see the same animal, we say the animal is real; what if three people see the same idea?"

The newcomer to the brain lab is awed by the high-tech rites of spike counting and frequency measurement, by intracellular amplifiers, signal averagers, and voltage-controlled oscillators. Rats are conditioned in computerized shuttle boxes that print out histograms of their reflexes, amid drinking and feeding monitors and startle-reflex meters. The brain is explored with "vibroslice tissue cutters"; radioimmunoassay antisera for bombesin, somatostatin, Substance P; scanning electron microscopes; osmotic pumps that deliver measured amounts of drugs to an animal's brain around the clock; and many other intimidating tools.

If he or she is lucky or skilled or both, a neuroscientist may snare a faint trace of mind. A conditioned gill-withdrawal reflex in *Aplysia californica*, a neuron that "recognizes" vertical lines, a statistical correlation between suicide and a breakdown product in spinal fluid, a "shadow of thought" (in Alan Gevins's phrase) in an EEG. Yet apparitions remain. The late Karl Lashley, trying to catch one with his scalpel, patiently cut up rat brains for twenty-five years, with the "memory center" always receding before him like a watery blue mirage on the Nevada highways. The cause of schizophrenia has proved so elusive that many researchers, we were told, have given up and gone into the depression business instead. Of the estimated 200 chemical transmitters in our heads, more than 150 are still incognito.

When we ask "Is the mind in the brain?" we assume we know what we mean. But after our journey around the organ of thought, the mind appears a far murkier thing than Descartes's *res cogitans*. Where is the mind under anesthesia, in a coma, in the final stages of Alzheimer's disease? Where is the mind of a multiple personality when an alter ego is on stage? Can a Korsakoff's patient who has lost all his memories be said to have a mind?

Do dogs possess consciousness? Does a disconnected right hemisphere? A disconnected left hemisphere? A newborn baby? A baby in utero? A talking chimpanzee? *Aplysia californica?* A computer?

When he divided the world into mind and matter, Descartes was consulting his senses. Matter was *res extensa*, a solid body occupying physical space, while mind (*res cogitans*) could not be apprehended by the senses. "It is ironic that such important problems should be frozen into old molds," Don Walter remarks. On a certain night in the early 1600s, he tells us, Descartes had a series of dreams on which he based much of his philosophy. Reexamining those seminal dreams three centuries later, a psychoanalyst named B. D. Lewin concluded that Descartes actually suffered an unrecognized epileptic fit and that the divorce between his cogitating self and his extended self was a dream solution to his feelings of loss of bodily control. What a curious irony—if the classic formulation of the mind/body problem were the result of a brain pathology!

In any case the line of demarcation between the mental and the material seems less certain now than it did in the seventeenth century. To Descartes's eyes, walking was a simple mechanical act that did not require a "mind." But we now know walking is a highly complex performance, no less "mental" perhaps than calculating. Indeed machines can solve advanced algebra problems with ease, but navigating in three-dimensional space is a Herculean task for a robot with a computer brain. And what would Descartes have made of a massless particle like the neutrino or of the schizoid existence of light as both particle and wave?

The philosopher Gilbert Ryle, of ghost-in-the-machine fame, called the mind/body problem a "philosopher's myth." It all came from a "category mistake" of Descartes, who, said Ryle, was rather like a bewildered foreign student on a guided tour of Oxford. As the library, the dormitories, the chapel, and so on are pointed out to him in turn, the student keeps asking, "Yes, but where's the *university*?" Asking "Where's the mind?" and finding it nowhere in physical space, Descartes granted it a spectral existence. But mind, says Ryle, is not a thing but a *process*.

Some philosophers liken the brain/mind to the "wavicle" in quantum mechanics. Under certain conditions light behaves as a wave; under other conditions as a particle. Whether it is a particle or wave in a given instance depends on the angle of observation. So it is with the mind/brain. Perhaps dualism is, as Karl Pribram puts it, "the product of conceptual procedures—not of any basic duality in nature." The mind/body problem, in short, may be in the eye of the beholder.

"Go back to the fertilized egg where it all began," psychologist Theodore Barber tells us when we ask him whether he thinks the mind is in the brain, "and then ask where mind comes in. It's obvious that it's both mind and matter from the very beginning. The molecules have mental as well as physical properties in that they have plan and purpose, which are attributes of mind."

Please show us (the seat of consciousness, the memory center, the headquarters of will) on this map.

An illustration from the 1930s depicts the brain as "The Control Station of Your Body." In their separate offices sit a "Manager of Speech," a "Brain Headquarters (in Cerebrum)," a "Manager of Reflex Actions (Cerebellum)," a "Tester of Foods," while in the "Camera Room" industrious "camera operators" run the giant projector of the eye.

Of course, we all know this factory-brain is about as realistic as those ancient maps of the world with their leviathan-infested seas ("Here be dragons") and enchanted isles. But we tend to confuse our more sophisticated "maps"—such as the simplified textbook diagrams of nerve pathways—with the real thing. Hence the reductionist dream of a point-to-point correspondence between a mental event and a brain event, as if, ultimately, our entire mental life could be mapped onto the surface of the cortex. But the more we learn about the organ of consciousness, the further we seem to be from such a wiring diagram.

"What you will be thinking a few minutes from now," says John Hopfield, "is extraordinarily sensitive to what was happening a few minutes ago. And we don't know what relatively minor physical influences—such as light energy of a star shining at night—might affect the state of the system several days from now." Thus no EEG apparatus ever dreamed of could plot the course of the stream of consciousness. Nor can obsession, paranoia, or creativity be explained by measuring microscopic amounts of chemicals or by trying to label neuroreceptors as if they were stuck on a circuit board. "Much of nature," says Mandell, "including this bonded electrochemical jelly in our heads, is like a cat. It'll move and you can relate to it, but you can't control it. You can't make it orderly." The mind is not unlike the Red Queen's croquet game in *Alice in Wonderland*, where the mallets were live flamingos, the balls live hedgehogs that uncurled themselves and ran away at the approach of another "ball," and the soldiers who doubled over to make the "arches" were continually wandering off the field.

The Rat Is Always Right

B.F. SKINNER, king of the behaviorists, once remarked, "The rat is always right."

An exemplary tale: To make autoradiographic maps of neuroreceptors, you must first sacrifice a rat. Laboratory rats are beheaded with miniature guillotines—a fairly humane method, but death is death. On one of our visits to the NIMH we found Candace Pert and her laboratory up in arms. They had just been told to decapitate their rats in the lab rather than in the "animal room" down the hall. The reason: The animal room was full of hundreds of rats in cages, all subjects in various experiments, and someone had just figured out that whenever a rat was killed in the presence of other rats, the other rats *knew*. Indeed, they freaked out, and this mortal fear was contaminating every experiment in the room.

Moral: Even rats live in a world of "ideas." If you do not take these ideas into account, all your graphs, quotients, indices, schedules, and rating scales—the effects of Fluorazepam on sleep latency, motor-activity counts as measured in a Motron Produkter apparatus, baseline blood-pressure readings and EEG recordings prior to shock-induced fighting, the $P<03$ and mg/kg figures—will be meaningless.

A few days later, in a lab full of rows of labeled rat brains, we talk to Miles Herkenham about the mind/body problem. He mentions a philosopher who tried to solve the problem by examining freshly decapitated heads during the French Revolution and who was disturbed to see the bodies jerking after their heads were gone.

"Every time you guillotine a rat," he tells us, "you try not to get the animal all upset. If the rat gets upset, its body will twitch more vigorously even though it's no longer attached to the head. There's this weird time delay. You throw the headless body in the corner of the counter and thirty seconds later it is twitching. Some stress signal got to the body before the head was removed and the body is still responding. . . ."

"But surely there's no *consciousness*?" we ask.

"I don't know," he says. "If I were Aristotle and I saw that, I'd reach some real strange conclusions."

The sight of chickens running around with their heads cut off convinced Aristotle that the mind was in the heart, not the brain. Now we know better, or at least we know the heart is not the organ of thought. But Herkenham doesn't think that luminous star charts of radioactive receptors will solve the mind/brain problem any more than Aristotle's barnyard observations did. After fifteen years of patient scrutiny of the rat cerebrum, he is a confirmed agnostic. "I guess the mind is in the brain, but studying the brain as an organ doesn't answer the question.

"It was because of my original interest in the problem of consciousness that I study the cerebral cortex," he adds. "And I guess it's possible to keep the grand questions in mind when you do research. But here I am spending all my time looking at differences between iodine tritium and some other isotope for autoradiography. I phone up radiation physicists and ask them, 'Is it X rays, gamma rays, or electron emissions that are affecting the film?' How did I get from consciousness to these questions?"

"There's this funny thing that happens to neurophysiologists at about the age of thirty-five or forty," Don Walter tells us. "They get *discouraged*.

"The unspoken ideal of science, is, 'Well, I have to approximate a little in my experiment today, but next week when I get my new instrument I can do better, and next year even better, and eventually it will all become *deterministic*. Scientists treat the P300 wave, for example, as a real object that is obscured by a little noise, and if you just average a little more and take out the noise, you can determine the thing more and more precisely. But that's wrong. You're sitting inside a little telephone booth, getting limited messages from the outside. Maybe the 'noise' is meaningful.

"The metamorphosis that we'll see in neuroscience," he continues, "will be more profound and more existentially upsetting than quantum mechanics. What will our new brain models be like? Well, they might be something like dreams—*Der Traumwerk*, or the 'dreamwork,' as it is rather inelegantly translated in *The Interpretation of Dreams*. A lot of our thinking is like that. Not like Descartes's 'clear and distinct ideas,' but like the stories we tell about the funny things that happen to us in our dreams."

Aphasia, alexia (inability to understand the printed word), hallucinations, delusions, hyperkinesia, tremors, echolalia (parroting of words), echopraxia (parroting of actions), satyriasis (excessive sexuality). Tics, automatisms, catatonia, catalepsy (rigidity of posture), agrypnia (total inablity to sleep), coma, choreas (involuntary "flickering" muscle movements), aphagia (inability to swallow), agnosia (perceptual difficulties), amorphia (inability to judge form), anorexia, orexia (incontinent gluttony). Aboulia (lack of will or initiative), bradykinesia (slowness of movement), tachykinesia (excessive speed of movement), ophthalmoplegia (paralysis of gaze), coprolalia, amimia (loss of expressive capabilities), algolagnia (lust for pain), paralysis, blindness, dementia.

These are a few of the misfortunes that can befall people when their brains are diseased or injured. Like the liturgy of a black mass, the terms conjure worlds infernal, unearthly, unspeakable; zones of nonbeing, of damnation, of eternal torment such as that endured by Prometheus, Sisyphus, and Dante's Paolo and Francesca. Although lobotomy mogul Walter Freeman once pronounced lobotomies no more hazardous than tooth extraction, most of us feel instinctively that the brain is something more than "just another organ."

Computers can do many impressive things: prospect for oil, land a man on the moon, prove mathematical theorems, impersonate a psychiatrist, play chess, design new molecules, and build Chevrolets. But only a brain can synthesize dopamine, adapt to a changing climate, wiggle the big toe, grow new proteins, monitor the environment for enemies, decode wavelengths, invent a new kind of computer, monitor body temperature and gastric fluids, send messages to the glands, and reflect on its own nature—all at the same time.

So where are we? After all the lab rats have been beheaded, all the nerve cells stained with horseradish peroxidase, all the receptors illumined with radioactive ligands, what final truth is revealed to the neuroscientist? Is the brain just a marvelous machine, an accident of evolution, that can be mastered and controlled like any other machine?

We asked Candace Pert, the brilliant, flamboyant discoverer of the opiate receptor, a final question about her science. "Einstein and other physicists," we said, "have described experiencing an almost religious awe when contemplating the laws of the universe. Do you ever feel that way about the brain?"

"No," she said, "I don't feel an awe for the brain. I feel an awe for God. I see in the brain all the beauty of the universe and its order—constant signs of God's presence. I'm learning that the brain obeys all the physical laws of the universe. It's not anything special. And yet it's the most special thing in the universe."

Brainspeak:
A Traveler's Lexicon

action potential the nerve impulse, a transient change in electrical potential across the neural membrane.

affect feeling or mood, general emotional state.

agonist in pharmacology, a drug that mimics the action of a neurotransmitter at the synapse.

alpha wave an EEG pattern of a characteristic frequency (eight to twelve hertz) signifying relaxed wakefulness.

Alzheimer's disease a progressive dementia caused by the death of neurons in a region of the brain called the nucleus basalis.

amplitude the height of a waveform.

amygdala an almond-shaped structure in the limbic system thought to control such emotions as aggression, fear, and rage.

antagonist in pharmacology, a drug that blocks the action of a neurotransmitter at the synapse; the opposite of an **agonist**.

aphasia loss of language ability.

Aplysia an invertebrate marine animal resembling a large, shell-less snail, sometimes referred to as a "sea slug" or "sea hare."

association areas parts of the cortex occupied with higher integrative or symbolic functions rather than direct sensory processing.

automatism a robotlike state in which one performs involuntary acts as if on "automatic pilot."

axon the neuron's "output" side: a single fiber that carries the nerve impulse away from the cell body.

basal ganglia a region at the base of the brain below the cerebral hemispheres comprising the globus pallidus, putamen, and caudate nucleus.

behaviorism a school of psychology that focuses on the objective, measurable parts of behavior (stimulus and response) and ignores the subjective, inner life of the person or animal.

benzodiazepine the class of Valium-like chemicals for which the brain possesses special receptors.

beta-endorphin a morphinelike brain chemical; one of the family of natural opiates collectively known as **endorphins**.

blood-brain barrier a network of membranes between the circulating blood and the brain that prevents some drugs (but not others) from passing into the brain.

brain stem the central core of structures between the spinal cord and the cerebral hemispheres, including the medulla, pons, and midbrain.

Broca's area   a localized center (in the left hemisphere in right-handed people) governing the production of speech.

central nervous system   the brain and spinal cord.

cerebellum   a large, convoluted structure above the pons concerned with motor coordination.

cerebrospinal fluid   the clear fluid filling the ventricles of the brain and the spinal canal.

cerebrum   the largest and uppermost portion of the brain.

chaotic systems   physical systems whose dynamics cannot be predicted with certainty.

chlorpromazine   an antipsychotic drug and major tranquilizer used to treat schizophrenia.

classical conditioning   a paradigm invented by Ivan Pavlov in which an animal is taught to associate a neutral stimulus (such as a bell) with a meaningful one (e.g., food, electrical shock); also known as *Pavlovian conditioning*.

corpus callosum   sheet of white matter connecting the cerebral hemispheres.

cortex   layer of nerve cells forming the outer covering, or "bark," of the cerebrum.

déjà-vu   an inexplicable feeling of familiarity as if everything had happened before; a phenomenon sometimes encountered in temporal lobe epilepsy.

dendrite   one of the fine filaments that branch off from the body of a nerve cell; along it are located multiple synapses, where the neuron receives messages.

diencephalon   one of the major subdivisions of the vertebrate brain, containing the hypothalamus and the thalamus.

dopamine   a neurotransmitter closely related to norepinephrine (noradrenaline) and associated with arousal, mood, etc.; deficient in Parkinson's disease and abnormal in schizophrenia.

dualism   the philosophical doctrine that mind and matter are two separate substances.

electrode   a wire or other conductor used to stimulate the brain with an electrical current or to record spontaneous neural activity.

electroencephalogram (EEG)   the recording of the brain's electrical patterns through electrodes placed on the scalp.

endorphin   the class of natural opiates made by the brain.

engram   memory trace, a putative physical record of a past event.

enkephalin   a brain opiate, a short fragment of the larger beta-endorphin molecule.

enzymes   catalysts produced by living cells that speed up chemical reactions.

event-related potential   the electrical response of the brain to a given stimulus or task; sometimes known as an *evoked potential*.

feature detector   a neuron specialized to perceive one particular feature of the physical world, such as greenness, verticality, etc.

frequency   the number of times an event occurs during a certain period.

frontal lobe   the frontmost of the four major subdivisions of the cortex.

glial cell   a type of brain cell that provides support and nourishment for the neurons; traditionally not thought to play a role in information processing.

glucose   a sugar used in metabolism.

Golgi stain   a dye that stains entire neurons (including the cell body, axons, and dendrites) so that they can be seen under a microscope.

grandmother cell   the ultimate extension of the feature-detector concept—a hypothetical neuron whose exclusive task is to perceive one's grandmother.

gyrus   one of the ridges or convolutions on the brain surface.

habituation   a reduced response to a repeated or constant stimulus.

hemisphere   the right or left half of the cerebrum.

hippocampus   a large, curved structure in the limbic system believed to play an important role in memory.

Huntington's chorea   a hereditary disease in which the neurons of the basal ganglia deteriorate, causing involuntary, jerky muscle movements (*choreas*) and progressive dementia.

hypothalamus   a small structure near the base of the brain that regulates such functions as hormonal activity, thirst, hunger, temperature, sex, and sleep.

idealism   the doctrine that physical objects are really ideas in the mind of some beholder; the opposite of **materialism**.

identity theory   the theory that every mental state is identical with a state of the brain; also known as *psychoneural identity theory*.

ions   charged atoms.

Korsakoff's disease   an alcoholic dementia marked by profound memory loss, disorientation, confabulation, etc.

lesion   tissue damage caused by disease, trauma, or deliberate experiment.

limbic system   a linked ring of structures deep in the forebrain, thought to be the primary seat of the emotions.

lobes   the four major divisions of the cortex.

locus coeruleus   a group of cells in the brain stem that regulates overall arousal as well as the cycles of REM (dreaming) sleep.

materialism   a philosophy that seeks to explain everything in terms of material (physical) laws.

microelectrode   a thin electrode used to record from single neurons.

monism   the philosophy that everything is reducible to a single substance or principle (e.g., matter); the opposite of **dualism**.

motor cortex   a region of the parietal cortex concerned with movement and coordination.

near-death experience (NDE)   the experience of clinical death and subsequent revival.

neural net   an interconnected network of neurons.

neuroleptic   one of the class of major tranquilizers used in the treatment of schizophrenia.

neuron   nerve cell, the structural unit of the nervous system.

neuropeptide   one of the newly discovered family of "brain hormones" (made up of short chains of amino acids) to which endorphins belong.

neurotransmitter   a chemical messenger released by one neuron to act on another at the synapse.

NIH   National Institutes of Health.

NIMH   National Institute of Mental Health.

norepinephrine (noradrenaline)   an excitatory neurotransmitter related to adrenaline; manufactured in the brain by the neurons of the locus coeruleus.

occipital lobe   the hindmost division of the cortex, containing the centers for vision.

ocular dominance columns   in the visual center, alternating bands of neurons representing the input from the right and left visual fields.

opiates   chemicals with a morphinelike structure and similar physiological effects, including heroin, Darvon, methadone, opium, etc.

parietal lobe   the middle division of the cortex, arching over the top of the head and containing the motor and somatosensory areas.

Parkinsonism   a condition of disabling tremors, masklike stare, and muscular rigidity or paralysis, caused by diseased motor pathways in the brain.

pineal gland   a mysterious little gland deep in the brain behind the thalamus; imagined by Descartes to be the liaison between mind and body.

pituitary   an important gland at the base of the brain, once considered the endocrine system's master control center.

positron emission tomography   an imaging technique that maps the brain's chemical activity in cross sections.

receptor   a specialized site where a molecule of a natural transmitter or a drug binds to a nerve cell.

reductionism   a method of explaining complex phenomena by reducing them to simpler, more elementary components.

REM (rapid eye movement) sleep   characteristic fluttering eye movements accompanying periods of dreaming.

reticular activating system   a network of fibers in the core of the brain stem that regulates wakefulness and alertness; also known as the *reticular formation*.

schizophrenia   a serious mental illness usually characterized by hallucinations, delusions, disorders of thought, withdrawal from reality, bizarre emotions, and so on.

sensitization   increased sensitivity to a stimulus.

serotonin   a neurotransmitter made by cells in a part of the brain called the *raphe nucleus*; involved in sleep, mood, appetite, and (possibly) depression and suicide.

somatosensory cortex   a region of the parietal cortex that processes sensations from the body surface—pressure, touch, pain, temperature, and so on.

split brain   a brain divided surgically into autonomous left and right hemispheres.

striate cortex   the primary visual center, located on the undersurface of the occipital lobe.

strange attractor   an abstract mathematical object that describes the dynamics of many natural phenomena, from neurons to waterfalls to the behavior of crowds; also known as a *chaotic attractor*.

sulcus   a groove or furrow in the surface of the brain.

synapse the point where neurons communicate.

synaptic cleft the miniscule gap between the membranes of two neurons.

temporal lobe the region of the cortex above the ears, site of the primary auditory areas.

thalamus a group of sensory relay centers located at the top of the brain stem.

Tourette's syndrome a neurological disorder whose symptoms include uncontrollable bursts of obscene language, grunting, and vocal tics.

triune brain the concept of a three-in-one human brain, composed of semiautonomous reptilian, old mammalian, and human subdivisions.

ventricles fluid-filled cavities within the brain.

wavelength the distance from the crest of one wave to the crest of the succeeding wave.

Wernicke's area a localized center (in the left hemisphere of right-handed people) specialized for the comprehension of speech.

Bibliography

Abraham, Ralph, and Shaw, Chris. *Dynamics: The Geometry of Behavior*. Santa Cruz, Calif.: Aerial Press.

Ayer, A. J. *Philosophy in the Twentieth Century*. New York: Vintage Books, 1982.

Bogen, Joseph E. "The Other Side of the Brain: An Appositional Mind." *Bulletin of the Los Angeles Neurological Societies* 34(3):135–162 (July 1969). (Reprinted in Ornstein [ed.], *The Nature of Human Consciousness*)

Bohm, David. *Wholeness and the Implicate Order*. London: Routledge & Kegan Paul, 1980.

The Brain: A Scientific American Book. New York: Scientific American, 1979.

Bronowski, Jacob. *The Identity of Man*. Garden City, N.Y.: The Natural History Press, 1971.

Brown, Gerald L.; Goodwin, Frederick K.; and Bunney, William E., Jr. "Human Aggression and Suicide: Their Relationship to Neuropsychiatric Diagnoses and Serotonin Metabolism." In *Serotonin in Biological Psychiatry*, edited by B. T. Ho et al. New York: Raven Press, 1982.

Bunge, Mario. *The Mind-Body Problem: A Psychobiological Approach*. Oxford, England: Pergamon Press, 1980.

Bylinsky, Gene. *Mood Control*. New York: Charles Scribner's Sons, 1978.

Calvin, William H., and Ojemann, George A. *Inside the Brain: Mapping the Cortex, Exploring the Neuron*. New York: The New American Library, 1980.

Carroll, Lewis. *The Annotated Alice*. Introduction and Notes by Martin Gardner. New York: The New American Library/A Meridian Book, 1974.

Chomsky, Noam. *Language and Mind*. New York: Harcourt Brace Jovanovich, 1972.

Cooper, Jack R.; Bloom, Floyd E.; and Roth, Robert H. *The Biochemical Basis of Neuropharmacology*. New York: Oxford University Press, 1978.

Crick, Francis, and Mitchison, Graeme. "The Function of Dream Sleep." *Nature* (14 July 1983).

Crow, Timothy J. "Is Schizophrenia a Contagious Disease?" *The Lancet*: 173–175 (22 January 1983).

Crow, Timothy J. et al. "Infection of a Virus-like Agent in CSF of Patients with Schizophrenia, Affective Psychoses, Huntington's Chorea, and Some Neurological Conditions and Attempts to Demonstrate Its Transmission." In *Biological Psychiatry 1981*, edited by C. Perris, G. Struwe, and B. Jansson. Amsterdam: Elsevier/North Holland Biomedical Press, 1981.

Davidson, Julian M., and Davidson, Richard J., eds. *The Psychobiology of Consciousness*. New York: Plenum Press, 1980.

Davis, Glenn C.; Buchsbaum, Monte S.; van Kammen, Daniel P.; and Bunney, William E., Jr. "Analgesia to Pain Stimuli in Schizophrenics and Its Reversal by Naltrexone." *Psychiatry Research* 1:61–69 (1979).

Davis, Joel. *Endorphins: New Waves in Brain Chemistry*. Garden City, N.Y.: The Dial Press, Doubleday & Co., 1984.

Delgado, José M. R. *Physical Control of the Mind: Toward a Psychocivilized Society*. New York: Harper & Row, 1969.

Donchin, Emanuel. "The Use of ERPs to Monitor Non-conscious Mentation" (paper).

Eccles, John C. "Brain and Free Will." (In Globus et al., *Consciousness and the Brain*)

———. "Cerebral Activity and Consciousness." In *Studies of the Philosophy of Biology: Reduction and Related Problems*, edited by F. J. Ayala and T. Dobzhansky. Berkeley, Calif.: Berkeley University Press, 1974.

———. "How Dogmatic Can Materialism Be?" (In Globus et al., *Consciousness and the Brain*)

———. *The Human Mystery*. Springer International, 1979.

Evans-Wentz, W.Y., ed. and comp. *The Tibetan Book of the Dead*. London: Oxford University Press, 1927.

Freeman, Walter J. "A Physiological Hypothesis of Perception." *Perspectives in Biology and Medicine* 24:561–592 (Summer 1981).

Freud, Sigmund. *The Interpretation of Dreams*. Translated and Edited by James Strachey. New York: Avon Books, 1965.

Garfinkel, Alan. "A Mathematics for Physiology." *American Journal of Physiology* 245:R455–R466 (1983).

Gazzaniga, Michael S. "The Split Brain in Man." *Scientific American* (August 1967).

Gazzaniga, Michael S., and Smylie, Charlotte S. "Dissociation of Language and Cognition." *Brain* 107: 145–153 (1984).

Geschwind, Norman. "Specializations of the Human Brain." *Scientific American* (September 1979).

Gevins, Alan et al. "Electrical Potentials in Human Brain During Cognition: New Method Reveals Dynamic Patterns of Correlation." *Science* 213: 918–921 (21 August 1981).

Globus, Gordon G. "The Causal Theory of Perception: A Critique and Revision Through Reflection on Dreams," 1982 (paper).

Globus, Gordon G.; Maxwell, Grover; and Savodnik, Irwin, eds. *Consciousness and the Brain: A Scientific and Philosophical Inquiry*. New York: Plenum Press, 1976.

Goldstein, Avram. "Thrills in Response to Music and Other Stimuli." *Physiological Psychology* 8(1):126–129 (1980).

Goleman, Daniel, and Davidson, Richard J., eds. *Consciousness: Brain, States of Awareness, and Mysticism*. New York: Harper & Row, 1979.

Greenough, William T. "Structural Correlates of Information Storage in the Mammalian Brain: A Review and Hypothesis." *Trends in NeuroSciences* 7(7):229–233 (July 1984).

Gregory, R. L. *Eye and Brain: The Psychology of Seeing*. New York: McGraw-Hill/World University Library, 1966, 1972, and 1977.

Group for the Advancement of Psychiatry (GAP). "What Mysticism Is." From *Mysticism: Spiritual Quest or Psychic Disorder?*, 1976. (Reprinted in Goleman and Davidson, *Consciousness*)

Harlow, Harry F., and Harlow, Margaret K. "Social Deprivation in Monkeys." *Scientific American* (November 1962).

Harth, Erich. *Windows on the Mind: Reflections on the Physical Basis of Consciousness.* New York: William Morrow & Co., 1982.

Heath, Robert J. "Brain Function and Behavior." *Journal of Nervous and Mental Disease* 160(3):159–175 (1975).

———. "Modulation of Emotion with a Brain Pacemaker: Treatment for Intractable Psychiatric Illness." *Journal of Nervous and Mental Disease* 165(5):300–317 (1977).

Heath, R. J.; Rouchell, A. M.; Llewelyn, R. C.; and Walker, C. F. "Cerebellar Patients: An Update." *Biological Psychiatry* 16(10):953–962 (1981).

Herkenham, Miles, and Pert, Candace B. *"In Vitro* Autoradiography of Opiate Receptors in Rat Brain Suggest Loci of 'Opiatergic' Pathways." *Proceedings of the National Academy of the Sciences*, September 1980.

Hofstadter, Douglas R. *Gödel, Escher, Bach: An Eternal Golden Braid.* New York: Basic Books, 1979.

Hofstadter, Douglas R., and Dennett, Daniel C. *The Mind's I: Fantasies and Reflections on Self and Soul.* New York: Basic Books, 1981.

Hubel, David H. "The Brain." *Scientific American* (September 1979).

Hubel, David H., and Wiesel, Torsten N. "Brain Mechanisms of Vision." *Scientific American* (September 1979).

Huxley, Aldous. *The Doors of Perception.* New York: Harper & Row, 1954.

James, William. *The Principles of Psychology* (1890). New York: Dover, 1950.

———. *The Varieties of Religious Experience: A Study in Human Nature.* New York: Collier Books, Collier-Macmillan Ltd., 1961.

Johnstone, E. C.; Owens, D. G. C.; Crow, T. J.; and Jagoe, R. "A CT Study of 188 Patients with Schizophrenia, Affective Psychosis and Neurotic Illness." In *Biological Psychiatry 1981*, edited by C. Perris, G. Struwe, and B. Jansson. Amsterdam: Elsevier/North Holland Biomedical Press, 1981.

Kandel, Eric R. "Psychotherapy and the Single Synapse: The Impact of Psychiatric Thought on Neurobiological Research." *New England Journal of Medicine* 301:1028–1037.

Kandel, Eric R., and Schwartz, James H. *Principles of Neural Science.* New York: Elsevier-North Holland, 1981.

Kaushall, Philip I.; Zetkin, Mark; and Squire, Larry R. "Single Case Study: A Psychosocial Study of Chronic, Circumscribed Amnesia." *Journal of Nervous and Mental Disease* 169(6):383–389 (1981).

King, Roy; Raese, Joachim D.; and Barchas, Jack D. "Catastrophe Theory of Dopaminergic Transmission: A Revised Dopamine Hypothesis of Schizophrenia." *Journal of Theoretical Biology* 92:373–400 (1981).

LaBerge, Stephen. "Lucid Dreaming: Directing the Action as It Happens." *Psychology Today* (January 1981).

———. *Lucid Dreaming: The Power of Being Awake and Aware in Your Dreams.* Los Angeles: Jeremy P. Tarcher, 1985.

Lem, Stanslaw. *The Futurological Congress*. New York: Avon Books/A Bard Book, 1981.

Lilly, John C. *The Center of the Cyclone: An Autobiography of Inner Space*. New York: Bantam Books, 1979.

———. *The Scientist*. New York: Bantam Books, 1981.

Loftus, Elizabeth F., and Loftus, Geoffrey R. "On the Permanence of Stored Information in the Human Brain." *American Psychologist* 35(5):409–420 (May 1980).

Luria, A. R. *The Mind of a Mnemonist: A Little Book About a Vast Memory*. Chicago: Henry Regenery Co., 1968.

———. *The Working Brain: An Introduction to Neuropsychology*. New York: Penguin Press, 1973.

MacLean, Paul. "Brain Evolution Relating to Family, Play, and the Separation Call." *Archives of General Psychiatry* 42:405–417 (April 1985).

———. "On the Evolution of Three Mentalities." In *New Dimensions in Psychiatry: A World View*, Vol. 2, edited by Dr. Silvano Arieti and Dr. Gerard Chrzanowki. New York: John Wiley & Sons, 1977.

MacDonald, Norma. "Living with Schizophrenia." *Canadian Medical Association Journal* 82 (1960). (Reprinted in Goleman and Davidson, *Consciousness*)

Mandell, Arnold J. *Coming of Middle Age: A Journey*. New York: Summit Books, 1978.

———. *The Nightmare Season*. New York: Random House, 1976.

———. "Statistical Stability in Random Brain Processes: Possible Implications for Polydrug Abuse in the Borderline Syndrome." In *Advances in Substance Abuse: Behavioral and Biological Research*, Vol. 2, edited by Nancy K. Mello. Greenwich, Conn.: JAI Press, 1980.

———. "The Sunday Syndrome." *Journal of Psychedelic Drugs* 10: 379–383 (1978).

———. "Toward a Psychobiology of Transcendence: God in the Brain." (In Davidson and Davidson [eds.], *The Psychobiology of Consciousness*)

McCarley, Robert W., and Hobson, J. Allan. "The Neurobiological Origins of Psychoanalytic Dream Theory." *American Journal of Psychiatry* 134(11):1211–1221 (November 1977).

Miller, Jonathan. *States of Mind*. New York: Pantheon Books, 1983.

Mishkin, Mortimer; Malamut, Barbara; and Bachevalier, Jocelyne. "Memories and Habits: Two Neural Systems." In *The Neurobiology of Learning and Memory*, edited by J. L. McGaugh, G. Lynch, and N. M. Weinberger. New York: Guilford Press, in press.

Moody, Raymond, Jr. *Life After Life*. New York: Bantam/Mockingbird Books, 1976.

Mountcastle, Vernon B. "The View from Within: Pathways to the Study of Perception." *Johns Hopkins Medical Journal* 136:109–131 (1975).

Ninan, P. T.; Insel, T. M.; Cohen, R. M.; Cook, J. M.; Skolnick, P; and Paul, S. M. "Benzodiazepine Receptor-mediated Experimental 'Anxiety' in Primates." *Science* 218:1332–1334 (24 December 1982).

Ornstein, Robert E., ed. *The Nature of Human Consciousness: A Book of Readings*. San Francisco: W. H. Freeman & Co., 1968.

Panksepp, Jaak. "The Biology of Social Attachments: Opiates Alleviate Separation Distress." *Biological Psychiatry* 13(5):607–618 (1978).

Penfield, Wilder. *The Mystery of the Mind: A Critical Study of Consciousness and the Human Brain*. Princeton, N.J.: Princeton University Press, 1975.

Pert, Candace B., and Snyder, Solomon H. "Opiate Receptor: Demonstration in Nervous Tissue." *Science* 179:1011–1014 (9 March 1973).

Phelps, Michael E., and Mazziotta, John C. "Positron Emission Tomography: Human Brain Function and Biochemistry." *Science* 228(4701):799–809 (17 May 1985).

Pietsch, Paul. *Shufflebrain: The Quest for the Hologramic Mind*. Boston: Houghton Mifflin Company, 1981.

Popper, Karl R., and Eccles, John C. *The Self and Its Brain: An Argument for Interactionism*. Springer International, 1977.

Pribram, Karl H. "Behaviourism, Phenomenology and Holism in Psychology: A Scientific Analysis." *Journal of Social and Biological Structures* 2:65–72 (1979).

———. *Languages of the Brain: Experimental Paradoxes and Principles in Neuropsychology*. Monterey, Calif.: Brooks/Cole Publishing Co., 1971.

Prigogine, Ilya, and Stengers, Isabelle. *Order Out of Chaos: Man's New Dialogue with Nature*. New York: Bantam Books, 1984.

Progoff, Ira, trans. and commentary. *The Cloud of Unknowing*. New York: Dell Publishing Co., 1957.

Restak, Richard M. *The Brain*. New York: Bantam Books, 1984.

———. *The Brain: The Last Frontier: An Exploration of the Human Mind and Our Future*. New York: Doubleday & Co., 1979.

Ring, Kenneth. "The Nature of Personal Identity in the Near-Death Experience: Paul Brunton and the Ancient Tradition." *Anabiosis* 4(1) (Spring 1984).

Robinson, Daniel N. *The Englightened Machine: An Analytical Introduction to Neuropsychology*. Encino, Calif.: Dickenson Publishing Co., 1973.

Rose, Steven. *The Conscious Brain*. New York: Alfred Knopf, 1973.

Rucker, Rudy. *Infinity and the Mind: The Science and Philosophy of the Infinite*. New York: Bantam Books, 1983.

Russell, Bertrand. *A History of Western Philosophy*. New York: Simon & Schuster, 1945.

Ryle, Gilbert. *Concept of Mind*. London: Hutchinson & Co., 1949.

Sabom, Michael. *Recollections of Death: A Medical Investigation*. New York: Harper & Row, 1982.

Sacks, Oliver. *Awakenings*. New York: E. P. Dutton, 1973 (paperback, 1983).

Sagan, Carl. *The Dragons of Eden: Speculations on the Evolution of Human Intelligence*. New York: Ballantine Books, 1977.

Savage, C. Wade. "An Old Ghost in a New Body." (In Globus et al., *Consciousness and the Brain*)

Shepherd, Gordon M. *Neurobiology*. New York: Oxford University Press, 1983.

Siegel, Ronald K. "Hallucinations." *Scientific American* (October 1977).

———. "The Psychology of Life After Death." *American Psychologist* 35(10):911–931 (October 1980).

Shutts, David. *Lobotomy: Resort to the Knife*. New York: Van Nostrand Reinhold Co., 1982.

Snyder, Solomon H. *Biological Aspects of Mental Disorder*. New York: Oxford University Press, 1980.

————. "Drug and Neurotransmitter Receptors in the Brain." *Science* 224:22–31 (6 April 1984).

Sperry, Roger W. "The Eye and the Brain." *Scientific American* (May 1956).

————. "Mental Phenomena As Causal Determinants in Brain Function." (In Globus et al., *Consciousness and the Brain*)

Squire, Larry R., and Cohen, Neal J. "Human Memory and Amnesia." In *Handbook of Behavioral Neurobiology*, Vol. 10, edited by J. McGaugh and R. Thompson. New York: Plenum Press, in press.

Swami Prabhavananda and Isherwood, Christopher, trans. and comps. *How to Know God: The Yoga Aphorisms of Patanjali*. New York: The New American Library/A Mentor Book, 1969.

————. *The Song of God: Bhagavad-Gita*. New York: The New American Library/A Mentor Book, 1951.

Swami Prabhavananda and Manchester, Frederick, trans. and comps. *The Upanishads: Breath of the Eternal*. New York: The New American Library/A Mentor Book, 1957.

Tart, Charles T. "Marijuana Intoxication: Common Experiences." *Nature* 226(5247):701–704 (1970).

————. *States of Consciousness*. New York: E. P. Dutton, 1975.

————, ed. *Altered States of Consciousness*. New York: Doubleday/Anchor Books, 1969, 1972.

Teyler, Timothy. *A Primer of Psychobiology: Brain and Behavior*. San Francisco: W. H. Freeman & Co., 1975.

Torrey, E. Fuller. *Surviving Schizophrenia: A Family Manual*. New York: Harper & Row, 1983.

Torrey, E. Fuller, and Peterson, Michael R. "The Viral Hypothesis of Schizophrenia." *Schizophrenia Bulletin* 2:136–145 (1976).

Torrey, E. Fuller; Yolken, Robert H.; and Winfrey, C. Jack. "Cytomegalovirus Antibody in Cerebrospinal Fluid of Schizophrenic Patients Detected by Enzyme Immunoassay." *Science* 216:892–894 (May 1982).

Underhill, Evelyn. *Mysticism*. New York: E. P. Dutton, 1961.

Watts, Alan. *Does it Matter?: Essays on Man's Relation to Materiality*. New York: Pantheon Books, 1970.

Weinberger, Daniel R.; Wagner, R. L.; and Wyatt, R. J. "Neuropathological Studies of Schizophrenia: A Selective Review." *Schizophrenia Bulletin* 9:193–212 (1983).

Wiener, Norbert. *God and Golem, Inc.: A Comment on Certain Points Where Cybernetics Impinges on Religion*. Cambridge, Mass.: The M.I.T. Press, 1964.

Wilson, Sheryl C., and Barber, Theodore X. "The Fantasy-prone Personality: Implications for Understanding Imagery, Hypnosis, and Parapsychological Phenomena." In *Imagery: Current Theory, Research, and Applications*, edited by A. A. Sheikh. New York: John Wiley & Sons, 1982.

Zaidel, Eran. "The Elusive Right Hemisphere of the Brain." *Engineering and Science* (September/October 1978).

Index

Abraham, Ralph, 360–61, 364, 365, 373
acetylcholine, 97, 157
action potentials, 30
adenosine, 95–96
Adey, W. Ross, 365, 375–77, 380
adrenocroticotropic hormone (ACTH), 88, 89, 96, 97
aggression, *see* violence
agoraphobia, 126
alcoholism: P300 waves in, 136; *see also* Korsakoff's syndrome
Alkon, Daniel, 198
Allen, Woody, 153, 218
Allison, Ralph, 238
Alpert, Richard, 353
altered states of consciousness (ASCs), 251–57
Altschule, Mark, 181
Alzheimer's disease, 96, 97; PET scans and, 123–25
American Psychiatric Association, 353
amnesia, 186–87, 204–9; in multiple personality disorder, 240–41
amygdala, 32, 36; memory and, 208; violence and, 182–83
anhedonia, 153
anomia, 56
Anthony, St., 342, 353
aphasia, 55–56
aphrodisiacs, 99–100
Aristotle, xiv, xvii, 388
artificial intelligence, 12
association areas, 50
autism, 81
autoimmune theory of schizophrenia, 118–19
autoscopic experience, 306–8
axons, 30

Barber, Theodore X., 344–45, 386
basal ganglia, 127
Bateson, Gregory, 280
Baudelaire, Charles, 242
B-CEE, 68–69, 94, 100
Begleiter, Henri, 136

behaviorism, 15–16, 49, 57, 58
benzodiazepines, 68
Berger, Hans, xviii
Berger, Philip, 70, 328
Berkeley, Bishop George, 6, 19, 20, 85, 301
Bianchi, Kenneth, 192–93, 241
biocybernetics, 137–38
Blake, William, 324–26, 332
Bleuler, Eugen, xviii, 108, 111, 368
blindsight, 210–11
blood-brain barrier, 120
Bloom, Floyd, 99–100
Blum, Kenneth, 81
Bogen, Joseph E., xix, 210, 221, 223, 226, 236
Bohn, David, 352
Borges, Jorge Luis, 185–86, 286
Bourguignon, Erica, 257
brain electrical activity mapping (BEAM), 107
brain pacemaker, 154–55, 173, 176
brain stem, 32, 45
Braun, Bennett, 240, 241
Broca, Pierre Paul, xvii, 55
Broca's area, 38, 55–56, 143, 223
Brody, Jonathan, 127
Bronowski, Jacob, 12, 57, 370
Brown, Gerald, 169–73
Brown, Warren, 138
Buchsbaum, Monte, 238, 327
Buddha, 342
Bunge, Mario, 317
Buono, Angelo, 193
Butterfly Effect, 362
Bylinski, Gene, 99

Carrington, Patricia, 257
Carroll, Lewis, 55, 218, 301
Castaneda, Carlos, 299
CAT (computerized axial tomography) scans, 107, 121; of schizophrenic brains, 114–15
catastrophe theory, 368
Catherine of Genoa, St., 353
Catherine of Siena, St., 353

caudate nucleus, 127
cell bodies, 30
Central Intelligence Agency (CIA), 137
cerebellum, 32, 34; memory and, 200–201; pacemaker implanted in, 154–55; violence and, 173–76
cerebral hemispheres, 32, 36; *see also* split-brain research
cerebrum, 36
chaos, 103–4, 359–90; brain and, 365–67; consciousness and, 383–87; as higher form of order, 375–77; paradoxical order and, 364–65; self-organization and, 378–81; strange attractors and, 371–75; topology and, 369–70
Chapman, Robert, 139
Chase, Thomas, 122, 124–25, 132
child abuse, 177–78; multiple personality disorder and, 241–42
chlorpromazine, 75, 111
cholecsytokinin (CCK), 89
Chomsky, Noam, 54, 57–59, 67, 139
Christianity, 179; charismatic, 332, 334; medieval, 5
Chuang-tzu, 302
Chung, David, 77
Churchland, Patricia, 12
"cinematic vision," 355
cingulate gyrus, 36, 48
classical conditioning, 198, 200
cognitive science, 12
Cohen, Neal, 209
Coleridge, Samuel Taylor, 281
collective properties, 216–17
Comanches, 177
confabulation, 204–5
consciousness, 388; altered states of, 251–57; chaos and, 383–87; dreams and, 296, 299; dual, 212–13, evolution of, 50–52; memory and, 210–12; near-death experiences and, 304; nonhuman, 53–54; split-brain research and, 221–22, 226–27; as uniquely human, 52–53; *see also* self
Copernicus, Nicholas, 5
coprolalia, 125
Corkin, Suzanne, 206
cortex, 32, 33, 36–37; evolution of, 59–60; geography of, 37–43
cortical mapping studies, 122–27
corticotropin releasing factor (CRF), 88, 89
Cowan, Jack, 264, 269–71, 366

Craik, Kenneth, 340
Crick, Francis, 10, 291–92, 326, 327, 351
Crow, Timothy J., 116, 117
culture, influence on brain development of, 60
cytomegalovirus (CMV), 116–17
Cytowic, Richard, 354

Dampiere, Marquise of, 125
Dante, 105, 180, 335, 389
Darwin, Charles, 89
declarative memory, 203–4, 209–10
Deikman, Arthur, 254
déjà vu, 37
Delgado, José, xix, 145–51, 158, 181, 183, 184
Delisi, Lynn, 119
dementia praecox, 108
Democritus, 5
dendrites, 30, 31
dendritic spines, 30, 31
Dennett, Daniel C., 138
Department of Defense (DOD), 136–37
depersonalization, 314
Descartes, René, xvii, 6–8, 11, 12, 17, 27, 51, 67, 213, 298, 301, 385–86, 389
DeValois, Karen and Russell, 351
"devil's tuning fork," 339
Diderot, Denis, 378
diencephalon, 32, 35
diet pills, 99
dissociation, 314
Donchin, Emanuel, 134–37
dopamine, 75; PET scans and, 128–29; schizophrenia and, 111–12, 368
Dostoevski, Fyodor, 330
Drachman, David, 97
dreams, 267–68, 281–302, 389; computer model of, 291–92; Descartes's, 386; EEGs during, 254, 255; lucid, 281–89; as neural events, 293–95; perception in, 296–300; reality and, 300–302; theories of, 289–91
drugs, 8; antischizophrenic, 75, 111, 112, 127; aphrodisiac, 99–100; chaos and, 374; consciousness-altering, 252, 258–67, 270, 275–79, 324–25, 328, 332; to control aggression, 162–63; diet, 99; meditation, 98–99; memory, 96–97; neurochemistry and, 68–72; painkiller, 97–98; plea-

sure center and, 157; psychoactive, 101; receptors and, 93–94, 129–30
dualism, 6; near-death experiences and, 317
Duara, Ranjin, 124, 126
Duncan-Johnson, Connie, 135–36
DU 27716, 162–63
Dylan, Bob, 269
dynorphin, 77
dyskinesias, 369
dyslexia, 227–28

Eccles, Sir John, 17, 51–53, 72, 187–88, 222, 234, 343
Eckhart, Meister, 317, 329
Edelman, Gerald, 62
ego, 225–26
Ehlers, Cindy, 370–71, 375
Einstein, Albert, 351, 362
electrical activity of brain, 29–31
electrical stimulation of brain (ESB), 145–61, 173, 335; memory and, 189–91
electroencephalography (EEG), 29, 107, 132–44; behavior patterns and, 370–71; chaos and, 375–77; dreams and, 283, 287; ESB and, 146, 153, 156–57; language and, 138–39, 141–42; military interest in, 136–37; P300 wave in, 134–36; split-brain research and, 228–29; states of consciousness and, 254–55
Eliot, T. S., 162, 327, 361
emergentism, 17
emotions: blunted, in schizophrenia, 109; cerebellum and, 174–75; electrical stimulation of, 145–61; limbic system and, 43, 45; neuropeptides and, 80, 89–92; right hemisphere and, 223
endorphins, 77, 80–81; as brain's reward system, 86, 88; and response to external reality, 86–87
engrams, 188–89
enkephalin, 77, 97, 98
Enright, Craig, 271
environment, brain development and, 63–66
epilepsy: automatism in, 211–12; chaos and, 366–67; ESB for, 149; religious experience in, 329–30; split-brain surgery for, 218, 229
episodic memory, 203
Erhard, Werner, 280
Ervin, Frank R., 181, 183, 184

Escher, M. C., 339, 340
Eswaran, Eknath, 196
event-related potential (ERP), 134–39
evoked potential, *see* event-related potential

faces, inability to recognize, 57
fantasy-prone personalities (FPPs), 344–45
Farmer, Doyne, 364, 371–72, 382
Farmer, Francis, 41
feature detectors, 337
Feynmann, Richard, 280
5-HIAA, 169–73
fixed point attractor, 363
food, neuropeptides in, 100–101
forebrain, 32
Fourier transfer, 348–49
Fouts, Roger, 54, 346
Fox, George, 352
Freeman, Walter, 39–41, 340–41, 381, 389
Freud, Sigmund, xvii, 11, 27–28, 43, 73, 103, 106, 107, 110, 120, 151, 158, 191, 281, 286, 293–95, 297, 353, 372–74
Fricker, Lloyd, 98
Friedman, David, 136
frontal lobes, 39–43
Frost, J. James, 128

Gabbard, Glenn, 314–15
Gabor, Dennis, 346–47
Gackenbach, Jayne, 285
Gage, Phineas, xvii, 39
Gajdusek, Carleton, 116
Galileo, 5
Gall, Franz Joseph, xvii, 27, 28, 36, 55, 57, 174–75
Gallup, George, Jr., 311
García Márquez, Gabriel, 55
Gardiner, Martin, 301
Gardner, Beatrix, 53
Gardner, R. Allen, 53, 54
Garfinkel, Alan, 365, 366, 369–71, 375, 378–80
Gazzaniga, Michael, 222, 230–36
Gelenberg, Alan, 101
Geschwind, Norman, 57, 228, 235, 236
Gelenberg, Alan, 101
Geschwind, Norman, 57, 228, 235, 236
Gevins, Alan, 140–44, 228–29, 385
"ghost in the machine," 16, 383–87
glial cells, 30
Gilles de la Tourette, George, 125

gliosis, 114
Globus, Gordon, 295–300
glucose mapping, 73–75
Gödel, Kurt, 277
Gold, Philip, 88
Goldstein, Avram, 77, 85
Golgi, Camillo, xvii, 29
Goodwin, Frederick, 169–71
Gray, Eden, 251
Green, Alyce and Elmer, 254
Greenough, William, 64–66
Gregory, Richard, 336, 339
Griffin, Donald, 51
Grossberg, Stephen, 360
Group for the Advancement of Psychiatry (GAP), 353
Guillemin, Roger, 35
gyri, 32

habit memory, 204
Haldane, J. B. S., 276
hallucinations, 258–80; chaos and, 366; drug-induced, 258–67, 270, 275–79; mechanics of, 269–71; near-death experiences and, 311–16; in schizophrenia, 268–69
Harlow, Harry F., xix, 173–74, 176
Heath, Robert G., xviii, 118–19, 152–61, 173–77, 180
Hebb, Donald O., xviii, 7, 63, 196, 199, 216
Heimberger, R. R., 182
Henn, Fritz, 112, 117
Herkenham, Miles, 25, 26, 50, 82–85, 88, 388
Hess, Walter, 146
Hillyard, Steven, 138
Hinckley, John, 114
hindbrain, 32
hippocampus, 32, 36; amnesia and, 208; in schizophrenia, 113
Hippocrates, xvii, 212
Hobbes, Thomas, 7
Hobson, J. Allan, 293–95, 382
Hodgkin, Alan L., xviii, 11
Hofmann, Albert, xviii, 260, 328–30
Hofstadter, Douglas, 138, 203–4
holographic brain theory, 345–52
homunculus, 39, 40
Honorton, Charles, 342–43
Hopfield, John, 214–17, 378, 387
hormones, 87, 88
Howard, William E., 178
Hubel, David H., xix, 28, 37, 65, 73, 74, 298, 336–38, 366, 380

Hughes, John, xix, 77, 78
Huichol Indians, 262–64
Hume, David, 19, 20, 85
Huntington's disease, 125, 130, 132
Husserl, Edmund, 299
Huxley, Aldous, 157, 324–27
Huxley, Andrew, xviii, 11
hypothalamus, 32, 35; electrical stimulation of, 146

id, 225–26
idealist philosophy, 6
identity theory, 13
immune system, schizophrenia and, 118–19
informational memory, 204
isolation tanks, 272, 274, 276–77, 280

Jackson, Hughlings, 189, 263
jamais-vu, 37
James, William, 324–25, 332, 333, 336, 352–54
Jaspers, Herbert, 189
Jaynes, Julian, 53
Jefferson Airplane, 25
Jesus, 329
Joan of Arc, 345
John of the Cross, St., 179, 332, 342
Johnson, Samuel, 6
Johnstone, Eve, 116
Jones, Bob, III, 335
Jouvet, Michel, 289, 293
Julesz, Bela, 338
Jung, Carl G., 103, 318–20, 322, 373

K, 376–79
Kamiya, Joe, 254
Kandel, Eric, xix, 197–99, 360
Kant, Immanuel, 337–38, 341
Kastenbaum, Robert, 323
Katz, Sir Bernard, 71
Kaushall, Philip I., 205
Kedzierski, Beverly, 281–85, 287–89
Kety, Seymour, 118–19
King, Roy, 367–69, 371
Kissinger, Henry, 167
Klein, Mark, 199
Klüver, Heinrich, 261, 270
Koestler, Arthur, 47
Koob, George, 89
Korsakoff's syndrome, 125, 204, 206–7
Kosterlitz, Hans, xix, 77, 78
Kovelman, Joyce, 113
Kramer, Milton, 295
Kretchmer, Norman, 178, 180

Krishna, Gopi, 332
Krishnamurti, Jiddu, 352
Kübler-Ross, Elisabeth, 304–5, 312
Kuhar, Michael, 129–30
!Kung bushmen, 254
kuru, 116
Kutas, Marta, 138

LaBerge, Stephen, 255–56, 282–89, 302
Laing, R. D., 110, 111
language: consciousness and, 53–54; disorders of, 55–56; EEG and, 138–39, 141–42; genetic basis of, 57–59; right hemisphere, 219, 224–25, 230–35
Lao-tzu, 332, 352
Laplace, Pierre Simon, Marquis de, 362
Lashley, Karl, xviii, 188–89, 191, 208, 348, 384
lateral geniculate nucleus, 35
Lawrence Livermore National Laboratories, 163
Leary, Timothy, 161, 261
Leiber, Justin, 138
Leibniz, Gottfried von, 6, 318, 366
Lem, Stanislaw, 92
Levine, Allen, 99
levodopa (L-dopa), 75–76
Levy, Jerre, 222–23, 227
Lewin, B. D., 386
Li, C. H., 77
Lida, 377
Liebeskind, John, 80
life after death, 311, 312
Lilly, John, xviii, 257, 271–80, 302, 342
limbic system, 32, 36, 43, 48–49; CMV and, 116–17; electrical stimulation of, 146, 147; in schizophrenia, 114
limit cycles, 363
Linnoila, Markku, 171
Llinas, Rudolfo, 35
lobotomies, 39–42
Locke, John, 52, 53
locus coeruleus, 32, 293
Loewi, Otto, xviii
Loftus, Elizabeth, 192–94
Loftus, Geoffrey, 193–94
long-term memory, 196, 203
Lorenz, Konrad, 49–50, 337
Lorenz, Edward, xix, 359–60, 363
love, violence versus, 176–80

LSD, 260, 261, 263–67, 270, 274–78, 284, 328
lucid dreams, 281–89
Ludlow, Christie, 240
Luria, A. R., 41–42, 186, 354–55
luteinizing-hormone-releasing-hormone (LHRH), 99

McCarley, Robert W., 293–95, 382
McCarthy, John, 141
McConnell, James V., 195
McCormick, David, 200
MacDonald, Norma, 109, 325
McGaugh, James, 97
McGuire, Michael, 164–67, 169–70
MacLean, Paul, xviii, 36, 43–49, 67, 109, 181, 211, 236, 335
Madsen, Douglas, 166
Mahesh Yogi, Maharishi, 254–55
mammillary bodies, 36
Mandell, Arnold, 68, 102–3, 236–37, 278, 329–34, 360, 366, 371–75, 378, 382
Maoris, 177
mapping of brain, 61–63; with PET scans, 122–27
Marangos, Paul, 93, 95–96
Mark, Vernon H., 181, 183, 184
Marsh, James, 139
Mason, William A., 174
materialist philosophy, 7
Matthysse, Steven, 112
Mayer, André, 181
Mazziotta, John, 122, 123, 132
medial geniculate nucleus, 35
meditation, 255; drug-induced, 98–99
memory, 8, 185–217; computer model of, 214–17; consciousness and, 210–12; declarative versus procedural, 209–10; development and, 65; dreams and, 290–91; drugs to improve, 96–97; engrams and, 188–89; holographic theory of, 348–49; kinds of, 230–34; localization of, 200–201, 208–9; loss of, *see* amnesia; manufactured, 192–95; neural mechanics of, 197–200; neuropeptide theory of, 195–96; Proustian, 201–2; P300 waves and, 135; self and, 187–88, 212–13; synapses and, 196, 198–99; temporal lobes and, 189–92
Mendelson, Wallace, 99
Merleau-Ponty, Maurice, 299
Merton, Thomas, 332
Merzenich, Michael, 61–63

midbrain, 32
MILD (mnemonic induction of lucid dreams), 284–85
Milk, Harvey, 180
Miller, Jonathan, 235
Milligan, William, 239
Milner, Brenda, 209
Milner, Peter, xviii, 147
Minsky, Marvin, 12
Mirsky, Allan F., 109
Mishkin, Mortimer, 204, 208, 210, 211
Mitchison, Graeme, 291–92
monism, 13
Moniz, Egas, xviii, 39, 40
Monod, Jacques, 7
Montague, Ashley, 181–82
Moody, Raymond, 303, 305, 311, 312, 316
Morely, John, 99
Moscone, George, 180
Mountcastle, Vernon, xix, 13, 19, 399, 366
multiple personality disorder, 8, 237–47; amnesia in, 240–41; child abuse and, 241–42; reintegration in, 242–47
mystical state, *see* religious experience

naltrexone, 99
Nathan, Peter, 220
near-death experiences, 256, 273–74, 303–23; autoscopic, 306–8; hallucinations and, 311–16; out-of-body perception in, 308–9; Platonic dualism and, 317–18; psychodynamic explanations of, 314–15; synchronicity and, 318–20; transcendental, 320–23
Necker cube, 339
neocortex, 36, 43, 48, 49
neurons, 29–30, 33
neuropeptides, 80, 88–89; emotions and, 89–92; foods containing, 100–101; memory and, 195–96; structure of, 87; *see also specific chemicals*
neurotransmitters, 71–73; specific behaviors and, 75, 76
Newton, Isaac, 5, 381–82
N400 waves, 138–39
norepinephrine, 75, 97
Noyes, Russell, 314
nuclear magnetic resonance (NMR), 107

occipital lobe, 37
ocular dominance columns, 73

Offray de la Mettrie, Julien, xvii, 7
Olds, James, xviii, 146–47, 152, 160, 161, 183
opiates, 101–2; natural, *see* endorphins; PET scans and, 129; receptors for, 76–77, 83–85
Osis, Karlis, 304, 383–84
out-of-body experiences (OBEs), 308–9, 383–84

pacemaker, brain, 154–55, 173, 176
painkillers, 98
Panksepp, Jaak, 81
paradoxical order, 364–65
parapsychology, 383–84
parietal lobes, 38–39
Parkinson's disease, 18, 75–76, 125
Pasternak, Gavril, 98
Patterson, Penny, 54
Paul, St., 1–3, 16, 326, 329, 330, 332, 352
Paul, Steven, 68–69, 95
Pavlov, Ivan, xvii, 10, 11, 198
PCP ("angel dust"), 101
Penfield, Wilder, xviii, 189–91, 194, 211–13, 315, 316
perception, 9; dreams and, 296–300; reality versus, 336–41
periodic attractor, 363
Pert, Candace B., xix, 42, 70, 72, 76–79, 81–85, 88–92, 101–4, 107, 119, 127, 130, 326–28, 335, 387, 390
PET (positron emission tomography) scans, 9, 73, 106–8, 120–32; biochemical mapping with, 122–27; receptors and, 127–31
Phelps, Michael E., 108, 120–22
phrenology, 28
Piaget, Jean, 53
Pickar, David, 105–6, 117
Pietsch, Paul, 351
pineal gland, 35
pituitary, 35
Plato, xvii, 302, 317, 326
pleasure center, 8–9, 147, 152–54, 157, 160–61
Plotinus, 332
pons, 32; dreams and, 289, 293
power relationships, 163–67
preestablished harmony, 318
Prescott, James W., 174–80
Pribram, Karl, 42, 52, 197, 211–12, 330, 338, 345–50, 352, 386
Prigogine, Ilya, 381
procedural memory, 203–4, 209–10

proprioception, 175
prosopagnosia, 57
Proust, Marcel, 15, 191–92, 201–2
psychedelic drugs, *see* drugs, consciousness-altering; LSD
psychic ability, tests of, 342–44
psychokinesis (PK), 343
psychophysical parallelism, 6, 318
P300 waves, 133–37, 139, 140
putamen, 127
Putnam, Frank, 238–42

Raichle, Marcus, 126, 131
Raleigh, Michael J., 164
Ram Das, 353
Ramón y Cajal, Santiago, xvii, 29–30
Rapp, Paul, 367
receptors, 76–80, 82–85; antibodies to, 119; chaos and, 365–66; in drug research, 93–94; perception filtered by, 326–28; PET scans of, 107–8, 127–31
reductionism, 14–17
Reivich, Martin, 73
religious experience, 9, 328–36, 352–55; epilepsy and, 329–30; holographic brain theory and, 349–52; on LSD, 328–29, 332; psychopathology of, 352–53; sensory deprivation and, 342; strange attractors and, 372–73
REM (rapid eye movements) sleep, 254, 257; dreaming and, 282, 283, 288–95
reticular activating system (RAS), 32, 289
Rilke, Rainer Maria, 152
Rimbaud, Arthur, 354
Ring, Kenneth, 305, 316, 317, 321
Robinson, Daniel N., 16, 59, 318, 338
Rose, Steven, 60–61, 72
Rosenzweig, Mark, 63
Ross, Elliott, 223
Rossler, Otto, 362, 373
Rubin, Jerry, 280
Rucker, Rudy, 385
Ruelle, David, 363
Ryle, Gilbert, 7, 386

Sabom, Michael, 303–12, 314–17, 323
Sacks, Oliver, 75, 355
Sagan, Carl, 46
Saltzberg, Bernard, 178
Saperstein, Alan, 364–65
Sartre, Jean-Paul, 61

Savage, C. Wade, 51
Schally, Andrew, 35
Scheibel, Arnold, 113
schizophrenia, 105–20, 335; autoimmune theory of, 118–19; deprivation and, 174; dopamine and, 111–12; EEG and, 153–54, 158, 160; hallucinations in, 268–69; neurochemistry and, 75; organic brain damage in, 112–16; PET scans and, 120, 126–27; psychological theories of, 110–11; P300 waves in, 136; reduced perception in, 327; stereotypic behavior in, 367–68; virus theory of, 116–18
Schopenhauer, Arthur, 341
Schwartz, James B., 197, 198
scotophobin, 195
Scott, George C., 271, 275
self, 218–47; memory and, 187–88, 212–13; in multiple personality disorder, 237–47; representations of, 235–37; split-brain research and, 218–35; *see also* consciousness
self-organization, 378–81
semantic memory, 203
Senoi people, 302
sensitization, 198
sensory deprivation, 342–43; *see also* isolation tanks
septum, electrical stimulation of, 147, 156
serotonin, 75, 97; defects in, violence and, 169–73; dominance and, 164–67; religious experience and, 330–31
Shakespeare, William, 25
Shaw, Rob, 361–64
Sherrington, Sir Charles, xviii, 17, 30, 220
short-term memory, 196, 203
Shulgin, Alexander, 330
Shutts, David, 41
Siegel, Ronald K., 253, 255–69, 271, 276, 278, 302, 305, 311–16, 322
Simon, Neil, 351
Skinner, B. F., xviii, 14, 58, 387
Skolnick, Phil, 68–69, 94
slime mold, 378–81
slow viruses, 116
Smith, Carolyn, 73, 75
Snyder, Solomon H., xix, 76–78, 93–94, 96, 98, 110, 128, 130
social order, 378–81
Society for Neuroscience, 6, 10, 15, 200

Sokoloff, Louis, 73, 74, 120–21, 126–27
somatostatin, 89
spatial memory, 203
speech, *see* language
Sperry, Roger, xix, 16–17, 50, 218–23, 233, 236, 378
split-brain research, 8, 218–35; ego and id and, 225–26; language in, 219, 224–25
split personality, *see* multiple personality disorder
Squire, Larry, 204, 205, 207, 209, 210
Stafford, Peter, 266
state-specific science, 252
Stein, Larry, 86
Stevens, Janice, 113–14
Stevens, Wallace, 235, 359
strange attractors, 362–64, 371–75
Stratton, G. M., 50
striate cortex, 74, 337
Stryker, Michael, 61
Substance P, 88, 89, 91–92
suicide, 170–71
sulci, 32
Sweet, William, 183
synapses, 30, 31; memory and, 196, 198–99; neurotransmitters and, 71–73
synaptic clefts, 30
synchronicity, 318–20
synesthesia, 354
Szasz, Thomas, 111

tabula rasa theory, 49
tachistoscopes, 219
Takens, Floris, 363
taraxein, 118–19
Tart, Charles, 251–53, 255, 256, 280, 288
temporal lobes, 37–38; memory and, 189–92
Tesla, Nikola, 256
thalamus, 32, 35
Theresa, St., 179, 352
Thomas, Lewis, 305, 315
Thompson, Hunter, 68
Thompson, Richard F., 200–201
Tibetan Book of the Dead, 269, 321–22
Tiger, Lionel, 167–68
topology, 369–70
Torrey, E. Fuller, 108–10, 112, 116
Tourette's syndrome, 125
Travanti, Daniel J., 180

triune brain, 43–49; violence and, 181–82
Twemlow, Stuart, 315
tyrosine, 100, 101

Valium, 68–70, 94–95, 100
vasopressin, 88–89, 96
ventricles, enlarged, 114
verbal memory, 203
violence, 162–84; amygdalectomy to control, 182–83; cerebellum and, 173–76; drugs to control, 162–63; love versus, 176–80; serotonin and, 164–67, 169–73; suicide and, 170–71; triune brain and, 181–82
Virkunen, Matti, 171
virus theory of schizophrenia, 116–18
Vonnegut, Kurt, 1, 145, 150, 161, 380
von Neumann, John, 188

Wagner, Henry N., 127–30
Walter, Don, 365, 366, 386, 389
Warrington, Elizabeth, 211
Washington, Yolanda, 193
Watson, James, 10, 11
Watson, John B., xviii, 14, 49, 91
Watson, Lyall, 21
Watson, Stanley, 80
Watts, Alan, 328
Weimer, Walter, 299
Weinberger, Daniel, 114, 116, 238
Weingartner, Herbert, 96, 97, 241
Weiskrantz, Lawrence, 211
Wernicke, Carl, xvii, 56
Wernicke's area, 38, 56, 143, 223
Wheeler, Michael, 181
White, Dan, 180
Wiener, Norbert, 132, 364
Wiesel, Torsten, xix, 28, 37, 65, 73, 74, 298, 336–38, 366, 380
Willis, Thomas, xiv
Wilson, Sheryl, 344
Wolf, Alfred, 120
Worrell, Olga, 382
Wurtman, Judith, 101
Wurtman, Richard, 100, 101

Yalow, Rosalyn, 35
Young, J. Z., 375

Zaidel, Eran, 56, 219, 224–26, 228, 233
Zen Flesh, Zen Bones, 328
Zetkin, Mark, 205
zimelidine, 97